Advanced Chinese
Intention, Strategy, and Communication

高级汉语
意图，技巧与表达

汤雁方

Yanfang Tang

College of William and Mary

陈青海

Qinghai Chen

University of Michigan

Yale University Press

New Haven • London

Publisher: Mary Jane Peluso
Production Controller: Maureen Noonan
Editorial Assistant: Gretchen Rings
Manuscript Editor: Joyce Ippolito
Production Editor: Margaret Otzel
Printed in the United States of America

Library of Congress Cataloging-in-Publication Data

Tang, Yanfang.
    Advanced Chinese : intention, strategy, and communication / Yanfang Tang, Qinghai Chen = [Gao ji Han yu : Yi tu, Ji qiao yu biao da / Tang Yanfang, Chen Qinghai].
        p. cm.—(Yale language series)
    Parallel title in Chinese characters.
    ISBN 13: 978-0-300-10463-9
    ISBN 0-300-10463-4 (pbk. : alk. paper)
    I. Chen, Qinghai. II. Title. III. Series.

PL1129.E5T35 2004
495.1'82—dc22   2004048470

A catalogue record for this book is available from the British Library.

The paper in this book meets the guidelines for permanence and durability of the Committee on Production Guidelines for Book Longevity of the Council on Library Resources.

10 9 8 7 6 5 4 3

目录

Narration 叙述

Description 描写

Persuasion 议论

Exposition 说明

Lyrical Expression 抒情

Acknowledgments

We would like to express our sincere gratitude to all the colleagues, students, and friends who have encouraged or assisted us during the lengthy period of the textbook's development. In particular, we would like to thank Judy Dyer of University of Michigan English Language Institute, who offered comments and suggestions in reading an early sample lesson and proofread the English part of the entire manuscript. Special thanks also go to Jianhua Bai for selecting our textbook (in manuscript) for use at the Middlebury College Summer Chinese School, and to Fengtao Wu for providing us with valuable feedback through his piloting experience with this textbook. We also want to express our appreciation to Wei Liu, who devoted many hours to the recording of the sound files that accompany this book, and to Stephen Field of Trinity University, Madeline Chu of Kalamazoo College, and Jerome Packard of the University of Illinois, Urbana-Champaign, whose reviews helped to improve the general quality of this course.

We are indebted to various departments and units at the University of Michigan (the Department of Asian Languages and Cultures and the Language Resource Center particularly), and the College of William and Mary for the multifaceted support that we received during the period of research, writing, and editing leading to the publication of this text. Part of this support was from the Freeman Foundation through the University of Michigan.

We would also like to thank the authors of the selected essays for giving us permission to use their works, Chunxiang Li of Tianjin Copyright Agency (PRC) for locating and contacting these authors for us, and Yale University Press staff for guiding us through the publication procedures.

Finally, we would like to thank our spouses, Ronald Rosenberg and Binglin Xiang, whose never-failing support for us in this important work has been crucial.

Introduction

In recent years, language educators have become increasingly interested in the question of how to advance the language ability of advanced-level students. It has been widely realized that, despite their sustained effort and the increasingly difficult text materials, many advanced students still function at the intermediate level in both speaking and writing. There seems to be an unusually large gap between the two levels that makes the transition difficult, and in the case of average students it sometimes appears doubtful whether a transition from the intermediate to the advanced levels is possible.

This integrated course in advanced Chinese is designed with this issue in mind. We believe that the main problem is a lack of a conscious, systematic, and rigorous training in the advanced language skills. For decades, the field of Chinese language pedagogy has been under the influence of the age-old thinking that the learning and instructional emphasis at the advanced level should be on "reading comprehension" (*yuedu lijie*). The theory behind such thinking is that the more students understand, the better their language abilities will be. However, it is one thing to be able to understand the content of a text, and quite another to be able to digest and use productively the language of that text. To achieve the latter, students must master the words, the expressions, and the sentence structures therein. Since the instructional materials at the advanced level are often authentic and formal, quite unlike the pedagogical language that students are taught at the beginning and intermediate levels, students must first of all know how to analyze and synthesize the rich linguistic data in the texts. They must then be able to transform their linguistic knowledge gained through such an analysis and synthesis into active skills, so that they can communicate their intentions accurately, appropriately, and effectively.

We believe that the instructional focus on "reading comprehension" leaves much that is not studied. The vast linguistic territory of formal Chinese texts needs to be charted, and students need comprehensive and systematized guidance as they cope with what often seems to be an endless supply of new words and other linguistic items as they study these texts. A simple vocabulary list is insufficient; so too are brief explanations of sentence structures as they randomly occur in the selected texts. Because there are systems in every language, and such systems appear as "patterns" in the formation of words, expressions, sentences, and texts, we believe that advanced students should have knowledge and command of these patterns. These students are in a position to understand these patterns, having already an empirical knowledge of the target language, and these patterns will also help them make better sense of the language they are attempting to acquire. This kind of training not only aids retention of old linguistic items, but it also helps students to perceive recurring patterns in new items, and by so doing to finally acquire them. The knowledge gained through analyzing patterns will also enhance students' desire and ability to use language creatively, thereby enabling them to form expressions of their own without stepping out of the bounds of the linguistic rules.

Most importantly, to learn a foreign language is to be able to communicate in that language. Neither interpreting textual meanings nor decoding linguistic patterns leads naturally to the productive skills needed for this ultimate task, although such "input" of linguistic knowledge is crucial. We have concluded that practice, in a conscious but meaningful way, is the key to successful transformation of input knowledge into productive output skills. At the advanced level, this training in productive skills entails a much more rigorous task than is expected of students at lower levels. If students are expected to communicate their intentions *correctly* at the beginning and intermediate levels, at the advanced level, they should be able to express themselves *better* or more *effectively*. The content of this advanced training extends beyond grammar into the areas of semantics, pragmatics, and rhetoric. Because there are many linguistic ways of expressing one intention, advanced students should be able to choose from the various strategies at their disposal and know which will best serve their needs under given circumstances.

The discussion above defines the mission and the tasks of this textbook. At one end of the "input-output" spectrum, this course endeavors to introduce students to the underlying systems of the Chinese language by helping them uncover the hidden patterns in the formation of characters, words, and sentence structures. Explanations are contextualized, and linguistic facts are introduced specifically as strategies to serve communicative purposes. Because the ultimate goal of this course is to help students communicate their intentions more effectively, a large number of rhetorical techniques are introduced with explanations as to why, how, and in what context they are used. At the other end of the "input-output" spectrum, and to push students to apply these techniques in their own communicative practice, we have developed many exercises within each of the fourteen lessons. These exercises are of different kinds, grammatical and rhetorical, mechanical and creative, and range over various linguistic levels including the lexical, sentential, and textual. These integrated exercises are intended to train students to speak and write accurately, appropriately, and effectively. To be effective communicators is the goal for students at the advanced level. Hence, every effort has been made to design these exercises in such a way that students are trained to express themselves more vividly, more succinctly, more cohesively, more elegantly, more forcefully, etc.

The text materials in this course are composed of essays (*sanwen*), a genre that traditionally falls under the category of "literary writings." The question has lately been debated as to whether literary writings are the best or most appropriate language teaching materials, considering the language in light of the practicality of communicating in everyday life. On this important issue, our opinions are as follows: 1) If the "formality" (in the sense of "seriousness") of the language is the concern, this question regarding suitability could be asked of any formal authentic writings, be they journalistic, technical, or any other. Unless a case can be made to discredit the role formal language plays in second language acquisition, literary writing is no different from any other form of writing as language teaching material. 2) Not all literary writings are "literary" or "artistic" to the extent that they have no application in ordinary spoken and written communication. In choosing the texts for this course, we have intentionally not selected writings that feature extremely artistic ways of expression. Neither have we considered the fame of the authors, as our attention is focused primarily on the level, the nature, and the quality of the language in the texts. A glimpse at the texts in this course will show that most are "personal essays" (*zawen* or *xiaopinwen*), in the spirit of the reaction papers American students frequently write at college and university. Even the two "descriptive essays" (*miaoxie sanwen*) and the one "lyrical essay" (*shuqing sanwen*) are free from the ornate diction and the lyrical tendency that normally characterize such literary writing.

Our decision to choose literary, rather than journalistic, essays as text materials is based on a third and most important consideration that is in direct accord with the pedagogical purposes of this course. As previously mentioned, our goal in this course is to help students speak and write more effectively in the sense of more vividly, cohesively, and forcefully. We believe that carefully selected literary essays will best assist us in achieving this purpose. As is the general consensus in Chinese culture, literature represents the best use of language, and in literature are to be found the best examples of writings composed for different purposes. Good writers are first of all good users of language. To achieve their purposes, they use language creatively, applying all the linguistic and rhetorical strategies at their disposal to best express their ideas. They draw analogies to create vivid comparisons, exaggerate to emphasize, and repeat words or segments of sentences to engage the reader's attention. Depending on their intentions and intended readers, they vary their writing styles from casual to formal, and from laudatory to sarcastic. When they can make a statement, they use a question, and when they can affirm something using a positive sentence, they use double negation to increase the force of their tone. They even organize characters to make sentences look symmetrical and sound rhythmical. Such creative and calculated use of language is not to be found in ordinary journalistic and technical writing, and yet our students need to learn these strategies to manipulate their language to express their ideas orally and in writing. If it appears that our standards are set too high, it is because we believe the efficacy of strict standards. As the Chinese put it: "If the standard is set high, the result may be at the middle; however, if the standard is set at the middle, the result may only be at a lower level" (*fa hu qi shang, de hu qi zhong; fa hu qi zhong, de hu qi xia*). As teachers we are quite satisfied if students, while attempting to reach the highest level, achieve the goal we set for them at or above the middle.

Finally, the essays in this textbook are all short, limited to approximately one standard printed page. We believe that while "extensive" reading is helpful to language acquisition, "intensive" analysis of language is particularly necessary. We hold the position that extensive reading of authentic texts should occur only after students have performed a comprehensive and detailed analysis of their vast but patterned linguistic data. Furthermore, engaging new texts and what seem to be new linguistic items is necessary, but we feel that reinforcing the mastery of the old texts and linguistic items is equally important. The short length of the texts in this course keeps the linguistic data manageable for analysis, and makes the process of learning reinforcement possible and effective.

Yanfang Tang, Ph.D.
College of William and Mary
yxtang@facstaff.wm.edu

Qinghai Chen, Ph.D.
University of Michigan
chenq@umich.edu

前言

近年来，如何进一步提高高年级汉语学生语言能力的问题得到了越来越多的关注。人们普遍认识到，尽管高年级的学生不断努力，教材的难度也不断增加，但是他们的口、笔头表达能力却仍然停留在二、三年级的水平。在"高级"和"中级"之间似乎存在着一道难以逾越的鸿沟，而一般的学生究竟能否实现从"中级"到"高级"的过度，有时竟显得疑团重重。

我们编写这本高级汉语教程就是为了解决这个问题。我们认为，"高年级"学生之所以水平不"高"，是因为缺乏在高级语言技能方面的自觉、系统和严格的训练。在过去的几十年里，汉语教学界受到一种陈旧观念的影响，认为高年级的教学重点应该是"阅读理解"。支持这种观念的理论是：学生懂得越多，他们的语言能力就会越强。但事实上，理解一篇文章的内容是一回事，而消化及习得文中的语料却是另一回事。为了提高语言表达能力，学生必须切实掌握其中的词语与句型。高年级所用的教材常为原作，语言也比较正式，跟学生在低、中年级所接触的专为教学而设计的语言甚为不同。所以，高年级学生必须首先学会如何分析和综合课文中的丰富语料，然后将获得的语言知识转化为可以实际应用的语言能力。只有这样，他们才可能在语言交流中精确地、恰当地、有效地表达自己的意思。

我们认为，把"阅读理解"作为教学重点是一种放任自流的、极不充分的教学方法。我们有必要向学生说明汉语作品中丰富的语言特点，在他们学习这些作品而常常需要对付似乎是无穷无尽的生词和其他语言现象时，向他们提供全面系统的指导。仅仅给一个词汇表是不够的，简单地解释所选作品中随机出现的句子结构也是不够的。既然每一种语言都有自己的体系，而这种体系在词语、句子和篇章的构成中表现为这样或那样的规律，那么，高年级学生就应该学习并掌握这些规律。他们已经具备了一定的目的语基础，所以他们比较容易理解这些规律；同时，有关这些规律的知识又会帮助他们去更好地理解目的语。这样的训练不仅使学生比较容易记住已学的语言材料，而且也因为各种语言规律在新的语料中不断复现而使学生比较容易掌握它们。与此同时，通过分析语言规律而获得的知识也会增强学生创造性地使用语言的欲望和能力，使他们得以在语言的规范内逐步自如地表达自己。

更为重要的是，学习一门外语的目的是为了能用它来进行交流。虽然理解课文的内容和分析语言的规律都是很关键的"输入"，但是它们都不会自然地产生实现这一最终目的所需要的语言表达能力。要把语言知识成功地转换成语言能力，唯一的途径是自觉地开展富有实际意义的语言实践活动。在高年级进行这种表达能力的训练要比在低年级严峻得多。在低年级只要求学生表达得正确，而在高年级，学生则应该有能力表达得更好或更有效。换言之，高年级的训练内容应该超越语法而进入语意、语用和修辞的范畴。既然同一种意图可以通过不同的语言技巧来表达，那么高年级的学生就应具备随心所欲地选用语言技巧的能力，并懂得如何在一个特定的情景里运用某种技巧来达到最佳的效果。

以上的讨论说明了本书的编写意图与任务。从"输入"的角度而言，它致力于帮助学生了解字、词、句的各种构成规律，并籍此向他们介绍汉语的语言体系。书中的解释尽可能地结合上下文来进行，而且把语言现象都作为实现特定交流目的的技巧来介绍。为了帮助学生更有效地实现自己的交流意图，书中介绍了大量的修辞技巧，并对为什么使用、怎么使用以及在何种情况下使用进行了说明。另一方面，从"输出"的角度而言，为了促使学生在语言实践中运用这些技巧，我们为十四课教材的每一课编写了大量的练习。这些练习属于不同的种类，或语法，或修辞，或机械，或活用，涵盖了词句篇章等各种语言层次。高年级学生的目标是使自己表达得更精确、更恰当、更有效，因而我们在练习的编写中不遗余力，尽可能地帮助他们表达得生动些、简洁些、有力些、紧凑些、文雅些、正式些，等等。

本教程所用的课文都是散文，传统上属于"文学作品"的范畴。部分教师对文学语言在日常生活中的实用性问题心存疑虑，因而认为文学作品不适合作为语言教材。我们的意见是：1) 如果所担心的是文学语言的"正式性"（或"严肃性"），那么，任何使用正式语言的原作，不论是新闻作品、科技作品还是其他作品，都会有是否适合做教材的问题。除非能证明在第二语言习得中不该有正式语言的一席之地，文学作品跟别的作品一样，完全可以作为语言教材。2) 并非所有文学作品的"文学性"或"艺术性"都强烈到使它们在日常的口头和书面交流中失去实用性的地步。在挑选课文的时候，我们刻意排除了在表达方式上过于艺术化的作品。我们也没有考虑作者的知名度问题，因为我们的注意力全都集中在语言的难度、语言的性质和语言的质量上。只消看一眼所选的课文就会知道，它们中的大多数是杂文或小品文，类似美国学生在大学里用母语常写的议论文一样。即便是其中两篇用于描述和一篇用于抒情的散文，也不带有这类文学作品通常会有的华丽辞藻和浓烈的抒情色彩。

我们决定选用文学性的散文而不是新闻材料，还有第三个、也是最为重要的一个原因。这个原因是跟本教程的教学目的直接相关的。如前所述，本教程旨在帮助学生改善口头和书面的表达能力。我们相信，经过精心挑选的文学作品最有助于实现这一目标。中国文化中的一个共识是：文学代表了使用得最好的语言，在文学中能找到用于不同目的的最佳范文。优秀的作家首先是语言大师。为了达到一定的效果，他们创造性地运用语言，随意调动一切修辞技巧，从而最有效地表达自己的思想。例如：他们用打比方来进行比较，用夸张来实现强调，用重复来抓住读者的注意力。他们根据自己的意图和作品的对象来使用不同的文体，时而随便，时而正式，时而褒扬，时而讽刺。在可以直陈时，他们改用一个反问句。在可以用肯定句表示肯定时，他们换用双重否定来加强语气。他们甚至斟酌词语的字数和音调来实现句子的对称性和节奏感。这样的创意和功力在一般的新闻作品和科技作品中是无处寻觅的，而我们的学生却正需要学习这些语言技巧来提高自己的表达能力。如果说我们把标准定得偏高，那是因为我们相信高标准的效果。"法乎其上，得乎其中；法乎其中，得乎其下。”只要学生在力争达到高标准的时候实现了中等或中等以上的目标，我们就会感到心满意足。

最后，本书选用的散文都很短小，篇幅均限于一页左右。我们认为，尽管“泛读”有助于语言学习，但“精读”却是必不可少的。学生泛读原作应该安排在他们全面、详尽地分析了体现各种语言规律的语料之后。同时，尽管有必要让学生学习新课文和新的语言现象，但巩固已学的课文和已学的语言现象具有同样重要的意义。本教程中短小的课文既便于对新语料进行分析，也使复习巩固的过程变得更为可行和有效。

威廉玛丽学院　　　　密歇根大学
汤雁方博士　　　　　陈青海博士
yxtang@facstaff.wm.edu　　chenq@umich.edu

Suggestions on Teaching the Course

Description of the textbook

This textbook includes both a core section and a supplementary section containing extra reading materials. The core comprises fourteen lessons that make up a yearlong integrated study of Chinese at the fourth-year level. These fourteen lessons are organized under five major units according to the general styles in which the essays are written: narration, description, persuasion, exposition, and lyrical expression. Such a categorization is based on the tradition according to which literary essays are normally divided. Linguistically, these essays share many commonalities in the use of language, as there is description in narration, narration in persuasion, and so forth. By the same token, the labeling of the essays is by no means intended to highlight a curricular emphasis on writing styles, although students are expected to know how to structure an essay in a given form after finishing this course. Our main concern lies with how to train students to understand authentic and formal language, and to communicate their intentions correctly and effectively in both speaking and writing. The emphasis, in other words, is not so much on the composition of an essay as on the acquisition of linguistic skills.

Each lesson is composed of nine sections briefly described as follows:

<u>Introduction</u> (without being labeled such)

This section serves as a general introduction to the new lesson. It tells students what to expect in terms of writing style, and the primary linguistic techniques that the author uses to achieve his or her intention. It highlights the major tasks students are expected to learn and perform in this lesson.

Part I: <u>Guide to the Text</u>

This section provides a simplified version of the original text to be studied. The reasons for this are, first, the simplified version will help students to understand the meaning of the original text, and second, it provides students with a convenient opportunity to observe the differences between informal or less formal language and its formal counterpart.

Part II: <u>Guide to the Words and Expressions</u>

This section is designed to simplify the study of the new words and expressions in a text, and it contains words and expressions the meaning of which can be guessed by students based on their existing knowledge of radicals (introduced in the first lesson) and the characters they already know. Some of these words are ambiguous standing alone, but given the context in which they are used, their meanings are clear. We believe that the process of making intelligent guesses makes it easier for students to remember the words being studied. It also trains students to "infer the unknown from the known," a skill much needed in learning a language as difficult as Chinese.

Part III: <u>Text</u>

The original text is provided in both simple and traditional characters, followed by questions for students' reflection. Most of the essays in this course are philosophical in nature, with interesting topics ranging from descriptions of events or activities to commentaries of social issues. They are mostly in the style of the "personal essay," in which the authors either hint or openly express their personal views on a variety of subjects. They serve as good examples for students of how to narrate an event, explain a point, demonstrate an argument, and so forth.

Part IV: <u>New Words and Expressions</u>

With the help of the first two sections, "Guide to the Text" and "Guide to Words and Expressions," the lists of new vocabulary in many of the lessons has been drastically reduced. The task of acquiring new words is thus much less daunting than with a traditional approach.

Part V: <u>Words, Expressions, and Sentence Patterns</u>

This section is devoted to the explanation of the usage of words, expressions, and sentence patterns. Attention is focused on "discourse" words or structures that look familiar but the meanings and usage of which are rather fluid with shades of nuances that can be made clear only by context. For this reason, many examples are given, and explanations are focused on context rather than on the language itself. Linguistic terms are kept to the minimum.

Part VI: <u>Knowledge and Rhetorical Skills</u>

This section provides information on the "facts" of the Chinese language, and introduces students to most, if not all, the rhetorical strategies that native speakers use to express their thoughts and feelings. Such information is not available in ordinary grammar books for students; neither can it be found in other language textbooks currently on the market. Taken as a whole, the discussions in this section actually give an overview of the Chinese language by exposing its structural "patterns" at various linguistic levels, by highlighting its characteristics with comparisons drawn from English, and by systematizing its linguistic or rhetorical tools that a speaker or writer can adopt to effectively communicate his or her intentions. This section can also be read as stand-alone reference material.

Part VII: Exercises

As in the previous section, this section also sets this textbook apart from its predecessors in that it incorporates a large amount of highly integrated and meticulously designed exercises. Divided into three parts, "Words, Expressions, and Sentence Patterns," "Knowledge and Rhetorical Skills," and "Creative Application," these exercises are of various kinds, each designed with a specific purpose. Every effort has been made to ensure that the learning cycle proceeds from the simple to the complicated, and prior knowledge and skills are sufficiently recycled.

Part VIII: Dialogues Using the Language of the Text

To show students how formal language is used in oral communication, and to provide students with examples of how the words, expressions, and sentence patterns they have learned can actually be used in conversation, we have structured this section using two dialogues focusing on the language of the text being studied. The two parties of the dialogue either play the roles of the characters in the text or assume the stance of third-party observers further arguing, for example, the issue raised by the author of the original essay. These dialogues are both entertaining and serve to explain the original text. Realistically, things may not always be said in such a formal manner as they are in the dialogues. Our aim through these dialogues is to raise students' language level, however, and the feeling for language students get from rehearsing such formal dialogues will help to achieve this purpose.

The supplementary section is composed of seventeen essays arranged under the same categories as the main texts. The instructor can choose a text that fits the text of the lesson being studied thematically or stylistically. We did not distribute the supplementary readings in the individual lessons in order to allow the course as much flexibility as possible. The instructor can make his or her own decision as to whether to have a component of supplementary readings.

The sound files for the course, in the form of a CD-ROM, are also packaged with the textbook.

Suggestions for Instructors

The following is the teaching procedure that we have adopted in the past two years of piloting this textbook in several Chinese language programs. We provide it here for reference, while realizing that further improvement is possible to ensure greater success than we have achieved so far.

Day 1	Part I, Guide to the Text
	Part II, Guide to Words and Expressions
Day 2	Part V, Words, Expressions, and Sentence Patterns
	Part VII, Exercises, "Words, Expressions, and Sentence Patterns"
Day 3	Part III, Text
	Part IV, New Words and Expressions
Day 4	Part VI, Knowledge and Rhetorical Skills
	Part VII, Exercises, "Knowledge and Rhetorical Skills"
Day 5	Part VII, Exercises, "Creative Application"
Day 6	Supplementary Reading
Day 7	Part VIII, Dialogues Using the Language of the Text
Day 8	Test

Several points are worth noting:

1) The decision as to whether to include supplementary readings should be made according to the ability and the demand of the students. Further, if the size of the class is small and the rehearsal of the dialogues can be achieved in a short time, the test can be given on the same day as the dialogues. This reduces the number of days devoted to a lesson to six or seven.

2) To push students to practice their oral skills, great effort must be made to optimize such opportunities. In addition to the opportunities built into this teaching plan, we suggest, for

example, that the two texts (the simplified and the original) should first be retold and discussed before the line-by-line check on comprehension is conducted. We also suggest reading the main text aloud to the instructor in his or her office, if not in class.

3) Some exercises can be done as take-home assignments. We suggest that the homework contain only the exercises on "facts" or "achievement knowledge," whereas those designed and suited for training oral skills should be practiced before class and performed during class.

4) In order for the students to remember and use the language of the original text, we have found a mandatory recitation of selected segments after it is discussed to be helpful. Although American students may dislike such a form of practice, it is highly useful even though the benefits might not be felt until later. The recitation can occur on days 4 and 5 and should take only a short period of class time.

5) Not all the linguistic explanations in the text need to be discussed in class. Since these are in English, students can go over many of them by themselves. Some difficult points should be explained in class, however, as not all the students may read these discussions, preferring to listen to the teacher's grammar explanations. To ensure their self-study of this section, some mechanism can be set up for inspection (such as a five-minute quiz). Students' self-study of these discussions is important, otherwise the class might turn into a lecture and this would seriously affect the anticipated results.

6) For supplementary readings, the instructor can either use those provided at the end of the textbook or prepare his or her own readings written in other forms (such as journalistic or technical) to provide a thematic and stylistic balance. Materials culled from newspapers or magazines can provide students with a set of vocabulary related to the social sciences (i.e., economics, politics, etc.). Because the employed sentence structures are often plain and repetitive, however, their capacity to develop students' rhetorical skills is limited. After undergoing training in much more varied and sophisticated language types provided by this textbook, students should have little problem grammatically or pragmatically in dealing with journalistic or other types of professional writing.

7) Quizzes on vocabulary or other linguistic knowledge can be scheduled as the instructor sees fit.

We believe that a textbook provides a means for achieving an anticipated purpose, and the possibility of achieving this purpose lies in the effort of the students and the instructor's effective use of the learning material. This particularly applies to the present textbook. The instructor may design his or her own teaching plan that best fits his or her students. He or she may even choose to use some components of a lesson, while ignoring others. What we have tried to accomplish with this textbook is to provide our colleagues with a tool. We have made available a comprehensive and in-depth tool for teaching and learning Chinese at the advanced level, and we trust our colleagues' best judgment as to how to use this tool effectively.

Yanfang Tang, Ph.D.   Qinghai Chen, Ph.D.

College of William and Mary   University of Michigan

yxtang@facstaff.wm.edu   chenq@umich.edu

教学建议

本教材的特点

本教材包含正文和补充阅读材料两大部分。正文分为十四课，供四年级整个学年使用。该十四课又根据所选课文的功能分成"叙述"、"描写"、"议论"、"说明"和"抒情"五个单元，即按照传统上散文的分类来编排。这样的分类并非为了在教学中强调文体，而是为了便于学生以指定的功能来练习表达。事实上，从语言的角度来看，这些散文具有许多相同之处，因为叙述中往往带有描写，议论中又常包含叙述，等等。我们的主要目的是通过训练帮助学生理解道地和正式的语言，并以口头和书面的形式正确、有效地表达自己的意图。换言之，教学的重点不在写作，而在于语言技能的习得。

教材中的每一课均由九个部分组成，现分别简单介绍如下：

提示（在课中未用此标题）

这是对新课的总的介绍，使学生对课文的文体以及作者赖以实现特定意图和效果的基本语言技巧有一个大致的了解，并让他们明确本课的主要学习任务。

第一部分：课文导读

这里提供的是经过简写的课文，其目的首先是帮助学生理解原文的意思，其次是为学生提供一个机会，让他们对非正式或不太正式的语言及其相应的较为正式的语言进行对比。

第二部分：词语导学

本部分用以简化新词语的学习，引导学生运用偏旁的知识（在第一课中作了介绍）和已经掌握的汉字来猜测新词语的意思。有些词孤立起来看词义不明显，但通过对比或置于上下文中词义就清楚了。我们认为，这样一个猜测的过程会使学生比较容易记住所学的词语，同时也培养他们"融会贯通，举一反三"的能力。这种能力在学习汉语这样一种难学的语言时是尤其必要的。

第三部分：课文

所选的原文先后以简体字和繁体字给出，接着是供学生在初读时思考的问题。大部分的课文是哲理性的，题材饶有趣味，包括对事件和活动的描写以及对社会问题的述评等等。这些课文多半是杂文，作者针对各种问题含蓄地或公开地发表自己的意见，在如何叙述一个事件、如何解释一个观点及如何阐明一种争议等方面，为学生起到良好的示范作用。

第四部分：新词语

因为"课文导读"和"词语导学"这两个部分分散了难点，许多课的词语表得以大幅度地缩短。跟传统的教法相比，在本教程中学习生词的难度得以降低。

第五部分：词语与句型

本部分用于解释生词、词组和句型的用法，重点放在跟语段有关的词语和结构上。这些词语和结构可能看上去并不陌生，但它们的意思和用法只有在上下文里才变得清楚。正因为如此，这里提供了大量的例句，所作的解释重在语境而不在语法，而且尽可能避免了术语的使用。

第六部分：语言知识与技巧

该部分提供了有关汉语的各种知识，介绍了汉语中绝大部分的修辞技巧。这样的知识在其他现有的汉语（作为外语的）教材中似未提及，在学生的语法书里也难找到。通过介绍汉语各语言层次上的规律，突出与英语的比较，以及把修辞技巧系统化，本部分事实上概括了汉语的基本特点，因此也可被作为一种参考资料而单独使用。

第七部分：练习

与前一部分相同，这一部分也是本教程的特色。大量精心编写而融为一体的练习，使本教程区别于所有现存的高级汉语教材。练习分为"词语与句型"、"语言知识与技巧"、"活学与活用"三组，种类繁多，目的各异。练习的编写还特别注意了语言学习的规律，力求做到循序渐进和大量复现。

第八部分：课文材料对话

本部分提供的两个对话使用了大量该课课文中的语言，目的是显示较为正式的语言在口头交流中的应用，给学生树立榜样，鼓励他们将学过的词语与句型实际应用到对话中去。这两个对话中的双方，或是课文中的角色，或是处于旁观地位的第三者对作者提出的问题发表意见。它们不但呼应了课文，而且引人入胜。尽管在生活中并不总是会使用这样正式的语言，但我们的目的是拔高学生的语言水平，而学生通过练习这些较为正式的对话所获得的语感将有助于达到这一目的。

补充阅读材料含有 17 篇散文，按照与主课文相同的分类方法编排。教师可配合主课文的教学选用题材上或文体上相应的材料供学生补充阅读。我们未将这些材料分别插入各课，是为了使本教程具有较大的灵活性。是否使用及如何使用这些补充材料，应由教师本人酌情而定。

我们的建议

在过去两年对本教材的试用中，我们基本上依循了一定的步骤，现介绍于此，供大家参考。应该指出的是，通过进一步改进教法来获取更好的效果是完全可能的。

第1天	第一部分 课文导读
	第二部分 词语导学
第2天	第五部分 词语与句型
	第七部分 练习（词语与句型）
第3天	第三部分 课文
	第四部分 新词语
第4天	第六部分 语言知识与技巧
	第七部分 练习（语言知识与技巧）
第5天	第七部分 练习（活学与活用）
第6天	补充阅读
第7天	第八部分 课文材料对话
第8天	测验

有几个问题需要说明：

1) 是否使用补充阅读材料应视学生的语言能力和学习要求而定。再者，如班级很小，对话表演占时不多，测验也可在同一天进行。这样，一课的教学时间有可能缩短到6-7个课时。

2) 为了促使学生进行口头练习，必须在教学计划安排的口头活动之外，进一步优化口头练习的机会。例如，在逐行检查学生对简易课文和主课文的理解之前，可先开展复述和讨论等口头活动。要求学生朗诵主课文的做法也值得提倡。

3) 部分练习可作为回家作业。这些通常是有关语言知识的练习和较为机械的练习。凡是可用作口头训练的练习，应要求学生在课前准备，然后在课上进行。

4) 为了让学生记住并运用课文中的语言，可在讨论课文后规定学生背诵文中的指定部分。学生可能不喜欢背诵，但这种做法确实有效，持之以恒，必有好处。背诵如在课上进行，所占的时间不应很多。

5) 并非教材中所有对语言的解释都需要在课上讨论。因为解释是由英语提供的，其中许多内容可由学生自学，在课上只须处理某些难点。有些学生喜欢在课上听老师讲解而可能不在课前自学。在这种情况下，可采取某种措施（如一个五分钟的小测验）来确保他们自学。学生对这些内容的自学极为重要。如果做不到这一点，课上便会充满教师的讲解而难以获得语言学习的预期效果。

6) 教师可选用书中的补充阅读材料，也可以不用这些材料而改用自选的其他形式的作品（如新闻或科技作品）。新闻材料能向学生提供与社会科学（如经济、政治等）有关的各种词汇，但它们的语言较为平淡并缺少变化，在修辞技巧方面对学生的帮助极为有限。由于本教材包含了丰富的高级语言材料，使用过本教材的学生在阅读新闻或其他类型的作品时，大致上不会有太多语法和语用方面的问题。

7) 各种要求的测验可由教师酌情安排。

众所周知，教材只是为达到某种目的提供了一种手段，而能否达到既定的目的取决于学生与教师对它的有效使用。在使用本教材时，教师应根据学生的情况来制定教学计划，比如只选用一课中的某些部分而不面面俱到等等。我们的目的是通过这本教材为同行们提供一种方便，一种具有广度和深度的高年级汉语教学的工具。我们深信，广大汉语教师会各显神通来用好它。

威廉玛丽学院   密歇根大学

汤雁方博士   陈青海博士

yxtang@facstaff.wm.edu   chenq@umich.edu

Abbreviations

adj	adjective
adv	adverb
Adv	adverbial
aug	augmentative
conj	conjunction
lit	literal or literally
m	measure word
n	noun
num	numeral
O	object
onm	onomatopoeia
P	predicate
part	particle
prep	preposition
pro	pronoun
S	subject
v	verb

Advanced Chinese

第一课　寂静的山林

In this first unit, we introduce three essays of narration (叙述, *xùshù*). Narrating an event or activity involves participants (i.e., characters) and the circumstance under which such an event or activity takes place. Description (描写, *miáoxiě*) of the details such as the scenes, the conflicts, and the psychological processes of the main characters is necessary, and a narrative is about how to connect these details to move the story forward. Sentence connection (句子连接, *jùzi liánjiē*) is important because it provides a temporal framework within which the story unfolds. It also helps reveal the complexities of the conflict and the details of the mental activities of the characters.

Sentence connectives (连接词, *liánjiēcí*) help achieve these purposes, but unlike English, Chinese does not rely heavily on sentence connectives to organize sentences or thought processes. In other words, although sentence connectives, such as "but," "yet," and "just as," help reveal the author's opinions and feelings, the nature of the Chinese language is such that even without use of these words, the author is able to demonstrate his or her opinions and feelings. The message of the following text is effectively delivered not only by the plot of the story but also by the ways in which the author presents the details. Sentence connectives are used, but the text is mostly composed of "short sentences" (短句, *duǎnjù*) juxtaposed without much use of these linguistic devices.

I. 课文导读 (Guide to the Text) ❧

　　一天早晨，一只母鹿 (lù, n., deer) 和一只小鹿在山林里的草地上玩。山林静静的 (jìngjìngde, adj., quiet)，没有风，没有小鸟的叫声，太阳也很好。母鹿和小鹿都很高兴，他们在草地上躺下 (tǎngxia, v., lie down) 了。一个猎人 (lièrén, n., hunter) 站在树的后面。他离得很近，只要开枪 (kāiqiāng, v., shoot)，就能打到母鹿。可是他把枪举 (jǔ, v., lift) 起来，放下，又举起来，又放下。他没有开枪，因为他想到了自己的妻子和儿子。

　　这个猎人，别人都觉得他很凶狠 (xiōnghěn, adj., fierce)。他的妻子已经离开了他，家里只有一个四岁的儿子。现在他看着母鹿就想到妻子，看着小鹿就想到儿子。他又把枪放下了。他觉得，草地上和树叶上的露珠 (lùzhū, n.,

1

dewdrops) 都象是他妻子的<u>眼泪</u> (yǎnlèi, n., tears)。他一定要去把她接回来，而且要带着儿子一起去接。

　　猎人从树林里走出来。虽然他有点儿饿，身上也有点儿冷，可是他觉得今天早晨的太阳和山林都比<u>平时</u> (píngshí, adv., at ordinary times) 更可爱。

II. 词语导学 (Guide to New Words and Expressions)

1. Match each item on the left with an item on the right based on the radicals and the character(s) you know:

1) 山林　shānlín　　　　　　　　n. clearing in a wood
　　林间　línjiān　　　　　　　　n. open ground
　　空地　kòngdì　　　　　　　　n. wood in a mountain

2) 跳跃　tiàoyuè　　　　　　　　v. jump
　　移动　yídòng　　　　　　　　v. gleam
　　闪动　shǎndòng　　　　　　　v. move

3) 头顶　tóudǐng　　　　　　　　n. surrounding area
　　高处　gāochù　　　　　　　　n. high place
　　周围　zhōuwéi　　　　　　　　n. the top of the head

4) 食指　shízhǐ　　　　　　　　　n. neck
　　脖子　bózi　　　　　　　　　n. index finger
　　泪水　lèishuǐ　　　　　　　　n. tears

5) 鸟巢　niǎocháo　　　　　　　　n. twig
　　树枝　shùzhī　　　　　　　　n. clusters of tall grass
　　草丛　cǎocóng　　　　　　　　n. bird's nest

6) 饥饿　jī'è　　　　　　　　　　adj. hungry
　　愧恨　kuìhèn　　　　　　　　adj. thin and weak
　　瘦弱　shòuruò　　　　　　　　n. remorse

7) 温热　wēnrè　　　　　　　　　adj. warm (water)

2

温暖　wēnnuǎn　　　　　adj. chilly
凉　　liáng　　　　　　　adj. warm (sunlight)

2. Select an appropriate meaning for the underlined word or phrase in each sentence according to the context and the character(s) you know:

1) 大家都睡了，寂静 (jìjìng, adj.) 的马路上没有一个人。
   a. busy　　b. quiet　　c. crowded

2) 从这儿到那儿是 1,000 米 (mǐ, n.)，要走十多分钟。
   a. meter　　b. mile　　c. foot

3) 他不时 (bùshí, adv.) 地写信回家，所以我们对他的情况很了解。
   a. often　　b. never　　c. sometimes

4) 老人知道死神 (sǐshén, n.) 正在走近自己。他想离开医院回家去看看。
   a. the doctor　　b. Death (personified)　　c. the mail carrier

5) 太阳很亮，走到外面的人都眯 (mī, v.) 着眼睛。
   a. close　　b. open　　c. narrow

6) 我掩 (yǎn, v.) 在大树后面，不让别人看见。
   a. stand　　b. reach　　c. hide

7) 我一叫他的名字，他就应声 (yìngshēng, v.) 站起。
   a. respond to the sound　　b. utter a sound
   c. ignore the sound

8) 小女孩依偎 (yīwēi, v.) 在妈妈身上，不愿意跟妈妈分别。
   a. stay away from　　b. keep jumping around　　c. lean closely on

9) 今晨 (jīnchén, n.) 虽然太阳很好，他仍觉得有些凉。
   a. today　　b. yesterday morning　　c. this morning

III. 课文 (Text)

寂静的山林　刘章盛

3

　　猎枪举了起来，又放下了，又举了起来，又放下了。几十米远的一块林间空地上，绿草萋萋，一只母鹿和一只小鹿在那里嬉戏。小鹿在母鹿的周围跳跃着，不时从母鹿肚下钻过。母鹿的身体有些瘦弱，皮毛还是很漂亮的。它的头随着小鹿的跳跃移动着，不时用嘴在小鹿的身上拱着，微眯的眼睛里流露出幸福的神色。周围的山林静静的，连鸟的叫声都听不见；早晨的阳光从林间透过，在草地上洒下了斑斓的色彩。

　　他掩在粗粗的桦树后面，望着眼前的情景；只要他举起猎枪，一扣扳机，母鹿就会应声倒下。距离太近了，这种机会是很难遇到的；但不知为什么，这个被村里人认为鲁莽凶狠的汉子，今天一举起猎枪，却感到有一种东西在心里撞击着，牵扯着他的手臂。这种神秘的感觉，只有在妻子离去之后，四岁的儿子依偎在他身上时，心里才产生过。

　　今天的山林怎么这么寂静？鸟都飞到什么地方去了？山风怎么也不吹了？青草上的露珠在阳光下闪动，多象妻子眼里的泪水啊！

　　母鹿和小鹿还在那里嬉戏，不知道死神正向它们走近。他又举起了猎枪，瞄准了母鹿的前胸，食指贴向了扳机。母鹿躺下了。它是感到有些站累了，四腿一屈卧倒在草地上，小鹿也在母鹿的身旁卧下，依偎在母鹿的身上。

　　他轻轻地出了一口气，又放下了手里的猎枪。

　　草丛里飞出一只黄色的小鸟，落在他头顶的树枝上。他抬起头，看见枝桠间有一所小小的鸟巢，小鸟嘴里衔着一条小虫，亮晶晶的眼睛向下望着，看到他站在树下，便"忽"地飞向了高处的树枝。几滴露珠从树叶上滚下，落进他的脖子里，凉丝丝的；象什么呢？妻子流下的眼泪，落到他的脖子上，是温热的。

　　想到妻子，望着眼前的小鹿，又想到儿子，他心里涌起一丝愧恨。他忽然决定：今天去把妻子接回来，一定要去，并且带着儿子；还要对妻子说些什么呢？对，就说今天……

　　他又望了一眼依偎在一起的母鹿和小鹿，轻轻地抽回猎枪，离开了树林。虽然今晨起得早，肚里已有些饥饿，露水打湿了裤子，贴在腿上有些凉意，但是他觉得今天的阳光特别温暖，山林也特别美丽。

（选自新地出版社１９８８年《甜甜的泥土》）

繁體字課文 (Text in Traditional Characters)

寂靜的山林　劉章盛

　　獵槍舉了起來，又放下了，又舉了起來，又放下了。幾十米遠的一塊林間空地上，綠草萋萋，一隻母鹿和一隻小鹿在那裡嬉戲。小鹿在母鹿的周圍跳躍著，不時從母鹿肚下鑽過。母鹿的身體有些瘦弱，皮毛還是很漂亮的。牠的頭隨著小鹿的跳躍移動著，不時用嘴在小鹿的身上拱著，微瞇的眼睛裡流露出幸福的神色。周圍的山林靜靜的，連鳥的叫聲都聽不見；早晨的陽光從林間透過，在草地上灑下了斑斕的色彩。

　　他掩在粗粗的樺樹後面，望著眼前的情景；只要他舉起獵槍，一扣扳機，母鹿就會應聲倒下。距離太近了，這種機會是很難遇到的；但不知為什麼，這個被村裡人認為魯莽兇狠的漢子，今天一舉起獵槍，卻感到有一種東西在心裡撞擊著，牽扯著他的手臂。這種神秘的感覺，只有在妻子離去之後，四歲的兒子依偎在他身上時，心裡才產生過。

　　今天的山林怎麼這麼寂靜？鳥都飛到什麼地方去了？山風怎麼也不吹了？青草上的露珠在陽光下閃動，多像妻子眼裡的淚水啊！

　　母鹿和小鹿還在那裡嬉戲，不知道死神正向牠們走近。他又舉起了獵槍，瞄准了母鹿的前胸，食指貼向了扳機。母鹿躺下了。牠是感到有些站累了，四腿一屈臥倒在草地上，小鹿也在母鹿的身旁臥下，依偎在母鹿的身上。

他輕輕地出了一口氣，又放下了手裡的獵槍。

草叢裡飛出一隻黃色的小鳥，落在他頭頂的樹枝上。他抬起頭，看見枝椏間有一所小小的鳥巢，小鳥嘴裡銜著一條小蟲，亮晶晶的眼睛向下望著，看到他站在樹下，便"忽"地飛向了高處的樹枝。幾滴露珠從樹葉上滾下，落進他的脖子裡，涼絲絲的；像什麼呢？妻子流下的眼淚，落到他的脖子上，是溫熱的。

想到妻子，望著眼前的小鹿，又想到兒子，他心裡湧起一絲愧恨。他忽然決定：今天去把妻子接回來，一定要去，並且帶著兒子；還要對妻子說些什麼呢？對，就說今天……

他又望了一眼依偎在一起的母鹿和小鹿，輕輕地抽回獵槍，離開了樹林。雖然今晨起得早，肚裡已有些饑餓，露水打濕了褲子，貼在腿上有些涼意，但是他覺得今天的陽光特別溫暖，山林也特別美麗。

思考題 (Questions to Think About)

今天有两只鹿就在猎人的眼前，但是他没有开枪。在他离开林子的时候，他的感觉却非常好。这是为什么？

IV. 新词语 (New Words and Expressions)

猎枪	lièqiāng	n.	hunting gun
萋萋	qīqī	adj.	lush
嬉戏	xīxì	v.	play
肚	dù	n.	abdomen
钻	zuān	v.	make one's way into
拱	gǒng	v.	push with one's shoulders or head
微	wēi	adv.	slightly

流露	liúlù	v.	reveal
神色	shénsè	n.	look
透	tòu	v.	penetrate
洒	sǎ	v.	shed (light)
斑斓	bānlán	adj.	multicolored
桦树	huàshù	n.	birch
望	wàng	v.	look into the distance
情景	qíngjǐng	n.	scene
扣	kòu	v.	pull (a trigger)
扳机	bānjī	n.	trigger
距离	jùlí	n.	distance
遇到	yùdào	v.	run into
鲁莽	lǔmǎng	adj.	crude and rash
汉子	hànzi	n.	fellow
撞击	zhuàngjī	v.	clash
牵扯	qiānchě	v.	tug
神秘	shénmì	adj.	mysterious
瞄准	miáozhǔn	v.	aim at
胸	xiōng	n.	chest
贴	tiē	v.	keep close to
屈	qū	v.	bend
卧	wò	v.	(of animal) crouch
落	luò	v.	fall
枝桠	zhīyā	n.	branch
衔	xián	v.	hold in the mouth
亮晶晶	liàngjīngjīng	adj.	sparkling
忽	hū	onm.	sound of a bird's sudden flight
凉丝丝	liángsīsī	adj.	slightly cool

涌	yǒng	v.	surge
抽	chōu	v.	draw back (a gun)
打湿	dǎshī	v.	wet

V. 词语与句型 (Words, Expressions, and Sentence Patterns)

1. …, 又 (adv.)　　　　　　　　　　猎枪举了起来，又放下了，…

Among other uses, 又 may also be used to indicate a contradiction in one's thinking and actions. The action of the verb following 又 normally contrasts with that preceding it.

他学了一年中文，又不学了。
妹妹出去了，又回来了。
我想写日记，又怕没时间。

2. 还是 (conj.)　　　　　　　母鹿的身体有些瘦弱，皮毛还是很漂亮的。

In this context, the phrase suggests that, after a second thought, the speaker or the subject of the verb makes a different judgment. There is normally an incongruity between the statements before and after 还是.

他的英文不行，中文还是挺好的。
现在没问题了，以后还是会有的。
他们在美国住了二十年，最后还是回到了中国。

3. 随着 (prep.)　　　　　　　它的头随着小鹿的跳跃移动着，…

A 随着 phrase contains an action that goes along with the action represented by the main verb. It often implies the cause of the main verb. If not emphasized, it is placed after the subject of the sentence. The above sentence can be changed to a more emphatic form: 随着小鹿的跳跃，母鹿的头移动着。

More examples:

很多花儿随着春天的到来开了。

8

随着春天的到来，很多花儿开了。

图书馆随着开学又忙起来了。
随着开学，图书馆又忙起来了。

4. 连 N 都 V　　　　　　　　周围的山林静静的，连鸟的叫声都听不见，…

This structure, where N is the actual subject or object of V, is used to describe the extent to which something happens or does not happen.

他讲故事讲得很好，连大人都爱听。
他讲故事讲得不好，连小孩都不爱听。

她们很喜欢吃中国菜，连筷子都会用。
她们不喜欢吃中国菜，连筷子都不会用。

5. 不知为什么　　　　　　　但不知为什么，这个被村里人认为…

This phrase indicates that it is not clear to the speaker why something happens or does not happen. It is usually used at the beginning of a sentence.

不知为什么，她今天没来。
不知为什么，他们很早就起床了。

6. 却 (adv.)　　　　　　　这个…汉子，今天一举起猎枪，却感到…

This word introduces a situation or fact that is in contrast to what has previously been said. It is more formal than 可是 and is only used in front of the verb.

今天的阳光特别温暖，猎人腿上却感到有些凉意。
小鹿和母鹿在那里嬉戏，猎人的儿子却没跟他在一起。
这位年轻人爬到了山顶却什么也没看见。

7. 怎么 (adv.)　　　　　　　　今天的山林怎么这么寂静？

怎么 differs from 不知为什么 in usage. While the latter expresses the doubt of the speaker

9

in the form of a statement, 怎么 does so by means of a question. Depending on the context, this question does not necessarily need an answer and is therefore a rhetorical question.

山风<u>怎么</u>也不吹了？

Compare: 不知为什么，山风也不吹了。

他今天<u>怎么</u>有一种神秘的感觉？

Compare: 不知为什么，他今天有一种神秘的感觉。

8. 多…(啊)!　　　　　　　　　　青草上的露珠…, <u>多</u>象妻子眼里的泪水<u>啊！</u>

This is an equivalent to the English pattern "how Adj . . .!" or "what N . . .!" 多 is usually the short form for 多么. The optional 啊 carries an emotional weight.

今天的山林<u>多</u>寂静<u>啊！</u>

活着<u>多</u>好<u>啊！</u>

9. 一　　　　　　　　　　它是感到有些站累了，四腿<u>一</u>屈卧倒在草地上，…

In the sentence from the text as well as in the following contexts, 一 indicates that an action occurs just once, or lasts for only a short while.

望<u>一</u>眼，喝<u>一</u>口，笑<u>一</u>下儿，等<u>一</u>会儿；

看<u>一</u>看，尝<u>一</u>尝，笑<u>一</u>笑，等<u>一</u>等；(一 can be omitted in this usage)

四腿<u>一</u>屈，两眼<u>一</u>闭，双手<u>一</u>撑，单脚<u>一</u>跳.

Look again at the four-character expressions in the above. They are all formed by "body part(s) + 一 + V."

一 may also be paired with 就 (or 便, see 10) to suggest that the action of the verb following 一 happens in such a short time that its occurrence immediately leads to that of the action indicated by the second verb.

只要他<u>一</u>扣扳机，母鹿<u>就</u>会应声倒下。

老师<u>一</u>来，他们<u>就</u>走了。

我<u>一</u>见他<u>就</u>生气。

10. 便 (adv.)　　　　　　　　（小鸟）看到他站在树下，便"忽"地飞向了⋯

This word is a formal equivalent to 就 and is used in written language to indicate a) the outcome caused by a certain condition, or b) that one action leads to the other.

他昨天睡得太晚，今天便起不来了。

她一到家便忙着打电话。

In both examples, 便 can be replaced by the colloquial 就.

VI. 语言知识与技巧 (Knowledge and Rhetorical Skills)

1. *Mastering Chinese characters by analyzing their composition*

Analyzing (分析, *fēnxi*) the composition of a character can be very helpful in making an intelligent guess about the meaning and/or pronunciation of that character. This is because around 90 percent of Chinese characters are made up of two parts, with one part suggesting meaning (known as "radical" or 形旁, *xíngpáng*), and the other suggesting sound (声旁, *shēngpáng*). Understanding the meaning of a radical is crucial because it classifies a character and thus makes it much easier to understand its meaning. Although the pronunciation suggested by the phonetic component (often a simple character or a phonetic component of a different composite character) is not always accurate or reliable, it provides a general idea as to how a character is actually pronounced.

Study the characters in the following two sections. In Section A, note the shared radical in each group of words along with the meaning it suggests; in Section B, pay attention to the shared phonetic component in each group of characters and how these characters are pronounced.

A. Example	Related Meaning
河酒渴洗深	water
林桦枝桌桥	wood
地场城墙塔	earth; ground
铁钱针镜钟	metal
灯烟热照烧	fire
明晴晚暗时	sun; time
肺肝脚腿肥	body part

11

雪雷雾露霜	meteorological phenomenon
打扫接换挤	hand
跑踢跳跟路	foot
想忘怕懂情	heart; feeling
眼睛睡眯瞄	eye
嘴吃喝叫唱	mouth
说语词课谢	word; speech
家室宫宿客	roof; house
妈姐姑奶好	female
孩孙孤学孝	child
神礼祝祥福	religious ritual
衬衫裤裙袖	clothes
线绸纸织缝	textile
花草菜茶药	plant; grass
笔筷篮箱篇	bamboo
秋种稻税季	crops
碗砖破矿砍	stone
贵货贸财败	money
船艇舱舵航	boat; ship
迎进迟远道	walking; road
狮猫狼狂猎	animal
饭饮馆饿餐	food
病疼瘦痴疤	disease

B. <u>Example</u>　　　　　　　<u>Related Sound*</u>

1) 恼脑瑙垴　　　　　　　nǎo

僵疆礓缰　　　　　　　jiāng

辟壁璧避臂　　　　　　bì

薛嬖襞

2) 谩蔓鳗馒	mán	man
曼漫慢熳谩墁	màn	
蔓幔镘缦		
泾茎经	jīng	jing
刭颈	jǐng	
劲径胫痉迳弪	jìng	
3) 青清	qīng	qing
情晴	qíng	
请	qǐng	
精菁睛腈	jīng	jing
靖婧	jìng	
4) 决诀抉	jué	jue
快块	kuài	kuai

In short, an informed guess based on knowledge of radicals and phonetic components will help you master a large number of Chinese characters efficiently and effectively.

2. *Sentences within a sentence: nature and effect of "short sentences"*

Chinese is marked by "short sentences" characterized by simple grammatical structures with relatively few words. Short sentences refer not only to short independent sentences ending with a period but also to grammatically self-contained segments, separated from one another by commas, in a long and traditionally defined sentence. Short sentences are characteristic of spoken language (口头语, *kǒutóuyǔ*), although they also occur frequently in written language (书面语, *shūmiànyǔ*). In Chinese, the grammatical relations of the words in a sentence are indicated by word order and the use of "empty words" or "function words" (虚词, *xūcí*). If a sentence is too long with too many empty words, such as sentence connectives, the grammatical relations of the words become too complicated. This makes it difficult not only for the speaker/writer to organize a sentence, but also for the listener/reader to understand such a sentence. Consequently, Chinese speakers tend to use short sentences in writing as well as in speaking.

Using short sentences in writing can make language terse (简洁, *jiǎnjié*), lively (活泼, *huópō*), and forceful (有力, *yǒulì*). For this reason, writers often consciously use them to enhance the clarity and force of their descriptions or arguments. In the text of this lesson, for example, the author uses short sentences whenever possible. The commas and semicolons used to separate the short sentences function as pauses in our silent reading, evoking a sense of rhythm and succinctness:

> 猎枪举了起来，又放下了，又举了起来，又放下了。

> 他又举起了猎枪，瞄准了母鹿的前胸，食指贴向了扳机。

> 草丛里飞出一只黄色的小鸟，落在他头顶的树枝上。他抬起头，看见枝桠间有一所小小的鸟巢，小鸟嘴里衔着一条小虫，亮晶晶的眼睛向下望着，看到他站在树下，便"忽"地飞向了高处的树枝。

> 几滴露珠从树叶上滚下，落进他的脖子里，凉丝丝的；象什么呢？妻子流下的眼泪，落到他的脖子上，是温热的。

> 想到妻子，望着眼前的小鹿，又想到儿子，他心里涌起一丝愧恨。他忽然决定：今天去把妻子接回来，一定要去，并且带着儿子；还要对妻子说些什么呢？对，就说今天……

The effect would be different if the author connected the short sentences into longer ones. Compare the following pairs of sentences:

> 周围静静的山林里连鸟的叫声都听不见，从林间透过的早晨的阳光在草地上洒下了斑斓的色彩。

> 周围的山林静静的，连鸟的叫声都听不见；早晨的阳光从林间透过，在草地上洒下了斑斓的色彩。

> 他又举起猎枪瞄准了母鹿的前胸并把食指贴向了扳机。

> 他又举起了猎枪，瞄准了母鹿的前胸，食指贴向了扳机。

When reading the sentences above, you can probably tell that the second sentence in each pair sounds much more rhythmical and forceful than the first. The use of short sentences in writing relates to the use of punctuation marks, which we shall discuss later in this course.

14

3. *Various ways of saying the same thing*

Like English, or any other language, Chinese allows a variety of ways of expressing essentially the same idea. These diverse expressions produce different effects on the reader. Compare the following sentences:

1) 今天的山林很寂静。 *= desolate, quiet*
   adj. modified, declarative
2) 今天的山林寂静极了。
3) 今天的山林真寂静！
4) 今天的山林太寂静了！
5) 今天的山林多寂静啊！
6) 今天的山林怎么这么寂静？ *rhetorical*

1) and 2) differ only in the way the adjective is modified. Although 2) sounds more emphatic than 1), they are both declarative sentences. The other four examples, however, represent different sentence types, with 3), 4), and 5) being exclamations, and 6) a (rhetorical) question. All the sentences describe the quietude in the woods, and yet each conveys a different degree of force or even a different shade of feeling. Look also at the following:

1) 还要对妻子说，今天…
2) 还要对妻子说什么呢？对，就说今天…

The expression in the form of question and answer, as in 2), is clearly more vivid and expressive than a plain declarative statement, as in 1).

4. *Connecting sentences to increase clarity (1)*

Depending on your communicative needs, in many circumstances you may want to connect sentences in ways that express your ideas more cohesively and thus more clearly. In other words, whether you are describing an event or making an argument, you may want to reveal the sequence in which things develop, or the logical steps of your thinking, so that the listener or reader can better understand you. In these circumstances, you can use many sentence connectives in Chinese to help you achieve this purpose. These sentence connectives either display the order in which things happen or provide explanations why things happen in the way they do. The following represent three scenarios that require you to use certain specific sentence connectives. Scenarios that require the use of other sentence connectives will be introduced later.

1) When you narrate an event, you normally follow a temporal order in your description of the occurrences. You may use these sentence connectives to make this temporal order clear to your listener or reader: 先, 接着, 然后, 以后, 后来, 于是, 终于, 就, 便, 又, 一...就... etc. Of course, if the context is clear, you may simply list the sentences one after another according to the order in which things happened without the use of these sentence connectives.

猎枪举了起来，<u>又</u>放下了，<u>又</u>举了起来，<u>又</u>放下了。

小鸟嘴里衔着一条小虫，看到他站在树下，<u>便</u>"忽"地飞向了高处的树枝。

想到妻子，他心里涌起一丝愧恨。<u>于是</u>他决定：今天去把妻子接回来。

猎人<u>先</u>轻轻地抽回猎枪，<u>然后</u>离开了树林。

猎人举起了猎枪，瞄准了母鹿的前胸，食指贴向了扳机。

2) Sometimes in your narration, you may want to make a contrast (对比, *duìbǐ*) in the things you describe to make your idea clearer. In such a scenario, instead of continuing what you are saying, you may make an abrupt turn (转折, *zhuǎnzhé*) and say the opposite to heighten the contrast. The following sentence connectives or sentence patterns can help you do this: 虽然…但是…, 可是, 却, 然而, 不过, etc.

机会太好了，<u>不过</u>，他没有开枪。

猎人可以打到两只鹿，<u>然而</u>他空手回家了。

<u>虽然</u>腿上有些凉意，<u>但是</u>他觉得阳光特别温暖。

这个鲁莽凶狠的汉子，今天<u>却</u>感到有一种东西在心里撞击着。

3) In a third scenario, where you want to emphasize the conditions (条件, *tiáojiàn*) under which something can happen or cannot happen, you can use such sentence patterns as 只要…就…, 只有…才…, and 除非…才…to connect the sentence that indicates the condition with the one that suggests the result.

<u>只要</u>他一扣扳机，母鹿<u>就</u>会应声倒下。

这种感觉，<u>只有</u>儿子依偎在他身上时，心里<u>才</u>产生过。

<u>除非</u>他去把妻子接回来，儿子<u>才</u>会高兴。

In cases where you want to express the idea that, regardless of the condition, something is bound to happen, or not to happen, you can use the sentence pattern 不管／不论／无论…都／也／还….

不管母鹿站着还是卧着，小鹿都在她周围跳跃。

不论妻子说什么，他也要接她回家。

VII. 练习 (Exercises)

词语与句型

1. Based on the text, give the Chinese equivalents for the English phrases below, and then fill in the blanks of the following sentences:

to raise the hunting gun	an open space in the woods
sparkling eyes	bright colors
not knowing why	along with
a scene before one's eyes	to fall at (or responding to) the sound
a crude and rash fellow	a mysterious feeling

1) 他心里有 ＿＿＿＿＿＿＿＿ 。

2) 小鸟 ＿＿＿＿＿＿＿＿ 正在看着他。

3) 草地上 ＿＿＿＿＿＿＿＿ 非常美丽。

4) 他 ＿＿＿＿＿＿＿＿ 瞄准母鹿。

5) 母鹿和小鹿在 ＿＿＿＿＿＿＿＿ 上嬉戏。

6) 这个 ＿＿＿＿＿＿＿＿ 今天要去把妻子接回来。

7) 看到 ＿＿＿＿＿＿＿＿ ，他慢慢放下了猎枪。

8) 猎人一扣动扳机，母鹿就会 ＿＿＿＿＿＿＿＿ 。

9) ＿＿＿＿＿＿＿＿ ，没有人愿意帮助他。

10) ＿＿＿＿＿＿＿＿ 新年的到来，每个人又大了一岁。

2. Use the words or expressions given in parentheses to rewrite the following sentences to make

17

them more formal:

   1) 孩子们课间都到操场上玩儿。（嬉戏）

   2) 小姑娘靠在妈妈的身上。（依偎）

   3) 在历史课上，他常常提出奇怪的问题。（不时）

   4) 天黑了，她身上觉得有些冷。（凉意）

   5) 因为太累了，他一下子躺倒在草地上。（卧）

   6) 早晨起床时，他有一种饿的感觉。（饥饿）

   7) 孩子们的眼睛里有一种幸福的样子。（神色）

   8) 他知道自己错了，心中有一些难受。（一丝愧恨）

3. Expand the phrases into sentences by following the examples:

   1) 他把枪举了起来，<u>又</u>放下了。

      我／想吃鱼汤／不想自己做

      小李／当了三年老师／做了三年学生

      姐姐／定做了衣服／不要了

      他／喜欢睡觉／没有时间睡觉

   2) 她身体不好，学习<u>还是</u>很好<u>的</u>。

      我爸爸／不会写文章／他的字／写得很好看

      电脑／不容易学／工作机会／很多

      他自己／觉得没唱好／鼓掌的人／不少

      丽莎／没有去过中国／她对中国／很了解

   3) 房间很小，<u>连</u>两个人<u>都</u>坐不下。

      昨天的舞会／非常重要／校长／来了

      这些字／很容易／小学生／会写

      房间很小，<u>连</u>坐的地方<u>都</u>没有。

      大家／玩得太高兴／时间／忘记了

天气／不冷／帽子／不用戴

4) 你刚吃过饭，<u>怎么</u>又饿了？

　　这部电影／他看过好几遍了／还要看

　　同学们／都来了／小王没来

　　你／很喜欢那辆车／把它卖了

　　你们／去看电影／不告诉我

5) 他很喜欢照相，我们<u>便</u>常收到他寄来的照片。

　　学校放假了／校园里／很安静

　　屋子里太热／大家／坐到外边的树下

　　中国去不了／他们／去了日本

　　她父母研究文学／家里／有许多书

6) 他住在学校宿舍，<u>却</u>自己做饭。

　　他／刚离开北京／很想再回去

　　猎人／瞄准了母鹿／没有开枪

　　死神／正向他们走近／他们／不知道

　　雨水／打湿了裤子／腿上／没有凉意

7) <u>只要</u>想到妻子，他心里<u>就</u>涌起一丝愧恨。

　　站在树下／你／能看见那只鸟巢

　　天气好／我们／去爬山

　　打个电话过去／汽车／会开过来

　　住得离商店近／买东西／很方便

8) <u>不管</u>草地湿不湿，我们每天早晨<u>都</u>去打排球。

　　遇到谁／他／问这个问题

　　树丛里有什么／猎人／进去看一看

　　心里怎么想／嘴上／不要说

　　下不下雨／路上／很脏

19

语言知识与技巧

4. Match the groups of characters in the left column with their implied meanings in the right column:

Characters		Implied Meanings
____ 海洋江湖	a)	stone
____ 跃踩跪跨	b)	textile
____ 焰烫煮熟	c)	clothes
____ 根森床柴	d)	boat; ship
____ 线绒绳丝	e)	disease
____ 袄袜襟袋	f)	water
____ 碟碎矿磐	g)	wood
____ 舰舶舫艘	h)	fire
____ 宅安牢宾	i)	hand
____ 巡退逃途	j)	sun; time
____ 痫疯痛疗	k)	plant; grass
____ 愁念惊懒	l)	foot
____ 抓指掌拜	m)	roof; house
____ 芽芳蕉苗	n)	walking; road
____ 暗时旦晨	o)	heart; feeling

5. Based on your knowledge of the radicals, study the meanings of the words below and then fill in the blanks of the following sentences:

怯懦 qiènuò	拖拽 tuōyè	堤坝 dībà
清澈 qīngchè	划艇 huátǐng	狂吼 kuánghǒu
白痴 báichī	马褂 mǎguà	讥讽 jīfěng
臂膀 bìbǎng	蝴蝶 húdié	松树 sōngshù

1) 他在女人面前是个 _____ (idiot)。

20

2) 远处的河上，有一条长长的 ＿＿＿＿＿＿＿ (dam)。

3) 他举起 ＿＿＿＿＿＿＿ (arms) 向我走来。

4) 她看到很多 ＿＿＿＿＿＿＿ (butterfly) 飞来飞去。

5) 风很大，＿＿＿＿＿＿＿ (rowboat) 走得很慢。

6) 许多年以前的 ＿＿＿＿＿＿＿ (mandarin jacket)，现在已经没有人穿了。

7) 这样的人常常受到别人的 ＿＿＿＿＿＿＿ (ridicule)。

8) 几个人 ＿＿＿＿＿＿＿ (haul) 着一辆坏车，不知是去哪儿。

9) 院子里的两棵 ＿＿松树＿＿ (pine tree) 长得太快了。

10) 因为 ＿＿＿＿＿＿＿ (timidness)，我失去了很多机会。

11) 狮子的 ＿＿＿＿＿＿＿ (wild roar)，大家都听见了。

12) 我们爱去 ＿＿清澈＿＿ (clear) 的湖水里游泳。

6. Connect the sentences in sections A, B, and C below using the connectives in parentheses:

A. You want to indicate the temporal order in which things take place:

1) 他轻轻地出了口气。他放下了手里的书。（然后）
2) 老师们看完了电影。他们回家了。（便）
3) 弟弟妹妹听说月亮出来了。他们都到窗口去看。（于是）
4) 他去了好几家书店。他买到了那本书。（终于）
5) 她跟男朋友分手了。男朋友又有了新的女朋友。（接着）

B. You want to make a turn or contrast in the meaning:

1) 父母亲希望他学医。他进了工学院（虽然…但是…）
2) 我们都要去中国旅行。只有我一个人会去上海。（不过）
3) 许多人认为考试对学生有帮助。也有人认为考试没好处。（然而）
4) 他心里非常高兴。他不能对别人说。（却）
5) 她喜欢外语。学习外语是要花很多时间的。（而）

21

C. You want to set up a condition under which things do or do not happen:

1) 学生住在校内。他们能熟悉校园生活。（只有…才）

2) 你得了什么病。你要找大夫看一看。（不管…都）

3) 我有空儿。我会请你吃饭。（只要…就）

4) 你做完作业。你可以看一会儿电视。（除非…才）

5) 那家饭馆怎么小。它是一家好饭馆。（不论…还）

7. Express the meaning of each of the following sentences in ways that suggest different degrees of emphasis (refer to VI.3 if necessary):

1) 母鹿的皮毛很漂亮。

2) 这种感觉真神秘。

3) 今天的阳光特别温暖，山林特别美丽。

4) 露珠象妻子流下的眼泪。

8. Rewrite the following passages using short sentences, so that the narratives sound concise, lively, and forceful:

1) 林间空地上的一只母鹿和一只小鹿正在草地上嬉戏。他们没有看到掩在大树后面正在向他们瞄准的猎人。鲁莽凶狠的猎人没有开枪的原因（"reason"）是他想到了自己的妻子和儿子。他决定今天就要带着儿子去把已经离开他的妻子接回来。

2) 吴教授的好朋友刘先生听说吴教授病了住在医院里。他想到医院去看望吴教授可是又不知道吴教授住在哪一个医院。刘先生打过电话去的医院都说没有这么一个病人。他没有给吴太太打电话的原因是吴太太现在不在家而是去美国照顾（"take care of"）刚生孩子的女儿了。

活学与活用

9. Using the expressions provided, narrate or describe the scene, the characters, and the details of the story in the text.

1) 今天早晨的山林是什么样子？

　　寂静／连鸟的叫声都听不见

　　阳光透过树林／草地上到处是斑斓的色彩

　　青草上和树叶上的露珠／在阳光下闪动

2) 母鹿和小鹿在做什么？

　　在林间空地上嬉戏／在草地上躺下／依偎在一起

　　流露出幸福的神色

3) 猎人为什么举起了猎枪又放下？

　　不知为什么／心里有一种神秘的感觉

　　望着眼前的情景／想到／又想到

　　心里涌起一丝愧恨

4) 猎人是个什么样的人？

　　村里的人认为／鲁莽凶狠的汉子

　　我认为／……

10. Answer the following questions based on your own opinions and experiences:

1) 你打过猎吗？你对打猎有什么看法？

2) 在山林里除了打猎还可以有些什么活动？谈谈你所熟悉的一种活动。

3) 你在生活中有没有碰到过鲁莽凶狠的人？这样的人也有感情吗？说一说你知道的一件事。

4) 动物有感情吗？人的感情和动物的感情一样吗？

5) 你什么时候有过神秘的感觉？说一下当时的情况。

11. Write an essay about a memorable field trip. Narrate the event including the details of time, place, people, and activities. Make sure that you also include some descriptions of how or what the main characters think. Use short sentences and appropriate sentence connectives.

VIII. 课文材料对话 (Dialogues Using the Language of the Text) 🎧

A

甲：这幅画儿画的是一块林间空地，周围的山林漂亮极了。

乙：是啊，你看空地上那两只依偎在一起的鹿，眼睛里还好象有一种幸福的神色呢。

甲：这种情景在生活中是很难看到的。可是，我最喜欢的还是这幅画儿的色彩。你看，阳光透过树枝，树叶上和青草上的露珠都亮晶晶的。

乙：快看这儿。这棵最粗的大树后面还躲着一个人呢。

甲：画的是猎人吧。他跟鹿的距离这么近，可是他的猎枪为什么不是举着的呢？

乙：我想，看到这两只鹿亲热的样子，他心里一定有一种神秘的感觉吧。

B

母鹿：孩子，我站得有些累了。

小鹿：妈妈，你身体太弱了，还是到那边草丛里躺一下吧。

母鹿：可是不知为什么，我觉得死神正在向我们走近。

小鹿：这不是真的，妈妈。这里这么安静，连鸟的叫声都听不见。今天的阳光又特别温暖，这样的天气是很少有的。

母鹿：谁知道有没有猎人正在向我们瞄准呢？只要他一扣扳机，我们就都完了。

小鹿：妈妈，我看到你的眼泪了。不，它们掉到我的脖子上了。那好吧，我们就赶快离开树林吧。

第二课　高处何所有

Generally speaking, narrators are of two kinds: one speaks in the first person singular (第一人称, *dìyī rénchēng*) as a character in the story, and the other assumes the stance of a third person (第三人称, *dìsān rénchēng*) who describes things and events from a "detached" position. Whatever voice the narrator adopts, a typical narration involves direct speech (直接引语, *zhíjiē yǐn yǔ*), indirect speech (间接引语, *jiànjiē yǐn yǔ*), or both. We generally assume that direct speech is informal (非正式, *fēi zhèngshì*) or casual (随便, *suíbiàn*), since it is normally a written representation of oral speech. This, however, is not always the case. In real-life communicative situations, a person can speak formally or informally depending on his or her age, educational background, and social status. In writing, the author makes the characters speak formally or informally based on his or her perception of the reader's educational and social background. This point is exemplified in the text of this lesson, which is dedicated by the author to a group of students graduating from college. The characters in this text speak using a formal style (正式语体, *zhèngshì yútǐ*) normally attributed to written language. Can you determine what in particular makes their speech sound so formal?

I. 课文导读 (Guide to the Text)

从前，在一个很远的地方，一位老<u>酋长</u> (qíuzhǎng, n., chief of a tribe) 病得快要死了。他让村里三个最好的年轻人去<u>爬</u> (pá, v., climb) 一座大山，而且一定要爬到最高的地方。这些年轻人回来以后得告诉他看到了什么，听到了什么。

三天以后，第一个年轻人回来了。他穿着漂亮的衣服和鞋子，笑得很开心。他说他看到了路的两边有很多很多花，<u>泉水</u> (quánshuǐ, n., spring water) 在流，小鸟在叫，声音很好听。可是老酋长说那不是<u>山顶</u> (shāndǐng, n., mountain top)，那只是山脚。

一个星期以后，第二个年轻人回来了。他看起来很累，好像受了很多<u>苦</u> (kǔ, n., hardships)。他到过的地方有很多高大的<u>松树</u> (sōngshù, n., pine tree)，又有<u>老鹰</u> (lǎoyīng, n., eagle) 飞来飞去。老酋长说那个地方也不是山顶，而是山腰。

第三个年轻人过了一个月才回来。大家看到他走每一步路都有<u>困难</u>

(kùnnan, n., difficulty)，身上的衣服都破了，头发和嘴唇 (zuǐchún, n., lips) 也都干了，只有眼睛还是亮亮的。他说他到过的地方什么都没有。在天和地之间，他能看到的只有他自己。老酋长说，那才是真的山顶。他让这第三个年轻人做了新酋长。

一个真正的英雄 (yīngxióng, n., hero) 会怎么样呢？他的身上会有很多伤口，他会一个人在一条很长的路上走，他会觉得自己没什么了不起 (liǎobuqǐ, adj., extraordinary)。

II. 词语导学 (Guide to New Words and Expressions)

1. Match each item on the left with an item on the right based on the radicals and the character(s) you know:

1) 蝴蝶 húdié   n. vulture
   秃鹰 tūyīng   n. flowers of all kinds and colors
   繁花 fánhuā   n. butterfly

2) 见闻 jiànwén   n. what one sees and hears
   伤痕 shānghén   n. wound
   智慧 zhìhuì   n. intelligence

3) 祝福 zhùfú   v. arrive
   攀登 pāndēng   v. bless
   到达 dàodá   v. climb

4) 神圣 shénshèng   adj. insignificant
   疲倦 píjuàn   adj. weary
   渺小 miǎoxiǎo   adj. sacred

5) 天意 tiānyì   n. mood
   心情 xīnqíng   n. the will of Heaven
   神情 shénqíng   n. facial expression

2. Select an appropriate meaning for the underlined word in each sentence according to the context and the character(s) you know:

1) 孩子过了半夜还没回家，父母很<u>担心</u> (dānxīn, v.)。
   a. feel worried　　b. feel excited　　c. feel interested

2) 一<u>周</u> (zhōu, n.)共有七天，我们只工作五天。
   a. month　　b. week　　c. day

3) 打<u>长途</u> (chángtú, n.)电话，白天比晚上贵。
   a. local　　b. collect　　c. long distance

4) 我们<u>当年</u>(dāngnián, adv.)住在纽约的时候，你还是个小学生。
   a. in those years　　b. last year　　c. in these years

5) 只要看一个人的<u>眼神</u> (yǎnshén, n.)，就知道他在想什么。
   a. eyes　　b. eyeballs　　c. expression in the eyes

6) 他爸爸<u>一向</u> (yíxiàng, adv.) 喜欢看足球比赛，每次比赛都要看。
   a. all along　　b. often　　c. seldom

7) 雨下得这么大。看你，<u>全身</u> (quánshēn, n.) 都是水了。
   a. the upper part of the body　　b. the whole body　　c. the lower part of the body

8) 他回来时带着<u>满脸</u> (mǎnliǎn, n.) 的血。
   a. a part of the face　　b. a half of the face　　c. the whole face

9) 他是英国人，<u>不过</u> (búguò, conj.)已经在美国住了很多年了。
   a. although　　b. but　　c. not to mention

10) 这件事他忙了好几个月，真是<u>难为</u> (nánwei, v.) 他了。
    a. be a tough job to　　　　b. be a good experience for
    c. be a rare opportunity for

3. Guess the meanings of the following four-character expressions:

1) 身强体壮　　（强: qiáng, adj., strong; 壮: zhuàng, adj., strong）

2) 智慧过人　　（过: guò, v., surpass）

3) 流泉淙淙　　（淙淙: cóngcóng, onm., gurgling of flowing water）

27

4) 鸟鸣嘤嘤　　（鸣：míng, n., chirping of a bird or birds）
5) 鸟语花香　　（香：xiāng, v., send forth fragrance）
6) 满脸风霜　　（霜：shuāng, n., frost）
7) 一步一蹭　　（蹭：cèng, v., move slowly）
8) 衣不蔽体　　（蔽：bì, v., cover）
9) 蓝天四垂　　（垂：chuí, v., hang down）
10) 一无所见　　（无：wú, n, nothing）

III. 课文 (Text)

高处何所有　　张晓风

赠给毕业同学

很久很久以前，在一个很远很远的地方，一位老酋长正病危。

他找来村中最优秀的三个年轻人，对他们说：

"这是我要离开你们的时候了，我要你们为我做最后一件事。你们三个都是身强体壮而又智慧过人的好孩子，现在，请你们尽其可能地去攀登那座我们一向奉为神圣的大山。你们要尽其可能爬到最高的、最凌越的地方，然后，折回头来告诉我你们的见闻。"

三天后，第一个年轻人回来了，他笑生双靥，衣履光鲜：

"酋长，我到达山顶了，我看到繁花夹道，流泉淙淙，鸟鸣嘤嘤，那地方真不坏啊！"

老酋长笑笑说：

"孩子，那条路我当年也走过，你说的鸟语花香的地方不是山顶，而是山麓。你回去吧！"

一周以后，第二个年轻人也回来了，他精神疲倦，满脸风霜：

28

"酋长，我到达山顶了。我看到高大肃穆的松树林，我看到秃鹰盘旋，那是一个好地方。"

"可惜啊！孩子，那不是山顶，那是山腰。不过，也难为你了，你回去吧！"

一个月过去了，大家都开始为第三位年轻人的安危担心，他却一步一蹭，衣不蔽体地回来了。他发枯唇燥，只剩下清炯的眼神：

"酋长，我终于到达山顶。但是，我该怎么说呢？那里只有高风悲旋，蓝天四垂。"

"你难道在那里一无所见吗？难道连蝴蝶也没有一只吗？"

"是的，酋长，高处一无所有。你所能看到的，只有你自己，只有'个人'被放在天地间的渺小感，只有想起千古英雄的悲激心情。"

"孩子，你到的是真的山顶。按照我们的传统，天意要立你做新酋长，祝福你。"

真英雄何所遇？他遇到的是全身的伤痕，是孤单的长途，以及愈来愈真切的渺小感。

（选自长江文艺出版社１９９５年《精美散文》哲理·文化卷）

繁體字課文 (Text in Traditional Characters)

高處何所有　張曉風

贈給畢業同學

很久很久以前，在一個很遠很遠的地方，一位老酋長正病危。

他找來村中最優秀的三個年輕人，對他們說：

"這是我要離開你們的時候了，我要你們為我做最後一件事。你們三個都是身強體壯而又智慧過人的好孩子，現在，請你們盡其可能地去攀登那座我們一向奉為神聖的大山。你們要盡其可能爬到最高的、最凌越的地方，然後，折回頭來告訴我你們的見聞。"

三天後，第一個年輕人回來了，他笑生雙靨，衣履光鮮：

"酋長，我到達山頂了，我看到繁花夾道，流泉淙淙，鳥鳴嚶嚶，那地方真不壞啊！"

老酋長笑笑說：

"孩子，那條路我當年也走過，你說的鳥語花香的地方不是山頂，而是山麓。你回去吧！"

一週以後，第二個年輕人也回來了，他精神疲倦，滿臉風霜：

"酋長，我到達山頂了。我看到高大肅穆的松樹林，我看到禿鷹盤旋，那是一個好地方。"

"可惜啊！孩子，那不是山頂，那是山腰。不過，也難為你了，你回去吧！"

一個月過去了，大家都開始為第三位年輕人的安危擔心，他卻一步一蹭，衣不蔽體地回來了。他髮枯唇燥，只剩下清炯的眼神：

"酋長，我終於到達山頂。但是，我該怎麼說呢？那裡只有高風悲旋，藍天四垂。"

"你難道在那裡一無所見嗎？難道連蝴蝶也沒有一隻嗎？"

"是的，酋長，高處一無所有。你所能看到的，只有你自己，只有'個人'被放在天地間的渺小感，只有想起千古英雄的悲激心情。"

"孩子，你到的是真的山頂。按照我們的傳統，天意要立你做新酋長，祝福你。"

真英雄何所遇？他遇到的是全身的傷痕，是孤單的長途，以及愈來愈真切的渺小感。

思考題 (Questions to Think About)

为什么第三个年轻人被立为新酋长？你觉得这篇文章要说明什么？

IV. 新词语 (New Words and Expressions)

何	hé	adj.	what
赠	zèng	v.	bestow
病危	bìngwēi	v.	be dying of illness
优秀	yōuxiù	adj.	outstanding
尽	jìn	v.	exhaust
其	qí	pro.	your (his, her, its, their)
奉	fèng	v.	revere
凌越	língyuè	adj.	paramount
折	zhé	v.	turn back
靥	yè	n.	dimple
衣履	yīlǚ	n.	clothes and shoes
光鲜	guāngxiān	adj.	bright and new
夹道	jiādào	v.	line up at both sides of a road
嘤嘤	yīngyīng	onm.	chirping of a bird or birds
山麓	shānlù	n.	foot of a mountain
肃穆	sùmù	adj.	solemn and quiet
盘旋	pánxuán	v.	circle
可惜	kěxī	adv.	regrettably
安危	ānwēi	n.	safety
枯	kū	adj.	dry
燥	zào	adj.	dry
剩下	shèngxia	v.	be left with
清炯	qīngjiǒng	adj.	(of eyes) clear, bright, and piercing
终于	zhōngyú	adv.	finally
悲	bēi	adv.	sorrowfully
旋	xuán	v.	see 盘旋

千古	qiāngǔ	adj.	of all ages
悲激	bēijī	adj.	solemn and indignant
按照	ànzhào	prep.	in accordance with
传统	chuántǒng	n.	tradition
立	lì	v.	appoint
何	hé	pron.	what
孤单	gūdān	adj.	lonely
愈	yù	adv.	愈…愈…: the more... the more...
真切	zhēnqiè	adj.	vivid

V. 词语与句型 (Words, Expressions, and Sentence Patterns)

1. 要 (v.) 　　　　　　　　　　　这是我<u>要</u>离开你们的时候了，…

　　要 is a very useful word if you can ascertain its various meanings in different contexts. Study the following sentences and pay attention to the changed meaning of 要 in different contexts:

> 这是我<u>要</u>离开你们的时候了。(be going to)
> 我<u>要</u>你们为我做最后一件事。(want)
> 这个周末，我<u>要</u>你来参加我的婚礼。(would like)
> 你们<u>要</u>努力爬到最高的地方。(must; should)
> 爬到山顶<u>要</u>半个月的时间。(need; take)

2. 而又 (conj.) 　　　你们三个都是身强体壮<u>而又</u>智慧过人的好孩子，…

　　Like 又…又…, 而又 may be used to connect two verbs, adjectives, or phrases to indicate that two or more actions, states, or qualities coexist. Unlike 又…又…, 而又 is often used in formal language, and the item following 而又 is often more desirable and yet less expected than that preceding it.

> 你们都是身强体壮<u>而又</u>智慧过人的好孩子。(formal)
> Compare: 你们都是<u>又</u>身强体壮<u>又</u>智慧过人的好孩子。(less formal)

32

这是一座具有传统特点<u>而又</u>现代化的城市。(formal)

Compare: 这是一座<u>又</u>具有传统特点<u>又</u>现代化的城市。(less formal)

For monosyllabic modifiers, however, 又⋯又⋯ is more natural:

这是一座<u>又</u>老<u>又</u>新的城市。

他走进一座<u>又</u>高<u>又</u>大的房子。

3. 其 (pro., adj.)　　　　　　　　　　　请你们尽<u>其</u>可能的去攀登那座⋯大山。

　　It is used in formal language to represent various pronouns such as subject pronouns (he/you/they/it), possessive pronouns (her/your/their/its), and demonstrative pronouns (that/those), etc.

你们要尽<u>其</u>可能爬到最高的、最凌越的地方。
You must do all that <u>you</u> can to climb to the highest spot.

只闻<u>其</u>声，不见<u>其</u>人。
Only hear <u>his/her/its</u> voice but not see <u>him/her/it</u>.

我们应该让所有的人各得<u>其</u>所。
We should let each person be in <u>his/her</u> proper position (or situation).

4. 一向 (adv.)　　　　　　　　请你们⋯去攀登那座我们<u>一向</u>奉为神圣的大山。

　　一向 is the same as 向来. It stresses the fact that up until now something or somebody's thinking has remained unchanged.

我们<u>一向</u>认为那是一座神圣的山。

这个<u>一向</u>鲁莽凶狠的汉子，今天举起猎枪，却扣不了板机。

你<u>向来</u>都吃三个面包，今天怎么只吃两个？

5. 不是⋯，而是⋯　　　　　　你说的鸟语花香的地方<u>不是</u>山顶，<u>而是</u>山麓。

　　This is similar to 不是⋯，是⋯, but a little more formal because of 而. 而 also makes the structure more emphatic and balanced.

那<u>不是</u>马，<u>而是</u>鹿。

我们<u>不是</u>来学习的，<u>而是</u>来旅游的。

6. 难为 N 了　　　　　　　　　　　　不过，<u>也难为</u>你<u>了</u>，你回去吧！

By using this expression, the speaker acknowledges that someone has done, or is presented with, something rather difficult. The speaker is often apologetic or thankful to the person if this difficulty was caused by him or her. Otherwise, the speaker simply apologizes or expresses pity for this person. The expression is often preceded with 也 or 真.

你们帮了那么多忙，<u>真难为</u>你们<u>了</u>。

前两位年轻人虽然没爬到山顶，<u>也难为</u>他们<u>了</u>。

别<u>难为</u>他<u>了</u>，这件事让我来做吧。

7. 难道…(吗)?　　　　　　　　　　　你<u>难道</u>在那里一无所见<u>吗</u>?

This structure is used to add force to a rhetorical question. The optional 吗 serves as a softener.

你在那里<u>难道</u>什么都没看见<u>?</u>

Implication: 你在那里一定看见什么了。

你到过的地方<u>难道</u>是山顶<u>吗</u>?

Implication: 你到过的地方一定不是山顶。

<u>这难道</u>是为了我<u>吗</u>?

Implication: 这一定不是为了我。

8. 所 V 的，只有/只是 N　　　　　你<u>所</u>能看到<u>的</u>，<u>只有</u>你自己，…

The N in this structure represents the object of the verb whose exclusiveness is stressed by 所. The structure is more emphatic than the statement expressed in a regular 只 structure. It is also more formal than the latter because of the word 所. 所 can be omitted, thus making the structure less formal. 只有 can be replaced by 只是.

我<u>所</u>看到<u>的</u>，<u>只有</u>我自己的书。

Compare: 我看到的，<u>只有</u>我自己的书。 (less formal)

我只看到我自己的书。 (less emphatic and less formal)

他<u>所</u>想到<u>的</u>，<u>只是</u>妻子和儿子。

Compare: 他想到的，<u>只是</u>妻子和儿子。 (less formal)

他只想到妻子和儿子。 (less emphatic and less formal)

鸟巢里<u>所有的</u>，<u>只是</u>一只小鸟。

Compare: 鸟巢里有的，<u>只是</u>一只小鸟。 (less formal)

鸟巢里只有一只小鸟。 (less emphatic and less formal)

9. 何所 V / 一无所 V   高处<u>何所有</u>？

是的，酋长，高处<u>一无所</u>有。

The unmarked order, in the grammatical sense, of the rather formal question-form structure 何所有 is 所有何, in which 何 is the object of 有. Other examples are:

<u>何所</u>遇	what to encounter (as seen in the text)
<u>何所</u>求	what to request/demand
<u>何所</u>思	what to think about

Similarly, the grammatically unmarked order of the structure (一)无所见 is 所见(一)无, meaning "to see nothing." 一 adds force to the structure, which means "not to see even one thing." Other examples are:

<u>一无所</u>求	to ask for not even one thing
<u>一无所</u>知	to know not even one thing
<u>一无所</u>得	to gain not even one thing

10. 以及 (conj.)   他遇到的是 …，<u>以及</u>愈来愈真切的渺小感。

以及 or 及 is the formal equivalent of 和, positioned before the last item in a series of listed items. It is particularly preferred to 和 when the list is long, and when 和 has already been used previously in linking one or more of the items.

他遇到的是伤痕，孤独，<u>及</u>渺小感。

草地上的母鹿和小鹿，树桠间的小鸟，<u>以及</u>猎人自己，都喜欢温暖的阳光。

夹道的繁花，淙淙的流泉，嘤嘤的鸟鸣，盘旋的秃鹰，<u>以及</u>肃穆的松树林，所有这些在山顶上都没有。

11. 愈来愈   他遇到的是 …，以及<u>愈来愈</u>真切的渺小感。

This is similar to 越来越, but more formal. It is used only in written language.

他<u>愈来愈</u>感到孤单，<u>愈来愈</u>感到自己渺小。

病危的老酋长<u>愈来愈</u>想立一位年轻人做新酋长。

看着眼前的情景，猎人<u>愈来愈</u>不想开枪。

VI. 语言知识与技巧 (Knowledge and Rhetorical Skills)

1. *Learning to speak and write formal language (1)*

Although language is commonly distinguished as formal and informal, such a distinction does not necessarily characterize written and spoken language respectively. Written language (书面语) may often contain elements characteristic of spoken language (口头语), so that it is not as formal as it is often thought to be. On the other hand, spoken language may take on elements of written language, and as a result it can be formal and even literary. To distinguish these phenomena, we may call the former "colloquial style in written language" (口语体的书面语) and the latter "formal style in spoken language" (书面语体的口头语).

In our everyday life we use both formal and informal language to interact with a variety of people on different occasions. As our communicative needs are different, our intentions are better achieved if we possess the linguistic ability to adjust our language to different interpersonal or social circumstances. The ability to use formal language style (正式语体) in both writing and speech is the hallmark of an educated person in Chinese culture. With regard to a second language learner of Chinese, it is an indicator of a high level of proficiency in the target language.

The text of this lesson features direct speech, which is normally understood to be a representation of what people say in actual conversations. The text is much more formal than that of the previous lesson, however, which is written in a purely narrative style. One factor that contributes to the formal characteristics of this text is the heavy use of four-character expressions (四字词语), which, by their very nature, are considered formal. There are many other reasons why one essay or speech may be more formal than another. You will learn these various means to speak and write formally as you proceed in this course.

2. *Raising language level by using four-character expressions*

[handwritten note: helps write / memorize / to better express ideas (concisely)]

Four-character expressions are a unique feature of modern Chinese. They are syntactically and phonologically fashioned by the nature of the language. They are actively employed by native speakers to express their thoughts and feelings because of their expressiveness and effectiveness.

Firstly, four-character expressions have an air of antiquity about them, derived as they are from classical documents and literary texts. They occur predominantly in written language, and thus, used in conversation, particularly evoke a feeling of formality and elegance. Secondly, the four syllables of a four-character expression are normally arranged according to certain syntactical and tonal patterns. This tendency toward structural and phonological regularity adds rhythm to speech, making it sound brisk, rhythmical, and forceful. Thirdly, although composed of only four characters, such expressions are rich in implication and can express complicated ideas concisely and clearly. Finally, and probably most importantly, many four-character expressions make use of concrete objects to suggest, rather than directly state, ideas and feelings. This imagistic orientation creates a visual dimension, which contributes to the particular effectiveness of four-character expressions in oral as well as written communication.

A great many four-character expressions have become set phrases, referred to as 成语. Many others are structurally more flexible in the sense that the component characters are movable or replaceable. In Lesson Six you will learn to analyze the structural composition of four-character expressions. For now your attention should be focused on how to approach a four-character expression semantically. One way to understand a four-character expression is to guess its meaning based on the characters you already know.* Look at the familiar characters and study the unfamiliar ones in their context. You should then confirm your understanding of the expression itself in the context where it occurs. If you still have difficulty in figuring out the overall meaning of the four-character expression, look up the character(s) in a dictionary. To illustrate the point, let us examine the following four-character expressions:

鸟语花香，雨过天晴，聪明过人，一天到晚，终有一日，
不大不小，又高又瘦，走马看花，如鱼得水，泪如雨下

Look at every character in each of these expressions. Is there any character that you do not know? Perhaps you have learned all four characters separately but have not seen them in this particular context. Now, study the four characters in relation to each other and make a guess at the meaning of the expression. As you do so, remember to read beyond the surface of the expression for any metaphorical meaning it may suggest.

Here is another group of four-character expressions:

面红耳赤，坐立不安，三心二意，张口结舌，手舞足蹈，
应有尽有，好事多磨，不计其数，万众一心，阳奉阴违

Do you know every word in them? Perhaps there are one or two characters that you have not met before. Can you figure out the meaning of the unfamiliar character(s) in the context of the ones you know? If not, look up this character in the dictionary.

Four-character expressions are not as daunting as they seem to be. More often than not, you can guess the meaning of an expression without using a dictionary. Even if you have to use a dictionary, following the above steps will not only save you time but also help you better understand, memorize, and use the four-character expression under study.

(*Another way to understand a four-character expression is to locate the characters representing concrete objects and phenomena, and study the rest of the character(s) in relation to these. We shall discuss this strategy in Lesson Ten.)

3. *Using onomatopoeia to make expression more vivid*

Like any other languages, Chinese has its own set of onomatopoeia words. By imitating the sound of an insect, an animal, or a natural phenomenon, you make the description of an event, activity, or situation more vivid (生动, shēngdòng). There is no particularly good way to learn these sound words other than memorizing them each time they occur. In this and previous lessons, we have come across the following onomatopoeia words:

忽 (hū): sound of a bird's sudden flight

淙淙 (cóngcóng): gurgling of flowing water

嘤嘤 (yīngyīng): chirping of a bird or birds

Are these imitations of the natural sounds similar to those in English?

In Lesson 4, the following sound words will appear:

哄 (hōng): sound of a group of people's sudden laughter

嘻嘻哈哈 (xīxī hāhā): sound of laughter

38

蹬蹬蹬 (dēngdēngdēng): sound of a person's heavy footsteps

VII. 练习 (Exercises)

词语与句型

1. Based on the text, give the Chinese equivalents for the English phrases below and then fill in the blanks in the following sentences:

> to smile showing two dimples
> birds sing and flowers send forth fragrance
> with hardships (represented by wind and frost) shown on the face
> with clothes hardly covering the body
> (of a person) strong and sturdy
> to see not even one thing
> to excel in wisdom
> to be dressed in bright and new clothes and shoes

1) 那儿什么都没有，我在那儿 _____。

2) 这么重的活儿，只有 _____ 的人才干得了。

3) 这真是一个 _____ 的好地方。

4) 要解决这个问题，一定得找到一个 _____ 的人。

5) 瞧你脸上这 _____ 的样子，有什么喜事了？

6) 别看他 _____，其实身上连一分钱都没有。

7) 当年他穷得 _____，现在可大不一样了。

8) 这位老人 _____，他过去一定吃过很多苦。

2. Using the words or expressions given in parentheses, rewrite the following sentences to make them more formal or concise:

1) 这些学生都非常好，以后会很有前途。（优秀）

2) 你们不用为他着急，他一定会回来的。（为…担心）

3) 妻子死了，孩子走了，老人过着一个人的生活。（孤单）

4) 他总是到得很早，今天一定有什么事了。（一向）

5) 只要走得再近些，就看得更清楚。（真切）

6) 猎人看到一只山鹰在头顶上飞来飞去。（盘旋）

7) 虽然他远离家乡，但亲人们一直把他的情况放在心上。（安危）

8) 从中国人一向的做法来看，春节是一个重要的节日。（按照…的传统）

9) 第三个年轻人觉得很累，他想好好休息一下。（疲倦）

10) 他刚从中国回来，我们都很希望有机会听他谈谈他了解到的情况。（见闻）

3. Fill in the blanks in the following sentences with these monosyllabic verbs:

A. 拱，掩，扣，抽，折，垂，蹭

1) 他轻轻地 _____ 回猎枪，离开了树林。

2) 只要一 _____ 扳机，母鹿就会应声倒下。

3) 她坐在一把椅子上，头和手都向下 _____ 着。

4) 小女孩 _____ 在门后，为了不让妈妈看到。

5) 他又累又饿，只能一步一步往前 _____ 。

6) 母鹿不时地用嘴在小鹿身上 _____ 着。

7) 他在去打猎的路上把猎枪丢了，只能又 _____ 回来。

B. 爬，钻，躺，屈，贴，眯

1) 老酋长 _____ 着身子， _____ 在床上。

2) 他们俩 _____ 着身子，互相依偎着。

3) 小男孩 _____ 到树顶，看到了鸟巢里的小鸟。

4) 小狗 _____ 到桌子底下，不肯出来。

5) 她 _____ 着眼睛，流露出幸福的神色。

C. 尽，奉，立，遇

　　1) 每一件事情，我都会 ＿＿＿ 力去做。

　　2) 中国人一向把孔子 ＿＿＿ 为圣人。

　　3) 像老酋长这样的人，是很难 ＿＿＿ 到的。

　　4) 大家都想 ＿＿＿ 一位英雄做他们的领袖。

4. Expand the phrases into sentences by following the examples:

　　1) 我<u>要</u>你们做一件事，你们<u>一定要</u>努力爬到山顶。

　　　　我／你们／听一句话／你们／把中文学好

　　　　我／你们／去一个地方／你们／把在那儿的见闻告诉我

　　　　他们／我／帮一个忙／我／尽力去做

　　　　老师／我们／写一篇作文／我们／在本周完成

　　2) 他<u>是</u>一个身强体壮<u>而又</u>智慧过人的孩子。

　　　　她／一个／聪明能干／美丽动人／姑娘

　　　　猎人／一个／鲁莽／凶狠／汉子

　　　　那／一种／神秘／亲切／感情

　　　　我所看到的／一种／让人喜爱／让人担心／情景

　　3) 第三位年轻人<u>终于</u>到达了山顶。

　　　　猎人／没有开枪

　　　　他／把妻子接了回来

　　　　孩子们／在林间找到了一块草地

　　　　那位满脸风霜的老人／回到了家乡

　　4) 山顶上<u>难道</u>没有蝴蝶吗？

　　　　草地上／有露水

　　　　你们／也为中国担心

　　　　你／不认识这位英雄

这样的机会 / 不好

5) 他<u>所</u>看到<u>的</u>, <u>只有 / 只是</u>他自己。

　　他 / 想到 / 高风悲旋的情景

　　我 / 爱的 / 你一个人

　　大家 / 能听懂的 / 几个简单的词

　　我们 / 学过的 / 美国历史

6) 这种渺小感<u>愈来愈</u>真切。

　　我们 / 喜欢在松树林里玩

　　死神 / 走近他们

　　猎人 / 感到愧恨

　　流泉淙淙、鸟鸣嘤嘤的地方 / 少

7) 那<u>不是</u>山顶, <u>而是</u>山腰。

　　那 / 步枪 / 机枪

　　这种感觉 / 饥饿感 / 疲劳感

　　我们 / 去攀登大山 / 去山林里打猎

　　这 / 夫妻之间的问题 / 男人和女人之间的问题

语言知识与技巧

5. Study the following four-character expressions and check what you think they mean by matching each of them with an English meaning on the right. Pay special attention to the items in B, whose meanings extend beyond the surface meanings of the component characters.

A. 1) 美丽动人　　　　find it hard or embarrassing to say something

　　2) 年轻有为　　　　without parallel in history

　　3) 有口难言　　　　with no relatives to turn to for help

　　4) 力不从心　　　　young and promising

　　5) 举目无亲　　　　pretty and attractive

　　6) 前无古人　　　　unable to do as much as one would like to

B. 1) 眼高手低　　　　　it is hard to succeed without support

2) 小题大做　　　　　crude and careless

3) 粗枝大叶　　　　　all by oneself

4) 单枪匹马　　　　　come straight to the point

5) 孤掌难鸣　　　　　have high standards but low ability

6) 开门见山　　　　　make a fuss over a trifle

6. Study the four-character expressions given below and work out their meanings based on the characters you already know:

坐立不安　　　　吃喝玩乐　　　　天意如此

唇焦口燥　　　　夹道欢迎　　　　繁花似锦

语重心长　　　　迷途知返　　　　充耳不闻

机会难得　　　　愧恨交加　　　　此情此景

一无所长　　　　饱经风霜　　　　满脸喜气

不思上进

7. Based on the English version provided below, complete the Chinese passage that follows by using the four-character expressions from the previous exercise. (This is for practice only! It is not good style to use so many four-character expressions in such a short passage.)

An old man who had experienced tremendous hardship felt upset when he saw his son eating, drinking, enjoying himself, and having fun all day long with no interest in self-improvement. The old man talked to his son earnestly to the extent that his lips and mouth got dry, but his son turned a deaf ear to him. One day, he and his son came to a mysterious place with beautiful flowers of all shapes and colors. To show their hospitality, the local people all came out and lined up on the street welcoming the visitors, and every face beamed with happiness. On seeing this, the son suddenly realized that he was good for nothing and was filled with a deep sense of remorse. For the old man, this represented a really rare opportunity. "This must be God's will," he thought, "to have my son mend his ways."

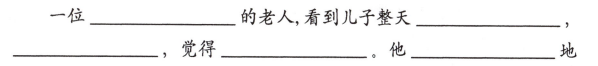

　　一位 ＿＿＿＿＿＿＿ 的老人,看到儿子整天 ＿＿＿＿＿＿＿,

＿＿＿＿＿＿＿, 觉得 ＿＿＿＿＿＿＿。他 ＿＿＿＿＿＿＿ 地

劝告儿子，说得 ＿＿＿＿＿＿＿＿＿ ，可是儿子 ＿＿＿＿＿＿＿＿＿ 。一天，他和儿子来到一个 ＿＿＿＿＿＿＿＿＿ 的神秘的地方。当地人有好客的传统，都出来 ＿＿＿＿＿＿＿＿＿ 这两个客人，个个 ＿＿＿＿＿＿＿＿＿ 。儿子看到 ＿＿＿＿＿＿＿＿＿ ，忽然觉得自己 ＿＿＿＿＿＿＿＿＿ ，因而 ＿＿＿＿＿＿＿＿＿ 。对老人来说，这真是 ＿＿＿＿＿＿＿＿＿ 。"这一定是 ＿＿＿＿＿＿＿＿＿ ，"他想，"要我儿子 ＿＿＿＿＿＿＿＿＿ 。"

8. Match the sound words in the left column with the sounds they imitate in the right column:

1)

砰砰的	雷声
呼呼的	哭声
沙沙的	枪声
蹬蹬蹬的	风声
喀嚓喀嚓的	脚步声
轰隆轰隆的	铃声
呜呜的	钟声
丁零丁零的	照相机声
当当的	雨声

2)

汪汪的	鸡叫声
咯咯的	敲门声
朗朗的	掌声
丁丁冬冬的	狗叫声
哗哗的	读书声
丝丝的	电流声
扑通扑通的	泉水声
喔喔喔的	笑声
嘭嘭的	心跳声

活学与活用

9. Answer the following questions using the expressions provided.

1) 老酋长对三个年轻人说什么？

要离开你们的时候／最后一件事
尽其可能／攀登／那座神圣的大山
爬到最高、最凌越的地方
然后／折回头来／告诉我你们的见闻

2) 这三个年轻人是什么样的人？

44

　　　　村中 / 最优秀

　　　　身强体壮 / 智慧过人

3) 说一下这三个年轻人的情况：

　　　　第一个年轻人 / 三天以后 / 鸟语花香的地方 / 山麓

　　　　第二个年轻人 / 一周以后 / 松树林和秃鹰 / 山腰

　　　　第三个年轻人 / 一个月以后 / 一无所有 / 山顶 / 祝福 / 新酋长

4) 一个真正的英雄会遇到什么？

　　　　全身的伤痕 / 孤单的长途 / 真切的渺小感

5) 作者为什么给快要毕业的学生讲这个故事？

　　　　年轻人 / 祝福

　　　　人生 / 攀登 / 会遇到什么

10. Using your own words, answer the following questions based on your own opinions and experiences:

1) 你中学毕业以前做的最后一件事是什么？

2) 你在什么地方爬过山？有没有到达山顶？说一说那天的情况。

3) 介绍一个你去过的好地方。你当时去那儿做什么？

4) 你有过渺小感吗？你是在什么时候什么地方有这种感觉的？

5) 你想过要当英雄吗？你认为一个人怎样才能成为英雄？

11. Graduation is drawing near. After four years of study in college, you have something important you want to share with your friends. You would like to do so by publishing a story in the campus newspaper. The story involves a professor and his students, and it conveys a rather philosophical message. Use direct speech to make your description more vivid. Also, use as many four-character expressions as you know to make your description of the story sound formal.

VIII. 课文材料对话 (Dialogues Using the Language of the Text)

A

甲："高处何所有"说的是什么？

乙：难道你没听说过这个故事吗？它说的是一位病危的老酋长怎么立了一位新酋长。

甲：酋长一定得身强体壮，特别聪明才行，最好是年轻人。

乙：是啊，老酋长找了三个最优秀的年轻人，让他们尽力去攀登一座神圣的大山。不过，只有一个真正到达了山顶。

甲：他在山顶看到了什么？

乙：山顶一无所有。这位年轻人在那儿看到的，除了蓝天，只有他自己。他觉得自己真渺小啊！

甲：我想这一定就是老酋长要找的英雄，也真难为他了。

乙：是的，老酋长终于按照传统，立了一位新酋长。

B

年轻人一：看你这满脸风霜的样子！你对老酋长说过你的见闻了吗？

年轻人二：说过了。我到的地方只见大片大片的松树林，还有秃鹰在天上飞来飞去。可是不知道为什么，老酋长说那不是山顶，而是山腰。那么你呢？你倒是满脸笑容，身上整整齐齐。你爬到山顶了吗？

年轻人一：也没有。老酋长说我连山腰也没到。

年轻人二：你看到什么了？

年轻人一：我看到的是一个鸟语花香的地方，那儿还有淙淙的泉水呢。

年轻人二：可惜啊！你只到了山麓。

第三课　混浊

The previous lesson introduced you to formal language using four-character expressions. There are other factors that can also make language sound formal. You will encounter these factors in the text of this lesson. Because of these factors, the text of this lesson is a little more difficult.

Technically speaking, when we communicate with others, we often like to use analogies (比喻, *bǐyù*) to make our ideas concrete (具体, *jùtǐ*) and vivid. How do we draw an analogy (打比方, *dǎ bǐfang*) in Chinese? What are the typical metaphors that native speakers of Chinese like to use? If metaphors represent the way that humans think, as some scholars argue, what do the metaphors used by Chinese people show us about their ways of thinking?

I. 课文导读 (Guide to the Text)

　　一座大坝 (bà, n. dam) 把大河分成上游 (shàngyóu, n., upper reaches of a river) 和下游 (xiàyóu, n., lower reaches of a river) 两段 (duàn, n., length of distance)。大坝底下的泄流孔 (xièliúkǒng, n., water-discharging hole) 和山边的排沙 (páishā, n., sand-discharging) 泄流洞让河水从上游流到下游。山边的排沙泄流洞是一条隧道 (suìdào, n., tunnel)，穿过隧道的河水流得特别快。

　　在大河的上游有一条小船，船上的两个人一个胖一个瘦。那条船就象被一条大鱼拉着，很快地往山边的洞口滑 (huá, v., slide) 过去。周围的人看见了，都大叫："快回来！"船上的人也想让小船回过来。他们拼命 (pīnmìng, adv., with all one's might) 努力，可是没有用。忽然，胖子从船上跳进了水里，他以为这样可以活下来。不知为什么，瘦子没有跳，他还留在船上。这时候，小船被吸 (xī, v., suck) 进了洞里。

　　胖子在水里游了一会儿，很快就死了。可是小船却从下游的洞口出来了。瘦子还在船上，他还活着。

　　有人说胖子很勇敢 (yǒnggǎn, adj., brave)，他为了求生 (qiúshēng, n., seeking

47

survival) 而跳进水里；瘦子不勇敢，因为他不**敢** (gǎn, v., dare) 离开小船，他没有死只是因为<u>运气</u> (yùnqi, n., luck) 好。也有人说瘦子很勇敢，因为他敢留在船上从隧道穿过；胖子不勇敢，因为他不敢留在船上穿过隧道。

　　大家都想知道瘦子的想法，可是他<u>呆呆地</u> (dāidāide, adv., dully) 望着大河，什么也没说。

II. 词语导学 (Guide to New Words and Expressions)

1. Match each item on the left with an item on the right based on the radicals and the character(s) you know:

1)　吞　tūn　　　　　　　　　v. swallow
　　躲　duǒ　　　　　　　　　v. hide
　　搅　jiǎo　　　　　　　　　v. stir

2)　桨　jiǎng　　　　　　　　n. light boat
　　钩　gōu　　　　　　　　　n. hook
　　艇　tǐng　　　　　　　　　n. oar

3)　岸　àn　　　　　　　　　　n. bank
　　沙　shā　　　　　　　　　n. tail
　　尾　wěi　　　　　　　　　n. sand

4)　巨兽　jùshòu　　　　　　　n. fly
　　苍蝇　cāngying　　　　　　n. coward
　　懦夫　nuòfū　　　　　　　n. giant beast

5)　堤坝　dībà　　　　　　　　n. cliff
　　山崖　shānyá　　　　　　　n. river course
　　河道　hédào　　　　　　　n. dam

6)　地狱　dìyù　　　　　　　　n. buoy
　　漩流　xuánliú　　　　　　　n. hell
　　浮标　fúbiāo　　　　　　　n. eddy

48

7) 感叹　gǎntàn　　　　　　　　　n. wild roar

　　询问　xúnwèn　　　　　　　　v. inquire

　　狂吼　kuánghǒu　　　　　　　v. sigh with feeling

8) 矗立　chùlì　　　　　　　　　v. cut off

　　截断　jiéduàn　　　　　　　　v. stand tall and upright

　　穿越　chuānyuè　　　　　　　v. pass through

2. Select an appropriate meaning for the underlined word or phrase in each sentence according to the context and the character(s) you know:

1) 他站在船头 (chuántóu, n.), 举起猎枪, 瞄准头顶的秃鹰。

　　　a. front end of the boat　　b. middle of the boat　　c. rear end of the boat

2) 她坐在草丛里, 木然 (mùrán, adv.) 地望着远处的山腰。

　　　a. certainly　　　b. stupefiedly　　　c. suddenly

3) 他把报纸摊开 (tānkāi, v.), 让大家一起看。

　　　a. fold up　　b. put away　　c. spread out

4) 大夫从孩子的鼻孔 (bíkǒng, n.) 里拿出一条小虫。

　　　a. nostril　　　b. nose　　　c. opening

5) 汽车走上山顶时, 车身不时地颤动 (chàndòng, v.)。

　　　a. run　　b. jump　　c. shake

6) 年轻人在漫天 (màntiān, adj.) 的风雪中走了一晚, 终于回到家乡。

　　　a. lasting for days　　b. waterlogged　　c. all over the sky

7) 有母鹿在身旁, 小鹿就不会感到怯懦 (qiènuò, adj.)。

　　　a. timid and scared　　b. appreciated　　c. encouraged

8) 老酋长只有在听了第三个年轻人的见闻后, 心里才觉得平静 (píngjìng, adj.)。

　　　a. interested　　b. excited　　c. calm

9) 那天山间的天气真好, 连雾 (wù, n.) 都没有。

49

a. fog　　　b. cloud　　　c. hail

10) 在山上最高的地方发生了一个<u>奇迹</u> (qíjì, n.)：天上有两个太阳。
　　　a. funny thing　　　b. miracle　　　c. interesting sign

11) 一个地方只要有<u>通路</u> (tōnglù, n.)，就一定有人来过。
　　　a. a broad road　　　b. a short cut　　　c. an open road

III. 课文 (Text)

混浊　　杨东明

一条混浊的大河。

灰色的堤坝在两山之间冷漠地矗立而起，截断了它那大漠狂沙般的黄色的热情。上游的水依旧是黄色的，平静得象一张摊开的饼。下游的水自然是黄色的，坝底的泄流孔和山边的隧道排沙泄流洞犹如巨兽的鼻孔，喷出漫天的黄雾。

一只小小的划艇载着一胖一瘦两个人，沿着堤坝在上游的河道里漂。瘦子坐在船头，胖子坐在船尾，因而那船便微微翘起来，颤动着，象是坠着鱼钩的浮标。

水底莫非有一条吞了钩的大鱼？那船好似被拖拽着，顺着堤坝向岸边的山崖滑去，船底那怪异的大鱼是要进洞的吧？——排沙泄流洞就在那山崖下，一边发出怒不可遏的狂吼，一边搅起黄风般的漩流。

坝上和崖边的人见了，禁不住声声发喊，"快回！"船上的人不呆，胖子和瘦子一起拼命打圆了桨，小船象只被粘住的苍蝇似的鼓着翅挣着腿。然而，那船依然向深幽幽的洞口滑……

岸上的人都看见了，胖子忽然跃起身，坚决地从船上跳进了水里；岸上的人也都看见了，瘦子忽然弯下腰，坚决地向船里一缩……

小船被吸进了洞中。

胖子拼命游了一段，终于沉了底。小船却奇迹般地穿越了几百米隧道，从下游的洞口弹射而出，将瘦子平安地载回。

有人感叹胖子死得勇敢，他勇于跳入水中求生。躲在船上的是懦夫，而懦夫总是容易侥幸地在世上活着。

有人赞叹瘦子活得勇敢，他敢于留在船上，穿越那地狱般的隧道。而胖子的勇敢本身即是一种怯懦，他怯于穿越那可怕的通路。

人们询问瘦子，彼时他们想了些什么，说了些什么。他却哑了似的沉默着，只木然地望着大河。

河水是混浊的，似乎永远也不会澄清。

（选自上海文艺出版社１９９２年《世界华文微型小说大成》）

繁體字課文 (Text in Traditional Characters)

<h1 style="text-align:center">混濁　　楊東明</h1>

一條混濁的大河。

灰色的堤壩在兩山之間冷漠地矗立而起，截斷了牠那大漠狂沙般的黃色的熱情。上游的水依舊是黃色的，平靜得像一張攤開的餅。下游的水自然是黃色的，壩底的泄流孔和山邊的隧道排沙泄流洞猶如巨獸的鼻孔，噴出漫天的黃霧。

一隻小小的划艇載著一胖一瘦兩個人，沿著堤壩在上游的河道裡漂。瘦子坐在船頭，胖子坐在船尾，因而那船便微微翹起來，顫動著，像是墜著魚鉤的浮標。

水底莫非有一條吞了鉤的大魚？那船好似被拖拽著，順著堤壩向岸邊的山崖滑去，船底那怪異的大魚是要進洞的吧？——排沙泄流洞就在那山涯下，一邊發出怒不可遏的狂吼，一邊攪起黃風般的漩流。

壩上和崖邊的人見了，禁不住聲聲發喊，"快回！"船上的人不歇，胖子和瘦子一起拚命打圓了槳，小船像只被粘住的蒼蠅似的鼓著翅掙著腿。然而，那船依然向深幽幽的洞口滑……

岸上的人都看見了，胖子忽然躍起身，堅決地從船上跳進了水裡；岸上的人也都看見了，瘦子忽然彎下腰，堅決地向船裡一縮……

小船被吸進了洞中。

胖子拚命游了一段，終於沉了底。小船卻奇蹟般地穿越了幾百米隧道，從下游的洞口彈射而出，將瘦子平安地載回。

有人感嘆胖子死得勇敢，他勇於跳入水中求生。躲在船上的是懦夫，而懦夫總是容易僥幸地在世上活著。

有人讚嘆瘦子活得勇敢，他敢於留在船上，穿越那地獄般的隧道。而胖子的勇敢本身即是一種怯懦，他怯於穿越那可怕的通道。

人們詢問瘦子，彼時他們想了些什麼，說了些什麼。他卻啞了似的沉默著，只木然地望著大河。

河水是混濁的，似乎永遠也不會澄清。

思考題 (Questions to Think About)

胖子死了，可是瘦子还活着。当人们问瘦子，在那个生死关头 ("life and death moment") 他们想了些什么，说了些什么，为什么瘦子哑了似的沉默着？

IV. 新词语 (New Words and Expressions)

混浊	hùnzhuó	adj.	muddy
冷漠地	lěngmòde	adv.	indifferently
漠	mò	n.	desert; 沙漠

狂	kuáng	adj.	mad
般	bān	part.	just like
依旧	yījiù	adv.	as before
犹如	yóurú	v.	好像
喷	pēn	v.	spurt
载	zài	v.	carry
沿着	yánzhe	prep.	along
漂	piāo	v.	drift (in water)
翘	qiào	v.	tilt up
坠	zhuì	v.	hang down
莫非	mòfēi	adv.	can it be that
好似	hǎosì	v.	好像
顺着	shùnzhe	prep.	along; 沿着
怪异	guàiyì	adj.	strange
怒	nù	n.	anger
遏	è	v.	check
禁不住	jīnbuzhù	v.	can not help (doing)
发喊	fāhǎn	v.	shout out
粘	zhān	v.	glue
鼓翅	gǔ chì	v.	pluck wings
挣腿	zhèng tuǐ	v.	struggle to get legs free
依然	yīrán	adv.	still; 还是, 依旧
深幽幽	shēnyōuyōu	adj.	deep and dark
弯	wān	v.	bend
坚决地	jiānjué	adv.	resolutely
缩	suō	v.	(of body) huddle up
沉	chén	v.	sink
弹射	tánshè	v.	shoot off (as with a catapult)

将	jiāng	prep.	把
侥幸地	jiǎoxìng	adv.	by luck
赞叹	zàntàn	v.	praise highly
彼时	bǐ shí	adv.	at that time
哑	yǎ	adj.	mute
沉默	chénmò	v.	be silent
似乎	sìhū	adv.	as if; 好象
澄清	chéngqīng	v.	(of liquid) become clear

V. 词语与句型 (Words, Expressions, and Sentence Patterns)

1. V 而 V　　　　　　　　　　灰色的堤坝在两山之间冷漠地矗立而起，…

In four-character expressions such as the following, the meaning of 而 is not very clear. It is needed perhaps to form or maintain the four-character structure. The preceding two characters, normally a verbal phrase, specify the cause or manner of the action represented by the verb following 而.

矗立而起　(stand up tall)

一跃而起　(jump up)

弹射而出　(shoot out)

一闪而过　(flash past)

结伴而行　(travel in a group)

2. 那 (pron.)　　　　　　　…，截断了它那大漠狂沙般的黄色的热情。

Depending on the context, 那 can mean 那种, 那个, etc. It can be omitted without affecting the meaning of the sentence, but using it adds force and balance to the sentence structure.

瘦子敢于留在船上，穿越那 (个) 地狱般的隧道。

你能在高处感到的，只有那 (种) 渺小感。

3. N 般　　　　　　　　…，截断了它那大漠狂沙般的黄色的热情。

This is used in written language to introduce an analogy. 般 is a short form for 一般. The colloquial equivalent is 像 N 一样.

大漠狂沙<u>般</u>的热情	<u>象</u>大漠狂沙<u>一样</u>的热情
兄弟<u>般</u>的友情	<u>象</u>兄弟<u>一样</u>的友情
奇迹<u>般</u>地穿越隧道	<u>象</u>奇迹<u>一样</u>地穿越隧道

4. 一 Adj / V 一 Adj / V　　　　　　　　一只小小的划艇载著<u>一</u>胖<u>一</u>瘦两个人。

Each of the two 一 in this structure is followed by a monosyllabic adjective or verb that is opposite in meaning. The two adjectives indicate contrast in the appearance, characteristics, position, or state of being of the people or things being described. The verbs indicate that the two actions are occurring simultaneously or alternately.

两只鞋，<u>一</u>大<u>一</u>小。

从外面<u>一</u>前<u>一</u>后走进两个人来。

电视机<u>一</u>开<u>一</u>关很容易坏的。

记者与这位作家<u>一</u>问<u>一</u>答，谈话进行得很顺利。

5. 因而 (conj.)　　　　　　　　胖子坐在船尾，<u>因而</u>那船便微微翘起来，…

因而 is the same as 因此 (所以 being the colloquial form). Both indicate the result of the action expressed in the previous clause.

瘦子没有跳入水中，<u>因而</u>他随着小船穿越了几百米隧道。

Compare: 瘦子没有跳入水中，所以他随着小船穿越了几百米隧道。

酋长病危，<u>因此</u>，他想要立一位新酋长。

Compare: 酋长病危，所以他想要立一位新酋长。

6. 莫非…?　　　　　　　　　　　水底<u>莫非</u>有一条吞了钩的大鱼<u>?</u>

莫非 is used in written language to form questions such as "can it be that...?" or "is it possible that...?" Its colloquial equivalent is 难道… 吗? This structure indicates suspicion on the part of the speaker. Refer to Part V.7 of Lesson Two.

水底<u>莫非</u>有一条大鱼<u>?</u>
Compare: 水底<u>难道</u>有一条大鱼<u>吗</u><u>?</u>

瘦子沉默着，他<u>莫非</u>哑了<u>吗</u><u>?</u>
Compare: 瘦子沉默着，他<u>难道</u>哑了<u>吗</u><u>?</u>

山顶上<u>莫非</u>一无所有<u>?</u>
Compare: 山顶上<u>难道</u>一无所有<u>吗</u><u>?</u>

7. 禁不住 V　　　　　　坝上和崖边的人见了，<u>禁不住</u>声声发喊，"快回！"

The English equivalent of this structure is "can't help doing something." 禁不住 can be replaced by the similar but more formal variant 不禁 without a change in meaning.

人们<u>禁不住</u>高喊："快回来！"
Compare: 人们<u>不禁</u>高喊："快回来！"

大家都<u>禁不住</u>为他的安危担心。
Compare: 大家都<u>不禁</u>为他的安危担心。

猎人<u>禁不住</u>想起自己的妻子和儿子。
Compare: 他<u>不禁</u>想起自己的妻子和儿子。

8. Adj 于 V　　　　　　　　　胖子死得勇敢，他<u>勇于</u>跳入水中求生。

When used after an adjective, the meaning of 于, an indicator of formal language, is rather vague. It is perhaps used to form a disyllabic word with the adjective, indicating the disposition and emotional state of the individual(s) performing the action of the verb.

老酋长<u>急于</u>立一位新酋长。可是，他<u>苦于</u>找不到真正的英雄。
瘦子<u>敢于</u>留在船上。
胖子<u>怯于</u>穿越那可怕的通路。

9. (然)而 (conj.)　　　　　　　　　　躲在船上的是懦夫，而懦夫总是…

而 is used to connect two SV structures to suggest contrast, or to provide more information about the subject of the first SV structure. Compare:

山顶上一无所有，而山腰和山麓却什么都有。 (contrast)

瘦子活得勇敢，而胖子的勇敢却是一种怯懦。 (contrast)

这个机会太好了，而这种机会是很难遇到的。 (more information)

躲在船上的是懦夫，而懦夫总是容易活着。 (more information)

10. 总是 (adv.)　　　　　　　…，而懦夫总是容易侥幸地在世上活着。

The expression 总是 often implies a complaint or a criticism on the part of the speaker.

老师总是让我们做听写。 (complaining)

我跟你说过多少次了，你总是不听。 (criticizing)

总是要吃完了饭再走吧。 (disapproving)

懦夫总是容易侥幸地在世上活着。 (showing contempt)

11. (好像/仿佛) Adj 似的　　　　　　他却哑了似的沉默著，…

This is often used to describe a person doing something in a way that shows an abnormal state of mind.

他（好象）哑了似的沉默着。

她（好象）疯了似的对周围的人又打又踢。

瘦子（仿佛）聋了似的什么都听不见。

When preceded by 好像, the above sentences would sound less formal. However, they would sound more formal if preceded by 仿佛. 好像 and 仿佛 can also be used by themselves:

河水是混浊的，好象永远也不会澄清（似的）。

流水淙淙，鸟鸣嘤嘤，大自然 ("mother nature") 仿佛在唱歌（似的）。

VI. 语言知识与技巧 (Knowledge and Rhetorical Skills)

1. *Learning to speak and write formal language (2)*

As mentioned earlier, written language need not necessarily be formal, and spoken language need not necessarily be casual. However, written language is generally more formal than spoken language because, after all, in daily conversations even educated people speak in casual style. In addition to four-character expressions, there are many other ways to make writing formal, including the choice of words and sentence structures. It is difficult to specify the extent to which certain words, expressions, and sentence structures are formal. However, the formality of language depends on word choice and use of sentence patterns. In the following list, you will find expressions and sentence structures from the first three lessons of this course that are formal or more formal, and which have less formal or casual equivalents that you may already know.

Formal or More Formal	Less Formal or Casual
嬉戏	玩
跳跃	跳
依偎	靠
询问	问
饥饿	饿
瘦弱	瘦
以及	和
寂静	静，安静
依然	还，还是
不时	常，常常，经常
好似	象，好象
求生	逃命
美丽	漂亮
跳入水中	跳到水里
彼时	那时
怯于	害怕

将	把
便	就
其	他／她／它（们）（的）
犹如	就象
莫非	难道
然而	但是
…而又…	又…又…
…，因而…	（因为）…，所以…
…般	象…一样
所V的，只有…	只V…
愈来愈	越来越
何所遇	碰到什么

We can discern several things from this list of words and sentence patterns. Among others, it appears that one character in casual or less formal style is often represented by two characters in formal style. In other words, words in formal style tend to be composed of two syllables. This is perhaps decided by the orientation of modern Chinese toward two-syllable words. Such a tendency is particularly apparent in written language.* Also, although formal language is derived from spoken language, it also retains traces of classical Chinese. Many words and expressions in the above list, such as 便, 其, 彼时, 怯于, 犹如, 莫非, "所V的，只有…，" 愈来愈, 何所遇, etc., contain elements of classical Chinese at both lexical and syntactical levels. This is why using formal language can effect a feeling of antiquity, elegance, and refinement.

(*The paradox is that due to the influence of classical Chinese, the central feature of which is brevity, some monosyllabic words such as 因, 曾, 如, 望, and 即 sound more formal than their two-syllable equivalents 因为, 曾经, 如果, 希望, and 立即. This phenomenon is particularly evident in formal business letters. We shall discuss this topic later in this course.)

2. Drawing analogies: a way to make statements more vivid

Whether we are aware of it or not, we constantly draw analogies to express ourselves. According to one theory this is because humans actually think in metaphors. Another theory attributes this phenomenon to the innate characteristics of a given language. A third theory holds that drawing analogies is simply a rhetorical means humans adopt to express themselves. Regardless of these diverse opinions, one thing is certain: drawing analogies helps render our thoughts and feelings concrete and thus more vivid.

As with other cultures, in drawing analogies, native speakers of Chinese use objects, things, and phenomena from the natural world as "vehicles" to express their thoughts, often referred to as "tenor." Certain words are typically used to connect the two counterparts, such as (好)象, (犹)如, 似(的), 若, (一)般 and 仿佛. These words can be used by themselves, but they can also be used in combination. For example:

Used by themselves:

> 从树叶上滚下的露珠<u>象</u>妻子的眼泪。
>
> 堤坝截断了大河那大漠狂沙<u>般</u>的热情。
>
> 上游的水平静得<u>象</u>一张摊开的饼。
>
> 坝底的泄流孔<u>犹如</u>巨兽的鼻孔，喷出漫天的黄雾。

Used in combination:

> 她们长得就<u>象</u>亲姐妹<u>一样</u>。
>
> 他坐在椅子上不停地动来动去，<u>好象</u>脖子里有很多头发<u>似的</u>。
>
> 露珠在阳光下闪动，<u>象</u>满地的宝石<u>一般</u>。
>
> 年轻人两眼血红，<u>仿佛</u>几天几夜没睡过觉<u>似的</u>。

The two entities being compared may also appear in a more direct manner with the help of such words as 是, 当做, 变成. For example:

> 他的肚子<u>是</u>无底洞，给他多少，他就能吃多少。
>
> 他们把留学生<u>当作</u>自己的亲人。
>
> 结果，爬山<u>变成</u>了一次考试。

In a still more direct way, analogy is used without any connecting words, and sometimes the tenor is even completely omitted, leaving the reader or listener to infer the meaning by virtue of the mere suggestion of the vehicle:

> 你们还很年轻，<u>前面</u>的<u>路</u>还很长。 (meaning "life")
>
> 生活中有<u>阳光</u>，也有<u>风雨</u>。 (meaning "ups and downs")
>
> <u>胳膊</u> ("arms") <u>拧</u> ("wrestle") 不过<u>大腿</u>。

(meaning "the weak cannot compete with the strong.")

鸡蛋里面<u>挑</u> ("pick") <u>骨头</u> (" bone")。 (meaning "finding faults with what is actually a perfect situation or state.")

In a broad sense, drawing an analogy includes the use of the rhetorical means of personification (拟人, nǐrén). Through this device, non-human beings think and behave like humans, and inanimate entities are filled with life, as if they are mortal:

<u>母鹿和小鹿</u> <u>不知道</u>死神正向他们走近。
<u>长城</u> <u>迎来了</u>世界各地的客人。

In this present essay, there are many instances of personification:

灰色的<u>堤坝</u>在两山之间<u>冷漠</u>地矗立而起，截断了它那大漠狂沙般的黄色的<u>热情</u>。

<u>排沙泄流洞</u>就在那山崖下，一边<u>发出怒不可遏的狂吼</u>，一边<u>搅起黄风般的漩流</u>。

<u>小船</u>象只被粘住的苍蝇似的<u>鼓着翅挣着腿</u>。

大河 and 堤坝 are personalized with the words 热情 and 冷漠, used to describe feelings that only humans have. Similarly, an inanimate object, 小船, becomes animate when it is described as 鼓着翅挣着腿 like a fly.

3. *Making sense of two-syllable words*

By now, you may have noticed that some Chinese two-syllable compounds are composed of antonyms (反义词), and yet this does not appear to affect their capacity to convey a central meaning:

A. 东西 (thing)， 安危 (safety)， 开关 (switch)， 买卖 (trade)，
长短 (length)， 大小 (size)， 多少 (amount)，早晚 (sooner or later)，
动静 (movement)

If you look closely, you will realize that these compounds all express an abstract idea, which does not necessarily correspond to either one of the two component characters. Therefore, interpreting the meanings of compounds like these based on one of the two characters is not a reliable approach. Such an approach, however, can be employed when you try to master certain other types of two-syllable compounds. In the latter case, if you know the meaning of one character or word, you may know more or less the meaning of the entire word or compound. Study the following:

B. 跳跃，饥饿，询问，寂静，清楚，凶狠，鲁莽，怪异，平安，语言，思想，图画，真实，生产

C. 学习，见闻，堤坝，山崖，瘦弱，兄弟，国家，窗户，手足，山水，皮毛，眉目

D. 漩流，通路，粗心，热爱，晚会，讲演，火车，鸡毛

E. 摊开，澄清，说明，打倒，缩小，变成，提高

In Group B, the two words or characters of a compound are synonyms (同义词). One word actually repeats or defines the other; in Group C, the two characters or words are not synonyms, but they relate to each other in a certain way and the meaning they suggest is traceable to one or both of them. In Groups D and E, the two words are juxtaposed according to a hierarchical order: in the former the second word of the compound is the main word, the first being a qualifier; in the latter, the main word of the compound is the first word, the second being a supplement normally indicating result. If you understand the main words of the compounds in these two groups, you will grasp the basic meanings of these two-syllable compounds.

VII. 练习 (Exercises)

词语与句型

1. Give the Chinese equivalents for the English phrases based on the text, and then fill in the blanks in the following sentences:

to give out wild roars	to praise highly
to keep silent as if dumb	to be in an uncontrollable rage
to tilt slightly upward	to drift along the dam
to sink to the bottom	to row with all one's might

1) 大家都想听他的见闻，他却 _____ 。

2) 谁都不愿意打桨，就让小艇在河道里 _____。

3) 桌子这一头压得太重，所以那一头便 _____。

4) 他做的小纸船在水上只漂了一会儿就 _____。

5) 全身伤痕的巨兽一边 _____，一边向猎人扑去。

6) 尽管每个人都 _____，船还是被漩流冲到了崖边。

7) 面对着这个凶狠的汉子，老酋长 _____。

8) 许多人 _____ 他勇于攀登高峰的精神。

2. Rewrite the following sentences with the words or expressions given in parentheses:

A. to make them more formal:

    1) 病危的人也可能因为运气好而活下来。（侥幸）

    2) 第三个年轻人到最后总算平安地回来了。（终于）

    3) 在混浊的河边有着一座神圣的大山。（矗立）

    4) 难道真的有地狱？（莫非）

    5) 草地上的露珠就象妻子的眼泪。（犹如）

    6) 我真的到了山顶。但是，我该怎么说呢？（然而）

B. to make them more vivid:

    1) 他用出全身的力气向岸边游去。（拼命）

    2) 汽车走过隧道的时候一定要开灯。（穿越）

    3) 小鸟听到声音，把脖子收回去，躲了起来。（一缩）

    4) 看他生气的样子，就象要把我一口吃下去似的。（吞）

    5) 怪兽一用力，就把小鹿弄进了嘴里。（吸）

    6) 她笑得差一点把饭吐到我脸上。（喷）

3. Fill in the blanks in the following sentences with the monosyllabic verbs:

    喷，漂，滑，坠，划，搅，躲，翘，沉

1) 只要拿筷子来 _____ 一下，汤就做好了。

2) 大家都在找你，你怎么 _____ 起来了？

3) 不会游泳的人在水里自然要 _____ 下去。

4) 路边的水管破了，水_____ 得很高。

5) 屋后桦树的枝桠上 _____ 着一只风铃 ("wind-bell")。

6) 老人家 _____ 起大拇指，赞扬我们中文说得好。

7) 水上怎么 _____ 着这么多的树叶？

8) _____ 水是我最喜欢的运动。

9) 他们 _____ 着小船进入河边的那个洞口。

4. Expand the phrases into complete sentences following the examples:

1) 船上坐着<u>一胖一瘦两个人</u>。

　　林间空地上／躺着／一只大鹿和一只小鹿
　　路边／放着／一把高椅子和一把低椅子

　　山腰上<u>两个洞一东一西</u>。

　　河道里／一条船在前一条船在后
　　电视上／一个人问一个人答

2) 周围的人<u>禁不住</u>问了他两个问题。

　　我们／又看了一遍这个电影
　　孩子们／一直跑到山上
　　老酋长／笑了起来
　　胖子／从船上跳到水里

3) 他<u>弯下腰</u>，又<u>直起腰</u>，觉得自己身强力壮。

　　猎人／低头／抬头／看到树顶上有一个鸟巢
　　姑娘／垂眼／抬眼／向远处望去

我／放手／举手／希望老师会叫自己的名字

瘦子／放腿／翘腿／不知道做什么好

4) 胖子<u>勇于</u>跳入水中。

猎人／急／把妻子接回来

胖子／怯／留在船上

英雄／常常／苦／孤单

年轻人／应该／敢／攀登高峰

5) 到达山顶的是英雄，<u>而</u>英雄总是活得太累。

这里／经常有雾／有雾／总是晴天

我们／终于找到了她／她／却哑了似的不说话

妻子／眼里闪动着泪水／泪水／也打动不了丈夫的心

她／又聪明又美丽／聪明美丽／是人人都喜欢的

6) 大家都在考试，<u>而</u>他却在家里睡觉。

猎人正在瞄准／小鹿还在嬉戏

树上落下的露珠是凉丝丝的／妻子流下的眼泪是温热的

第一个年轻人到了山腰／第二个年轻人只到了山麓

上游的水十分平静／下游的水却流得很快

7) 鸟语花香的地方<u>总是</u>好地方。

早晨的山林／这么寂静

他这个人／满脸倦容

你这个孩子／让大家担心

勇敢的人／遇到更多的机会

8) 这孩子<u>哑了似地</u>不说话。

猎人／呆／没有开枪

哥哥／聋／没听到我叫他

秃鹰／瞎／一头撞到山上

　　苍蝇／疯／在屋子里飞来飞去

9) 小鹿一边跳跃着，一边发出欢快的叫声。

　　他们／爬山／看蝴蝶

　　躺在草地上的两个人／望着蓝天／听着音乐

　　猎人／把食指贴向扳机／瞄准母鹿

　　小鸟／衔着一条小虫／眼睛向下望着

10) 有人眼中涌出热泪，有人嘴里发出欢呼。

　　一直走到终点／中途就折回来了

　　流露出担心的神色／一点也不在意

　　喜欢《寂静的山林》／爱读《高处何所有》

　　认为胖子死得勇敢／觉得瘦子活得勇敢

语言知识与技巧

5. Rewrite the following passages to make them more formal. Locate the appropriate substitutes for the underlined words and phrases from the texts of this and previous lessons:

1) 一只母鹿和一只小鹿在一块森林中间的空地上玩。小鹿在母鹿的周围跳着，常常从母鹿的肚皮底下钻过。(L.1)

2) 你们三个都是身体非常好而又比别人聪明的好孩子。现在，请你们尽你们的能力去爬那座我们一向看作是神圣的大山。(L.2)

3) 真英雄碰到的是什么？他碰到的是全身的伤疤，是只有自己一个人走的一条很长的路，和一种越来越清楚确实的觉得自己渺小的感觉。(L.2)

4) 灰颜色的大坝在两座山中间高高地站着，切断了河水那跟大沙漠里疯狂的沙一样的热情。上游的水还是黄的，下游的水当然是黄的。大坝底下的泄流孔和山边上的泄流洞就象一头很大的野兽的鼻孔，喷出满天的黄颜色的雾。(L.3)

5) <u>大家</u> <u>问</u>瘦子，<u>当时</u>他们想了<u>些什么，说了些什么。他却</u><u>象哑了一样地</u><u>不说话</u>，<u>只是</u> <u>呆呆地</u>望着大河。(L.3)

6. In the following sentences, underline the more formal equivalents to the words and expressions given in parentheses:

1) 母鹿和小鹿依然在林间空地上嬉戏。莫非它们不知道死神正在向它们走近？（还是，玩，难道）

2) 第一个年轻人到了一个天堂般的地方，以为那就是山顶。然而，那只是山麓。（象…一样，但是）

3) 彼时的大河犹如一头猛兽，不时发出狂吼。（那时，就象，常常）

4) 他曾去过台湾，虽很想再去，却苦于没钱。（曾经，虽然，可是）

5) 老师因病未能来校，我们便自行复习。（因为，生病，没，到学校来，就，自己）

6) 我家小狗于昨日走失，如在您处，望即将其送回，十分感谢。（在，昨天，不见了，如果，您那儿，希望，马上，把，它，很）

7. Following the examples, rewrite each of the sentences using various comparison forms:

1) Examples:　　小船<u>象（是）</u>一只被粘住的苍蝇（<u>似的</u>）。
　　　　　　　　小船（<u>就</u>）跟一只被粘住的苍蝇<u>一样</u>。
　　　　　　　　小船（<u>就</u>）<u>象</u>一只被粘住的苍蝇<u>一般</u>。
　　　　　　　　小船<u>好似</u>一只被粘住的苍蝇（<u>一般</u>）。
　　　　　　　　小船<u>犹如</u>一只被粘住的苍蝇（<u>似的</u>）。

Rewrite the following:

　　　　　　　　上游的水平静得象一张摊开的饼。
　　　　　　　　小船象是坠着鱼钩的浮标。

泄流孔犹如巨兽的鼻孔。

那船好似被拖拽着向山崖滑去。

2) Examples:　小船奇迹<u>般</u>地穿越了隧道。

小船<u>（象是）</u>奇迹<u>似地</u>穿越了隧道。

小船<u>就</u>象奇迹<u>一样地</u>穿越了隧道。

Rewrite the following:

瘦子象是哑了似地沉默着。

灰色的堤坝高山似地矗立而起。

大河就象发怒一样地吼叫着。

3) Examples:　划艇<u>是</u>河道里的一条小鱼。

划艇<u>变成了</u>河道里的一条小鱼。

划艇<u>被当做了</u>河道里的一条小鱼。

Rewrite the following:

知识就是力量，时间就是金钱。

英雄变成了高山上的青松。

几百米的隧道被当做了地狱。

8. Based on your knowledge of two-syllable words, match each of the underlined words with an English meaning on the right:

1)	没有<u>动静</u>	about	2)	<u>真实</u>的故事	strange
	三天<u>左右</u>	dispute		<u>重要</u>的人物	healthy
	互相<u>来往</u>	(sign of) movement		<u>奇怪</u>的想法	manufacture
	<u>是非</u>太多	all along		多<u>休息</u>几天	real
	并不<u>矛盾</u>	contradictory		身体很<u>健康</u>	rest
	<u>始终</u>在家	interaction		<u>制造</u>自行车	important
3)	<u>眉目</u>清楚	simple and easy	4)	一根<u>鸡毛</u>	pleasant to hear

68

头脑<u>冷静</u>	research and produce	喜欢<u>红茶</u>	boiled water
<u>血汗</u>钱	sober and calm	多喝<u>开水</u>	snow-white
<u>简易</u>的办法	opinion	<u>好听</u>的音乐	talk face to face
大家的<u>意见</u>	logic (of writing)	<u>雪白</u>的裙子	chicken's feather
<u>研制</u>新产品	blood and sweat	有事<u>面谈</u>	black tea

5)
<u>缩小</u>一半	improve
<u>翻开</u>报纸	raise
<u>改进</u>做法	keep
<u>留住</u>客人	shrink
<u>举起</u>双手	spurt
<u>喷出</u>水花	open

<u>活学与活用</u>

9. Retell the details of the incident described in the text using the expressions suggested:

1) 这个故事发生在一个什么样的地方？

混浊的大河／灰色的堤坝

上游的水／黄色／平静／象一张摊开的饼

下游的水／黄色

坝底／泄流孔

山边／隧道／排沙泄流洞

喷出／漫天的黄雾

2) 说一说小船和船上的人:

小小的划艇／上游的河道／漂

胖子／瘦子／船头／船尾

微微翘起来／颤动／象是坠着鱼钩的浮标

3) 小船碰到了什么问题？

好似被拖拽着／水底／吞了钩的大鱼

向岸边的山崖滑去

拼命打圆了桨／依然向深幽幽的洞口滑

4) 胖子怎么了？

忽然跃起身／坚决／跳入水中求生

拼命游了一段／沉了底

5) 瘦子怎么了？

忽然弯下腰／坚决／留在船上

穿越／地狱般的隧道

下游的洞口／弹射而出

平安／奇迹

6) 你怎么看胖子和瘦子？

勇敢／怯懦

英雄／懦夫

侥幸

10. Using your own words, answer the following questions based on your own opinions and experiences:

1) 你划过船吗？是在什么地方跟什么人一起划的？

2) 你父母什么时候为你的安危担心过？当时发生了什么事？

3) "懦夫总是容易侥幸地在世上活着。" 你能举一个例子吗？

4) 说一下你认为勇敢的人所做的一件勇敢的事。

5) 生活中有时很难分清什么是对，什么是错。你遇到过这样的情况吗？
请你介绍一下。

11. Write an essay in which you narrate an exciting sports event. Picture a close game in which either side could be the winner or the loser. Make the story as vivid as you can by drawing

analogies. Use as many two-syllable words as you can.

VIII. 课文材料对话 (Dialogues Using the Language of the Text)

A

甲：你看到上游河道里那条小船了吗？船上好象坐着两个人。

乙：看到了，一胖一瘦，瘦的在船头，胖的在船尾。

甲：不好了，那船顺着堤坝向岸边的山崖滑过去了！

乙：（对着河上大喊）快回来！快回来！

甲：来不及了。看，小船被吸到排沙泄流洞里去了。

乙：胖子先已经跳了水，可是瘦子……

甲：快看下游，小船穿过隧道从那边洞口冲出来了。瘦子还活着。他能留在船上，真勇敢。

乙：可惜啊！胖子死了。不过我觉得真正勇敢的还是胖子，因为他敢于跳到水里求生。而瘦子呢，只是一个侥幸活着的懦夫而已。

B

瘦子：船翘起来了，又在颤动，会不会有问题？

胖子：不会吧。那是因为你坐在船头，我坐在船尾。

（过了一会儿）

瘦子：这是怎么一回事？船好象被什么东西拖着在走。

胖子：是啊，难道水底有一条吞了钩的大鱼？船怎么滑得这么快？

瘦子：不好了，船要进洞了。

（坝上和崖边的人高声大喊："快回来！""快回来！"）

瘦子：快，用力划。

胖子：好，用力划……来不及了。

　　（胖子突然跳入水中。瘦子向船里一缩。小船进入隧道。）

第四课　"柿把儿" 老师

Description is an integral part of narration, but it is also an independent literary form in itself. In essays that are highly descriptive, the author often introduces a person, a scene, or an object with many details. Sometimes the author describes a person or a thing for their own sake, but frequently the author uses them to convey a moral message. In this second unit of the course, you will find two articles written according to these conventions.

Description is actually also very common in our everyday life. In describing a person we like or dislike, we normally focus on his or her character, personality, or temperament reflected in the ways he/she thinks and behaves. The tone of voice (语气 or 口气) in which we present the person is very important. Through intonation, tone words, and other verbal means, our tone not only reveals our attitude toward the person but also can persuade the listener to like or dislike the person being described. Even a difficult person can become lovable if we use a proper tone. This is exactly what happens in our text with Mr. Zhao, a schoolteacher with many unattractive personal characteristics.

I. 课文导读 (Guide to the Text) ✼

　　赵老师个子很矮，戴眼镜，嘴上长着小胡子 (húzi, n., moustache)，不太好看，也不太难看。第一次给学生上课，他就说了 180 个 "是吧"。因为 "是吧" 和 "柿把 (shìbà, n., persimmon stem)" 说起来声音很象，所以大家就叫他 "柿把儿" 老师。

　　上课的时候，同学们喜欢学他的样子说 "是吧"，他很生气。有一次他真的发火 (fāhuǒ, v., lose one's temper) 了，大家都不敢说话。可是，想不到他自己又说了一个 "是吧"，同学们都笑了起来。这样，他就更生气了。虽然他上课上得不好，可是他写文章写得很好。大家经常在报纸和杂志上看到他写的东西，都很喜欢他。

　　他快要到 30 岁了，可是还没有结婚。有一个漂亮的姑娘，爸爸是局长 (júzhǎng, n., head of a government bureau)，因为喜欢他的文章，所以也就喜欢上了他这个人。只要他同意去局办公室工作，姑娘就会跟他结婚。这真是一件大好事，可是他说要想一想。那一天，姑娘到他住的地方来问他想得怎么样，他说："我还是爱我的学生。离开他们，我就没有<u>灵感</u> (línggǎn, n., inspiration)了。是吧！"姑娘多生气啊！她马上就走了。"柿把儿"老师自己也差一点流下眼泪来。

同学们知道了这件事都很感动。第二天，有人在讲桌上放了一个花瓶。瓶里是一把漂亮的<u>野</u> (yě, adj., wild) 花。一张小纸条上写着："我们全班同学都爱你。我们不再叫你'柿把儿'老师了。"赵老师看着纸条说不出话。过了很长时间，他突然说了一个"是吧！"这一次，教室里<u>静悄悄</u> (jìngqiāoqiāo, adj., quiet) 的，没有一个人笑。

II. 词语导学 (Guide to New Words and Expressions)

1. Match each item on the left with an item on the right based on the radicals and the character(s) you know:

1) 背影　bèiyǐng　　　　　　　n. eye socket
   鼻尖　bíjiān　　　　　　　　n. back viewed from behind
   眼眶　yǎnkuàng　　　　　　　n. tip of the nose

2) 拜读　bàidú　　　　　　　　v. read with respect
   考虑　kǎolǜ　　　　　　　　　v. reprimand
   训斥　xùnchì　　　　　　　　v. consider

3) 寒舍　hánshè　　　　　　　　n. wonderful thing
   美事　měishì　　　　　　　　n. your great writing (honorific)
   大作　dàzuò　　　　　　　　　n. my humble home (humble)

4) 有心　yǒuxīn　　　　　　　　adj. with a mind set to do something
   完全　wánquán　　　　　　　　adj. complete
   老实　lǎoshí　　　　　　　　　adj. honest

5) 青年 qīngnián   n. young person

    千金 qiānjīn   n. someone's daughter (honorific)

    大人 dàrén   n. official (old way of addressing, honorific)

6) 讲桌 jiǎngzhuō   n. slip of paper

    教鞭 jiàobiān   n. podium

    纸条 zhǐtiáo   n. pointer

7) 花茎 huājīng   n. bead of sweat

    水平 shuǐpíng   n. flower stem

    汗珠 hànzhū   n. level

8) 前途 qiántú   n. respect

    敬意 jìngyì   n. language and literature

    语文 yǔwén   n. future

9) 喝 hè   v. kiss

    亲 qīn   v. blink

    眨 zhǎ   v. shout loudly

10) 告别 gàobié   v. turn around

     失去 shīqù   v. say "good-bye"

     转身 zhuǎnshēn   v. lose

2. Select an appropriate meaning for the underlined word or phrase in each sentence according to the context and the character you know:

1) 近日 (jìnrì, adv.), 我遇到了一个多年不见的老朋友。
    a. nearly   b. closely   c. recently

2) 在学校里我最喜欢的课是写作 (xiězuò, n.)。
    a. calligraphy   b. writing   c. painting

3) 巨兽张开 (zhāngkāi, v.) 嘴巴, 一口吞下了小鹿。
    a. open   b. close   c. hold

4) 大家都觉得他肯定 (kěndìng, adv.) 会平安地回来。
    a. definitely   b. probably   c. necessarily

5) 他<u>暗地里</u> (àndìli, adv.) 告诉我他明天一大早就走。
  a. in a dark field b. sadly c. secretly

6) <u>爱情</u> (àiqíng, n.) 是男女之间的一种神秘的感觉。
  a. love b. respect c. admiration

7) 她的眼睛长得<u>出奇</u> (chūqí, adv.) 的美。
  a. strangely b. extraordinarily c. certainly

8) 去北京工作？这<u>分明</u> (fēnmíng, adv.) 是个好机会。
  a. possibly b. especially c. obviously

9) 他已经<u>谈</u> (tán, v.) 过好几个女朋友，可惜谁都不喜欢他。
  a. spoke to b. dated c. talked with

3. Guess the meanings of the following expressions:

1) 好心人
2) 下课铃　　　（铃: líng, n. bell）
3) 自我介绍
4) 报刊杂志
5) 笑成一片
6) 鸦雀无声　　（鸦: yā, n., crow; 雀: què, n., sparrow）
7) 孑然一身　　（孑然: jiérán, adj., alone）
8) 爱屋及乌　　（及: jí, v., reach; 乌(鸦): wū(yā), n., crow）
9) 艳福不浅　　（艳: yàn, adj., amorous; 浅: qiǎn, adj., shallow）
10) 千载难逢　　（载: zǎi, n., year; 逢: féng, v., come across）

III. 课文 (Text) ❧

"柿把儿" 老师　赵广存

  他姓赵，个子很矮，比拿破仑肯定还矮几公分。满脸的青春美丽豆。小小的眼睛上罩副近视镜。厚厚的嘴唇上蓄着两撇小胡子。

第一堂语文课，他自我介绍说："我嘛，就这副尊容，是吧！好也好不到哪里去，差也差不到哪里去。是吧！" 就那一堂课，有心的同学做了次不完全统计，他总共说了 180 个 "是吧"。平均每分钟 4 个，平均每个人 5 个。于是大家暗地里叫他 "是吧" 老师。因 "是吧" 与 "柿把" 谐音，而这里多的是柿子，大家就管他叫 "柿把儿" 老师。

以后上课，他在上面说一个 "是吧"，同学们在下面学一个。有时，他还没说 "是吧"，同学们就先说了。他很生气，却不好发作。谁叫他满嘴的 "是吧" 呢！有一次，他真的生了气，一甩教鞭训斥大家："以后，只许老师说'是吧'，不许你们说'是吧'，谁再说'是吧'，就滚出去。" "柿把儿" 老师从来没发过这么大的火，这一下把大家给镇住了，教室里变得鸦雀无声。谁料，他最后又来了一个 "是吧"！教室里 "哄" 地一声又笑成一片。气得他的那两撇小胡子一抖一抖的。这时候下课铃响了，他走出教室时，向同学们告别，竟说 "老师再见！" 同学嘴张开了，还没问出声，"哄" 地又笑了。

他的课确实讲得不好，甚至可以说比较糟。可他的写作水平却出奇的好。还是市作协的会员呢！同学们常在报刊杂志上拜读他的大作。老实说，在同学们心中某个角落，还装着对他的敬意呢！每堂课都在嘻嘻哈哈中结束，他走时，鼻尖上尽是细细的汗珠。

他在爱情上也是失败的。快 30 岁的人了，至今孑然一身。听说谈过的不少，可没一个成功的。近日，又有好心人给他介绍了一位，是文学青年，长得特俊，又是 X 局局长大人的千金。姑娘因喜欢他的文章而爱屋及乌地喜欢上他。他还有啥说的。连别的老师都说："你家伙艳福不浅啊！" 姑娘有个条件，要把他调到 X 局办公室，以后朝政界发展，前途大大的。这哪里是条件呀，分明是千载难逢的美事一桩。他倒好，说要考虑考虑。

那一天，姑娘笑盈盈飘进他的寒舍来打探结果。他望了姑娘一眼，低下头说："我还是爱我的学生，我不能离开我的学生，离开他们，我就失去灵感了。是吧！"听了他的话，姑娘气红了脸，大喝一声："去你的'是吧'吧！"说着转过身"蹬蹬蹬"走了。他望着姑娘灵动的背影，眼泪在眼眶里打转儿。可终于没有流出来。

同学们知道这件事，一个个感动得直流泪，真想把"柿把儿"老师亲两口。

第二天，"柿把儿"老师去上课，发现讲桌上亭亭玉立着一个花瓶，瓶里插着一把鲜艳的野花，花茎上系着一张纸条，上面写着："赵老师，我们全班同学都爱你，我们不能没有你。我们不再叫你'柿把儿'老师了，我们以后要好好听你的课！"

"柿把儿"老师痴痴地望着纸条，眼睛眨也不眨，半天说不出一个字。只有那两撇小胡子在剧烈地抖动。突然嘴一张，迸出两个字"是吧"！听了他的话，教室里静悄悄的，没有一个人笑。

（选自复旦大学出版社１９９６年《千字文阅读与训练》）

繁體字課文 (Text in Traditional Characters)

"柿把兒"老師　趙廣存

他姓趙，個子很矮，比拿破崙肯定還矮幾公分。滿臉的青春美麗豆。小小的眼睛上罩副近視鏡。厚厚的嘴唇上蓄著兩撇小鬍子。

第一堂語文課，他自我介紹說："我嘛，就這副尊容，是吧！好也好不到哪裡去，差也差不到哪裡去。是吧！"就那一堂課，有心的同學做了次不完全統計，他總共說了１８０個"是吧"。平均每分鐘４個，平均每個人５個。於是大家暗地裡叫他"是吧"老師。因"是吧"與"柿把"諧音，而這裡多的是柿子，大家就管他叫"柿把兒"老師。

以後上課，他在上面說一個"是吧"，同學們在下面學一個。有時，他還沒說"是吧"，同學們就先說了。他很生氣，卻不好發作。誰叫他滿嘴的"是吧"呢！有一次，他真的生了氣，一甩教鞭訓斥大家："以後，只許老師說'是吧'，不許你們說'是吧'，誰再說'是吧'，就滾出去。""柿把兒"老師從來沒發過這麼大的火，這一下把大家給鎮住了，教室裡變得鴉雀無聲。誰料，他最後又來了一個"是吧"！教室裡"哄"地一聲又笑成一片。氣得他的那兩撇小鬍子一抖一抖的。這時候下課鈴響了，他走出教室時，向同學們告別，竟說"老師再見！"同學嘴張開了，還沒問出聲，"哄"地又笑了。

他的課確實講得不好，甚至可以說比較糟。可他的寫作水平卻出奇的好。還是市作協的會員呢！同學們常在報刊雜誌上拜讀他的大作。老實說，在同學們心中某個角落，還裝著對他的敬意呢！每堂課都在嘻嘻哈哈中結束，他走時，鼻尖上盡是細細的汗珠。

他在愛情上也是失敗的。快30歲的人了，至今孑然一身。聽說談過的不少，可沒一個成功的。近日，又有好心人給他介紹了一位，是文學青年，長得特俊，又是X局局長大人的千金。姑娘因喜歡他的文章而愛屋及烏地喜歡上他。他還有啥說的。連別的老師都說："你傢伙艷福不淺啊！"姑娘有個條件，要把他調到X局辦公室，以後朝政界發展，前途大大的。這哪裡是條件呀，分明是千載難逢的美事一樁。他倒好，說要考慮考慮。

那一天，姑娘笑盈盈飄進他的寒舍來打探結果。他望了姑娘一眼，低下頭說："我還是愛我的學生，我不能離開我的學生，離開他們，我就失去靈感了。是吧！"聽了他的話，姑娘氣紅了臉，大喝一聲："去你的'是吧'吧！"說著轉過身"蹬蹬蹬"走了。他望著姑娘靈動的背影，眼淚在眼眶裡打轉兒。可終於沒有流出來。

同學們知道這件事,一個個感動得直流淚,真想把"柿把兒"老師親兩口。

第二天,"柿把兒"老師去上課,發現講桌上亭亭玉立著一個花瓶,瓶裡插著一把鮮艷的野花,花莖上系著一張紙條,上面寫著:"趙老師,我們全班同學都愛你,我們不能沒有你。我們不再叫你'柿把兒'老師了,我們以後要好好聽你的課!"

"柿把兒"老師痴痴地望著紙條,眼睛眨也不眨,半天說不出一個字。只有那兩撇小鬍子在劇烈地抖動。突然嘴一張,迸出兩個字 "是吧"!聽了他的話,教室裡靜悄悄的,沒有一個人笑。

思考題 (Questions to Think About)

赵老师喜欢说"是吧"的毛病没有改,可是学生们不再笑他了,为什么?

IV. 新词语 (New Words and Expressions)

拿破仑	Nápòlún	n.	Napoleon Bonaparte
青春豆	qīngchūndòu	n.	pimple; 青春痘
罩	zhào	v.	cover
副	fù	m.	pair (of glasses)
近视镜	jìnshìjìng	n.	nearsighted eyeglasses; 近视眼镜
蓄	xù	v.	grow (moustache)
撇	piě	m.	strand (of moustache)
堂	táng	m.	(of a class) period
尊容	zūnróng	n.	distinguished face (note the ironic tone in the text)
统计	tǒngjì	n.	count

平均	píngjūn	adv.	at an average of
谐音	xiéyīn	v.	be a homophone with
发作	fāzuò	v.	flare up
甩	shuǎi	v.	toss
滚出去	gǔn chūqu	v.	get out
镇住	zhènzhù	v.	bring under control
料	liào	v.	expect
哄	hōng	onm.	sound of a group of people's sudden laughter
响	xiǎng	v.	(of a bell) ring
竟	jìng	adv.	unexpectedly; 竟然
确实	quèshí	adv.	indeed
甚至	shènzhì	conj.	so much so that
糟	zāo	adj.	poor
作协	zuòxié	n.	writers' society; 作家协会
会员	huìyuán	n.	member of an organization
角落	jiǎoluò	n.	corner
装	zhuāng	v.	fill with
嘻嘻哈哈	xīxī hāhā	onm.	sound of laughter
尽	jìn	adv.	all
失败	shībài	adj.	failed
俊	jùn	adj.	pretty
啥	shà	pro.	what; 什么
调	diào	v.	transfer
朝	cháo	prep.	in the direction of, 往
政界	zhèngjiè	n.	political circle
笑盈盈	xiàoyíngyíng	v.	be all smiles
飘	piāo	v.	drift (in the air)
打探	dǎtàn	v.	inquire about

结果	jiéguǒ	n.	result
蹬蹬蹬	dēngdēngdēng	onm.	sound of a person's heavy footsteps
灵动	língdòng	adj.	quick and nimble
亭亭玉立	tíngtíng yù lì	v.	(of a young woman) slim and graceful
鲜艳	xiānyàn	adj.	bright-colored
系	jì	v.	fasten
痴痴地	chīchīde	adv.	dumbfoundedly
剧烈地	jùliède	adv.	rapidly
抖动	dǒudòng	v.	tremble; 颤动
迸	bèng	v.	burst forth

V. 词语与句型 (Words, Expressions, and Sentence Patterns)

1. 比 N 还 Adj　　　　　　　　　个子很矮，比拿破仑肯定还矮几公分。

The presence or absence of 还 makes a difference in meaning (or shades of meaning) between the two otherwise similar structures. Compare the following two sentences and try to understand the different nuance effected by 还:

他比他爸爸矮几公分。

他比他爸爸还矮几公分。

The first sentence simply states a fact that "he" is shorter than "his father." The second sentence, however, indicates that "he" is so short that even "his father," who is already quite short, is taller than "him."

2. (Adj 也) Adj 不到哪里去　　　好也好不到哪里去，差也差不到哪里去。

This is a colloquial structure, indicating that, although the speaker generally agrees with what the adjective suggests, he or she still has some reservation. Repetition of the adjective is optional but more emphatic.

那座山（高也）高不到哪里去。

她丈夫（坏<u>也</u>）坏<u>不到哪里去</u>。

这孩子（聪明<u>也</u>）聪明<u>不到哪里去</u>。

3. 管 A 叫 B   大家就<u>管</u>他<u>叫</u>"柿把儿" 老师。

This is the same as "把 A 叫做 B" but is slightly more colloquial.

中国人<u>管</u>外国人<u>叫</u>"老外"，<u>管</u>外国人的孩子<u>叫</u>"小外"。

他们<u>管</u>你<u>叫</u>什么？

4. 谁叫 SV 呢？   <u>谁叫</u>他满嘴的 "是吧" <u>呢？</u>

This colloquial structure is used to justify the speaker's agreement with the consequence someone suffers from what the speaker thinks is a wrongdoing. In the above sentence, because Mr. Zhao uses so many "OKs" in his speech, the author thinks that he deserves to be called by such a nickname. (Note the undertone, though.) 叫 can be replaced by 让.

胖子死了。<u>谁叫</u>他不呆在船上<u>呢？</u> (So it is natural that he died.)

<u>谁让</u>你爬到山腰就折回来<u>呢？</u> (So you should not expect to be chosen as the tribe leader.)

<u>谁让</u>我听了你的话<u>呢？</u> (So it is natural that I am suffering from the bad consequence right now.)

5. 只许…, 不许…   <u>只许</u>老师说 '是吧'，<u>不许</u>你们说…

This is used to emphasize a contrast, which either indicates an unfair treatment or sets up a standard as to what is allowed and what is not.

<u>只许</u>他吃，<u>不许</u>我吃，这不公平 ("unfair")。

<u>只许</u>前进，<u>不许</u>后退。

<u>只许</u>州官 ("magistrate of a county") 放火，<u>不许</u>百姓 ("ordinary people") 点灯。
(A Chinese idiomatic saying indicating that a double standard is being practiced.)

6. (谁)再…就…   谁<u>再</u>说 '是吧'，<u>就</u>滚出去。

This colloquial structure is used to signal a warning. 再 introduces a condition under which the consequence represented by the 就 phrase would or could happen. 谁 is optional.

(谁)<u>再</u>说 "是吧"，我<u>就</u>发火了！

(谁)<u>再</u>把枪带到学校来，我们<u>就</u>把他抓起来。

(谁)<u>再</u>不走，<u>就</u>走不了了。

7. 从来没 V 过这么 Adj 的 N   "柿把儿" 老师<u>从来没发过</u>这么<u>大的</u>火，…

This emphasizes that something unexpected (represented by the verbal phrase) has happened. It is equivalent to the English "someone has never done such a thing" or "something like this has never happened."

我们<u>从来没看过</u>这么可怕<u>的</u>电影。

世上<u>从来没出现过</u>这么伟大<u>的</u>奇迹。

他<u>从来没遇到过</u>这么好<u>的</u>机会。

8. 这一下   <u>这一下</u>把大家给镇住了，…

This colloquial expression introduces the immediate effect of a certain action that has just happened.

老师真的发火了，<u>这一下</u>我们要吃苦头了。

小船被吸进了洞中，<u>这一下</u>岸上的人都吓坏了。

年轻人终于到达山顶，<u>这一下</u>他看到了别人所看不到的东西。

9. 谁料(到)   <u>谁料</u>，他最后又来了一个 "是吧" ！

This means "who would have thought that...." Used at the beginning of a sentence, it introduces a fact that is unexpected, and that normally runs counter to the situation presented in the preceding sentence. Its colloquial forms are 谁知道 and 想不到.

教室里静静的。<u>谁料</u>，几只苍蝇飞了进来。

Compare: 教室里静静的。<u>谁知道</u>，几只苍蝇飞了进来。

三个年轻人都很优秀。<u>谁料</u>，只有一个真正到达了山顶。

Compare: 三个年轻人都很优秀。<u>谁知道</u>，只有一个真正到达了山顶。

猎人一开枪就能打到母鹿。<u>谁料</u>，他又把枪放下了。
Compare: 猎人一开枪就能打到母鹿。<u>想不到</u>，他又把枪放下了。

10. V1 得 SV2　　　　　　　　　　　气<u>得</u>他的那两撇小胡子一抖一抖的。

SV2 here serves as a resultative complement of V1 to suggest the extent of an emotional state (indicated by V1). The normal structure is SV1 得 V2. However, the inverted structure sounds more forceful and idiomatic.

同学们又笑起来，气<u>得</u>老师小胡子一抖一抖的。
Compare: 同学们又笑起来，老师气得小胡子一抖一抖的。

猎人举起枪，吓<u>得</u>小鹿把头往草丛里钻。
Compare: 猎人举起枪，小鹿吓得把头往草丛里钻。

孩子没回家，担心<u>得</u>父母一夜没合眼。
Compare: 孩子没回家，父母担心得一夜没合眼。

11. 还…呢！　　　　　　可他的写作水平却出奇的好。<u>还</u>是市作协的会员<u>呢！</u>

This colloquial structure is used to emphasize a fact that is the result of the cause of the situation introduced in the preceding statement.

他教课教得出奇地好，<u>还</u>是优秀教师<u>呢！</u>
小鹿不知道死神正向它走近，<u>还</u>在那儿嬉戏<u>呢！</u>
我今天太忙了，到现在<u>还</u>没吃饭<u>呢！</u>

12. 老实说　　　　　　　<u>老实说</u>，在同学们心中某个角落，还装着…

The English equivalent to this colloquial expression is "to be honest with you" or "frankly speaking."

<u>老实说</u>，他的课确实讲得不好，甚至可以说比较糟。

<u>老实说</u>，你到过的地方根本就不是山顶！

13. 哪里是…，分明是… 这<u>哪里是</u>条件呀，<u>分明是</u>美事一桩。

The second sentence introduced by 分明是 stresses the truth of a fact, whereas the first beginning with 哪里是 introduces a statement that is clearly contrary to the fact. 分明 is interchangeable with 明明.

胖子<u>哪里是</u>勇敢，他<u>分明是</u>怯懦，才跳到水里。
胖子<u>哪里是</u>怯懦，他<u>明明是</u>勇敢，才跳到水里。
姑娘<u>哪里是</u>喜欢赵老师，她<u>分明是</u>喜欢赵老师写的文章。

分明 or 明明 can also be used in conjunction with 可是 or 可, which introduces a statement contrary to the fact in the 分明/明明 clause:

这<u>分明是</u>一件好事，<u>可是</u>他们说要考虑考虑。
她<u>明明是</u>生气了，<u>可</u>她说是身体不舒服。

14. S 倒好 他<u>倒好</u>，说要考虑考虑。

倒好 colloquially expresses a disappointment or dissatisfaction of the speaker with someone whose behavior has failed to live up to expectations.

大家都拼命打圆了桨，小王<u>倒好</u>，一个人躲在船尾睡觉。
人们对瘦子问长问短，瘦子<u>倒好</u>，沉默着一言不发。
我们都在为你担心，你<u>倒好</u>，到现在才打电话来。

15. V Adj 了 N 姑娘气红<u>了脸</u>，大喝一声…

In 气红了脸，脸红了 is the result of 气. Look at what follow the verbs in the following expressions. More often than not, they are exaggerations:

笑弯了腰，跑断了腿，吓昏了头，气炸了肺
哭干了眼泪，笑掉了大牙，喊哑了嗓子，讲干了喉咙

16. 去你的(…)吧！ <u>去你的</u> '是吧' <u>吧</u>！

This colloquial and impolite structure shows that the speaker has run out of patience or tolerance with someone, and is now angry or contemptuous.

去你的 "是吧" 吧！我以后再也不想见到你了。

去你的 "传统" 和 "天意" 吧！我们已经听够了。

去你的吧！难道你害我还害得不够吗？

17. 直 (adv.)   同学们知道这件事，一个个感动得直流泪…

直 is colloquial for "不停地."

同学们一个个直哭。

她站在狂风中直发抖。

小船直往深幽幽的洞口滑去。

18. V 也不 V   "柿把儿" 老师痴痴地望着纸条，眼睛眨也不眨，…

This means "someone does not even do something (indicated by the verbs)." 不 is replaceable with 没 for a past event.

瘦子痴痴地站着，头动也不动。

那个人坐也没坐就走了。

我在给你讲故事，你怎么听也不听？

VI. 语言知识与技巧 (Knowledge and Rhetorical Skills)

1. Speaking in the colloquial style of native speakers (1)

Colloquial style refers to the style of language normally adopted in oral communication. However, it can also refer to a style, typical of spoken language, that an author intentionally adopts in his/her writing to achieve a special effect. For the sake of differentiating the two situations, we may call the former "colloquial style in spoken language" (口语体的口头语) and the latter "colloquial style in written language" (口语体的书面语), of which the text of this present lesson is a good example.

There are two ways to make a written text informal or colloquial: one such method is to include simulated real-life conversation between the characters; the other is through the adoption of a colloquial, or even vernacular, style in one's description or narration. What is the purpose of adopting a colloquial style in a written text? The main goal is to add a realist touch to the text so as to make it sound more vivid, lively, and believable. Because colloquial style is common in real-life situations, using it in a written text enhances the credibility of the story and engenders in the reader a feeling of closeness to the author, and to the characters in the story. Word choice and the use of colloquial expressions and structures are the primary means to achieve this purpose. In addition, tone words (such as 嘛, 吧, 呢, 啊, 呀), sound words (e.g., "蹬蹬蹬," "嘻嘻哈哈"), exclamation marks, and so on all make a text sound casual as if the author is personally telling you the story.

2. Considering tone: subtlety as strategy

Tone is very important in verbal communication because words, expressions, and sentences are not fully meaningful unless they are expressed with a tone that indicates the speaker's thoughts, feelings, and attitude. Because tone varies from person to person and from situation to situation, however, it can be very complicated and thus represents a challenge for learners of a second language.

Tone has three main functions: the first is to denote the speaker's intent, including his/her intent to explain, question, beg, etc. The second function of tone is to indicate the speaker's emotional feelings such as joy, excitement, surprise, sadness, hatred, etc. The third function of tone is that it reveals the speaker's attitude toward the subject of his speech, which can be positive, negative, supportive, or critical. These functions of tone, indicating a wide range of intentions and emotions, can be expressed through intonation, sound stress, pause between syllables, tone words, exclamation words, adverbs, and pace of speech. Study the following examples, paying special attention to the underlined parts that suggest a tone for a specific purpose:

我嘛，就这副尊容，是吧！(affirm, ironic)

他很生气，却不好发作。谁叫他满嘴的"是吧"呢！(disapprove, seemingly critical)

以后，只许老师说'是吧'，不许你们说'是吧'，谁再说'是吧'，就滚出去。(order, angry)

他的课确实讲得不好，甚至可以说比较糟。可他的写作水平却出奇的好。还是市作协的会员呢！(appearing to criticize, complimentary)

姑娘因喜欢他的文章而爱屋及乌地喜欢上他。他还有啥说的。连别的

老师<u>都</u>说： "你家伙艳福不浅<u>啊！</u>" (blame, sarcastic)

Of all the means for effecting a specific tone, intonation and tone words seem to be the most important. We shall discuss tone words in detail in Lesson Five.

Note that using an appropriate tone is especially important when writing in a casual style, because the author seems to be engaged in leisurely talk, and because tone is most obvious and expressive in conversation. It should also be noted that although a certain tone can convey a certain meaning or feeling, under a different circumstance, the same tone may convey a different meaning or shade of emotion. For instance, in the text of this lesson, the author adopts a generally sarcastic tone to describe Mr. Zhao, often using words that are not complimentary. At first, we may think that the author dislikes his character for his idiosyncrasies and unattractive appearance. As we read on, however, we realize that the author's deep fondness for this eccentric school teacher is being expressed in an apparently disapproving or mocking tone, and this actually helps him to convey his feelings effectively. Please re-read the text and carefully consider its tone as well as its underlying emotions.

3. *Learning to speak and write formal language (3)*

Despite its general informal and casual atmosphere, the essay in this lesson still contains some features of formal language. (After all, it is not only a written text but also a literary text). In addition to many four-character expressions, the author has used words and expressions that are quite formal. (For example, instead of 骂, 尊敬, 政府工作, 明明, and 很快, the author uses 训斥, 敬意, 政界, 分明, and 剧烈 respectively.) Moreover, the author also uses expressions that are typical of formal polite language (礼貌语, *lǐmàoyǔ*). Spoken particularly by educated people in old times, many expressions of this polite language continue to be used in present times to show respect for others. Two sets of words exist for this purpose: those that honor others, and those that humble oneself. The following are some of the expressions used by the author in this essay, listed together with their antonyms for your reference:

<u>Honorific</u>	<u>Self-deprecating</u>
贵府 ("distinguished home")	寒舍
尊容	敝容 ("ugly appearance")
大作	拙作 ("a writing of poor quality")
千金	小女 ("a girl of insignificance")

It should be noted that under certain circumstances, or depending on the intention of the speaker, polite language can help achieve a totally different effect, including irony. At such times, the speaker is obviously not sincere with his or her flattering words, as exemplified by the following case from the text:

（姑娘）长得特俊，又是 X 局*局长大人*的*千金*。

By referring to the head of a government bureau as 大人 ("His Honor"), the author is clearly faking his respect. 大人 is a term of address used by people of a low social status to a high official in traditional China. To humble themselves further in front of their superiors, these people would often refer to themselves as 小民 or 下官. Because these terms are no longer used in present-day China where equality is emphasized (at least in theory), the term 大人 here carries a strong ironic or satirical tone.

In addition to showing respect for others, polite language can also be used simply to express one's appreciation or admiration for somebody, and the ability to do so often marks the speaker as educated and well-mannered. We shall discuss this aspect of using polite language in Lessons Twelve and Thirteen.

4. *Exaggerating for effect*

In the text of this lesson, the author tells us that Mr. Zhao is very short, so short that even Napoleon must be several inches taller than him. Is this a true or accurate description of the teacher? Probably not. Interestingly, we as readers do not really mind if the author has exaggerated, because exaggeration (夸张, *kuāzhāng*) is very natural and common in discourse. We often exaggerate in our own speech, and we do so because we want to emphasize our point and leave a vivid impression on the listener. Exaggeration is thus a rhetorical strategy.

When we exaggerate, we tend to make things bigger, stronger, or faster than they are. We also make things appear smaller, weaker, or slower than reality. Sometimes we create our own exaggerations, and sometimes we use words and expressions that have been used so often and so widely that we no longer think of them as representing exaggerations. For instance, the following expressions from the text are frequently used, but they are all exaggerations to varying degrees: 满脸的青春美丽豆, 180 个 "是吧", 满嘴的 "是吧", 笑成一片, 气得他的那两撇小胡子一抖一抖的, 局长大人的千金, 千载难逢的美事一桩, 痴痴地望着纸条.

Exaggeration often relies on metaphors, analogies, and personifications as means of execution. In other words, when we draw analogies, we often exaggerate things beyond their normal state or situation. The following passage from the text of the previous lesson exemplifies this point:

灰色的堤坝在两山之间冷漠地矗立而起，截断了它那大漠狂沙般的黄色的热情。上游的水依旧是黄色的，平静得像一张摊开的饼。下游的水自然是黄色的，坝底的泄流孔和山边的隧道排沙泄流洞犹如巨兽的鼻孔，喷出<u>漫天的黄雾</u>。

What a vivid description of the scene!

    One thing we should bear in mind is that when we use exaggeration, we should not lose sight of reality. Otherwise, we run the risk of losing credibility, and this in turn hinders us from expressing what we intend.

VII. 练习 (Exercises)

<u>词语与句型</u>

1. Based on the text, give the Chinese equivalents for the English phrases and then fill them in the blanks of the following sentences:

Get out!	with a mind set to do something
self-introduction	newspapers and magazines
(as a) result	at an average of ... per day
secretly	to speak honestly
(fall short of others' expectation)	(show anger or contempt)

1) 大家嘴上不说，但是 _____ 都在为他的安危担心。

2) 开学第一天，老师让每一个同学在课上作 _____ 。

3) 他很生气，指着门对我大喝一声："_____ 。"

4) _____ ，勇士和懦夫有时很难分得清。

5) 瘦子侥幸地活了下来，_____ ，他成了英雄。

6) 大家都在等你，你 _____ ，到现在才来。

7) 今天老师讲地理 ("geography"), _____ 的同学带来了一张世界地图。

8) 我上星期打了十几个长途电话，_____ 两个。

9) _____ "助人为乐" 吧！你就会说假话。

10) 许多 _____ 都介绍了他的优秀事迹。

91

2. Rewrite the following sentences using the words or expressions given in parentheses to make them more formal:

A. 1) 他妻子离去以后，到现在都没有回来。（至今）
   2) 李海调到局长办公室去工作了，今天来跟大家说再见。（告别）
   3) 没有人喜欢那个总是骂我们的老师。（训斥）
   4) 早回来的年轻人明明没有到过山顶。（分明）
   5) 村里人真的认为他很鲁莽。（确实）

B. 1) 这样的好姑娘是很难遇到的。（千载难逢）
   2) 学生们正在考试，教室里没有一点儿声音。（鸦雀无声）
   3) 老人家很孤单。他的妻子去年死了。（孑然一身）
   4) 我喜欢吃中国菜，也就这样爱上了中国文化。（爱屋及乌）
   5) 孩子们一看到小丑就都笑了起来。（笑成一片）
   6) 新来的老师先向大家问好，然后开始介绍自己。（自我介绍）

3. Expand the phrases into sentences by following the examples:

1) 他<u>比</u>我<u>还</u>矮几公分。

   这座大山／周围的大山／高／…公尺
   我们的划艇／他们的划艇／长／…英尺
   胖子／瘦子／小／…岁
   酋长用的猎枪／年轻人用的猎枪／重／…公斤

2) 他这副尊容（好也）好<u>不到那里去</u>。

   那块林中空地／大
   这两个人／勇敢
   掩在树后的猎人／凶狠
   赵老师讲的课／糟

3) 学生们<u>管</u>他<u>叫</u>"柿把儿"老师。
   学生们<u>把</u>他<u>叫做</u>"柿把儿"老师。

92

（以前） 中国人 / 外国人 / "洋鬼子"

（现在） 中国人 / 外国人 / "老外"

村里的人 / 那座大山 / "圣山"

我们 / 男女之间的这种感觉 / "爱情"

4) <u>谁叫</u>他说那么多的 "是吧" <u>呢</u>？

他 / 走到山麓就回来

猎人 / 在这时候想到妻子和儿子

胖子 / 不呆在船上

你 / 没吃早饭

5) <u>只许</u>老师用红笔，<u>不许</u>学生用红笔。

小船 / 大船 / 进入河道

年轻人 / 老年人 / 走那条路

<u>只许</u>说 "好"，<u>不许</u>说 "是吧"。

成功("succeed") / 失败

种桦树 / 种松树

6) <u>谁再</u>叫我 "柿把儿" 老师，<u>就</u>不是我的学生。

遇到这样的机会 / 一定要开枪

去那条河里游泳 / 不要回来见我

到山林里打猎 / 会死在那里

能活着回来 / 是奇迹

7) 我<u>从来没</u>发<u>过</u>这么大的火。

我 / 见 / 漂亮 / 蝴蝶

我们 / 爬 / 高 / 山

他们 / 吃 / 好吃 / 菜

猎人 / 遇到 / 这么好 / 机会

8) 大家感动<u>得</u><u>直</u>流泪。

　　爸爸妈妈／高兴／笑

　　孩子们／累／哭

　　在边上看的人／急／喊

　　大家／担心／叹气 ("sigh")

9) 老师又说了个"是吧"，乐<u>得</u>大家都笑出声来。

　　同学们又笑了／气／老师说不出话来

　　小船依然向着洞口滑去／吓／胖子跳入水中

　　小鹿和母鹿依偎在一起／感动／猎人放下了猎枪

　　第三个年轻人终于到达山顶／高兴／老酋长为他祝福

10) 我们都喜欢李老师，<u>还</u>准备给他送生日礼物<u>呢</u>！

　　那座山太高／没人爬过

　　河水流得很快／发出狂吼

　　今年冬天不冷／没下过雪

　　等车的人很多／排着长队

11) 胖子<u>哪里</u>是勇士，他<u>分明</u>是懦夫。

　　那些人／真心帮助你／他们／喜欢你的钱

　　这个年轻人／到了山顶／他／只到了山麓

　　猎人／不敢开枪／他／想到了妻子和儿子

　　小船／被大鱼拖拽着／它／被漩流吸进了洞中

12) 小鸟站在树上<u>动也不动</u>。

　　小鸟站在树上<u>动也没动</u>。

　　她／等／就回家了

　　我说了几个笑话／他们／笑

　　他们的条件／我／考虑

　　这么重要的话／你们／怎么／听

语言知识与技巧

4. Using the words and expressions provided, translate the English sentences into two Chinese versions. After you have finished, compare the two Chinese sentences and judge how they are different:

1) Dewdrops are like (his) wife's tears, but (his) wife's tears are warm.

   a. 好象，可是
   b. 犹如，然而

2) He is really more intelligent than other people.

   a. 真的，比…聪明
   b. 确实，智慧过人

3) The thin guy, still looking at the big river, did not say anything.

   a. 还是，看，啥也不说
   b. 依然，望，一言不发

4) The fat guy disappeared after jumping into the water.

   a. 跳到水里，就，不见了
   b. 跳入水中，便，不知去向

5) Students read your articles from time to time.

   a. 常常，看，文章
   b. 不时，拜读，大作

5. Use the suggested words and expressions to make the following into sentences with different tones:

1) (serious) 母鹿和小鹿还在那里<u>嬉戏</u>，<u>不知道</u>死神<u>正</u>向它们走近<u>。</u>

   (lighthearted) "啪嗒啪嗒"地跳过来跳过去

                它们怎么会知道

                正在…呢！

2) (lighthearted) 同学们<u>一个个</u>感动得<u>直</u>流泪，<u>真想</u>把老师亲两口。

(serious) 都

不停地

确实希望

吻老师两下

3) (sincere) 孩子，你<u>第一个回来</u>，<u>但是你到的地方不是山顶</u>。

(ironic) 我们的第一名

回来得好快

(但是)

真不坏啊！

4) (ironic) 这可是<u>千载难逢的美事一桩</u>，<u>你家伙的艳福不浅啊！</u>

(sincere) 难得的好机会

你

运气很好。

5) (complimentary) <u>瘦子</u><u>活得勇敢</u>，他<u>敢于</u>留在船上，<u>穿越那地狱般的隧道</u>。

(demeaning) 这个瘦子

竟还活着

不知为什么

这一下，成了英雄了。

6) (demeaning) 他姓赵，个子<u>很矮</u>，<u>比拿破仑肯定还矮几公分</u>。

(complimentary) 不算太矮

我爸爸

要高多了

6. Make sense of the underlined phrases in the following mini-dialogues, and learn how polite language is used in these situations:

1) A: <u>贵校</u>的学生比<u>敝校</u>的学生努力多了。

   B: <u>哪里，哪里</u>，还是<u>贵校</u>的学生更努力。

2) A. 时间不早了，不再<u>打扰</u>了。<u>拙文</u>就先留在您这儿吧。

   B: 那您请<u>慢走</u>。您的<u>大作</u>我明天一定<u>拜读</u>。

3) A: <u>令弟</u>勇于穿越那可怕的隧道，真是一位英雄。

   B: <u>不敢当</u>。<u>舍弟</u>留在船上只是因为不会游泳。

4) A: 您的<u>千金</u>刚才唱得真不错。

   B: <u>见笑，见笑</u>。<u>小女</u>才学了没几天呢。

5) A: 欢迎<u>光临</u> <u>寒舍</u>。欢迎，欢迎。

   B: 其实我早就想到<u>府上</u>来<u>拜访</u>了。

6) A: <u>不好意思</u>，今天又让您<u>破费</u>了。

   B: 快别这么说，我那件事还得请您多<u>费心</u>呢。

7. Exaggerate your points by using the words and expressions suggested:

1) 你怎么才来？我已经等了你很长时间了。（半天）

2) 这件事我跟你说了许多遍了。（几百遍）

3) 每天都有很多人来找他。（数不清的）

4) 这几天我忙得一点空儿都没有。（一秒钟的）

5) 他就是躲到很远的地方我也要找到他。（天边）

6) 他们家到处都是书。（满屋子）

7) 像这样的小玩意儿多得很，随便挑一个就是。（多如牛毛）

8) 她呆呆地看着镜子中的自己，流很多眼泪。（泪如雨下）

9) 对面那个女孩长得太美了。（象个天仙似的）

10) 他这个人一心想做大事。（心比天还高）

<u>活学与活用</u>

8. Tell some stories about Mr. Zhao using the expressions provided.

1) 介绍一下赵老师:

语文

个子／眼镜（眼睛）／小胡子（嘴唇）

快 30 岁／谈过的不少／孑然一身

2) 他的课上得怎么样？

不好／可以说比较糟

"是吧" ／ "柿把儿"老师

每堂课／嘻嘻哈哈

3) 学生笑他的时候，他怎么样？

生气／发火／甩教鞭

不许／只许

"滚出去"

4) 为什么同学们心中装着对他的敬意？

写作水平／出奇的好

作（家）协（会）的会员

在报刊杂志上／拜读／大作

5) 说一说赵老师千载难逢的艳福:

好心人／介绍

文学青年／特俊／局长的千金

条件／调到局办公室／朝政界发展

"不能离开我的学生" ／失去灵感

气红了脸／ "去你的…" ／转过身走了

6) 同学们很感动，他们做了什么？赵老师看了怎么样？

讲桌上／花瓶／一把鲜艳的野花

一张小纸条／都爱／不能没有／不再／以后要

痴痴地／半天说不出一个字／迸出两个字

9. Using your own words, answer the following questions based on your own opinions and experiences:

　　1) 你爸爸或妈妈长什么样儿？

　　2) 你有过一个会发火的老师吗？他（或她）发火的时候是什么样子？

　　3) 谈谈你的男朋友或女朋友。他（或她）做过什么事让你感动？

　　4) 你认识一个 "艳福不浅" 的人吗？介绍一下他的情况。

　　5) 一个人长得好看难看跟这个人是好是坏有关系吗？请你举一个例子。

10. Write an essay about a funny or strange person that you know. Try to show in what ways this person distinguishes himself/herself from others. Make sure you describe this person's appearance and the way he/she behaves. Indicate your attitude toward this person by using an appropriate tone.

VIII. 课文对话材料 (Dialogues Using the Language of the Text)

A

甲：你认识我们班的语文老师吧。

乙：你是说那个个子很矮、戴眼镜、嘴上蓄着两撇小胡子的赵老师吗？

甲：对，我们都管他叫 "柿把儿" 老师！

乙：这么叫他，难道他不生气吗？

甲：他当然很生气，但是却不好发作。谁叫他满嘴的 "是吧" 呢！

乙：听说他的课确实讲得比较糟，可他的写作水平却出奇地好，还是市作协的会员呢！

甲：是啊，我们常在报刊杂志上拜读他的大作。老实说，同学们心里对他可
　　尊敬啦！

B

赵：　局长大人的千金，今天来打探结果，是吧？

姑娘：告诉你，我是因为喜欢你的文章而爱屋及乌地喜欢上你的。你还有啥
　　　说的？可你倒好，总是说要考虑考虑。现在考虑好了吗？

赵：　很多人都说我的艳福不浅，这样的机会千载难逢。可你有个条件，是
　　　吧！要把我调到局长大人的办公室，朝政界发展，是吧！

姑娘：那怎么了，以后前途好着呢！

赵：　可我不能离开我的学生,是吧！一离开他们，我就失去灵感了，是
　　　吧！

姑娘：去你的"是吧"吧！（转过身"蹬蹬蹬"地走了。）

第五课　丑石

In the previous lesson, we had a chance to observe the "colloquial style in written language," as opposed to the "formal style in spoken language" we had dealt with earlier in Lesson Two. The author chooses to write in a casual, lighthearted style because it serves best to convey his tone, which is indicative of his attitude toward his main character. The author also uses various other strategies to make his text sound familiar and casual. These strategies, which have also been adopted by the author of the present essay for the same purpose, are discussed in detail in this lesson.

As with the story about Mr. Zhao, where the author first highlights his character's "negative" traits before exposing and commending his positive ones, so in this essay the author also begins with the "ugliness" of a piece of rock, the subject of his essay, and does not reveal its "beauty" until much later in the text. We now understand why the author of the previous essay chooses Mr. Zhao as his main character. The reason, however, for the author of the present essay to focus on a piece of "ugly rock" might not be clear perhaps even after we finish reading the story. What is special about this rock? What is its symbolism? Perhaps what baffles us most is when the author compares himself with this ugly rock at the end of his essay.

I. 课文导读 (Guide to the Text)

　　我家门前的那块大石头，黑黑的，样子像一头牛。没有人知道它是从什么时候开始躺在这里的，也没有人去管它。奶奶嫌 (xián, v., complain) 它占 (zhàn, v., occupy) 地方，总是说要把它搬走。它的样子很不规则 (guīzé, adj., regular)，方不方，圆不圆，造房子用不上它。而它的石质 (zhì, n., texture) 又不好，什么都做不了。这样，它静静地躺在那里，变得越来越难看，连我们这些孩子也讨厌 (tǎoyàn, v., dislike) 起它来。奶奶总是不许我们爬到它上面去玩，怕我们摔 (shuāi, v., fall) 下来。有一次我真的摔了下来，弄破了膝盖 (xīgài, n., knee)。这真是世上最难看的一块石头啊！

　　终于有一天，一个天文学家 (tiānwénxuéjiā, n., astronomer) 路过，发现 (fāxiàn, v., discover) 了这块石头。大家这才知道，它不是一般 (yìbān, adj., ordinary) 的石

头，而是一块了不起的<u>陨石</u> (yǔnshí, n., stony meteorite)，从天上掉下来已经有几百年了。随着它被小心地<u>运</u> (yùn, v., transport) 走，村子里的人都在谈论它。天文学家说，它确实很难看，可是它的难看就是它的漂亮，最最难看也就是最最漂亮。天文学家还说，正因为这块陨石不能用来做小东西，所以一般的人才不喜欢它。

我和奶奶的脸都红了。我觉得自己很<u>可耻</u> (kěchǐ, adj., shameful)，而那块石头真伟大。这么多年，大家都讨厌它，它却在沉默中<u>忍受</u> (rěnshòu, v., endure) 着，勇敢地<u>生存</u> (shēngcún, v., survive) 了下来。

II. 词语导学 (Guide to New Words and Expressions)

1. Match each item on the left with an item on the right based on the radicals and the character(s) you know:

1) 地面 dìmiàn   n. gable
   山墙 shānqiáng   n. surface of the ground
   坑凹 kēng'āo   n. hole

2) 污土 wūtǔ   n. hard rock
   顽石 wánshí   n. riverside
   河滩 hétān   n. filthy dirt

3) 时节 shíjié   n. night
   满月 mǎnyuè   n. season (for a certain agricultural activity)
   夜晚 yèwǎn   n. full moon

4) 遗憾 yíhàn   v. drink
   咒骂 zhòumà   v. regret
   喝饮 hēyǐn   v. curse

5) 刻字 kèzì   v. carve patterns or designs
   雕花 diāohuā   v. wash yarn
   浣纱 huànshā   v. beat cloth (i.e., wash cloth)

捶布 chuíbù	v.	carve or engrave characters
6) 补天 bǔ tiān	v.	glitter
发热 fārè	v.	mend the sky (see note in IV)
闪光 shǎnguāng	v.	emit heat
7) 垒 lěi	v.	carry on the shoulder
掮 qián	v.	long for
盼 pàn	v.	build by piling up (stones, etc.)
8) 干燥 gānzào	adj.	dry
光滑 guānghuá	adj.	surprised
惊奇 jīngqí	adj.	smooth

2. A character may represent the meaning of a word or an entire expression in a polysyllabic word or expression. Study the following words and expressions and match each of them with an English meaning on the right:

黑黝黝 hēiyōuyōu	v.	transport
模样 múyàng	adj.	fine and smooth
搬运 bānyùn	n.	weeds on a piece of desolate land
采用 cǎiyòng	adj.	jet-black
磕破 kē pò	v.	select and use
盛满 chéng mǎn	n.	ornamental knickknack
细腻 xìnì	n.	loneliness
荒草 huāngcǎo	n.	appearance
寂寞 jìmò	v.	fill (a container with sth.)
小玩意儿 xiǎowányìr	v.	hit (sth. hard) and break

If you happen to know both characters in a two-syllable word, your guess may be even more accurate. In the following, match each Chinese item on the left with its English meaning on the right:

破开 pò kāi	n.	sight
拉直 lā zhí	v.	grow

103

<u>眼光</u>	yǎnguāng	n.	misunderstanding
<u>平面</u>	píngmiàn	v.	break (sth.) into parts
<u>生长</u>	shēngzhǎng	n.	ancestors
<u>先祖</u>	xiānzǔ	v.	pull (sth.) straight
<u>误解</u>	wùjiě	n.	brightness
<u>光明</u>	guāngmíng	n.	flat surface

Sometimes, the character you know may not be sufficient for you to deduce the meaning of a compound word. The context where this compound word occurs, however, may help. Study the following sentences and match each Chinese word on the left with its English meaning on the right:

我们家 [盖房]，要用很多石头。

<u>盖房</u>　gài fáng　　　　　　　　　　　　　　v. look up at

大家坐在草地上，[仰望/翘望] 天上的明月。

<u>仰望</u>　yǎngwàng　　　<u>翘望</u>　qiàowàng　　v. build a house

来了几个 [石匠]，正在盖一座石屋。

<u>石匠</u>　shíjiàng　　　　　　　　　　　　　　v. shake one's head

他对我 [摇着头] 说"不"。

<u>摇头</u>　yáo tóu　　　　　　　　　　　　　　n. stonemason

III. 课文 (Text) 💿

丑石　　贾平凹

　　我常常遗憾我家门前的那块丑石呢：它黑黝黝地卧在那里，牛似的模样；谁也不知道是什么时候留在这里的，谁也不去理会它。只是麦收时节，门前摊了麦子，奶奶总是要说：这块丑石，多碍地面呦，多时把它搬走吧。

　　于是，伯父家盖房，想以它垒山墙，但苦于它极不规则，没棱角儿，也没平面儿；用錾破开吧，又懒得花那么大气力，因为河滩并不甚远，随便去搹一块回来，哪一块也比它强。房盖起来，压铺台阶，伯父也没有看上它。有一年，来了一个石匠，为我家洗一台石磨，奶奶又说：用这块丑石吧，省得从远处搬运。石匠看了看，摇着头，嫌它石质太细，也不采用。

它不象汉白玉那样的细腻，可以凿下刻字雕花，也不象大青石那样的光滑，可以供来浣纱捶布；它静静地卧在那里，院边的槐荫没有庇覆它，花儿也不在它身边生长。荒草便繁衍出来，枝蔓上下，慢慢地，竟锈上了绿苔、黑斑。我们这些做孩子的，也讨厌起它来，曾合伙要搬走它，但力气又不足；虽时时咒骂它，嫌弃它，也无可奈何，只好任它留在那里去了。

稍稍能安慰我们的，是在那石上有一个不大不小的坑凹儿，雨天就盛满了水。常常雨过三天了，地上已经干燥，那石凹里水儿还有，鸡儿便去那里喝饮。每每到了十五的夜晚，我们盼那满月出来，就爬到其上，翘望天边；奶奶总是要骂的，害怕我们摔下来。果然那一次就摔了下来，磕破了我的膝盖呢。

人都骂它是丑石，它真是丑得不能再丑的丑石了。

终有一日，村子里来了一个天文学家。他在我家门前路过，突然发现了这块石头，眼光立即就拉直了。他再没有走去，就住了下来；以后又来了好些人，说这是一块陨石，从天上落下来已经有二三百年了，是一件了不起的东西。不久便来了车，小心翼翼地将它运走了。

这使我们都很惊奇！这又怪又丑的石头，原来是天上的呢！它补过天，在天上发过热，闪过光，我们的先祖或许仰望过它，它给了他们光明，向往，憧憬；而它落下来了，在污土里，荒草里，一躺就是几百年了？！

奶奶说："真看不出！它那么不一般，却怎么连墙也垒不成，台阶也垒不成呢？"

"它是太丑了。"天文学家说。

"真的，是太丑了。"

"可这正是它的美！"天文学家说："它是以丑为美的。"

"以丑为美？"

"是的，丑到极处，便是美到极处，正因为它不是一般的顽石，当然不能去做墙，做台阶，不能去雕刻，捶布。它不是做这些小玩意儿的，所以常常就遭到一般世俗的讥讽。"

奶奶脸红了，我也脸红了。

我感到自己的可耻，也感到了丑石的伟大；我甚至怨恨它这么多年竟会默默地忍受着这一切？而我又立即深深地感到它那种不屈于误解、寂寞的生存的伟大。

（选自百花文艺出版社１９９２年《贾平凹散文选集》）

繁體字課文 (Text in Traditional Characters)

醜石　賈平凹

我常常遺憾我家門前的那塊醜石呢：它黑黝黝地臥在那裡，牛似的模樣；誰也不知道是甚麼時候留在這裡的，誰也不去理會它。只是麥收時節，門前攤了麥子，奶奶總是要說：這塊醜石，多礙地面呀，多時把它搬走吧。

於是，伯父家蓋房，想以它壘山牆，但苦於它極不規則，沒棱角兒，也沒平面兒；用鑿破開吧，又懶得花那麼大氣力，因為河灘並不甚遠，隨便去搥一塊回來，哪一塊也比它強。房蓋起來，壓鋪台階，伯父也沒有看上它。有一年，來了一個石匠，為我家洗一台石磨，奶奶又說：用這塊醜石吧，省得從遠處搬運。石匠看了看，搖著頭，嫌它石質太細，也不採用。

它不像漢白玉那樣的細膩，可以鑿下刻字雕花，也不像大青石那樣的光滑，可以供來浣紗捶布；它靜靜地臥在那裡，院邊的槐蔭沒有庇覆它，花兒也不在它身邊生長。荒草便繁衍出來，枝蔓上下，慢慢地，竟鏽上了綠苔、黑斑。我們這些做孩子的，也討厭起它來，曾合伙要搬走它，但力氣又不足；雖時時咒罵它，嫌棄它，也無可奈何，只好任它留在那裡去了。

稍稍能安慰我們的，是在那石上有一個不大不小的坑凹兒，雨天就盛滿了水。常常雨過三天了，地上已經乾燥，那石凹裡水兒還有，雞兒便去那裡喝飲。每每到了十五的夜晚，我們盼那滿月出來，就爬到其上，翹望天邊；奶奶總是要罵的，害怕我們摔下來。果然那一次就摔了下來，磕破了我的膝蓋呢。

人都罵它是醜石，它真是醜得不能再醜的醜石了。

終有一日，村子裡來了一個天文學家。他在我家門前路過，突然發現了這塊石頭，眼光立即就拉直了。他再沒有走去，就住了下來；以後又來了好些人，說這是一塊隕石，從天上落下來已經有二三百年了，是一件了不起的東西。不久便來了車，小心翼翼地將它運走了。

這使我們都很驚奇！這又怪又醜的石頭，原來是天上的呢！它補過天，在天上發過熱，閃過光，我們的先祖或許仰望過它，它給了他們光明，嚮往，憧憬；而它落下來了，在污土裡，荒草裡，一躺就是幾百年了？！

奶奶說："真看不出！它那麼不一般，卻怎麼連牆也壘不成，台階也壘不成呢？"

"它是太醜了。"天文學家說。

"真的，是太醜了。"

"可這正是它的美！"天文學家說："它是以醜為美的。"

"以醜為美？"

"是的，醜到極處，便是美到極處，正因為它不是一般的頑石，當然不能去做牆，做台階，不能去雕刻，捶布。它不是做這些小玩意兒的，所以常常就遭到一般世俗的譏諷。"

奶奶臉紅了，我也臉紅了。

我感到自己的可恥，也感到了醜石的偉大；我甚至怨恨它這麼多年竟會默默地忍受著這一切？而我又立即深深地感到它那種不屈於誤解寂寞的生存的偉大。

思考題 (Questions to Think About)

跟"丑石"相比，作者为什么感到自己可耻？他为什么甚至怨恨"丑石"这么多年默默地忍受着一般世俗的讥讽？

IV.新词语 (New Words and Expressions)

丑	chǒu	adj.	ugly
理会	lǐhuì	v.	pay attention to
麦收	màishōu	n.	wheat harvest (wheat, 麦子)
碍	ài	v.	be in the way of
于是	yúshì	conj.	so
伯父	bófù	n.	father's elder brother
棱角	léngjiǎo	n.	edges and corners
鏨	zàn	n.	chisel
懒得	lǎnde	v.	not feel like (doing sth.)
强	qiáng	adj.	better
压铺	yāpū	v.	hold and lay down
台阶	táijiē	n.	steps
洗	xǐ	v.	make (millstones)
石磨	shímò	n.	millstones
省得	shěngde	conj.	so as (for sth.) not (to happen)
汉白玉	hànbáiyù	n.	white marble
凿	záo	v.	chisel

108

供	gōng	v.	provide
槐荫	huáiyīn	n.	shade of a Chinese scholartree
庇覆	bìfù	v.	protect and cover
繁衍	fányǎn	v.	increase gradually in number or quantity
枝蔓	zhīmàn	v.	(of branches and tendrils) grow
锈	xiù	v.	be stained with
苔	tái	n.	moss
斑	bān	n.	spot
合伙	héhuǒ	v.	join forces to do sth.
足	zú	adj.	sufficient; 够
嫌弃	xiánqì	v.	dislike
无可奈何	wúkě nàihé	v.	have no alternative
任	rèn	v.	allow
稍稍	shāoshāo	adv.	a little bit
安慰	ānwèi	v.	comfort
果然	guǒrán	adv.	sure enough
终	zhōng	adv.	eventually
立即	lìjí	adv	immediately
小心翼翼	xiǎoxīn yìyì	adv.	very cautiously
原来	yuánlái	adv.	as it turns out
补天	bǔ tiān	v.	mend the sky (alluding to the story of Nǚ Wā, a mythical figure who is said to have fixed the collapsed sky with the colorful stones she smelted)
向往	xiàngwǎng	n.	longing
憧憬	chōngjǐng	n.	yearning for
遭到	zāodào	v.	suffer from
世俗	shìsú	n.	worldly convention
讥讽	jīfěng	n.	ridicule
怨恨	yuànhèn	v.	have a grudge against

| 一切 | yíqiè | n. | everything |
| 不屈于 | bùqū yú | v. | not yield to |

V. 词语与句型 (Words, Expressions, and Sentence Patterns)

1. 谁也/都 V　　　　　　　　　它黑黝黝地卧在那里，… 谁也不去理会它。

谁 here is used to form not a question, but an emphatic structure where it means "anybody," "everybody," or, if the sentence is in negative form, "nobody." Although in the negative form, both 都 and 也 are used, in the positive form, 都 is usually used.

谁也不知道丑石是什么时候从天上落下来的。

这块丑石真是太丑了，谁都讨厌它。

赵老师那么矮，谁都比他好看。

2. 以 (prep.)　　　　　　　　伯父家盖房，想以它垒山墙，…

This prepositional phrase indicates the means with which one does something. 以它垒山墙 means 拿它垒山墙 or 用它垒山墙 but is more formal.

人心不是以金钱可以收买的。

他们考虑以东山之石建西河之坝。

以眼还眼，以牙还牙。

3. … 吧，又…　　　　　　　用錾破开吧，又懒得花那么大气力，…

This indicates the speaker's hesitation in making a decision. What preceeds 吧 stands for an action being considered, yet what follows 又 introduces a fact that runs counter to this action, making its realization impossible. 又 indicates the contradiction.

把石头搬走吧，又不想花那个力气。

笑吧，又怕老师生气。

说瘦子勇敢吧，他又不敢离开小船跳入水中。

4. 哪一 M N…也/都　　　　　随便去捡一块回来，哪一块也比它强。

Depending on the item that follows 哪, the phrase can mean "any N" or "any time when."

湖上的划艇，<u>哪</u>一条<u>也</u>比我们（的划艇）走得快。

他<u>哪</u>一次打猎<u>都</u>不会空手回来。

不管上完<u>哪</u>一堂课，他鼻子上<u>都</u>有汗珠。

5. 省得 (conj.)　　　　　　　　　奶奶又说：用这块丑石吧，<u>省得</u>从远处搬运。

省得 is the colloquial form of 免得, which introduces a situation or action that the speaker hopes to prevent from happening. The prevention is made possible by the action of the verb in a preceding sentence. If translated into English, the phrase means something like "so as not to" or "so as to avoid."

还是我去吧，<u>省得</u>你来。

没有钱也好，<u>省得</u>担心了。

我们不叫他"柿把儿"老师了，<u>免得</u>他生气。

6. 嫌, 嫌弃 (v.)　　　　　　　　　石匠…<u>嫌</u>它石质太细，也不采用。

　　　　　　　　　…虽时时咒骂它，<u>嫌弃</u>它，也无可奈何，…

There is no a single, clear-cut definition for 嫌, which is also difficult to translate into English. 不喜欢 or 讨厌 in Chinese and "dislike" or "complain of" in English perhaps come closest to it, but they still do not convey all the nuances the word implies. Generally speaking, 嫌 implies a negative emotion or attitude of someone (toward something or somebody) that can be characterized as "dissatisfaction," "dislike," and "contempt" (or a combination of these feelings). Try to understand the nuances of the word in the different contexts of the following sentences:

他看了看船桨，<u>嫌</u>它太旧，不想用。 (He reacts negatively toward the oar, thinking it is too old to be used.)

胖子<u>嫌</u>瘦子太瘦，瘦子<u>嫌</u>胖子太胖。 (The fat man thinks the thin man is too skinny, and the thin man thinks the fat man is too fat.)

赵老师又矮又难看，姑娘却不<u>嫌</u>他，因为他的写作水平出奇的好。 (The girl did not mind Mr. Zhao being short and ugly, because he is an excellent writer.)

111

嫌弃, on the other hand, refers to an action rather than an attitude.

> 大家都<u>嫌弃</u>那把旧的船桨，没人用它。
>
> 不少姑娘<u>嫌弃</u>赵老师，因为他长得难看。

7. 任 N V　　　　　　　　　（我们）也无可奈何，只好<u>任</u>它留在那里去了。

This is another word that carries different shades of meaning in different contexts. In some contexts, it means that the subject of 任 has no other way but to let somebody do something. In other contexts, however, it does not have this shade of meaning, but means simply that the subject allows someone to do something as he or she pleases. In the latter case, the verbs after N are normally 选, 挑, 作, 取, etc.

> 她不肯去看电影，我们只好<u>任</u>她留在家里。
>
> 房子坏了就得修，决不能<u>任</u>它去。
>
> 这八道练习题，<u>任</u>你们选做五道。

8. 果然 (adv.)　　　　　　　　<u>果然</u>那一次就摔了下来，磕破了我的膝盖呢。

Separated from the rest of the sentence by a comma, the phrase means "sure enough" or "as expected."

> 一整天都是阴沉沉的，后来<u>果然</u>就下雪了。
>
> 猎人好像不愿意对母鹿开枪。过了一会儿，他<u>果然</u>把枪放下了。
>
> 岸上的人都说胖子活不了。<u>果然</u>，他拼命游了一段，还是沉了底。

9. Adj 得不能再 Adj（了）　　　　　它真是<u>丑得不能再丑</u>的丑石了。

This is an emphatic structure that often embodies an exaggeration. By describing 丑石 as 丑得不能再丑了, the speaker means that absolutely nothing could be uglier than this rock. Compare the following statements:

> 丑石很丑。
>
> 丑石真丑。
>
> 丑石太丑了.

丑石丑极了.

丑石多丑啊！

丑石怎么这么丑！

丑石<u>丑得不能再丑</u>了. (Consult Part VI.3 of Lesson One)

丑 can be replaced by many descriptive adjectives such as 漂亮, 干净, 安静, 难吃, 好喝, 脏, 吵, 胖, 瘦, 甜, etc.

10. 原来 (adv.)　　　　　　　　　　　这又怪又丑的石头, <u>原来</u>是天上的呢！

This expression indicates that something previously unknown has now been discovered.

听了老酋长的话, 第一个年轻人才知道自己<u>原来</u>只到了山麓。

为什么叫他 "柿把儿" 老师呢？<u>原来</u> "是吧" 与 "柿把" 谐音。

<u>原来</u>是你呀！两年没见, 认不出来了。

11. 一 V 就是 Num M N　　　　　　　而它…, <u>一躺就是</u>几百年了？！

This structure emphasizes the fact that once an action occurs, it continues or is carried out to an extreme extent.

第一个年轻人只去了三天, 而第三个年轻人<u>一去就是</u>一个月！

他<u>一</u>写信<u>就是</u>四页纸。

这个孩子<u>一</u>看电视<u>就是</u>几个小时。

12. 以 N1 为 N2　　　　　　　　　天文学家说: "它是<u>以丑为美</u>的。"

This means "to take N1 as N2." Thus the phrase 以丑为美 can be translated as "taking the ugly as the beautiful."

学生们<u>以</u>学校<u>为</u>家。

那个村子里的人<u>以</u>打鱼<u>为</u>生。

我这个人<u>以</u>忙<u>为</u>乐, 越忙越高兴。

13. 甚至 (adv.)　　　　　我感到自己的可耻, 也感到了丑石的伟大; 我<u>甚至</u>…

The word 甚至 means something like "even" or "V so far as to." It introduces a situation to show that the state mentioned in the previous sentence(s) has developed to an extreme extent. The word is often used together with 还.

瘦子不喜欢胖子，<u>甚至</u>讨厌他。

我帮助了她，她不但不感谢，<u>甚至</u>还生我的气。

我没出过国，<u>甚至</u>连美国的很多地方也没去过。

VI. 语言知识与技巧 (Knowledge and Rhetorical Skills)

1. *Empty word? The role of tone words*

One aspect of the Chinese language that constantly baffles second language learners is the tone words, or 语气词. Although inconspicuous and labeled as "empty words," tone words attached to the ends of sentences play a significant role in conveying the thoughts and feelings of the speaker, as demonstrated in the following:

他来了<u>的</u>。　(affirming the fact)

他来了<u>嘛</u>。　(the fact is obvious; no need for fuss)

他来了<u>吗</u>？　(asking a question about something not known)

他来了<u>吧</u>？　(being uncertain)

他来了<u>呢</u>！　(being surprised)

他来<u>啦</u>！　　(no need to worry now)

Essentially the same sentence can have different meanings with the use of different tone words. Therefore, studying and mastering tone words is highly important. Also, because native speakers of Chinese use tone words often, you will not sound idiomatic unless you use them appropriately and actively. There is, however, no systematic or clearly defined method to deal with tone words. It seems that the best way to master them is to listen to native speakers carefully, understand the nuances of the tone words they use in context, and try to memorize and use them in your own conversations.

The following is a list of sentences from the texts we have studied so far. Read these sentences aloud and try to absorb the meaning of the tone word at the end of each sentence:

母鹿的身体有些瘦弱，皮毛还是很漂亮<u>的</u>。 (L.1) (to emphasize)

可惜啊！孩子，那不是山顶，那是山腰。(L.2) (to express regret)

你难道在那里一无所见吗？难道连蝴蝶也没有一只吗？ (L.2) (to challenge)

船底那怪异的大鱼是要进洞的吧？ (L.3) (to guess)

他很生气，却不好发作。谁叫他满嘴的“是吧”呢！ (L.4) (to blame; to scorn)

老实说，在同学们心目中某个角落，还装着对他的敬意呢！ (L.4) (to express admiration)

这哪里是条件呀，分明是千载难逢的美事一桩。(L.4) (to express doubt; to challenge)

姑娘气红了脸，大喝一声：“去你的‘是吧’吧！ (L.4) (to express anger)

这块丑石，多碍地面呦，多时把它搬走吧。(L.5) (to complain; to request)

没棱角儿，也没平面儿；用錾破开吧，又懒得花那么大气力。(L.5) (to hypothesize)

果然那一次就摔了下来，磕破了我的膝盖呢。(L.5) (to emphasize)

人都骂它是丑石，它真是丑得不能再丑的丑石了。(L.5) (to emphasize)

这又怪又丑的石头，原来是天上的呢！ (L.5) (to express surprise)

2. ***Speaking in the colloquial style of native speakers (2)***

It is widely held that as students progress to the advanced level, they should begin studying 书面语, as if what they have learned by then is 口语, which, by implication, is easier than its formal counterpart. This is rather misleading because, strictly speaking, 口语 refers to the authentic and natural language that native speakers use in their daily communication. It is a product of impromptu conversations and is therefore very difficult to learn due to its complex tones, idiomatic expressions, and flexible sentence structures that are formed not according to grammar, but according to the situations in which the conversations take place. Unless students master these colloquial features of oral communication, however, they will not speak as naturally and authentically as native speakers do.

As discussed in the previous lesson, tone in spoken language is shown by stress, pace of speech, tone words, and intonation. Transcribed in writing, tone is shown by the use of tone words, sound words, exclamation words, and punctuation marks:

我<u>嘛</u>，就这副尊容，是<u>吧！</u>（L.4）（嘛: being ironical; 吧: being rhetorical）

这使我们都很惊奇<u>！</u>这又怪又丑的石头，原来是天上的<u>呢！</u>（L.5）（呢: indicating surprise and admiration; ! emphasizing the degree of the feelings）

教室里"<u>哄</u>"地一声又笑成一片。（L.4）（哄: sound of laugh）

听了他的话，姑娘气红了脸，转过身"<u>蹬蹬蹬</u>"走了。（L.4）（蹬蹬蹬: sound of fast and heavy steps）

它给了他们光明，向往，憧憬；而它落下来了，在污土里，荒草里，一躺就是几百年了<u>？！</u>（L.5）（？！: indicating surprise and admiration）

我感到自己的可耻…；我甚至怨恨它这么多年竟会默默地忍受着这一切<u>？</u>（L.5）（？: indicating surprise and regret）

In addition to tone, colloquial style in written texts (as well as in spoken language) is also manifest in vernacular words, words of reduplication, 儿 suffix, idiomatic structures, proverbs, localisms, slang words, and other types of colloquial expressions. Expressions of these various forms are vivid and rich in implication and are shared by the majority of Mandarin speakers. The examples from this and previous lessons that illustrate the use of some of these expressions are:

At word level:*

姑娘因喜欢他的文章而<u>爱屋及乌</u>地喜欢上他。他还有<u>啥</u>说的。（L.4）

同学们知道这件事，<u>一个个</u>感动得<u>直</u>流泪，真想把"柿把儿"老师<u>亲两口</u>。（L.4）

这哪里是条件呀，分明是千载难逢的<u>美事一桩</u>。他<u>倒</u>好，说要考虑考虑。（L.4）

老师从来没发过这么大的火，<u>这一下</u>把大家给镇住了。（L.4）

姑娘<u>有个</u>条件，要把他调到 X 局办公室，以后朝政界发展，前途<u>大大的</u>。（L.4）

116

伯父家盖房，想以它垒山墙，但苦于它极不规则，没棱<u>角儿</u>，也没平<u>面儿</u>。(L.5)

At sentence or discourse level:

奶奶<u>总</u>是要骂<u>的</u>，害怕我们摔下来。(L.5)

人都骂它是丑石，它真是<u>丑得不能再丑</u>的丑石了。(L.5)

我嘛，<u>就这副尊容</u>，是吧！<u>好也好不到哪里去</u>，<u>差也差不到哪里去</u>。(L.5)

<u>谁叫</u>他满嘴的"是吧"<u>呢！</u> (L.4)

他的课确实讲得不好，甚至可以说比较糟。<u>可</u>他的写作水平却出奇的好。<u>还是</u>市作协的会员<u>呢！</u> (L.4)

*The distinction between "word level" and "sentence or discourse level" is arbitrary and is made here only for the purpose of explanation.

It is natural that colloquial words and expressions often retain features of local dialects. Dialectal features can occur in an author's writings as a means to achieve a realistic effect. The two essays in this and the previous lesson reveal that the authors are from northern China, as they use such expressions as 特俊 (vs. 特别漂亮), 有啥说的 (vs. 有什么说的), 多时 (vs. 什么时候) and words with 儿 suffix such as 棱角儿, 平面儿, 水儿, and 鸡儿. We believe that advanced students should have some knowledge of local dialects, but we do not encourage them to use the dialects in their own speech.

Finally, colloquial style is marked by "short sentences" (refer to the discussion in Lesson One). In speech, short sentences are natural and necessary. In writing, depending on their intention, authors can take advantage of this general feature of Chinese and use short sentences to add to the colloquial color of their writings. In this and previous essays, short sentences predominate because both authors want to write in a casual style. To reinforce further the colloquial feeling, they tend to omit words (有个 instead of 有一个, 没 instead of 没有) and sometimes use loose or inverted sentences (气得老师 instead of 老师气得, 多的是柿子 instead of 柿子多的是, 磕破了膝盖 instead of 膝盖磕破了). All this contributes to the casual and colloquial atmosphere of the two essays.

3. *Connecting sentences to increase clarity (2)*

In Lesson One, we examined three communicative scenarios where you can use certain sentence connectives to make your expression more accurate, cohesive, and convincing. We shall now introduce another three scenarios where different sentence connectives should be used.

　　1) In order to explain or describe several related things or situations, or to elaborate on several aspects of one thing or one situation, you may simply list them in a series of short sentences according to a conceptually logical and sequential order. You may also use sentence connectives such as 同时, 也…也…, 又…又…, 既…又…, 一(方)面…一(方)面…, 一边…一边, 不是…而是…. Examples of these situations from the texts we have studied so far include:

　　我看到繁花夹道，流泉淙淙，鸟鸣嘤嘤。(L.2)

　　你能看到的，只有你自己，只有'个人'被放在天地间的渺小感，只有想起千古英雄的悲激心情。(L.2)

　　柿把儿"老师痴痴地望着纸条，眼睛眨也不眨，半天说不出一个字。(L.4)

　　小鸟嘴里衔着一条小虫，<u>同时</u>眼睛向下望着。(L.1)

　　排沙泄流洞就在那山崖下，<u>一边</u>发出怒不可遏的狂吼，<u>一边</u>搅起黄风般的漩流。(L.3)

　　有人给他介绍了一位，是文学青年，长得特俊，<u>又</u>是Ｘ局局长大人的千金。(L.4)

　　你说的鸟语花香的地方<u>不是</u>山顶，<u>而是</u>山麓。(L.2)

　　2) In case you want to emphasize further what you have said in a previous sentence by adding more information in the following sentence, use the structures of 不但(不仅, 不只, 不光)…而且(并且, 甚至)…, 不但… 还…, or 不但…也…. 而且, 并且, 甚至, 还, and 也 can also be used by themselves:

　　今天去把妻子接回来，一定要去，<u>并且</u>带着儿子。(L.1)

　　他的课确实讲得不好，<u>甚至</u>可以说比较糟。(L.4)

　　我感到自己的可耻，也感到了丑石的伟大；我<u>甚至</u>怨恨它这么多年竟会默默地忍受着这一切？(L.5)

　　3) In situations where you want to name the reason or cause for the occurrence of something, structures such as 因(为)…所以(就)… and 由于…因而… are helpful. You do not need to use both of the connectives in these structures because 因此, 因而, 所以 can be used independently

118

to introduce the result:

瘦子坐在船头，胖子坐在船尾，<u>因而</u>那船便微微翘起来。(L.3)

<u>因</u>"是吧"与"柿把"谐音，大家<u>就</u>管他叫"柿把儿"老师。(L.4)

<u>因为</u>河滩并不甚远，随便去掮一块回来，哪一块也比它强。(L.5)

<u>正因为</u>它不是一般的顽石，<u>当然</u>不能去做墙，做台阶，不能去雕刻，捶布。(L.5)

它不是做这些小玩意儿的，<u>所以</u>常常就遭到一般世俗的讥讽。(L.5)

Imagine yourself in the communicative situations described above, and learn to use the new set of sentence connectives introduced here.

4. *Making sense of Chinese short forms*

Many words of two or three syllables are formed by abbreviating the original phrases with a varying number of syllables. In fact, abbreviation is a means that accounts for a large number of words and expressions that have found their way into modern Chinese in the past few decades. Once abbreviated, these words tend to become set phrases. What is more, as time goes on, they can be used as components for inventing new words and expressions. Examples of short forms from the text of the previous lesson are 作协 and 语文, which are the abbreviated forms of 作家协会 and 语言文学 respectively. Further examples are:

地铁（地下铁路）　　　　　空调（空气调节器）

彩电（彩色电视机）　　　　　音像（录音和录像）

家教（家庭教师）　　　　　　师院（师范学院）

简历（简单历史）　　　　　　高考（高等学校入学考试）

环保（环境保护）　　　　　　婚龄（结婚年龄）

空姐（空中小姐）　　　　　　男足（男子足球队）

外办（涉外事务办公室）　　　港台（香港和台湾）

夏时制（夏季时间制度）

奥运会（奥林匹克运动会）

公安局（公共安全事务管理局）

119

老大难（老问题、大问题、难解决的问题）

From this list, you can see that most of these short-form words stand for new things or new phenomena in the changing society of China and that the Chinese language in modern times is oriented toward brevity and two-syllable words (cross-reference to Part VI.3 of Lesson Three).

VII. 练习 (Exercises)

词语与句型

1. Using the words or expressions given in parentheses, rewrite the following sentences to make them more colloquial or idiomatic:

  1) 这块石头的样子像一头牛。（模样）

  2) 苦于时间太少，我们没能把它做完。（因为）

  3) 同学们都觉得老师说得太快。（嫌）

  4) 这么热的天气，大家都不愿意走出去。（懒得）

  5) 胖子很勇敢，瘦子不能跟他比。（不像…那样…）

  6) 学生总是先说"是吧"，这样，老师就不用说"是吧"了。（省得）

  7) 孩子们每每在满月的日子到河滩上去看月亮。（常常）

  8) 猎人说要把妻子接回来，他果然这样做了。（真的）

  9) 这个年轻人很伟大，只有他一个人到了山顶。（了不起）

  10) 美到极处的东西，也许就不美了。（美得不能再美）

2. Fill in the blanks in the following sentences with the monosyllabic words:

  盼，运，盖，摔，插，蓄，调，镇

  1) 那一次我半夜从床上 _____ 下来，就醒了。

  2) 学校去年 _____ 了新图书馆，可是大不到哪里去。

  3) 他从来不留长发，可胡子总是 _____ 得长长的。

  4) 老酋长一说话，就把大家 _____ 住了。

5) 一大早就来了车，把石头都 ＿＿＿＿ 走了。

6) 老实说，我们都 ＿＿＿＿ 你往政界发展呢。

7) 那两个年轻人都 ＿＿＿＿ 到天文台去工作了，一个还当了台长。

8) 我平时把眼镜 ＿＿＿＿ 在上衣口袋里，看书时才拿出来。

3. Based on the hints given in numbers 1 through 10, write out some of the four-character expressions that you have learned from the first five lessons of this course:

1) 森林中的空地　　　　　＿＿＿＿＿＿＿＿＿＿

2) 一听到（枪）声就倒下　＿＿＿＿＿＿＿＿＿＿

3) 身体非常好　　　　　　＿＿＿＿＿＿＿＿＿＿

4) 用你们最大的可能　　　＿＿＿＿＿＿＿＿＿＿

5) 路的两边满是各种鲜花　＿＿＿＿＿＿＿＿＿＿

6) 神态和表情显得很累　　＿＿＿＿＿＿＿＿＿＿

7) 风在高处悲激地盘旋　　＿＿＿＿＿＿＿＿＿＿

8) 历史上的英雄们　　　　＿＿＿＿＿＿＿＿＿＿

9) 自己介绍自己　　　　　＿＿＿＿＿＿＿＿＿＿

10) 爱好文学的青年　　　　＿＿＿＿＿＿＿＿＿＿

4. Expand the phrases into sentences by following the examples. Pay attention to the colloquial or idiomatic features that the underlined words and phrases display:

1) <u>谁都</u>知道他是什么时候来的。

　　感到／这块丑石很一般

　　不相信／他是美国人

　　喜欢／听听她的中国见闻

　　不想／去地狱

2) 走路去学校<u>吧</u>，<u>又</u>太慢。

　　一个人去看电影／太孤单

跳到水里／不会游泳

把石头搬走／没车

朝政界发展／怕失去灵感

3) 你把什么都告诉他，<u>省得</u>他不高兴。

你还是去一次／他们来

大家要带着地图／走错路

不要训斥学生／别人误解

就买一个小的好了／多花钱

4) 人们都<u>嫌</u>这块陨石<u>太丑</u>。

他／自己的艳福／浅

来游泳的人／河里的水／浑浊

大家／院子里的荒草／长得快

人们都<u>嫌</u>这块陨石<u>不（够）</u>美。

孩子们／这儿的天气／暖

小鹿／山林里的青草／多

全班同学都／赵老师讲得／好

5) 孩子们<u>任</u>那块丑石留在那里。

Compare: 孩子们<u>不让</u>那块丑石留在那里。

母鹿／小鹿／从肚下钻过

村里的人／秃鹰／在山腰盘旋

胖子和瘦子／小船／在河道里漂

赵老师／学生／叫他"柿把儿"老师

6) 这座山高<u>得不能再高了</u>。

他上的课／糟

局长大人的千金／漂亮

船上的人／呆

今天的山林／寂静

7) 他<u>一</u>睡<u>就是</u>十个小时。

第三个年轻人／去／一个月

赵老师／写／几千个字

这块石头／在这里／躺／二三百年

猎人／在山上／住／好多天

语言知识与技巧

5. Read the following passage aloud and discuss the tone and the style with your classmates:

真带劲！我推着儿童车，朝公园的玫瑰花坛走去，心里别提多美了。车里，是我的小宝贝、小天使、小丫头—颖颖。今天 8 个月又 1 7 天了。瞧，又笑了。别光笑啊！你怎么不说话呀，我跟你说话就像跟大人说话一样。好，好，不说就不说。颖颖，你爸爸今天回来，夜里 1 1 点 1 0 分的火车。一走就是半年，唉，老是出差，出差……你摆手干吗？对，不怪他，工作第一。

（摘自复旦大学出版社《千字文阅读与训练》；何文安："公园奇遇"）

6. Connect sentences by applying designated sentence connectives.

A. You want to list the aspects of a situation or phenomenon:

1) 鸟都飞走了。山风不吹了。（也）
2) 真英雄会遇到孤单的长途。他会遇到真切的渺小感。（既…又）
3) 跳进水里求生的不是瘦子。跳进水里求生的是胖子。（不是…而是）
4) 他的课讲得很糟。他在爱情上是失败的。（一方面…，另一方面）
5) 丑石不能去做墙，做台阶。它不能去雕花，捶布。（同时）

B. You want to provide further information:

1) 他肚里有些饥饿。他身上有些凉意。（还）

2) 他们身强体壮。他们智慧过人。（不但…而且）

3) 小船穿越了几百米隧道。它将瘦子平安载回。（并且）

4) 学生们都很感动。赵老师很感动。（更）

5) 孩子们讨厌这块丑石。他们要合伙搬走它。（甚至）

C. You want to indicate the result of a cause:

1) 母鹿感到累了。它卧倒在草地上。（所以）

2) 第三个年轻人到的是真的山顶。天意立他做新酋长。（因而）

3) 瘦子在世上活着。他敢于留在船上。（之所以…是因为）

4) 姑娘喜欢他的文章。她喜欢上他。（因为…所以）

5) 它不是一般的顽石。它不是做小玩意儿的。（由于…所以）

7. Match the short forms with the full forms they represent:

1) 电大　　女子排球队　　　　2) 打假　　防止火灾

　　教改　　外国商人　　　　　　反恐　　治理沙害

　　文革　　足球协会　　　　　　申奥　　打击假货

　　家电　　教学改革　　　　　　入世　　禁止赌博

　　国安局　广播电视大学　　　　治沙　　加入世界贸易组织

　　女排　　毕业生工作办公室　　防火　　反对恐怖主义

　　外商　　社会科学院　　　　　禁赌　　参加比赛

　　毕办　　国家安全局　　　　　参赛　　申请举办奥运会

　　足协　　文化大革命

　　社科院　家用电器

活学与活用

8. Talk about the "ugly rock" by using the words and expressions suggested.

1) 说一说丑石的样子：

　　黑黝黝 / 牛似的模样
　　丑得不能再丑

2) 丑石为什么让作者遗憾？

　　谁也不知道 / 什么时候 / 留在这里
　　谁也不理会
　　奶奶总是要说 / 搬走

3) 伯父家盖房，为什么不能用这块丑石？

　　极不规则 / 棱角 / 平面
　　河滩 / 不太远 / 随便揪一块回来
　　哪一块 / 也 / 强

4) 孩子们喜欢丑石吗？

　　讨厌 / 咒骂 / 嫌弃
　　合伙 / 要搬走它 / 力气不足
　　无可奈何 / 任 / 留在那里

5) 丑石原来是一块什么样的石头？

　　陨石 / 天上 / 补过天 / 发过热 / 闪过光
　　落下来 / 躺 / 二三百年
　　不是一般的顽石 / 了不起的东西

6) 天文学家怎么说丑石？

　　以丑为美 / 丑到极处 / 美到极处
　　不是用来做小玩意儿的
　　遭到 / 一般世俗 / 讥讽

7) 作者怎么想丑石？

怨恨／这么多年来／默默地忍受

深深地感到／伟大

不屈于误解和寂寞／生存下来

9. Using your own words, answer the following questions based on your own opinions and experiences:

　　1) 你见过的最怪最丑的东西是什么？它怎么个怪法？怎么个丑法？

　　2) 什么东西让你讨厌？你为什么讨厌它？

　　3) 介绍一件你认为了不起的东西。你为什么觉得它不一般呢？

　　4) 有些伟大的东西在很多年里被人们误解和嫌弃。你能举一个例子吗？

　　5) 你自己在生活中被误解过吗？你当时是怎么对待的？

10. Write an essay about an interesting object that you have come across. Try to show in what way it is special and describe what you and other people think of it. Describe its appearance and share the thoughts that it has inspired in you. Use an appropriate tone.

VIII. 课文材料对话 (Dialogues Using the Language of the Text)

A

奶奶：门前那块丑石，黑黝黝的，你就把它搬去盖房吧。

伯父：这块石头，没棱角儿，也没平面儿，我看不上它。

奶奶：难道就不能把它破开吗？

伯父：谁也懒得花这么大的力气。随便去河滩掮一块石头回来，哪一块都比它强。您还是用它洗一台石磨吧。

奶奶：石匠看过了，嫌它石质太细，也用不上。

伯父：那就让它留在这儿吧。

B

作　　者：这又怪又丑的石头，原来是从天上落下来的呢！

奶　　奶：真看不出！它那么不一般，怎么会连墙也垒不成，台阶也垒不成呢？

天文学家：正因为不是一般的顽石，它不是用来做小玩意儿的。

作　　者：可是，这块丑石，真是丑得不能再丑了。

天文学家：它是太丑了，可这正是它的美！它是以丑为美的。

奶　　奶：以丑为美？！

天文学家：是的，丑到极处，就是美到极处。

作　　者：这么一件了不起的东西，怎么几百年来谁都讨厌它，咒骂它，嫌弃它呢？

天文学家：那是因为，不一般的东西，更容易遭到一般世俗的讥讽。

第六课　光与影之恋

In the third unit of this course you are going to study six essays that are written in a form called "persuasion" (议论, *yìlùn*). As suggested by the title, essays written in this style are intended to express the author's opinions and to persuade the readers to look at things from his/her perspective. The six essays included in this unit vary in topic, ranging from political and social issues to reflections on personal habits, interests, and beliefs. They also differ in the approach from which the author proceeds with his or her argument. Despite this variety in topics and approaches, however, the linguistic means the six authors adopt to achieve their intentions are similar, and it is these linguistic means that are our primary concern in studying these texts.

When narrating an event or describing a person or object, the author relies on an appropriate presentation of details for delivering his/her message. In persuasion, however, what matters are the tenability, persuasiveness, and force of the author's argument. The author's attention, in other words, should be focused on presenting his/her argument in a way that is most convincing and forceful. The author of the following essay discusses the lack of sunlight in the living environment of modern people (现代人), who are more interested in pursuing the material pleasures brought about by technology. Limited by space, the author cannot go into detail about her argument against this "unnatural" way of living. Yet the way the author argues for her points is so powerful that you may find yourself swayed by her opinions as you read the text. What are the linguistic or rhetorical strategies that the author uses to deliver her message so effectively?

I. 课文导读 ♥♪

一对新婚夫妇请我去做客。他们不但住的房子很好，而且家里什么东西都有。我能感觉到他们的幸福和<u>自豪</u> (zìháo, n., pride in oneself)。可是，当我向四面一看，就感到<u>气氛</u> (qìfēn, n., atmosphere) 有一丝<u>忧闷</u> (yōumèn, adj., depressive)。到底是什么地方不对头呢？却又说不出来。几天以后，我在一个宾馆里又有了同样的感觉。这时，我才突然明白，原来在宾馆和在朋友的家里都缺少阳光。

因为没有阳光，早晨醒来的时候就不觉得温暖；因为没有阳光，<u>黄昏</u> (huánghūn, adv., at dusk) 回家的时候就不觉得<u>浪漫</u> (làngmàn, adj., romantic)；因为没有阳光，放假的日子也得不到安慰。住在都市里的人，离开<u>自然</u> (zìrán, n., nature) 越来越远。一想到这一点，我的心马上就变得很寂寞。

于是，我知道自己做不了现代人，因为在我的生活中少不了风雨和阳光。我不能开着空调把自己关在房间里。如果我在外面，一天到晚忙得不能再忙，累得不能再累，只要一想到回家以后就有阳光，就有新鲜的空气，就有鲜花的清香，那么，我的心就有了欢乐和<u>温情</u> (wēnqíng, n., tender feeling)，我就不会再觉得<u>孤独</u> (gūdú, adj., lonely)。

一个家，就应该给人这样的一种感受。

II. 词语导学

1. In each group, match the Chinese words on the left with the English meanings on the right based on the characters you know:

1) 新居　xīnjū　　　　　　　　n. carpet
   家具　jiājù　　　　　　　　n. new residence
   地毯　dìtǎn　　　　　　　　n. stereo system
   音响　yīnxiǎng　　　　　　n. combination
   组合　zǔhé　　　　　　　　n. furniture

2) 岁月　suìyuè　　　　　　　n. bride
   现实　xiànshí　　　　　　　n. banquet
   宴席　yànxí　　　　　　　　n. (of human life) years
   新娘　xīnniáng　　　　　　n. reality
   居住　jūzhù　　　　　　　　n. living

3) 眼红　yǎnhóng　　　　　　v. flow away
   封闭　fēngbì　　　　　　　v. fill
   迎接　yíngjiē　　　　　　　v. envy
   流失　liúshī　　　　　　　　v. seal
   充满　chōngmǎn　　　　　v. greet

129

4)　自在　zìzài　　　　　　　　　　n. joy

　　欣悦　xīnyuè　　　　　　　　　n. lightness and gentleness

　　轻柔　qīngróu　　　　　　　　　n. comfort

5)　高级　gāojí　　　　　　　　　　adj. gentle and soft

　　温柔　wēnróu　　　　　　　　　adj. correct

　　对头　duìtóu　　　　　　　　　adj. top-grade

2. Based on the radicals and the characters you know, match the items on the left to the items on the right:

1)　挡　dǎng　　　　　　　　　　v. overflow

　　溢　yì　　　　　　　　　　　　v. shut oneself indoors

　　闷　mēn　　　　　　　　　　　v. block

2)　芬芳　fēnfāng　　　　　　　　n. worry

　　灿烂　cànlàn　　　　　　　　　n. fragrance

　　忧烦　yōufán　　　　　　　　　n. brilliance

3)　唤起　huànqǐ　　　　　　　　v. cast away

　　沐浴　mùyù　　　　　　　　　v. arouse

　　抛却　pāoquè　　　　　　　　v. bathe

3. Guess the meanings of the following four-character expressions. Use your imagination in cases where extended meanings are used:

1)　应有尽有

2)　坐立不安　　（不安: bù'ān, adj., uneasy）

3)　岁月沧桑　　（沧桑: cāngsāng, n., great changes. See the list of new words）

4)　青山绿水

5)　风风雨雨

6)　没完没了

III. 课文 🔊

光与影之恋　赵洁

那一天，我被邀去做客。

一对新婚夫妇的两房一厅，目前让许多广州人眼红的居住条件：地毯、空调、墙纸、组合家具和高级音响，应该是应有尽有了。

新娘子身着粉红轻纱，殷勤为客人送烟递水；新郎脸上溢出的笑容竟是如此的灿烂如此的自豪如此的幸福。

环顾四周，我却坐立不安；不知道什么地方，总有那么一点点不对头，明确点，我却又说不出。

过了几天，到外地出差，一下火车，朋友便订好了宾馆来接。

走在宾馆那铺着红地毯的走廊上，突然之间，那种感觉又来了，一丝不安，一丝不对头，一丝忧闷的气氛。

于是我明白了：

那宾馆里没有阳光。

朋友的新居里也缺少阳光。

每天清晨，醒来的第一眼，没有唤起生命与爱心的温暖。

每日黄昏，推开房门，迎接你的，不是光与影告别西窗前的那一片温柔与浪漫。

每个假日，躺在摇椅中晃着，却无法沐浴那一份代表了岁月沧桑年华流失的辉煌与灿烂。

只因为，房间里，没有阳光。

都市的人不再依恋青山绿水，相反地，他们将自然用厚厚的纱挡住，宁愿终日坐在空调的轰鸣中。

没有山的伟岸，没有海的飘然，没有风的轻柔也没有雨的忧烦。

在那一刹那间，心，充满落寞。

于是知道自己此生此世再也做不了现代人，因为怎也抛却不了那一丝属于情绪却不属于现实的东西。于是知道生活中永远少不了自然中的风风雨雨和阳光，因为我无法在空调中封闭自己。

就算一个人闷在宾馆里看电视，就算一天到晚被没完没了的稿件压得无法抬头，就算坐在一个没有空气的屋子里假笑着应付客人，就算宴席上周身充满了疲倦和不自在，只要一想到推开那一个小屋的门，便有阳光跳跃着来迎接，便有温柔的清风来照拂，便有花的芬芳草的清香，于是，我的心，便有了慰藉，有了欣悦，有了温情。

那是一种让你不会再孤独的感受，那是一种家的感受。

你的家，是否也给过你这一种感受？

（选自长江文艺出版社１９９５年《精美散文》青春·温情卷）

繁體字課文

<h1 style="text-align:center">光與影之戀　趙潔</h1>

那一天，我被邀去做客。

一對新婚夫婦的兩房一廳，目前讓許多廣州人眼紅的居住條件：地毯、空調、牆紙、組合傢俱和高級音響，應該是應有盡有了。

新娘子身著粉紅輕紗，殷勤為客人送煙遞水；新郎臉上溢出的笑容竟是如此的燦爛如此的自豪如此的幸福。

環顧四周，我卻坐立不安；不知道甚麼地方，總有那麼一點點不對頭，明確點，我卻又說不出。

過了幾天，到外地出差，一下火車，朋友便訂好了賓館來接。

走在賓館那鋪著紅地毯的走廊上，突然之間，那種感覺又來了，一絲不安，一絲不對頭，一絲憂悶的氣氛。

於是我明白了：

那賓館裡沒有陽光。

朋友的新居裡也缺少陽光。

每天清晨，醒來的第一眼，沒有喚起生命與愛心的溫暖。

每日黃昏，推開房門，迎接你的，不是光與影告別西窗前的那一片溫柔與浪漫。

每個假日，躺在搖椅中晃著，卻無法沐浴那一份代表了歲月滄桑年華流失的輝煌與燦爛。

只因為，房間裡，沒有陽光。

都市的人不再依戀青山綠水，相反地，他們將自然用厚厚的紗擋住，寧願終日坐在空調的轟鳴中。

沒有山的偉岸，沒有海的飄然，沒有風的輕柔也沒有雨的憂煩。

在那一剎那間，心，充滿落寞。

於是知道自己此生此世再也做不了現代人，因為怎也拋卻不了那一絲屬於情緒卻不屬於現實的東西。於是知道生活中永遠少不了自然中的風風雨雨和陽光，因為我無法在空調中封閉自己。

就算一個人悶在賓館裡看電視，就算一天到晚被沒完沒了的稿件壓得無法抬頭，就算坐在一個沒有空氣的屋子裡假笑著應付客人，就算宴席上周身充滿了疲倦和不自在，只要一想到推開那一個小屋的門，便有陽光跳躍著來迎接，便有溫柔的清風來照拂，便有花的芬芳草的清香，於是，我的心，便有了慰藉，有了欣悅，有了溫情。

那是一種讓你不會再孤獨的感受，那是一種家的感受。

你的家，是否也給過你這一種感受？

思考题

为什么作者认识到她当不了"现代人"？为什么阳光对作者这么重要？

IV. 新词语

恋	liàn	n.	love
邀	yāo	v.	invite
着	zhuó	v.	wear
殷勤	yīnqín	adv.	hospitably
递	dì	v.	pass over
新郎	xīnláng	n.	bridegroom
如此	rúcǐ	adv.	so; 这么; 这样
环顾	huángù	v.	look around
铺	pū	v.	spread
走廊	zǒuláng	n.	corridor
晃	huàng	v.	rock
沧桑	cāngsāng	n.	沧海桑田, a Chinese allusion referring to the quick passage of time as is seen in the change of seas into mulberry fields and vice versa.
年华	niánhuá	n.	(of human life) years
辉煌	huīhuáng	n.	splendor
依恋	yīliàn	v.	be emotionally attached to
相反	xiāngfǎn	adv.	on the contrary
宁愿	nìngyuàn	adv.	would rather
终日	zhōngrì	adv.	all day long
轰鸣	hōngmíng	n.	roar
伟岸	wěi'àn	n.	magnificence
飘然	piāorán	n.	gracefulness

一刹那	yíchànà	adv.	in an instant
落寞	luòmò	n.	despondence
属于	shǔyú	v.	belong to
情绪	qíngxù	n.	mood
稿件	gǎojiàn	n.	manuscripts
应付	yìngfù	v.	deal with
周身	zhōushēn	adv.	all over the body; 全身
照拂	zhàofú	v.	attend to
慰藉	wèijiè	n.	comfort

V. 词语与句型

1. 竟, 竟然 (adv.)　　　　　　　新郎脸上溢出的笑容<u>竟</u>是如此的灿烂…

This word emphasizes the fact or state it introduces as being completely unexpected by the speaker. It implies a fair degree of surprise on the speaker's part.

下课的时候, 赵老师<u>竟（然）</u>对学生们说"老师再见"。

慢慢地, 这块丑石<u>竟（然）</u>锈上了绿苔、黑斑。

在朋友的新家, 我<u>竟（然）</u>是那样地坐立不安。

2. 那么 (adv.)　　　　　　　不知道什么地方, 总有<u>那么</u>一点点不对头…

The meaning of 那么 in this context is rather vague. In fact, the word can be omitted without affecting the meaning of the sentence. In a context like this, however, using 那么 is more idiomatic than without it. 那么 also highlights or emphasizes the state or situation represented by the words and phrases after it.

我总有<u>那么</u>一种感觉, 终有一日你会回来的。
Compare: 我总有一种感觉, 终有一日你会回来的。

不知为什么, 你身上有<u>那么</u>一点与别人不同的地方。
Compare: 不知为什么, 你身上有一点与别人不同的地方。

135

3. … 的, …　　　　　　　　　　推开房门, 迎接你<u>的</u>, 不是… 那一片温暖与浪漫。

的 here is serving its normal function of connecting a noun with its qualifier. The noun is omitted because it is understood from the combination of the qualifier and 的.

高处一无所有。你所能看到<u>的</u>（东西）, 只有你自己。

稍稍能安慰我们<u>的</u>（一件事）, 是在那石上有一个不大不小的坑凹儿, 雨天就盛满了水。

4. 相反(地) (conj.)　　　　　都市的人不再依恋…, <u>相反地</u>, 他们将自然…

This word, when inserted between two sentences, means "on the contrary." Normally the first sentence is in the negative form, and the second sentence introduces a situation or fact that is opposite to what is expressed in the first sentence.

第三个年轻人爬到了山顶。他没觉得高兴, <u>相反地</u>, 他很失望。

丑石并不丑, <u>相反</u>, 它很美。

我并不觉得很成功 ("successful")。<u>相反地</u>, 我觉得自己失败了。

5. 宁愿 (adv.)　　　　　　　他们将自然挡住, <u>宁愿</u>终日坐在空调的轰鸣中。

宁愿 is the same as 宁可 or 宁肯, meaning "would rather." Sometimes it forms a structure with 也不, in which case it means "would rather...than...."

石匠嫌丑石石质太细, <u>宁愿</u>从远处搬石头过来。

这位中国朋友不喜欢吃美国饭, 他<u>宁可</u>饿着。

现代人<u>宁肯</u>爬楼梯, 也不愿坐电梯。

6. 再也不　　　　　　　　　于是知道自己此生此世<u>再也</u>做<u>不</u>了现代人…

It is similar to 不再, which means "no longer." However, 再也不 is more emphatic and its English equivalent should be "never again."

我们<u>再也不</u>叫你 "柿把儿" 老师了。

136

Compare: 我们<u>不再</u>叫你"柿把儿"老师了。

More examples:

这又怪又丑的石头，原来是天上的呢！我们<u>再也不</u>嫌它丑了。

那个天文学家发现了丑石以后<u>再也不</u>走了。

7. 就算…, (也/还是) …　　　　　　　　<u>就算</u>一个人闷在宾馆里看电视…

This is used at the beginning of a clause and normally with 也 and 还是 in the main sentence. It means "even if…, still…" and, sometimes, "although."

<u>就算</u>这房子让人眼红，要是没有阳光，住在里面<u>也</u>不舒服。

<u>就算</u>胖子从船上跳进了水里，这<u>也</u>不是勇敢。

<u>就算</u>你每天不睡觉，月底以前你<u>还是</u>写不完这篇文章。

8. 只要…便/就…　　　　　　<u>只要</u>一推开那一个小屋的门，<u>便</u>有阳光来迎接…

只要, meaning "if only," introduces a neccessary condition or a minimal requirement, whereas what follows 便 or 就 indicates the result of such a condition.

<u>只要</u>他举起猎枪，一扣扳机，母鹿<u>就</u>会应声倒下。

<u>只要</u>赵老师同意以后朝政界发展，姑娘<u>就</u>不会离开他。

9. 是否　　　　　　　　　　　　你的家，<u>是否</u>也给过你这一种感受？

是否 is the same as 是不是, but more formal.

你<u>是否</u>感到过丑石的伟大？

我可以跟他谈谈。他<u>是否</u>同意，我不知道。

这块陨石<u>是否</u>有用，我们最好去问天文学家。

VI. 语言知识与技巧

1. Using words of reduplication to make descriptions more vivid

In Lesson Two, we have said that onomatopoeia words contribute significantly to the vividness of expression, because the sounds they imitate work directly on the ear and directly affect one of the most important human sense faculties in cognition. In a loose sense, sound words can also include "words of reduplication" (叠字词, *diézìcí*) formed by the reduplication of one character in a two-syllable word or of two characters in a four-syllable word or expression. The character being reduplicated is normally an adjective or a verb. Grammatically, the reduplicated words function as modifiers, and sometimes as predicates. As modifiers, normally followed by 的 or 地, or preceded by 得, they emphasize the state of the noun, the degree of the quality indicated by the adjective, or the manner in which the action of the verb is carried out. Look at the following:

A. As modifiers:

1) modifying a noun

粗粗的桦树	小小的划艇
厚厚的嘴唇	细细的汗珠
高高的大楼	很远很远的地方

2) modifying a preceding adjective

亮晶晶的眼睛	凉丝丝的露珠
教室里静悄悄	深幽幽的洞口
黑黝黝地卧在那里	小心翼翼地搬走

3) modifying a verb

轻轻地出了一口气	痴痴地望着
默默地忍受	深深地感到
慢慢地绣上了绿苔	稍稍地安慰我们
声声发喊	微微翘起来
偷偷去看	常常要

4) modifying an adverb

很久很久以前

B. As predicates:

绿草<u>萋萋</u>	山林<u>静静</u>的
前途<u>大大</u>的	我再<u>考虑考虑</u>

Read these phrases aloud and while doing so, try to experience the sound of the reduplicated characters as well as the effect of this sound.

2. *Enumeration: a way to reinforce statements (1)*

"Enumeration" (排比, *páibǐ*) stands for a rhetorical device in Chinese that is employed by writers to enhance the force of their argument. Enumeration normally involves three or more sentences arranged one after another. These sentences contain shared expressions or sentence structures and are approximately the same in length or in the number of the characters they contain. Because they are neat in form and rhythmical in sound, sentences in the form of enumeration help enhance the force of the tone, reinforce the reader's impression through repetition (重复, *chóngfù*), and build the author's argument in a compelling manner. Sometimes, these sentences convey the same or related meanings: the author utters them at one stretch simply relying on the repetition to bring home his/her point to the reader. At other times, there is a progression of seriousness or importance in the order in which the sentences are arranged. Each sentence represents one step deeper in the author's reasoning, and the progression forces the reader to confront the argument that the author is advancing.

Enumeration is used in all kinds of writing. It is particularly common in essays of persuasion and lyrical expression. Repeating the same expressions or sentence patterns appears to be simple. However, much thought has to go into the choice of the component words in terms of their meaning, sound, and form. Such considerations are obviously based on, or made possible by, the unique features of the Chinese language. As is self-evident, Chinese characters are independent from one another in terms of meaning, sound, and form. As such they can be easily used as "building blocks" by a writer for intended sentence structures.

Enumeration occurs at various levels of the Chinese language. Using the present text as an example, we see them

A. at word level:

新郎脸上溢出的笑容竟是<u>如此</u>的灿烂<u>如此</u>的自豪<u>如此</u>的幸福。

突然之间，那种感觉又来了，<u>一丝</u>不安，<u>一丝</u>不对头，<u>一丝</u>忧闷的气氛。

B. at sentence level:

没有山的伟岸，没有海的飘然，没有风的轻柔也没有雨的忧烦。

C. at paragraph level:

每天清晨，醒来的第一眼，没有唤起生命与爱心的温暖。

每日黄昏，推开房门，迎接你的，不是光与影告别西窗前的那一片温暖与浪漫。

每个假日，躺在摇椅中晃着，却无法沐浴那一份代表了岁月沧桑年华流失的辉煌与灿烂。

The third paragraph from the last in the text is very interesting. The whole paragraph is actually one long complicated sentence, containing several enumerated or parallel structures at both word and sentence levels:

就算一个人闷在宾馆里看电视，就算一天到晚被没完没了的稿件压得无法抬头，就算坐在一个没有空气的屋子里假笑着应付客人，就算宴席上周身充满了疲倦和不自在，只要一想到推开那一个小屋的门，便有阳光跳跃着来迎接，便有温柔的清风来照拂，便有花的芬芳草的清香，于是，我的心，便有了慰藉，有了欣悦，有了温情。

The basic grammatical framework of this sentence is: 就算…，只要…，于是，我的心…. There are four sentences introduced by 就算, three by 便有, and three by 有了. Reading this long but rhythmical sentence, you may be able to feel the cadence effected by these enumerated sentences and the power of the author's voice conveyed by it.

3. *Making sense of four-character expressions*

In Lesson Two we introduced four-character expressions including their nature and the purpose of using them in oral and written communication. In the essay of this lesson, the author has also used a large number of four-character expressions, not only to make her essay terse, formal, and forceful, but also to take advantage of their phonological and syntactical regularity to effect enumeration and progression, in an attempt to enhance the general force of the author's argument. Not all the four-character expressions the author uses are set phrases; many of them are spontaneously put together by the author to help achieve the effect she intends.

Analyzing the formation of four-character expressions may help you to understand and use this highly effective linguistic means. Generally speaking, in terms of composition, there are three types of four-character expressions. Using the four-character expressions you have learned as examples, there are

A. those that are set phrases:

鸦雀无声	孑然一身
爱屋及乌	千载难逢
亭亭玉立	小心翼翼
应有尽有	坐立不安

B. those with replaceable elements (underlined as follows) in a set framework:

没完没了	自我介绍
火上加油	不太不小
又怪又丑	以丑为美
送烟递水	此生此世

C. those that are formed loosely and spontaneously:

环顾四周	矗立而起
声声发喊	平安载回
爬到其上	翘望天边
突然之间	一刹那间

In addition to the knowledge of the formation of four-character expressions, a grammatical analysis of their internal structures can also help you understand, memorize, and use four-character expressions. Study the grammatical structures of the following expressions:

衣履光鲜	(n + n) + (adj + adj)	S + P
身强体壮	(n + adj) + (n + adj)	SP + SP
繁花夹道	(adj + n) + v + n	S + P + O
高风悲旋	(adj + n) + adv + v	S + Adv + P

Knowing basic structures such as these, you can make up your own four-character expressions whenever possible.

4. *Punctuation marks (1)*

Punctuation marks (标点符号, *biāodiǎn fúhào*) are closely and importantly related to tone, because in written language tone is shown by punctuation marks, as well as tone words. The following three sentences composed of the same words have different meanings because of the different tones conveyed by the different punctuation marks:

小鹿跑了。

小鹿跑了？

小鹿跑了！

Punctuation marks are an integral part of written language also because they indicate pause (停顿, *tíngdùn*) in reading. In Chinese, where characters are independent from one another in sound, meaning, and form, this function of punctuation marks can directly impact the meaning of a sentence. Consider the following three sentences:

为了这个，酋长，我才这么做的。

为了这个酋长，我才这么做的。

为了这个，酋长我才这么做的。

These three sentences are composed of exactly the same characters. Punctuated differently, however, their meanings are quite different.

Chinese punctuation marks, borrowed from Western languages, overlap substantially with those of English in both form and usage. There are, still, a few things that need to be noted: a) three punctuation marks in Chinese are different in form from their counterparts in English: period (句号, "。"), ellipsis (省略号, "……"), and the book title mark (书名号, "《 》"); b) Chinese has a slight-pause mark (顿号, "、"), which is absent from English; c) the usage of period, comma (逗号), and colon (分号) differs from English. Our attention will be focused on these three marks and the slight-pause mark. We shall begin our discussion here with period, and continue with the other three marks in Lesson Twelve.

1) Period

A period is used at the end of a declarative sentence, whether this sentence is long or short, complicated or simple, or whether it includes one or several grammatically self-contained "short sentences." The latter fact is particularly important because, as we have said of short sentences previously, in Chinese the concept of a sentence is not defined by an internal logical grammatical relation. A period at the end of the sentence does not indicate that what is within the sentence is necessarily a structure of "subject--predicate (--object)" or a structure of "main clause--subordinate clause" as in English. Often, what defines a sentence in Chinese is the coherence of meaning, which means that a sentence ending with a period may include two or more grammatically self-contained sentences separated by commas. The following sentence from the text of Lesson One is a good example:

几十米远的一块林间空地上，绿草萋萋，一只母鹿和一只小鹿在那里嬉戏。

This sentence contains what would be considered two sentences separated by a period in English. Yet, in Chinese it is treated as one sentence because the two short sentences are coherent in meaning, and therefore their separation by a period is unnecessary. This being the case, the choice of punctuation marks in the following passage is not very appropriate:

熊猫的样子非常可爱。肥肥的身体，短短的腿＿ 头非常大，耳朵又这么小＿ 眼睛上象戴着墨镜一样。

In this paragraph, the second and third periods (underlined) should be changed to commas because all the short sentences are closely connected in meaning, concerned as they are with one topic--how the panda looks. Having said this, it should be pointed out that not all short sentences are separated by commas. Indeed, even if the topic is the same, sometimes a period is used to prevent the sentence from running on:

他在爱情上也是失败的。快 30 岁的人了，至今孑然一身＿ 听说谈过的不少，可没一个成功的。

In this passage, the second period (underlined) could be a comma since the next sentence continues the same topic--Mr. Zhao's failure in his personal life. However, the period seems more appropriate, because it truncates the sentence and makes the meaning more clear.

VII. 练习

词语与句型

1. Rewrite the following sentences with the words or expressions given in the parentheses.

    1) 那对刚结婚的人是我的好朋友。（新婚夫妇）

    2) 他们家应该有的东西全都有了。（应有尽有）

    3) 别忘了给客人送上香烟和茶水。（送烟递水）

    4) 我觉得坐着也不自在，站着也不自在。（坐立不安）

    5) 瘦子望着流不完的河水，一言不发。（没完没了）

    6) 我看，总有一个什么地方出了问题。（不对头）

    7) 她要到一个别的地方去办一些公事。（去外地出差）

    8) 老同学为我们在宾馆订了一个房间。（订好了宾馆）

2. Select the most appropriate four-character expression for each of the following sentences:

    鸟语花香，衣不蔽体，爱屋及乌，鸦雀无声，孑然一身，千载难逢，亭亭玉立，无可奈何，小心翼翼，坐立不安，应有尽有

    1) 这对新婚夫妇 ＿＿＿＿＿＿＿＿ 地把组合音响搬回了家。

    2) 四周 ＿＿＿＿＿＿＿＿ ，不见一个人影，好象一切都已经死去。

    3) 商店里什么东西都卖，真是 ＿＿＿＿＿＿＿＿ 。

    4) 他们的女儿今年十七岁，已经是一个 ＿＿＿＿＿＿＿＿ 的大姑娘了。

    5) 人们在山洞里发现他的时候，他 ＿＿＿＿＿＿＿＿ ，人不象人。

    6) 公园里山青水秀，＿＿＿＿＿＿＿＿ 。很多人带着孩子来玩。

    7) 她一想到住在医院里的丈夫，就觉得 ＿＿＿＿＿＿＿＿ 。

    8) 那位老人家一辈子没有结过婚，至今 ＿＿＿＿＿＿＿＿ 。

    9) 他太太是中国人，他也就 ＿＿＿＿＿＿＿＿ 地喜欢上了中国。

    10) 今天时间又不够了。他看了看手表，＿＿＿＿＿＿＿＿ 地摇了摇头。

    11) 要是错过了这个 ＿＿＿＿＿＿＿＿ 的机会，你一辈子都会遗憾的。

3. Select appropriate words or expressions to replace the underlined parts in the sentences to make them sound more formal:

    A. 便，甚，但，以，足，曾，将，虽，极

1) 他<u>虽然</u>很生气，<u>但是</u>却不好发作。

2) 赵老师<u>曾经</u>谈过不少女朋友。

3) 胖子一跳进水里<u>就</u>沉了底。

4) 猎人<u>用</u>小车把妻子接了回来。

5) 时间不<u>够</u>，谁也做不好这件事。

6) 这座山并不<u>太</u>高，<u>很</u>容易爬。

B. 无法，立即，如此，或许，新居，终日，环顾，是否

1) 朋友请我们去他的<u>新房子</u>做客。

2) 要是缺少阳光，就<u>没有办法</u>生活。

3) 他<u>一天到晚</u>闷在家里生气。

4) 没有人知道她<u>是不是</u>打过电话来。

5) 他们脸上的笑容是<u>这样</u>的自豪<u>这样</u>的幸福。

6) 我<u>看了看</u>四周，什么也没有发现

7) 你<u>马上</u>去河边，<u>也许</u>还能看到她。

4. Expand the phrases into sentences by following the examples:

1) 局长大人的千金竟（然）爱上了"柿把儿"老师。

这个年轻人／过了一个月才回来

瘦子／平安地穿越了隧道

山林静静的／连鸟的叫声都听不见

那块石头／是从天上落下来的

2) 年轻人对老酋长说<u>的</u>，（只）<u>是</u>他们自己的见闻。

猎人在这时候想到／他的妻子和儿子

堤坝上的人听到／河水发出的狂吼

姑娘喜欢／他的文章

让我讨厌／在空调中封闭自己

145

3) 瘦子没有跳到水里，<u>相反地</u>，他留在船上了。

前两个年轻人没有往高处走 / 他们回到了村子

猎人瞄准了母鹿却没有开枪 / 他离开了树林

村子里的人不再说丑石丑 / 大家都觉得它了不起

我不喜欢把自己关在没有空气的屋子里 / 我喜欢自然中的风雨和阳光

4) 伯父<u>宁愿</u>去河滩上捡石头回来，<u>也</u>不用那块丑石。

小鹿 / 在母鹿身旁卧下 / 再跳来跳去

老酋长 / 让年轻人先去爬山 / 先告诉他们为什么

胖子 / 跳入水中求生 / 留在船上等死

赵老师 / 留在学校教书 / 朝政界发展

5) 都市里的人<u>再也不</u>依恋青山绿水<u>了</u>。

同学们 / 笑话他们的语文老师

我们 / 觉得丑石难看

大家 / 到堤坝上游的河道里划船

这个鲁莽凶狠的汉子 / 打他的妻子

6) <u>就算</u>你有一个家，你<u>也</u>不一定幸福。

他的写作水平出奇的好 / 他 / 不是一个好老师

这是很难遇到的机会 / 他 / 没有开枪

<u>就算</u>你有一个家，你<u>还是</u>不一定幸福。

这块石头很丑 / 它 / 不一般

天意要立他做新酋长 / 他 / 觉得自己很渺小

7) <u>只要</u>生活中缺少阳光，人们<u>就</u>会感到忧闷。

他心里还有一丝愧恨 / 他 / 不是一个坏人

你到的地方鸟语花香 / 那 / 是山麓

一个人活得勇敢或死得勇敢 / 他 / 不是懦夫

他离开学生／他／会失去灵感

语言知识与技巧

5. Match the items in the left column with those in the right. After you finish, read the phrases aloud to note the effect of the words of duplication:

1) Modifying nouns

薄薄的	故事
尖尖的	眼睛
大大的	山林
静静的	信纸
很长很长的	衣服
很旧很旧的	塔顶

2) Modifying preceding adjectives

闹	油油（的草地）
热	冰冰（的面孔）
急	哄哄（的车站）
绿	皑皑（的雪山）
白	烘烘（的面包）
冷	匆匆（的行人）

3) Modifying verbs

重重地	抓住
暗暗地	出发
远远地	打人
死死地	走路
早早地	叫苦
一跳一跳地	观看

4) As predicates

身材	厚厚的
嘴唇	糟糟的
讲课	美美的
心里	商量商量
天气	瘦瘦的
大家	暖暖的

6. Complete the following sentences in your own words, using the suggested enumerated structures:

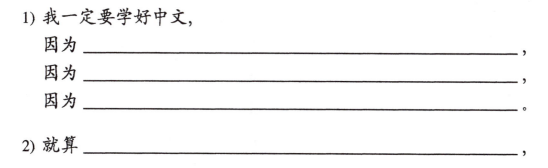

1) 我一定要学好中文，

因为 _____ ，

因为 _____ ，

因为 _____ 。

2) 就算 _____ ，

147

就算 ＿＿＿＿＿＿＿＿＿＿＿＿＿＿＿＿＿＿＿＿＿＿＿，

就算 ＿＿＿＿＿＿＿＿＿＿＿＿＿＿＿＿＿＿＿＿＿＿＿，

我也还自以为是一个好学生。我热爱自己的专业。在我的心中，

充满了 ＿＿＿＿＿＿＿＿＿，充满了 ＿＿＿＿＿＿＿＿＿，充满了

＿＿＿＿＿＿＿＿＿。

3) "一年之计在于春。"

春天，是 ＿＿＿＿＿＿＿＿＿＿＿＿＿＿＿＿＿＿ 的季节;

春天，是 ＿＿＿＿＿＿＿＿＿＿＿＿＿＿＿＿＿＿ 的日子;

春天，给我们带来 ＿＿＿＿＿＿＿＿＿＿＿＿＿＿＿＿。

7. Write out the four-character expressions according to the meanings provided:

1) 从早上一直到晚上　　　　从 ＿＿ 到 ＿＿

2) 不太早也不太晚　　　　　不 ＿＿ 不 ＿＿

3) 现在这个时刻　　　　　　此 ＿＿ 此 ＿＿

4) 很多个白天和夜里　　　　日 ＿＿ 夜 ＿＿

5) 从开头一直到结尾　　　　从 ＿＿ 到 ＿＿

6) 没个完，没个了　　　　　没 ＿＿ 没 ＿＿

7) 说起来会有很长的话　　　＿＿ 来 ＿＿ 长

8) 把很长的话说得短　　　　＿＿ 话 ＿＿ 说

9) 很多个男的和女的　　　　＿＿ 男 ＿＿ 女

10) 男的女的老的少的　　　　＿＿ ＿＿ ＿＿ ＿＿

11) 一个男的和一个女的　　　一 ＿＿ 一 ＿＿

12) 个子很高很大　　　　　　又 ＿＿ 又 ＿＿

13) 把学校当作家　　　　　　以 ＿＿ 为 ＿＿

14) 什么也没看见　　　　　　一 ＿＿ 所 ＿＿

15) 走过来又走过去　　　　　走 ＿＿ 走 ＿＿

16) 好了又更好　　　　　　　___ 上加 ___

活学与活用

8. Using the expressions provided, describe the author's experiences in, and opinions about, her friend's new residence.

1) 作者在新婚夫妇的家里看到什么？

两房一厅 / 应有尽有
新娘 / 粉红 / 殷勤
新郎 / 笑容 / 自豪 / 幸福

2) 作者有什么样的感觉？

坐立不安
什么地方 / 不对头 / 说不出

3) 作者后来去哪里？她明白了什么？

到外地出差 / 宾馆
不对头 / 不安 / 忧闷的气氛
没有阳光

4) 房间里没有阳光会怎么样？

清晨 / 醒来 / 没有温暖
黄昏 / 推开房门 / 没有温柔与浪漫
假日 / 在摇椅中 / 无法沐浴辉煌与灿烂

5) 作者的心为什么充满落寞？

都市的人 / 不再依恋青山绿水
厚厚的纱 / 挡住 / 自然
终日 / 空调 / 轰鸣

6) 作者为什么说自己做不了现代人？

149

抛却不了／属于情绪的东西

生活中／少不了风雨和阳光

7) 作者认为家的感受应该是什么？

阳光／清风／花草

慰藉／欣悦／温情

不会再孤独

9. Using your own words, answer the following questions based on your own opinions and experiences:

1) 你被什么新婚夫妇邀请去做过客吗？谈谈你当时的感觉。

2) 你曾经在谁的家里觉得坐立不安吗？那是因为什么地方不对头？

3) 你喜欢大自然吗？说一下你自己在大自然里的感觉。

4) 在你看来，家的感觉应该是什么样的？

5) 现代文明给我们的生活带来了什么好处和什么坏处？

10. Write an essay on an ideal place where you would like to live. You may want to start with a home you know, and comment on the things about it that you do not like. You may then go on to describe a new place where you would like to live, and argue how nice life would be if you lived in that environment. To add force to your argument, use enumeration whenever possible.

VIII. 课文材料对话

A

客人甲：这三房两厅的居住条件真让人眼红。

客人乙：是啊，地毯、空调、墙纸和组合家具，连高级音响都不缺，可以说是应有尽有了。

客人甲：新郎和新娘多么幸福多么自豪。我还从来没见过这么灿烂的笑容呢。

客人乙：（环顾四周）可是，不知为什么，这房间让我坐立不安，总有那么一点点不对头。

客人甲：我也感到气氛有些问题。难道是屋子里缺少阳光？

客人乙：果然是缺少阳光！老实说，这屋子哪儿都好，就是没有温暖，没有一种家的感受。

B

老年人：现在有许多人象你一样，把自然用厚厚的纱挡住，整天坐在装着空调的屋子里。你们那年轻的心，不会感到寂寞吗？

年轻人：当然不会。我们不再依恋青山绿水，我们喜欢在空调中封闭自己。那么您呢？您感到孤独吗？

老年人：如果在你这屋子里，是的。有一种属于情绪而不属于现实的东西，我怎么也抛却不了。离开了自然中的风风雨雨和阳光，我就没法生活。

年轻人：我跟您不同。我并不害怕闷在宾馆里看电视，也不讨厌在一个没有空气的屋子里假笑着应付客人。就算一天到晚被没完没了的稿件压得无法抬头，只要开着空调，我就心满意足了。

老年人：可是，我需要阳光、清风和花草，因为它们给我安慰和温暖，给我一种家的感受。

年轻人：我现在连家都不要，还要什么家的感受呢？！

第七课　妇人之见

The essay of the previous lesson comments on one physical phenomenon, the lack of sunlight in the living environment of modern people. In the essay of this lesson, the topic shifts to a sociological issue, one that is much debated in modern societies in many cultures: the difference between men and women. Although in America some books on gender relationships propose that men and women are different, the author of this essay vehemently argues that men are in some aspects inferior to women, and that to be a woman is much easier and better than to be a man. From what we have learned so far, in terms of the effect on the reader, we realize that *how* an author expresses himself/herself can be more important than *what* the author expresses. Here is another essay that shows us the importance of artful persuasion. The author speaks in a tone that immediately reveals her position. She also resorts to enumeration, and short sentences, that are typical of persuasive writing. In addition to these tactics, other rhetorical devices are also employed by the author as she proceeds with her argument. Whether we agree with the author's opinion or not, we feel compelled to see things from her perspectives because of the powerful linguistic and rhetorical tools she uses.

I. 课文导读 🎀

我很高兴我是个女人。

女人想怎么样就怎么样，不用担心被人小看。男人却不能这样，他一定得活得象个男人的样子。只要想到这一点，我们就会明白他们有多累。

女人就象大自然里的花草树木，每一秒钟都在感受这个世界。她的<u>一辈子</u> (yíbèizi, n., one's whole life) 是不打<u>折扣</u> (zhékòu, n., discount) 的。可是男人一天到晚总是在忙这忙那，随时准备听<u>上司</u> (shàngsī, n., boss) 的话。做个男人真烦人。

男人自然会有男人的<u>事业</u> (shìyè, n., career) 和<u>成功</u> (chénggōng, n., success)。他们自己觉得很伟大、很神圣、很了不起。他们这样感觉的时候，那种可爱的样子，就跟我们上小学一年级的儿子差不多。有一半男人自己以为在做很重要的事情，<u>其实</u> (qíshí, adv., as a matter of fact) 谁都知道，他们只是在做没有用的

152

<u>蠢事</u> (chǔnshì, n., stupid thing)。

　　就算一个男人聪明得不能再聪明，他在女人面前也是个<u>白痴</u> (báichī, n., idiot)。男人永远弄不懂女人，而女人却能一眼看透男人。男人在爱上一个女人的时候最聪明，女人在爱上一个男人的时候最<u>愚蠢</u> (yúchǔn, adj., stupid)。

　　这个世界其实什么都不重要，重要的是生活本身，而生活是离不开女人的。要是没有女人，这个世界就会不对头。女人要爱自己。只要女人可爱，世界就<u>至少</u> (zhìshǎo, adv., at least) 有一半是美好的了。

　　不管男人们怎么样，我们女人就是要高高兴兴！

II. 词语导学

1. In each group, match the Chinese words on the left with the English meanings on the right based on the characters you know:

1) 智力　zhìlì　　　　　　　n. waist measurement
   饭量　fànliàng　　　　　　n. social position
   腰围　yāowéi　　　　　　　n. invitation card
   X光　X guāng　　　　　　 n. power
   地位　dìwèi　　　　　　　 n. intelligence
   请帖　qǐngtiē　　　　　　 n. X-ray
   权力　quánlì　　　　　　　n. appetite

2) 明了　míngliǎo　　　　　 adj. complacent
   可怜　kělián　　　　　　　adj. clear
   得意　déyì　　　　　　　　adj. down-to-earth
   实在　shízài　　　　　　　adj. pitiful

3) 握手　wòshǒu　　　　　　 v. present flowers
   献花　xiànhuā　　　　　　 v. feel happy because things could be worse
   抢购　qiǎnggòu　　　　　　v. shake hands
   庆幸　qìngxìng　　　　　　v. rush to purchase

153

2. Guess the meanings of the following four-character expressions. Use your imagination in cases where extended meanings are used:

1) 目不斜视　　（斜视: xiéshì, v., look sideways）
2) 挺胸凸肚　　（挺: tǐng, v., stick out; 凸: tū, v., protrude）
3) 心不在焉　　（焉: yān, adv., here）
4) 一本正经　　（正: zhèng, adj., standard; 经: jīng, n., scripture）
5) 油盐酱醋　　（油: yóu, n., oil; 盐: yán, n., salt; 酱: jiàng, n., soy sauce; 醋: cù, n., vinegar）
6) 锅碗瓢盆　　（锅: guō, n., pot; 碗: wǎn, n., bowl; 瓢: piáo, n., ladle; 盆: pén, n., plate）

III. 课文

妇人之见　　李永芹

很庆幸是个女人。

女人想哭就哭，想笑就笑，害怕就害怕，脆弱就脆弱，不用担心被人小看。男人却不能，他除了别的许多顾虑外，最不爱听的一句话是：象个女人。他只有挺胸凸肚，只有目不斜视，只有二两的饭量咽三两，只有二尺的腰围撑三尺，借钱也要请客，醉死也要喝酒。

想想也替他们累。

女人一如自然界的花草树木，全身心都在感受这个世界，不会有一秒钟心不在焉。她的一辈子是实实在在不打折扣的一辈子。

男人西装口袋里插支钢笔，身上揣个本本，男人走五米路同三个人握手，随时准备对上司说："是是是"。当个男人烦人。

男人自会有轰轰烈烈的事业，自会有人献花、照相，自会每天收一大堆

154

信件、请帖，自会对女人一扬眉："不回来吃饭。"可怜那份热闹和愉快跟我们抢购漂亮衣裙时差不多，他们自认为很伟大很神圣很了不起的时候，你站在一边偷偷去看吧，那煞有介事的可爱象极了你上小学一年级的儿子。有一半男人自以为得意地在高高的大楼里绞痛眉头，其实干的都是些谁也不需要的蠢事。

再聪明的男人在女人面前也是个白痴。男人不屑其实是无法研究女人，他们永远也弄不懂女人。而女人能一眼看透面前的男人，如X光胸透那样简单明了。

男人最聪明的时候是爱上一个女人。

女人最愚蠢的时候是爱上一个男人。

人类的智力就这样拉平了。

男人瞧不起女人是因为他傻，女人瞧不起女人是因为没弄清自己需要什么。她眼红男人的权力和地位，她不懂得这个世界其实什么都不重要，重要的是生活本身。生活中少不得油盐酱醋，少不得锅碗瓢盆，少不得孩子老人，少不得星期日的烦琐星期六的温柔。没有女人，这世界该会多么乏味，多么不成个世界！

你要爱自己、欣赏自己，你要让自己每天漂亮，你要让自己更加可爱，世界就至少有一半是美好的了。

让男人们去一本正经吧，我们乐我们的！

（选自陕西旅游出版社１９９２年《散文诗精品》）

繁體字課文

婦人之見　李永芹

很慶幸是個女人。

155

　　女人想哭就哭，想笑就笑，害怕就害怕，脆弱就脆弱，不用擔心被人小看。男人卻不能，他除了別的許多顧慮外，最不愛聽的一句話是：像個女人。他只有挺胸凸肚，只有目不斜視，只有二兩的飯量嚥三兩，只有二尺的腰圍撐三尺，借錢也要請客，醉死也要喝酒。

　　想想也替他們累。

　　女人一如自然界的花草樹木，全身心都在感受這個世界，不會有一秒鐘心不在焉。她的一輩子是實實在在不打折扣的一輩子。

　　男人西裝口袋裡插枝鋼筆，身上揣個本本，男人走五米路同三個人握手，隨時準備對上司說："是是是"。當個男人煩人。

　　男人自會有轟轟烈烈的事業，自會有人獻花、照相，自會每天收一大堆信件、請帖，自會對女人一揚眉："不回來吃飯。"可憐那份熱鬧和愉快跟我們搶購漂亮衣裙時差不多，他們自認為很偉大很神聖很了不起的時候，你站在一邊偷偷去看吧，那煞有介事的可愛像極了你上小學一年級的兒子。有一半男人自以為得意地在高高的大樓裡絞痛眉頭，其實幹的都是些誰也不需要的蠢事。

　　再聰明的男人在女人面前也是個白痴。男人不屑其實是無法研究女人，他們永遠也弄不懂女人。而女人能一眼看透面前的男人，如X光胸透那樣簡單明瞭。

　　男人最聰明的時候是愛上一個女人。

　　女人最愚蠢的時候是愛上一個男人。

　　人類的智力就這樣拉平了。

　　男人瞧不起女人是因為他傻，女人瞧不起女人是因為沒弄清自己需要甚麼。她眼紅男人的權力和地位，她不懂得這個世界其實甚麼都不重要，重要的是生活本身。生活中少不得油鹽醬醋，少不得鍋碗瓢盆，少不得孩子老人，少不得星期日的煩瑣星期六的溫柔。沒有女人，這世界該會多麼乏味，多麼不成個世界！

　　你要愛自己、欣賞自己，你要讓自己每天漂亮，你要讓自己更加可愛，世界就至少有一半是美好的了。

　　讓男人們去一本正經吧，我們樂我們的！

思考题

　　"妇人"这个词常常带有不好的意思？，可是为什么作者一边把自己叫做"妇人"，一边又赞美女人？你同意作者对男人和女人的看法吗？为什么？

IV. 新词语

脆弱	cuìruò	adj.	fragile
顾虑	gùlǜ	n.	worry
两	liǎng	m.	unit of weight, equal to one-twentieth of a kilogram
咽	yàn	v.	swallow
尺	chǐ	m.	traditional unit of length, equal to one-third of a meter
撑	chēng	v.	maintain
醉	zuì	adj.	drunk
替	tì	prep.	for
一如	yìrú	prep.	just like
口袋	kǒudài	n.	pocket
揣	chuāi	v.	carry in one's hand or pocket
轰轰烈烈	hōnghōnglièliè	adj.	on a grand and spectacular scale
堆	duī	m.	pile
扬眉	yáng méi	v.	raise one's eyebrows
份	fèn	m.	used after 这 or 那 in reference of certain abstract

			things
偷偷	tōutōu	adv.	secretly
煞有介事	shà yǒu jiè shì	adj.	with a show of being serious
绞	jiǎo	v.	twist
眉头	méitóu	n.	eyebrows
不屑	búxiè	v.	disdain to do sth.
胸透	xiōngtòu	n.	X-ray examination of chest; 胸部透视
瞧不起	qiáobuqǐ	v.	look down upon
傻	shǎ	adj.	stupid
烦琐	fánsuǒ	n.	trifles
乏味	fáwèi	adj.	boring
欣赏	xīnshǎng	v.	appreciate

V. 词语与句型

1. 想 V 就 V　　　　　　　　　　　　　女人<u>想</u>哭<u>就</u>哭，<u>想</u>笑<u>就</u>笑，…

想 is coupled with 就 to convey the meaning that "if one wants to do something, one goes ahead and does it without a second thought." The structure suggests that the subject of the verb is impulsive and willful, or that he/she is simply being truthful to himself/herself.

同学们在"柿把儿"老师的课上<u>想</u>笑<u>就</u>笑，<u>想</u>说话<u>就</u>说话。
局长大人的千金<u>想</u>上班<u>就</u>上班，<u>想</u>不上班<u>就</u>不上班。
你们<u>想</u>什么时候来<u>就</u>什么时候来吧，我们一天都在家。

2. Adj / V 就 Adj / V　　　　　　　　　　　害怕<u>就</u>害怕，脆弱<u>就</u>脆弱，…

At first sight, this structure appears to be the same as the previous one. You can think of it this way if you take 想 as omitted here. Otherwise, the structure can mean something quite different in a different context. In the text, by saying 害怕就害怕，脆弱就脆弱, the author means that "if a woman is scared, then she acts scared" (she is being truthful to herself). In a different context, however, it can mean that "if you think I am scared, then I am scared." In this second scenario, the structure implies resignation, concession, or, conversely, that the speaker is

158

taking up a challenge by doing something he/she may not be willing to do.

> 我让他从船上跳下去。他说："跳<u>就</u>跳。"(taking up a challenge)
>
> 去<u>就</u>去，别以为我不敢。(taking up a challenge)
>
> 懒<u>就</u>懒吧，只要心不坏就好。(making a concession)
>
> 他们说我丑。丑<u>就</u>丑吧。有什么办法呢？(showing resignation)

3. 只有/只好 (adv.)　　　　　　　　　他<u>只有</u>挺胸凸肚，<u>只有</u>目不斜视，…

The English equivalent is something like "(one) can do nothing but...."

> 她没事可做，又不想去哪儿，<u>只好</u>呆在家里看电视。
>
> 丑石太重，孩子们<u>只好</u>让它留在那里。
>
> 姑娘走了，赵老师<u>只有</u>望着她的背影，眼泪在眼眶里打转儿。

4. (就是) V1 也 V2　　　　　　　　　借钱<u>也</u>要请客，醉死<u>也</u>要喝酒。

This means "in order to do (or not to do) something, one goes to such an extent as to...." The first verb spells out the extent to which the subject goes in order to achieve his/her purpose indicated by the second verb. It can be preceded by 就是 and the action it indicates is sometimes a hypothetical one. 也 contributes crucially to the nuance of the structure, which implies the stubbornness of the person who performs the actions of the verbs.

> 我（<u>就是</u>）一夜不睡<u>也</u>要看完这本小说。
>
> 他（<u>就是</u>）热死<u>也</u>不肯开空调。

The subjects of the two verbs in this structure can be different. In this case, the first SV serves as the extent to which the second SV will or will not occur.

> （<u>就是</u>）下大雨，我们<u>也</u>要去打猎。
>
> 他（<u>就是</u>）没有权力和地位，我<u>也</u>喜欢他。
>
> 小船（<u>就是</u>）被吸进洞里，船上的人<u>也</u>不会有危险。

5. 一如 (adv.)　　　　　　　　　　　女人<u>一如</u>自然界的花草树木，…

Here 一, which can be omitted, is used to suggest the meaning of "consistence." The sentence from the text means that "women have always been like flowers and trees in nature, enjoying the physical environment with both body and soul."

> 山边的排沙泄流洞<u>一如</u>巨兽的鼻孔，喷出漫天的黄雾。
> 孩子们<u>一如</u>欢快的小鹿在林间空地上嬉戏。
> 黑黝黝的丑石<u>一如</u>病危的老牛，默默地卧在那里。

6. 可怜　　　　　　　　　　<u>可怜</u>那份热闹跟我们抢购漂亮衣裙时差不多，…

可怜, which by itself means "pitiful," can be attached to the beginning of a sentence as an indicator of the speaker's sympathetic attitude. Depending on the circumstances, however, it can also carry a mocking tone, as in the sentence from the text. This author certainly does not "take pity" on men, but rather finds their behavior childish or foolish. More examples:

> 父亲去世了，<u>可怜</u>他小小年纪就要出去做工。(the speaker being sympathetic)

> 小船奇迹般地将瘦子平安载回。<u>可怜</u>胖子拼命游了一段，终于沉了底。(the speaker is being sympathetic or sarcastic depending on his/her attitude toward the fat man)

7. 自以为/自认为…，其实…　　　　男人<u>自以为</u>得意地在大楼里…，<u>其实</u>…

This means "one thinks one is ..., but in reality it is not the case." Pay attention to the sarcastic tone of this structure.

> 他<u>自以为</u>很聪明，<u>其实</u>愚蠢得不能再愚蠢。
> 男人<u>自以为</u>很伟大很神圣，<u>其实</u>他们在女人面前都是白痴。
> 我们嫌弃丑石，<u>自认为</u>很了不起。<u>其实</u>我们都很渺小。

8. 得意 (adj.)　　　　　　　男人自以为<u>得意</u>地在大楼里…，其实…

Serving as an adjective, this means "complacent" or "one is carried away by one's success."

> 这家伙自认为是英雄，<u>得意</u>极了。
> 你先别<u>得意</u>，当上司可不是一件容易的事。
> "柿把儿"老师艳福不浅，可他自己并不为此<u>得意</u>。

9. 再 Adj 也 V　　　　　　　　　　再聪明的男人在女人面前也是个白痴。

再 and 也 are used together in the structure to mean "no matter how... still ...." 再 is followed immediately by an adjective. Depending on the situation, however, the subject can appear either before 再 or after the adjective. In the later case, 的 is used to connect the adjective and the noun. Compare:

房子再好也得要有阳光。
再好的房子也得要有阳光。

一个人再笨也能做好这个工作。
再笨的人也能做好这个工作。

男人再聪明在女人面前也是个白痴。
再聪明的男人在女人面前也是个白痴。

10. 该会 (V 得) 多么 Adj !　　　　　　没有女人，这世界该会多么乏味，…

This is a more emphatic way of saying "without women this world would be very boring," or "没有女人，这世界会很乏味." 该会 or 应该会 adds force to the already emphatic structure of 多么！

有了爱情，生活该会多么幸福！
没有那一丝属于情绪的东西，日子该会多么难过！
抛却了世俗的讥讽，人们该会活得多么自在！

11. 让 N 去 V 吧　　　　　　　　　让男人们去一本正经吧。…

This means "leave someone alone to do whatever he or she likes." The structure implies that what the person does has no effect on things anyway. Hence, the above sentence means "let men pretend they are very important; we enjoy ourselves." A variation to this form is 让 N V 去吧, with 去 moved after the verb.

让她去训斥吧，没有人会听她的！
让她去哭吧，哭完了就不难受了。

让他去得意吧，其实他干的都是蠢事。

让学生们去笑吧，我不怕。

12. S V S 的 　　　　　　　　　　　　　　　…，我们乐我们的。

The verb 乐 can be replaced by any verb that indicates an action, while the subject should remain the same before and after the verb. The structure means "we (or I, he, they) do whatever we are supposed to do regardless of what is happening around us or what other people say about us." If the verb takes an object, the object should appear after 的 at the end of the sentence.

让女人们去笑吧，我们得意我们的。

她骂她的，我们玩我们的。

你看你的（书），我看我的（电视），好吗？

VI. 语言知识与技巧

1. Getting closer to the reader with subjectless sentences

In grammar books, the term "subjectless sentences" (无主句, *wúzhǔjù*) refers to those sentences where the subjects are absent due to the convention of language use, or are difficult to find if an attempt is made to expose them. Here "subjectless sentences" refers to the situations where subjects are purposely left out by an author or speaker to achieve a certain rhetorical effect. Examples from this essay are:

很庆幸是个女人。

想想也替他们累。

By leaving out the subject "I," which is obvious from the context, the author presents herself as a member of a large social group so that her voice acquires a universal, and hence more authoritative, tone. If the reader happens to be a woman, the omission of the subjects knocks down the wall between the author and the reader, evoking a feeling of closeness on the latter's part. This makes it easier for the author to talk to her readers and ensure their support. The omission, apparently, also makes the statements more succinct, adding a touch of force to what the author is saying.

There are other ways to help you get close to your readers, such as talking directly to them or including them in things that you yourself do, just as this author does at the end of the article:

你要<u>爱</u>自己、<u>欣赏</u>自己，<u>你</u>要让自己每天漂亮，<u>你</u>要让自己更加可爱。

让男人们去一本正经吧，<u>我们</u>乐<u>我们</u>的！

2. *Parallelism and the nature of Chinese characters again*

Like the author of the previous essay, the author of this essay also makes use of enumeration, the main function of which is to enhance the force of the tone through repetition and progression. Examples from this present essay include:

女人想哭<u>就</u>哭，想笑<u>就</u>笑，害怕<u>就</u>害怕，脆弱<u>就</u>脆弱。

他<u>只有</u>挺胸凸肚，<u>只有</u>目不斜视，<u>只有</u>二两的饭量咽三两，<u>只有</u>二尺的腰围撑三尺。

男人<u>自会</u>有轰轰烈烈的事业，<u>自会</u>有人献花、照相，<u>自会</u>每天收一大堆信件、请帖，<u>自会</u>对女人一扬眉："不回来吃饭。"

生活中<u>少不得</u>油盐酱醋，<u>少不得</u>锅碗瓢盆，<u>少不得</u>孩子老人，<u>少不得</u>星期日的烦琐星期六的温柔。

These progressive sentences are also characteristic of another rhetorical device, parallelism (对偶, *duì'ǒu*), which means the matching of the words in the corresponding positions of the two sentences. Take the second sentence above as an example: the four-character expression 挺胸凸肚 in the first short sentence is matched with another four-character expression 目不斜视 in the second short sentence; likewise, the seven-character phrase in the third short sentence 二两的饭量咽三两 is matched with the phrase of equal characters in the fourth short sentence 二尺的腰围撑三尺. Note that matching has several dimensions, such as meaning, sound, and the number of characters. Such multidimensional parallelism of multidimensions creates an aural as well as a visual effect. The aural effect adds to the rhythm of the language, and enhances the power of the argument the author tries to make.

Naturally, parallelism between two sentences is made possible by the nature of the Chinese language. As has been said, in Chinese a character stands for one sound and normally one meaning. Also, modern Chinese tends to be disyllabic, where a monosyllabic character or word serves as a component of a disyllabic word. Because a normal sentence is not composed of either only monosyllabic or only disyllabic words, but of an alternation of the two, provision is made for parallelism. The author would use monosyllabic words in positions corresponding to those in a previous sentence where monosyllables are used, and he/she does the same with disyllabic words or four-character expressions, making sure that they match their corresponding words and expressions in the previous sentence in terms of meaning, sound, and the number of characters. A major result of such conscious, or sometimes subconscious, matching by authors, and indeed general native speakers of Chinese, in writing is a pleasant and powerful sense of rhythm, which contributes greatly to the general force of the argument.

3. *Repetition: a way to reinforce statements (2)*

Enumeration using shared words and structures at least three times in a row is one way to achieve repetition, the primary purpose of which is to enhance the force of the language. The author of this present essay tries to increase the power of repetition further by purposely using the same words in a sentence. In the sentence 女人想哭就哭, 想笑就笑, 害怕就害怕, 脆弱就脆弱, in addition to 就, which is shared by all the four component sentences, the author also repeats the words 哭, 笑, 害怕, and 脆弱. Through the repetition of these words, typical female temperamental traits are vividly conveyed. Also, by twice using the structure 想 V 就 V, which implies a willfulness on the part of the subject, the author forcefully argues that women are more "natural" than men, because they act the way they want without feeling restricted by social expectations. Other examples of the technique of repetition in this text are:

她的一辈子是实实在在不打折扣的一辈子。

他们自认为很伟大很神圣很了不起。

没有女人, 这世界该会多么乏味, 多么不成个世界！

你要爱自己、欣赏自己, 你要让自己每天漂亮, 你要让自己更加可爱。

Repetition of this kind would produce a monotonous effect in English and therefore is discouraged. In Chinese, however, the opposite is true. Please read these sentences again and try to experience the force of the author's argument brought about by her deliberate repetition of words.

4. *The power of numbers*

Chinese people have a tendency to use numbers to express their ideas. We can only speculate the cause for such a linguistic or, perhaps, cognitive tendency, but using numbers certainly renders an expression more concrete and vivid. Numbers occur at every level of Chinese language use. At the lexical level, they have the tendency to become an integral part of set phrases through repeated use. Some examples are:

三心二意，九牛一毛，七手八脚，六神无主

At the syntactic level, the two examples from the text of this lesson are representative:

只有二两的饭量咽三两，只有二尺的腰围撑三尺。

男人走五米路同三个人握手。

Most of the numerical expressions have become stock phrases, but many are not as stable, and are thus subject to change or alternation by different speakers. You are encouraged to use whatever numerical expressions you have come across, but be aware that variations may exist, especially with those that have just come into use. You are also encouraged to invent your own numerical expressions as long as the numbers sound reasonable. For instance, when describing a child who does not eat his/her meal properly, you may say "吃三口吐两口" ("takes in three mouthfuls but spits out two"). In this case, the numbers "three" and "two" can be replaced by "two" and "one," or "five" and "three," depending on the circumstance. Numbers by no means need to be exact. They are used for depiction only and are thus highly subjective in nature.

VII. 练习

词语与句型

1. Fill in the blanks with the words and expressions provided:

A. To help make your language more expressive:

得意，一辈子，弄清，弄懂，眼红，可怜，实实在在，打折扣，
少不得，瞧不起

1) 每个人都得先 _____ 自己需要什么，而没有必要去_____
别人已经有的东西。

2) _____ 他在爱情上总是失败，_____ 孑然一身。

3) 为了 _____ 一个女人，_____ 要花时间研究。

4) 就算你觉得自己很 _____ ，也不能 _____ 别人。

5) 我说的这些话都是 _____ 的。你在转告他们的时候可不能

165

　　　　　　＿＿＿＿＿。

　B. To help make your language more formal:

　　随时，一如，至少，其实，庆幸，不屑于，自会，自以为/自认为

　　1) 有些人讨厌教书，＿＿＿＿＿做教师，＿＿＿＿＿教师的工作充满了
　　　慰籍和欣悦。

　　2) 先不要＿＿＿＿＿你的艳福不浅，你的女朋友＿＿＿＿＿都可能离
　　　你而去。

　　3) ＿＿＿＿＿岁月的流失，人的生命＿＿＿＿＿渐渐走向终点
　　　("destination")。

　　4) 我＿＿＿＿＿不傻，＿＿＿＿＿我知道怎么去应付别人。

2. Using the words or expressions given in parentheses, rewrite the following sentences to make them more succinct, vivid, and forceful.

　　1) 他走路的时候，眼睛从来都是只看着前方。（目不斜视）
　　2) 我不喜欢看你把胸部挺得高高的样子。（挺胸凸肚）
　　3) 我在一边偷偷地看他，发现他不知在想些什么。（心不在焉）
　　4) 他环顾四周，很认真似地对我说："我有女朋友了。"（煞有介事）
　　5) 上司脸上没有一丝笑容地走进来，眼光停在我的身上。（一本正经）
　　6) 局长说话，用的字很少，但是意思很清楚。（简单明了）
　　7) 厨房里做饭的家伙应有尽有。（锅碗瓢盆）
　　8) 不论做什么菜都少不得调味品。（油盐酱醋）

3. Create sentences of enumeration by repeating the underlined phrases:

　　1) 孩子们自会（长大，懂事，成家立业，有他们自己的前途）。
　　2) 老人的一生是（孤单寂寞，小心翼翼，饱经风霜）的一生。
　　3) 生活中少不得（阳光，空气，青山绿水，风风雨雨）。
　　4) 新婚夫妇的笑容是如此的（灿烂，自豪，幸福）。

5) 只要有了家的感受，<u>就有了</u>（慰籍，欣悦，温情）。

6) 人们对丑石<u>总是</u>（讨厌，怨恨，咒骂，嫌弃）。

7) <u>就算</u>（垒不成墙，铺不成台阶，洗不成石磨），丑石还是一件了不起的东西。

8) <u>只要</u>（静静地等待，默默地忍受，慢慢地努力），别人对你的误解就会变成理解。

4. Expand the phrases into sentences by following the examples:

1) 女人<u>想</u>哭<u>就</u>哭，<u>想</u>笑<u>就</u>笑，让人弄不清是为了什么。

　　你们／唱／跳／做什么都可以

　　同学们／来／走／不用跟老师说

　　这家伙<u>想</u>说什么<u>就</u>说什么，从来不好好考虑。

　　我／去哪儿出差／我自己说了算

　　你／怎么走／为什么要问我呢

2) 浪漫<u>就</u>浪漫，我们不怕别人说。

　　丑／随你怎么想

　　贵／买了再说

　　恨我／我不怕

　　长途搬运／可以用车拉

3) 盖房缺少石头，（他）<u>只好</u>去河滩捡一些回来。

　　为了灵感／赵老师／留在学校跟学生们在一起

　　天气太热／新娘子／关上窗子打开空调

　　稿件多得没完没了／大家／任它们堆在桌上

　　因为觉得孤独／我／去找一个热闹的地方

4) （就是）工作很忙<u>也要</u>让自己每天漂亮。

　　不回来吃饭／跟我说一下

碰到凶狠的人 / 勇敢

周身充满了疲倦 / 假笑着应付客人

没有事业上的成功 / 有一个幸福的家庭

5) 新婚夫妇<u>自以为</u>家里应有尽有, <u>其实</u>他们的新居缺少阳光。

他 / 智力很好 / 他聪明也聪明不到哪里去

这位年轻人 / 很了不起 / 他一无所长

姑娘 / 爱上了"柿把儿"老师 / 她爱的只是他写的文章

女人 / 能一眼看透男人 / 不是每个男人都能看透

6) （一个）<u>再</u>幸福的人<u>也</u>有忧烦的时候。

一个人<u>再</u>幸福<u>也</u>有忧烦的时候。

伟大 / 国家 / 要尊重别的国家

傻 / 孩子 / 不会做这样的事

勇敢 / 人 / 有害怕的时候

光明 / 地方 / 会有黑暗的角落

7) （要是）<u>没有</u>阳光, 我们的世界<u>该会多么</u>不同。

笑容 / 教室里的气氛 / 忧闷

堤坝 / 这条大河的下游 / 平静

爱心和亲情 / 这世界 / 冷漠

权力和地位 / 他的生活 / 自在

8) <u>让</u>他们男人<u>去</u>可怜自己<u>吧</u>。

她们 / 瞧不起我们

新郎新娘 / 自我安慰

现代人 / 把自己封闭在房间里

姑娘们 / 玩个痛快

9) 他<u>顾虑他的</u>, 我<u>干我的</u>。

他们 / 等 / 我们 / 走

他／得意／我／做

你／吃／我／吃

他／睡／你／玩

语言知识与技巧

5. Complete the following sentences using the designated structures:

1) 这件事让我很 _____，很 _____，很 _____。

2) 为了研究陨石，我们需要学习 _____，需要学习 _____，需要学习 _____。

3) 传统人的生活，多么 _____，多么 _____，多么 _____！
现代人的生活，多么 _____，多么 _____，多么 _____！

4) 我们应该 _____ 孩子们的 _____，_____ 孩子们的 _____，_____ 孩子们的 _____。

5) 按照 _____，按照 _____，按照 _____，李志强先生成为我们的新校长。

6) 一个人再 _____，再 _____，再 _____，也会有需要别人帮助的时候。

7) 我们大家都明白，这是一个 _____ 的机会，这是一个 _____ 的机会，这是一个 _____ 的机会。

8) 我很庆幸 _____，我很庆幸 _____ _____，我很庆幸 _____。

6. Observe the parallelism between the two components of each of the following sentences. Try to understand the words and phrases in the corresponding positions in terms of sound, meaning, and the number of characters:

1) 猎人掩在树后，小鹿卧于草中。

2) 年轻人词穷理尽，老酋长语重心长。

3) 山腰松林肃穆、高风悲旋，山脚阳光明媚、繁花夹道。

4) 瘦子只因怯懦而留在船上，胖子全凭勇敢才跳入水中。

5) 荒草满山，丑石遍地。

6) 城里人不再依恋青山绿水，乡下人却也热中暖气空调。

7) 男子汉关心事业，女人家热爱生活。

8) 书山有路勤为径，学海无涯苦作舟。

7. Based on your knowledge of the words and expressions acquired from this and previous lessons, try to understand the following passage, and pay special attention to the underlined four-character expressions:

　　"是是是"是我的顶头上司的外号。因为他总是对他的顶头上司说"是是是"，所以大家背地里都叫他"是是是"。我常跟"是是是"一起去外地出差，他很快就把我当成了朋友。即使在不出差的时候，他也会随时随地找我说话。当然，不管他对我说什么，我都只能洗耳恭听。

　　"是是是"告诉我，有权力有地位的人总是担心受怕，因为权力和地位是随时都可能失去的。他还说，男人比女人更容易自我欣赏、自鸣得意。很多男人做了些什么，甚至只是想了要去做些什么，就自认为了不起，就喜欢到处去说，弄得满城风雨。对于这样的男人，女人往往不屑一顾。女人更喜欢实实在在、每天回家吃饭的男人。

　　其实，"是是是"自己经常不回家吃饭。他做什么事都顾虑重重，有时候还偷偷摸摸，不让别人知道。结果，很多人怨恨他，我的另一个顶头上司甚至说他可耻。我绞尽脑汁，才让这两位上司握手言欢。

　　对于"是是是"，我喜欢不到哪里去，也讨厌不到哪里去。可是，我每天都得跟他说话。谁让我是他的下属呢！

8. Work out the meanings of the following expressions and sayings by envisioning in your mind the pictures suggested by the numbers. Refer to a dictionary if necessary:

1) 一清二楚　　　　　　2) 两面三刀

3) 三心二意   4) 三头六臂

5) 说三道四   6) 五湖四海

7) 五颜六色   8) 七嘴八舌

9) 四面八方   10) 三教九流

11) 以一当十   12) 十全十美

13) 百无一失   14) 百里挑一

15) 千方百计   16) 万水千山

17) 万众一心   18) 三天打鱼，两天晒网

19) 心里象十五个吊桶

("well-bucket") 打水，

七上八下

活学与活用

9. Discuss the author's general attitude toward men and women by using the expressions provided.

1) 作者为什么庆幸自己是个女人？

哭／笑

害怕／脆弱

不用担心被人小看

2) 作者为什么说"想想也替男人累"？

挺胸凸肚／目不斜视

饭量／腰围

请客／喝酒

3) 作者对男人的事业怎么看？

轰轰烈烈／献花／照相／信件／请帖

自认为／伟大／神圣／了不起

自以为得意／煞有介事

171

　　　　上小学一年级的儿子／蠢事

4) 作者怎么比较女人和男人？

　　男人：口袋／钢笔／本本／握手／"是是是"／烦人
　　女人：花草树木／全身心感受／实实在在／不打折扣

　　男人：白痴／弄不懂女人
　　女人：看透男人／X光胸透

　　男人：爱上一个女人／聪明
　　女人：爱上一个男人／愚蠢

5) 作者觉得这个世界重要的是什么？

　　生活本身
　　油盐酱醋／锅碗瓢盆／孩子老人
　　星期日的烦琐／星期六的温柔
　　没有女人／乏味／不成个世界

6) 作者认为女人要怎么样？

　　爱自己／欣赏自己
　　每天漂亮／更加可爱
　　至少一半的世界／美好
　　乐

10. Using your own words, answer the following questions based on your own opinions and experiences:

1) 你觉得男人和女人有什么相同和不同的地方？

2) 说一说你自己当个男人或女人的感觉。

3) 如果真有下辈子，你愿意当男人还是当女人？为什么？

4) 你觉得什么样的生活是乏味的？什么样的生活是美好的？

5) "这个世界其实什么都不重要，重要的是生活本身。"你同意这样的看法吗？　为什么？

11. Write an essay on behalf of women or men. To make your argument vivid and forceful, take advantage of any rhetorical devices you have learned in this lesson (e.g., subjectless sentences, enumeration, repetition, and numerical expressions). Also, prepare for a debate in class on gender differences and your personal "preference" for being a man or a woman.

VIII. 课文材料对话 🎧

A

女甲：我们女人就好象自然界的花草树木，全身心都在感受这个世界，不会有一秒钟心不在焉。

女乙：对啊。我们的一辈子是实实在在不打折扣的一辈子。

女甲：我们不需要眼红男人的权力和地位。这些东西，其实都不重要。

女乙：我同意。在这个世界上，最重要的是生活本身。油盐酱醋，锅碗瓢盆，孩子老人，哪一样都离不开我们女人。没有我们，这个世界还成个世界吗？

女甲：我们就是要爱自己，欣赏自己。只要我们让自己更加可爱，这世界就至少有一半是美好的了。

女乙：说得好！让男人们去一本正经吧，我们乐我们的。

B

男：你看我有轰轰烈烈的事业，每天在高高的大楼里写稿件、应付客人。象我这样的男人，可以说是聪明得不能再聪明了。

女：去你的"聪明"吧。你自以为很伟大很神圣很了不起，是吗？你每天煞有介事地做着谁也不需要的蠢事。在我的眼里，你只是一个可怜的白痴。

男：你从来没发过这么大的火。今天是怎么了？说真的，我永远也弄不懂你们女人。

女：可我却能一眼就看透你们男人，就象X光胸透那样简单明了。你知道吗？你是在最聪明的时候爱上了我，而我却是在最愚蠢的时候爱上了你。

男：你这么说，我就明白了，原来你们女人都很傻。

女：随便你说什么，我还是庆幸自己是个女人。我们女人想哭就哭，想笑就笑，不用担心被人小看。哪象你们男人？想想也替你们累。

第八课　眼睛的位置

In the text of Lesson Five, the author delivers a message about the virtue of endurance amidst misunderstandings. He couches this message in his description of an "ugly rock," which was despised and discarded by humans until the day when its true value was revealed. The "ugly rock" serves as a symbol of endurance, knowing its own worth, and not yielding to the mockery of unenlightened humans. The author recounts the story in a narrative style, and he does not comment on his own feelings and attitude until the end of the essay.

In the text of this lesson, the author discusses the "position of the eyes" as a metaphor for a moral message he means to deliver. There is no story to tell, and the author plunges into a discussion at the very beginning of the essay. We see him adopt a comparative approach, like the author of the previous essay on gender differences. Also like the previous author, he speaks in an ironic tone, clearly revealing his attitude toward what is right and wrong, and what is proper and abnormal. He does not use the technique of enumeration; rather, he chooses to use "long sentences" (长句), and various sentence connectives that represent the logical steps of his reasoning. As he proceeds, these sentence connectives find their way into his short speech: 不过, 但, 设想, 那, 倘若, 可是, 反之, 不然, 还是, 归根到底, 虽然, 究竟. Following these sentence connectives, can you tell the reasoning steps the author takes on his way to arriving at his final conclusion?

I. 课文导读 🔊

　　古时候，中国有位哲学家 (zhéxuéjiā, n., philosopher) 说过：世界上的事物，没有一件是没有道理 (dàolǐ, n., reason) 的。外国也有一位哲学家说过：一切事物都安排 (ānpái, v., arrange) 在最好的地方。我不懂哲学，可是按照常识 (chángshí, n., common sense)，我觉得眼睛是一定不能搬到别的地方的。

　　眼睛长在脸上，是为了向前看。这样，什么都能看得清，两只脚配合 (pèihé, v., coordinate) 得很自然，走和跑都没有问题。走新路的时候，心里不害怕，相反地，感到有把握 (bǎwò, n., certainty)。用一句话来说，眼睛长在前面，对前进有好处。设想 (shèxiǎng, v., imagine) 一下，要是眼睛长在脑后会怎么样呢？那就会把后方当成前方，把倒退看作前进。虽然眼睛在向后看，腿脚却要往前走，就算走的是以前走过的老路，也走不了，只好站着不动了。

　　如果两只眼睛都长在同一边，左边或右边，走路横 (héng, v., move sideways) 着走，腿脚照样不听话，一不小心就会摔倒。那么，像鸟一样，一只眼睛长在左边，一只眼睛长在右边，是不是什么问题都没有了呢？不是。虽然看清了左右，但是看不见前后，两只脚一个要向左，一个要向右，还是动不了。人跟鸟不同，身上没长着翅膀 (chìbǎng, n., wing)，不能向上飞，所以眼睛还是不要长在两边的好。

　　有的人，大家说他们的"眼睛长得比头顶还高"。眼睛长在头顶上，看不见周围的一切，自以为最了不起，看天上的东西又很方便。不过，前后左右怎么样，却一点儿都不知道，一开始走路，说不定就会掉到泥坑里去。这样，也还是只能站着不动。

　　说来说去，眼睛还是长在前面好。只有这样才便于往前走，才敢于走新路。当然，有些人不想自己走路，眼睛长着反正 (fǎnzhèng, adv., in any case) 也没用，他们的眼睛长在哪儿都可以。

II. 词语导学

1. Match each item on the left with an item on the right based on the radicals and the character(s) you know:

1) 螃蟹　pángxiè　　　　　　　　n. target

　　洼坑　wākēng　　　　　　　　n. crab

　　目标　mùbiāo　　　　　　　　n. holes in the ground

2) 跨　kuà　　　　　　　　　　　v. look

　　瞧　qiáo　　　　　　　　　　v. close

　　闭　bì　　　　　　　　　　　v. stride

3) 使唤　shǐhuàn　　　　　　　　v. stumble and fall

追踪　zhuīzōng　　　　　　　　n. order

跌交　diējiāo　　　　　　　　　v. trace

4) 熟路　shúlù　　　　　　　　　n. satellite

脚跟　jiǎogēn　　　　　　　　　n. destination

终点　zhōngdiǎn　　　　　　　　n. heel

卫星　wèixīng　　　　　　　　　n. familiar road (or route)

5) 说不定　shuōbudìng　　　　　v.　cannot tell

用不着　yòngbuzháo　　　　　adv. maybe

闹不清(楚)　nàobuqīng(chu)　　v.　not need

2. Select an appropriate meaning for the underlined word or phrase in each sentence:

1) 请在地图上找一下机场的<u>位置</u> (wèizhi, n.)。

　　　a. location　　　b. area　　　c. distance

2) <u>人家</u> (rénjia, pron.) 已经说过的话，你就不用再说了。

　　　a. family members　　　b. everybody　　　c. others

3) <u>看来</u> (kànlái, adv.) 他不会做菜，这些菜都很乏味。

　　　a. watching　　　b. coming　　　c. it seems

4) 听说外星人个子不大，可是<u>脑袋</u> (nǎodai, n.) 很大。

　　　a. brain　　　b. head　　　c. pocket

5) 很多人这样说。我很相信这种<u>说法</u> (shuōfǎ, n.)。

　　　a. speech　　　b. argument　　　c. method

6) 生活中用的东西，有很多不是自然的，而是<u>人造</u> (rénzào, adj.) 的。

　　　a. manmade　　　b. man-like　　　c. man-based

7) 路的<u>两旁</u> (liǎngpáng, n.) 种满了花草树木。

　　　a. both ends　　　b. both sides　　　c. both lanes

8) 我一看见她，便<u>抬步</u> (táibù, v.) 迎了上去。

　　　a. stand up　　　b. jump on one's feet　　　c. take steps

3. Guess the meanings of the following four-character expressions:

1) 万事万物
2) 莫不有理　　（莫: mò, adv., not; 理: same as 道理）
3) 左右兼顾　　（兼: jiān, adv., concurrently; 顾: gù, v., attend to）
4) 万事大吉　　（吉: jí, adj., auspicious）
5) 无所适从　　（适从: shìcóng, v., follow）
6) 唯我独尊　　（唯: wéi, adv., only; 尊: zūn, v., honor）
7) 归根到底　　（归: guī, v., return; 根: gēn, n., root）
8) 又当别论　　（当: dāng, v., should）

III. 课文 ✍

眼睛的位置　　金克木

眼睛的位置是在脸上，这有什么可说的！不过我听说古代中国有位哲学家朱熹说过：万事万物莫不有理。又听说古代外国有位哲学家莱布尼茨说过：一切事物都安排在最好的地方。我不懂哲学，但凭常识想，眼睛的位置确是不好移动。

眼睛长在脸上为的是向前看，看前面有什么，怎么走。这样，前面有洼坑，有石头，都可以迈过去，远望近看都方便，和两只脚配合起来很自然。无论是走，是跑，只管迈步，不怕跌交。看见前途，心有把握，敢走新路。总之是利于前进。

设想眼睛生在脑后，那就会把后方当作前方，眼睛见到的都是人家走过的熟路，心里很踏实，可是要走动，腿脚不方便了。眼睛把倒退看成前进，脚底下却是脚跟朝前不好走，膝盖转不过弯来，眼睛和腿脚发生矛盾，怎么是前进，怎么是后退，闹不清楚，只好站着不动了。

178

倘若是两只眼都长在左边，那就只好像螃蟹一样横行，一个劲儿向左跨大步，一心想快到终点，跳上目标，可是腿脚照样不听使唤，一不小心就会跌交。反之，若两只眼都长在右边，也是一样。那么，我一只眼长在右边，一只眼长在左边，平均分配，左右兼顾，像鸟一样，该是万事大吉了吧？不然。左右看清了，前后却看不见，两只脚一个要向左，一个要向右，无所适从，还是走不动。看来没长翅膀，不能向上飞，还是不要学习鸟把眼睛分长两边。鸡看前面的东西常常要歪着脑袋瞧，多难看。

听说有"眼高于顶"的说法，那么，眼睛长在头顶上应当很好。只望见天空，看不见周围一切，唯我独尊。人造卫星上天，我不用仰脖子就能追踪，多方便。可是前后左右都不知道，一抬步，说不定会掉进泥坑，还是只能站着不动，动起来太冒险。

归根到底还是眼睛长在前面好，为的是向前进。虽然也有时需要扭头转身看看走过的路和两旁情况，可是看得清前面新路怎么走，前途怎么样，究竟是比把眼睛长在脑后老看过去强。

不过对于不想自己走路的那就又当别论了。那就用不着眼睛了，不管长在哪里都行，反正是闭上眼睡大觉。

（选自中国人民大学出版社１９９１年《中国当代名家小品精选》）

繁體字课文

眼睛的位置　金克木

眼睛的位置是在臉上，這有甚麼可說的！不過我聽說古代中國有位哲學家朱熹說過：萬事萬物莫不有理。又聽說古代外國有位哲學家萊布尼茨說過：一切事物都安排在最好的地方。我不懂哲學，但憑常識想，眼睛的位置確是不好移動。

眼睛長在臉上為的是向前看，看前面有甚麼，怎麼走。這樣，前面有窪坑，有石頭，都可以邁過去，遠望近看都方便，和兩隻腳配合起來很自然。無論是走，是跑，只管邁步，不怕跌跤。看見前途，心有把握，敢走新路。總之是利於前進。

設想眼睛生在腦後，那就會把後方當作前方，眼睛見到的都是人家走過的熟路，心裡很踏實，可是要走動，腿腳不方便了。眼睛把倒退看成前進，腳底下卻是腳跟朝前不好走，膝蓋轉不過彎來，眼睛和腿腳發生矛盾，怎麼是前進，怎麼是後退，鬧不清楚，只好站著不動了。

倘若是兩隻眼都長在左邊，那就只好像螃蟹一樣橫行，一個勁兒向左跨大步，一心想快到終點，跳上目標，可是腿腳照樣不聽使喚，一不小心就會跌跤。反之，若兩隻眼都長在右邊，也是一樣。那麼，我一隻眼長在右邊，一隻眼長在左邊，平均分配，左右兼顧，像鳥一樣，該是萬事大吉了吧？不然。左右看清了，前後卻看不見，兩隻腳一個要向左，一個要向右，無所適從，還是走不動。看來沒長翅膀，不能向上飛，還是不要學習鳥把眼睛分長兩邊。難看前面的東西常常要歪著腦袋瞧，多難看。

聽說有"眼高於頂"的說法，那麼，眼睛長在頭頂上應當很好。只望見天空，看不見周圍一切，唯我獨專。人造衛星上天，我不用抑脖子就能追蹤，多方便。可是前後左右都不知道，一抬步，說不定會掉進泥坑，還是只能站著不動，動起來太冒險。

歸根到底還是眼睛長在前面好，為的是向前進。雖然也有時需要扭頭轉身看看走過的路和兩旁情況，可是看得清前面新路怎麼走，前途怎麼樣，究竟是比把眼睛長在腦後老看過去強。

不過對於不想自己走路的那就又當別論了。那就用不著眼睛了，不管長在哪裡都行，反正是閉上眼睡大覺。

思考题

　　在这篇文章里，"眼睛长在前面"是什么意思？作者最后说："不过对于不想自己走路的那就又当别论了。那就用不著眼睛了，不管长在哪里都行，反正是闭上眼睡大觉。"你怎样理解这句话的含义("implication")？

IV. 新词语

朱熹	Zhū Xī	n.	a Song dynasty philosopher (1130-1200)
莱布尼茨	Láibùnící	n.	Gottfried Wilhelm von Leibniz (1646-1719), a German philosopher
凭	píng	prep.	on the basis of
确	què	adv.	really; 确实
只管	zhǐguǎn	adv.	by all means
迈步	màibù	v.	take steps
利于	lìyú	v.	be of advantage to; 有利于
踏实	tāshi	adj.	free from anxiety
矛盾	máodùn	n.	contradiction
倘若	tǎngruò	conj.	if
一个劲儿	yígejìnr	adv.	persistently
分配	fēnpèi	v.	distribute
不然	bùrán		不是这样
歪	wāi	v.	tilt (to one side)
冒险	màoxiǎn	adj.	risky
扭头	niǔtóu	v.	turn around one's head
情况	qíngkuàng	n.	situation
究竟	jiūjìng	adv.	after all

V. 词语与句型

1. 凭 (prep.)　　　　　　　　我不懂哲学，但凭常识想，眼睛的位置确是不好移动。

This means "based on," "according to," or "on the strength of." It is often followed by 着 or 什么. When followed by 什么, the phrase carries a tone of challenge as if demanding an answer.

赵老师凭自己的写作水平，当上了市作协委员。

他凭着自己是个局长，想训斥人就训斥人。

他们凭什么说我象个女人呢？

2. 无论 (conj.)　　　　　　　　无论是走，是跑，只管迈步，不怕跌跤。

无论 is the same as 不论 and 不管 but more formal. It means that "no matter what the circumstance is, the result remains unchanged." It is often used in conjunction with 都.

无论有钱没钱，他都要吸烟喝酒。

妻子对猎人说："无论你说什么，我都不回去。"

3. 只管 (adv.)　　　　　　　　只管迈步，不怕跌跤。

It means that "one (can) go(es) ahead and do(es) something without any concern." The phrase is rather emphatic in tone.

母鹿对小鹿说："你只管去那边玩，别害怕。"

酋长对年轻人说："孩子，你只管说，你看见什么了？"

新娘子为客人递烟送水，新郎却只管自己吃饭。

4. 总之 (conj.)　　　　　　　　心有把握，敢走新路。总之是利于前进。

This is the same as the English phrase "in short" or "in a word." It is often followed by a pause in speech, or a comma in writing.

女人想哭就哭，想笑就笑。总之，她们不担心被人小看。

现代人的生活中没有风的轻柔也没有雨的忧烦。总之，他们喜欢在空调中封闭自己。

5. 设想 (v.)　　　　　　　　　设想眼睛生在脑后，那就会把后方当作前方，…

The English equivalents are "imagine" and "suppose." It introduces a hypothesis.

设想你处在我的位置上，你会怎么做呢？

我不是鸡，我没法设想一只眼长在左边一只眼长在右边会怎么样。

设想一下，一颗流星落到海上，搅起一阵狂风和漩流。

6. 一个劲儿(地) V　　　　　　　　那就象…，一个劲儿向左跨大步，…

This phrase is colloquial, meaning "one does something continuously or persistently."

石匠一个劲儿地凿，终于把石磨洗成了。

是谁在那儿一个劲儿地抽烟？空气太不好了！

别一个劲儿说了，我都听烦了。

7. 一心(想) (adv.)　　　　　　　一心想快到终点，跳上目标，可是…

Unlike 一个劲儿(地), which refers to action, 一心 refers to one's persistence in wishing or hoping for something to happen. It is often followed by 想 or 要.

你一心想当作家，可是当作家并不是一件容易的事情。

有人说，男人一心想的是权力和地位，而女人一心想的是生活本身。

他一心要出国，花很多时间学外语。

8. 反之 (conj.)　　　　　　　　反之，若两只眼都长在右边，也是一样。

反之 is the same as 相反 and 反过来, but more formal. Inserted between sentences or clauses, it means "on the contrary."

眼睛长在脸上，两条腿往前走很容易。反之，眼睛生在脑后，两只脚就只能往后退。

外国人在美国没有家的感觉。反之，美国人在外国也没有家的感觉。

男人永远弄不懂女人，反之也一样。

9. 看来 (conj.)   <u>看来</u>没长翅膀，不能向上飞。

This is an equivalent of the English "it seems that ...." It indicates the speaker's opinion or judgment and occurs at the beginning of a sentence.

<u>看来</u>眼睛长在脸上是最合理的。

我不喜欢空调的轰鸣。<u>看来</u>，我做不了"现代人"。

10. 还是 (adv.)   没长翅膀不能飞，<u>还是</u>不要学习鸟…

The phrase indicates that after weighing all the possibilities, the speaker decides on one option (introduced by 还是) as being the most proper or satisfactory.

下雨了，你<u>还是</u>明天走吧。

奶奶说："这块丑石，多碍地面呀，<u>还是</u>把它搬走吧。"

你<u>还是</u>不要学西班牙语了，就学汉语或日语吧。

11. 说不定 (adv.)   一抬步，<u>说不定</u>会掉进泥坑，…

This is equivalent to the English words "maybe" or "perhaps." It is often used with 呢 at the end of a sentence for emphasis.

姑娘气得走了。如果她真的喜欢赵老师，<u>说不定</u>还会回来。

<u>说不定</u>丑石是从火星上来的<u>呢</u>。

耳朵<u>说不定</u>长在腰的两边最好，那裤子就可以套在耳朵上，不用皮带了。

12. 究竟 (adv.)   可是看得清前面新路怎么走，…<u>究竟</u>是比…强。

究竟 is the same as 终究 and 毕竟, meaning "after all." The speaker uses the word to emphasize the heart of a matter or the essentials of a fact.

人总得向前走而不是横着走。人<u>究竟</u>不是螃蟹。

她<u>究竟</u>是个华人，还是喜欢吃中国饭。

Unlike 毕竟, however, 究竟 is also used in a question, where it indicates that the speaker is determined to find out the truth of a matter:

我想弄明白<u>究竟</u>是胖子勇敢还是瘦子勇敢。

你昨天<u>究竟</u>去哪儿了？你一定要说清楚。

13. 又当别论/另当别论　　　　不过对于不想自己走路的那就<u>又当别论</u>了。

This phrase means that what has been said is not applicable to a certain person or situation, about whom or which a different conclusion should be made. The phrase is normally preceded by 就 and followed by 了.

我不喜欢空调。可是天气太热的时候就<u>又当别论了</u>。

女人想哭就哭，想笑就笑。男人就<u>另当别论</u>了。

这个问题就这样解决。其他问题<u>另当别论</u>。

14. (不管…,) 反正…　　　　　　<u>不管</u>（眼睛）长在哪里，<u>反正</u>是…

反正, often used in conjuction with 不管("no matter what"), indicates that something is bound to happen or not to happen, or that something has or has not happened anyway regardless of the situation introduced by 不管.

<u>不管</u>你去不去，<u>反正</u>我要去。

你要生气就生气，<u>反正</u>我不回来吃饭。

<u>不管</u>是胖子勇敢还是瘦子勇敢，<u>反正</u>胖子死了瘦子还活着。

VI. 语言知识与技巧

1. *Using comparison and contrast to make statements clear and forceful*

The content of this and prior essays provides the two authors with a perfect opportunity to use the rhetorical strategy of "comparison and contrast" (对比 or 对照). The author of each essay compares what he or she advocates with an opposite situation or phenomenon, and the contrast resulting from the comparison presents a strong argument in itself. Look at the following:

<u>女人</u>想哭就哭，想笑就笑，害怕就害怕，脆弱就脆弱，不用担心被人

185

小看。<u>男人</u>却不能，…。他只有挺胸凸肚，只有目不斜视，只有二两的饭量咽三两，只有二尺的腰围撑三尺，借钱也要请客，醉死也要喝酒。(L7)

<u>男人</u>最<u>聪明</u>的时候是爱上一个<u>女人</u>。<u>女人</u>最<u>愚蠢</u>的时候是爱上一个<u>男人</u>。(L7)

<u>眼睛长在脸上</u>为的是向前看，看前面有什么，怎么走。这样，前面有洼坑，有石头，都可以迈过去，远望近看都方便，和两只脚配合起来很自然…。设想<u>眼睛生在脑后</u>，那就会把后方当作前方，眼睛见到的都是人家走过的熟路，心里很踏实，可是要走动，腿脚不方便了。(L8)

In the first example, instead of focusing on the "positive" traits of women, the author compares them with the "not-so-positive" traits of men. In other words, men serve as a foil for women's "superiority." In the third example, arguing that there must be a reason for the eyes to grow on the front of the head, the author compares the advantages of this fact with the disadvantages of other options. The contrast brought about by these comparisons not only sheds light on the point the author wishes to make, but it also leaves a vivid impression on the reader's mind.

Comparison and contrast can be made by juxtaposing sentences or clauses (usually two) together without using any sentence connectives, as is demonstrated by the second example above. However, if the sentences are not neatly parallel to each other, like those in the first and third examples, using sentence connectives can help better organize the comparison or contrast. Typical sentence connectives for this purpose are 可是, 然而, 而, 却, 而…却. (Refer to Part VI.4. 2 of Lesson One). Other examples of comparison and contrast from the texts we have studied so far are:

岸上的人都看见了，胖子<u>忽然跃起身</u>，<u>坚决地从船上跳进了水里</u>；岸上的人也都看见了，瘦子<u>忽然弯下腰</u>，<u>坚决地向船里一缩</u>…… (L3)

有人赞叹瘦子活得<u>勇敢</u>，他<u>敢于</u>留在船上，穿越那地狱般的隧道。<u>而</u>胖子的勇敢本身是一种<u>怯懦</u>，他<u>怯于</u>穿越那可怕的通路。(L3)

他的课确实讲得<u>不好</u>，甚至可以说比较糟。<u>可</u>他的写作水平却<u>出奇的好</u>。还是市作协的会员呢！(L4)

这又怪又丑的石头，原来是天上的呢！它补过天，在<u>天上发过热</u>，闪过光，我们的先祖或许仰望过它，它给了他们光明，向往，憧憬；<u>而它落</u>

<u>下来</u>了，在污土里，荒草里，一躺就是几百年了？！　(L5)

In addition to the sentence connectives that indicate contrast (underlined in the above), also pay attention to the words and expressions in the above examples (underlined also) that express opposite meanings.

2. *Connecting sentences to increase clarity (3)*

So far (in Lesson One and Lesson Five) we have introduced six scenarios in real-life communication where you should connect individual sentences to make your statement more cohesive and accurate. In doing so, you must rely on the use of sentence connectives, although sometimes you may be able to present your thinking or reasoning steps without them. The following represents three more of the most commonly encountered communicative situations in which connecting sentences is required.

1) In real-life situations, circumstances often require us to hypothesize or to imagine things and situations that have not yet happened, or will probably never happen. In English, "if" or "suppose" is used to introduce the hypothesis. In Chinese you can use 如果, 假如, 倘若, 若, or 要是 for the same purpose. Also use 就, 那么, 那, 便, or 还 in the main sentence to indicate the situation as a result of the realization of the hypothesis:

<u>倘若</u>是两只眼都长在左边，<u>那就</u>只好象螃蟹一样横行。

<u>若</u>两只眼都长在右边，<u>也</u>是一样。

<u>如果</u>（<u>要是</u>）你愿意，我<u>就</u>陪你去山上看看。

<u>假如</u>胖子没跳下水去，他也许<u>还</u>活着呢。

In the above examples, the result indicated in the main sentence is in agreement with the hypothesis. In other words, it is a natural consequence once the hypothesized situation is established or realized. If the result runs counter to the hypothesis, or, if the result is different or the same even if something hypothesized has happened, one of these conjuctions, 即使, 就是, 就算, 哪怕, should be used to introduce the hypothesis with 也 or 还 occurring in the main sentence:

<u>就算</u>他自以为了不起，别人<u>还是</u>小看他。

<u>即使</u>生活不是天天美好，我们<u>也</u>应该热爱生活。

<u>哪怕</u>会有人误解，我<u>也</u>要这么做。

2) When you want to make clear to your reader or listener the purpose (目的) to be achieved by a certain action, or under a certain circumstance, use the following phrases to introduce the purpose: 为, 为了, 为的是, 以, 以便, 用以, 好:

眼睛长在脸上<u>为的是</u>向前看。

请你留下你的电话和地址，<u>以便</u>今后联系。

<u>为了</u>把孩子喂养大，母亲辛苦地干了一辈子。

让他去看他的电视，我们<u>好</u>说话。

If, through some action, one wants to avoid something or some state of being, 省得, 以免, 免得 are a set of useful sentence connectives to indicate the situation or problem to be avoided:

奶奶说："用这块丑石吧，<u>省得</u>从远处搬运。"

麻烦你把这本书带给她，<u>免得</u>我自己跑一趟。

我把汽车检查了一遍，<u>以免</u>中途发生问题。

3) In our life we often run into situations where we have to make a choice among various options. When you express these circumstances, use the following sentence connectives: 或(者)A, 或(者)B; 是A, 还是B; 不是A, 就是B; 要么A, 要么B; 要就是A, 要就是B:

<u>或者</u>你去，<u>或者</u>他去，反正都一样。

<u>是</u>你去，<u>还是</u>他去？总得去一个人。

<u>不是</u>住这儿，<u>就是</u>住宾馆。我们今天不回去了。

<u>要么</u>住这儿，<u>要么</u>住宾馆，我们今天不回去了。

In situations where the preferred choice is very clear or where you are determined to do one thing instead of the other, such sentence connectives as 与其A, 不如B; 与其A, 宁可B; 宁可A, 也不B; 宁愿A, 也不愿B should be used:

赵老师<u>宁愿</u>留下来教书也<u>不愿</u>往政界发展。

<u>与其</u>住到缺少阳光的大楼里，我<u>宁可</u>住在这个阳光灿烂的小屋里。

<u>与其</u>做男人被别人小看，<u>不如</u>做个女人。

3. Accuracy and logic: analyze, understand, and use long sentences

In Lesson One we discussed short sentences as one striking syntactic feature of the Chinese language. We have said that short sentences are frequently used in written language because of their brevity, clarity, and forcefulness. However, this does not mean that long sentences should always be avoided. In fact, in some circumstances long sentences are preferred to short sentences because of certain advantages they provide.

There are two kinds of long sentences. The first kind has a simple grammatical structure, but with many words serving as qualifiers of the main sentence elements (such as the subject, the predicate, and the object). A good example can be found in the following sentence from the text of Lesson Three:

灰色的<u>堤坝</u>在两山之间冷漠地<u>矗立而起</u>，<u>截断了</u>它那大漠狂沙般的黄色的<u>热情</u>。(L3)

In this 33-character sentence, the basic structure is 堤坝矗立而起，截断了热情, as underlined. All the other parts are qualifiers of the subject, the predicate, and the object respectively. Thus, this type of long sentence provides more information in the form of qualifiers, and the detailed information naturally makes the expression more accurate (准确) and logical. Regarding understanding this kind of long sentence, one method is to first single out the main structure, along the line of "subject + predicate (+ object)," get rid of all the qualifiers, and then shorten the sentence to its bare and basic form. Once you understand the main structure, look at the qualifiers and try to understand their meanings in relation to the parts they modify.

The second type of long sentence (normally referred to as "complex sentences" or 复句) has a complicated grammatical structure with clauses linked to each other by sentence connectives. For example:

<u>就算</u>一个人闷在宾馆里看电视，<u>就算</u>一天到晚被没完没了的稿件压得无法抬头，<u>就算</u>坐在一个没有空气的屋子里假笑着应付客人，<u>就算</u>宴席上周身充满了疲倦和不自在，<u>只要</u>一想到推开那一个小屋的门，便有阳光跳跃着来迎接，便有温柔的清风来照拂，便有花的芬芳草的清香，<u>于是</u>，我的心，<u>便</u>有了慰藉，有了欣悦，有了温情。(L6)

This sentence, explained in Lesson Six, contains 132 characters, scattered in one main clause and five subordinate clauses. Its basic structure is: 就算⋯，就算⋯，就算⋯，就算⋯，只要⋯，(于是⋯,)我的心，便⋯. The main subject-predicate structure, "我的心，便有了⋯," has five subordinate clauses introduced by 就算 and 只要 indicating "concession" and "condition" respectively. (便, which introduces three enumerated sentences within the 只要 clause, is not underlined because these sentences are not directly related to the main clause.) This type of long sentence, in addition to providing more information, also provides the logical steps of a reasoning process. By connecting simple sentences in a certain order using appropriate sentence connectives, expression is more cohesive and logical.

　　Long sentences of the second type seem to be much more common than the first kind, simply because they reflect the ways humans think in the process of cognition or argument. On the other hand, this type of long sentence is more difficult to comprehend because of the grammatical relations between the main clause and the subordinate clause(s). One approach to tackling them is that you first locate the sentence connectives and figure out the main clause. After you understand the main clause, you can examine what is expressed in the subordinate clause(s). The sentence connective tells you the relation in which each subordinate clause stands to the main clause. In other words, it tells you whether the clause serves as a condition, a concession, or a cause, etc. for the main sentence. By cross-referencing between the main clause and the subordinate clause(s), you will gradually realize what the author is trying to say.

VII. 练习

词语与句型

1. Match each word in one column with its antonym in the other column:

1)

伟大	寒冷
勇敢	冷漠
温暖	黑暗
强壮	渺小
澄清	瘦弱
热情	混浊
光明	怯懦

2)

高级	冷清
封闭	愚蠢
脆弱	开放
热闹	无理
聪明	坚强
乏味	低级
有理	好看
难看	有趣

3)

上游	懦夫
船头	老路
勇士	死亡
终点	下游
生存	乡村
都市	船尾

4)

赞美	彼时
远望	后退
前进	咒骂
上天	相互
此时	近观
自我	入地

新路　　起点

5) 动　　　假
　 安　　　否
　 高　　　危
　 美　　　静
　 真　　　矮
　 是　　　送
　 接　　　丑
　 凉丝丝　暖烘烘
　 静悄悄　闹哄哄

2. In the following sentences, replace the English word with its Chinese equivalent given below:

设想（如果/要是/倘若）　　　　反之（相反地）
看来（看起来）　　　　　　　　这样
究竟（到底）　　　　　　　　　那么
无论（不论/不管）　　　　　　归根到底（总之）
反正

1) (Whether) 是男人还是女人，在生活中都需要有一份温情。

2) 还没有人去攀爬那座山崖。(It seems that) 喜欢冒险的人不多。

3) (Suppose) 你身上长着翅膀，你会愿意飞吗？

4) 几个人划船的时候，一定要相互配合。(In this way)，船才能走得好，走得快。

5) 前进 (after all) 比后退强。就算进步不大，也值得我们高兴。

6) 有时候，(in any case) 做不到左右兼顾，那就只好坚决只顾一头。

7) 你们嫌组合音响太贵，懒得去买。(Then)，现在打折扣了，你们买不买呢？

8) 要是喜欢冬天，你该住在北方；(on the contrary)，喜欢夏天的话，你就该住在南方了。

9) 男人讨厌油盐酱醋、锅碗瓢盆，不重视星期日的烦琐星期六的温柔，也永远弄不懂女人。(In a word)，他们不热爱生活。

3. Expand the phrases into sentences by following the examples:

1) 我们<u>凭（着）</u>感觉猜到了你的意思。

上小学三年级的女儿／地理知识／找到了那座大楼

有些人／自己的权力和地位／没完没了地做坏事

石匠／气力／把一块大石头掮了回来

新娘／好酒量／应付了很多客人

2) <u>无论</u>清晨<u>还是</u>黄昏，我<u>都</u>希望能见到阳光。

上游／下游／河水／是黄色的

失败／成功／我们／会感到自豪

男人／女人／不能忍受寂寞

山麓／山腰／不象山顶那样一无所有

3) 大家不怕累，<u>只管</u>往前走。

胖子和瘦子来不及说话／拼命划船

瘦子一言不发／木然地望着大河

同学们不怕老师发火／嘻嘻哈哈

小伙子上课心不在焉／痴痴地望着姑娘

4) 他们<u>一个劲儿地</u>怨恨丑石，嫌它难看。

年轻人／往山上爬／终于到达山顶

他／对上司说"是是是"／不敢说一个"不"字

孩子们／翘望天边／希望出现奇迹

小鹿／跳跃着／一点儿也不怕累

5) 猎人<u>一心</u>想把妻子接回来。

老酋长／立一位新酋长

胖子和瘦子／活下来

奶奶／把丑石搬走

局长大人的千金／让"柿把儿"老师朝政界发展

6) 我们<u>还是</u>想想丑石的美<u>吧</u>。

男人和女人／互相多研究一下吧

"柿把儿"老师／留在学校教书

眼睛／不要长到脑后

都市的人／不要把自然挡在窗外

7) 母鹿和小鹿<u>说不定</u>会遇到别的猎人。

这种孤独的感觉／很多人都有

X光胸透／对身体有坏处

自我欣赏／是一件好事

女人的一辈子／比男人的一辈子更伟大

8) 他上的课很糟，他写的文章<u>就又当别论了</u>。

在大海里游泳太冒险／在游泳池游泳

爱冒险的人可以试试这样做／不爱冒险的人

孩子跟孩子容易闹矛盾／孩子跟大人

丑石的丑遭人嫌弃／它的美

9) <u>不管</u>你们到哪里，<u>反正</u>都得回来把见闻告诉我。

前进多少／不能倒退

终点有多远／你一定得到达

你有没有目标／我有我的目标

男人强还是女人强／得在一块儿过日子

语言知识与技巧

4. Complete the following sentences using expressions or phrases that help you form vivid comparisons or contrasts:

1) 老师可以＿＿＿＿＿＿＿，学生却不可以＿＿＿＿＿＿＿。

2) 胖子＿＿＿＿＿＿＿，瘦子却＿＿＿＿＿＿＿。

3) 男人喜欢＿＿＿＿＿＿＿，而女人喜欢＿＿＿＿＿＿＿。

4) 前两个年轻人＿＿＿＿＿＿＿，而第三个年轻人＿＿＿＿＿＿＿。

5) 丑石的模样＿＿＿＿＿＿＿，可它的历史＿＿＿＿＿＿＿。

6) 新婚夫妇的笑容＿＿＿＿＿＿＿，可他们的新居＿＿＿＿＿＿＿。

7) 耳朵长在头上，＿＿＿＿＿＿＿＿＿＿＿＿＿。
   然而，要是它们长在腰里，＿＿＿＿＿＿＿＿＿。

8) 充满阳光的房间＿＿＿＿＿＿＿＿＿＿＿＿＿。
   反之，缺少阳光的房间＿＿＿＿＿＿＿＿＿＿。

5. Connect the sentences by using the designated sentence connectives:

A. You want to express a purpose:

1) 老酋长要立一位新酋长。他找来三个优秀的年轻人。（为了）
2) 姑娘希望赵老师调到局办公室工作。他可以朝政界发展。（以便）
3) 他们运走陨石时小心翼翼。他们不想把它碰坏。（以免）
4) 我们走路时要看清地上的洼坑石头。我们不想跌交。（免得）
5) 我看到不爱看的东西就闭上眼睛。我不想不高兴。（省得）

B. You want to make a hypothesis:

1) 眼睛长在脑后。眼睛会和腿脚发生矛盾。（如果…就…）
2) 女人瞧不起自己。她是没弄清自己需要什么。（假如…那么…）
3) 天文学家不到村子里来。丑石还会留在我家门前。（倘若…就…）
4) 你嫌弃自己。别人会小看你。（若…便…）

5) 我情绪不好。我宁愿呆在家里。（要是…就…）

C. You want to indicate a choice:

1) 你别以为我眼红他的钱。也别以为他眼红我的权。（或是）

2) 我们想坐火车去。我们也想坐飞机去（或者…或者…）

3) 她丈夫常常借钱请客。他也常常喝得大醉。（要么…要么…）

4) 你会留在船上吗？你会跳入水中吗？（…还是…）

5) 一个人的爱好可能属于情绪。一个人的爱好也可能属于现实。（不是…就是…）

6) 我希望生活中有青山绿水。我不做现代人。（宁可…也不…）

7) 不想让丑石留在那里。想合伙把它搬走。（与其…不如…）

6. Underline the sentence connectives in the following long sentences and try to identify the reasoning steps the authors take in their argument:

1) 设想眼睛生在脑后，那就会把后方当作前方，眼睛见到的都是人家走过的熟路，心里很踏实，可是要走动，腿脚不方便了。(L.8)

2) 倘若是两只眼都长在左边，那就只好像螃蟹一样横行，一个劲儿向左跨大步，一心想快到终点，跳上目标，可是腿脚照样不听使唤，一不小心就会跌交。(L.8)

3) 虽然也有时需要扭头转身看看走过的路和两旁情况，可是看得清前面新路怎么走，前途怎么样，究竟是比把眼睛长在脑后老看过去强。(L.8)

4) 我们这些做孩子的，也讨厌起它来，（虽）曾合伙要搬走它，但力气又不足；虽时时咒骂它，嫌弃它，也无可奈何，只好任它留在那里去了。(L.5)

5) 因"是吧"与"柿把"谐音，而这里多的是柿子，大家就管他叫"柿把儿"老师。(L.4)

6) 距离太近了，这种机会是很难遇到的；但不知为什么，这个被村里人

认为鲁莽凶狠的汉子，今天一举起猎枪，却感到有一种东西在心里撞击着，牵扯着他的手臂。(L.1)

7. Rewrite the following sentences:

A. Reduce the length of the sentences by getting rid of the qualifiers of the subjects, the predicates, and/or the objects:

1) 身为市作协委员的赵老师在上课的时候总是不知不觉地说很多他最爱说的"是吧"。

2) 这块从天上掉下来的了不起的陨石这么多年来竟会这么默默地忍受着全村的人们对它的误解。

3) 每个假日，新郎和新娘都躺在摇椅中沐浴那两房一厅带给他们的一份慰藉、欣悦和温情。

4) 归根到底，生活中少不得伟大、神圣而又轰轰烈烈的事业，也少不得愉快、温柔而又平平静静的繁琐。

B. Increase the length of the sentences by adding qualifiers to the subjects, the predicates, and/or the objects:

1) 孩子买书。
2) 人们去爬山。
3) 窗外是景色。
4) 墙上挂着照片。

8. Following the examples, create sentences with the words and expressions given in parentheses:

1) 看来没长翅膀，不能向上飞，还是不要学习鸟把眼睛分长两边。
（看来…，还是…）

2) 眼睛长在脸上为的是向前看，看前面有什么，怎么走。这样，看见前

196

途，心有把握。

（…为的是…。这样，…）

3) 设想眼睛生在脑后，和两只脚就配合不好了，只好站着不动。

（设想…，就…，只好…）

4) 听说两只眼长在同一边不行。那么，一只长在右边，一只长在左边，该是万事大吉了吧。

（听说…。那么，…，该是…了吧）

5) 对于不想自己走路的人，不管眼睛长在哪里都行，反正是闭上眼睡大觉。

（对于…，不管…都…，反正…）

6) 眼睛长在脸上，无论是走还是跑，只管迈步，不用害怕。

（…，无论是…还是…，只管…，不用…）

7) 倘若两只眼睛都长在左边，那就好象螃蟹一样横行。反之，若是两只眼睛都生在右边，也是一样。

（倘若…，那就…。反之，若是…，也是一样）

8) 归根到底眼睛还是长在前面好。虽然有时需要扭头转身看看后面和左右的情况，可是看得清前面新路怎么走，究竟是比把眼睛长在脑后强。

（归根到底…。虽然…，可是…，究竟是比…强）

活学与活用

9. Using the expressions provided, hypothesize about the position of the eyes and discuss the advantages and disadvantages of each option.

1) 为什么眼睛长在脸上利于前进？

远望近看／方便

和脚配合／自然

走／跑／只管迈步／不怕跌交

2) 眼睛生在脑后会怎么样？

把后方当作前方

把倒退看成前进

腿脚／眼睛／发生矛盾

膝盖／转不过弯来

只好站着不动

3) 如果两只眼睛都长在边上呢？

都长在左边／或／都长在右边

象螃蟹一样／横行

腿脚／不听使唤

一不小心／跌交

两只脚／无所适从／走不动

4) 要是眼睛长在头顶上会怎么样？

只望见天空／唯我独尊

周围的一切／前后左右／都不知道

动起来／太冒险

说不定／掉进泥坑

5) 什么样的人眼睛长在哪里都行？

不想自己走路

反正／闭上眼睡大觉

用不着眼睛／另当别论

10. Using your own words, answer the following questions based on your own opinions and experiences:

1) 眼睛向前看有利于向前进。这一点能说明生活中的什么道理？

2) 为什么眼睛长在前面而耳朵却长在两边？耳朵除了长在头上，还有更好的地方吗？

3) 你觉得在什么情况下开车心里有把握？在什么情况下开车心里不踏实？

4) 你最近的一次跌交是在什么时候？它给了你什么教训？

5) 举例说明"万事万物莫不有理"。

11. Write an essay specifying your preference for the direction in which your new room should face. Use the strategy of comparison and contrast in your hypotheses of other possibilities. Whenever possible, use appropriate sentence connectives to make your argument cohesive and logical.

VIII. 课文材料对话

A

甲：眼睛长在脸上为的是向前看。看见了前途，心里就有把握，就敢于走新路。

乙：眼睛长在前面当然有利于前进，可是看后面的东西就不方便了。

甲：不是可以扭头转身吗？。

乙：扭头转身的时候，眼睛倒是看着后面。可是，如果腿脚还在朝前走，就会和眼睛闹矛盾，就可能跌交。这样，就只好站着不动了。

甲：那你说怎么办？

乙：看来得有四只眼睛才行，在脑后再长两只。

B

丙：我爱说什么就说什么，爱干什么就干什么。普天之下，唯我独尊。

丁：听你这得意的口气，你的眼睛象是长在头顶上似的。

丙：你是说"眼高于顶"吧。眼睛朝天，难道不好吗？

丁：好是好，看天上的东西不用仰脖子，可是前后左右、周围的一切都看不见。一抬腿，说不定还会掉进泥坑，太冒险了。

丙：有什么险可冒的？反正我要插翅高飞。飞起来，该会多么自在！要东就东，要西就西，一飞就是几百里。天上总不会有泥坑吧！再说，从天上往下看，什么都清清楚楚，美着呢。

丁：原来你是要飞上天的！这么看来，你的眼睛还是得长在脸上。只有这样，往下看才方便。

第九课　黄粱梦里

Generally speaking, there are two ways to compose an essay of persuasion: one is to raise your argument at the beginning, and then support your argument in the rest of the essay by providing the reasons. The authors of the two previous essays adopted such a method. The second commonly adopted approach is to open your discussion with someone else's argument, and then refute this argument with your own findings or reasonings in the rest of the essay. The author of this present essay uses this less direct but equally effective approach. She argues that life is not an "empty dream," contrary to what many people have told her, and her arguments for this view constitute the main body of her essay. Almost every paragraph in this essay ends with a question. And yet these questions are more forceful and persuasive than plain statements, because they resonate in our minds and force us to reflect on what the author is trying to say.

I. 课文导读 📀

　　好多人都认为人生就象一场梦，在经历了许多事情之后，到头来却发现一切都是空的。

　　可我总是不<u>服气</u> (fúqì, v., be convinced)，我总觉得，生命的本身应该有一种意义。在这个世界上，有些东西是一直在<u>重复</u> (chóngfù, v., repeat) 和<u>继续</u> (jìxù, v., continue) 着的。我的母亲曾经抱过我，曾经一寸一寸地把我<u>喂养</u> (wèiyǎng, v., feed and raise) 长大。现在她老了，我却象她年轻时一样，抱自己的女儿，为自己的女儿<u>切洗</u> (qiēxǐ, v., cut and wash) <u>蔬菜</u> (shūcài, n., vegetables) 和水果。等到我老去的时候，我的女儿又会象今天的我一样，一寸一寸地把她的孩子养大。所有这一切，谁能说<u>仅仅</u> (jǐnjǐn, adv., merely) 是一场梦呢？

　　不管时间过得多快，也不管<u>景物</u> (jǐngwù, n., scenes and things) 怎么变换，大自然里的有些事物却是永远不变的。我在生活中曾经努力过，对这些努力的<u>记忆</u> (jìyì, n., memory) 也会永远留在那里，每次<u>翻寻</u> (fānxún, v., search)，每次都还在。这样的生命，我能不热爱吗？

当然，有人会说。我再努力也还是在一场梦里，我的一切还是会慢慢地过去。可是我却相信，总有一些什么会留下来，我的努力是不会<u>白费</u> (báifèi, v., waste) 的。

在连续不断的"梦"里，一定会有跟我想法相同的女子吧。当她在一千年以后翻看我写的东西时，一定会高兴地发现，虽然已经过去了许多年，虽然世间还有种种不好的事情，可是只要生活在继续，生命就还是<u>值得</u> (zhíde, v., be worth) 热爱的。

那么，我们为什么还要遗憾呢？

II. 词语导学

1. Match each item on the left to an item on the right based on the characters you know:

1) 悲欢　bēihuān　　　　n. hatred
    痛苦　tòngkǔ　　　　 n. sorrows and joys
    仇恨　chóuhèn　　　　n. sufferings

2) 时光　shíguāng　　　　n. thought
    心思　xīnsī　　　　　 n. time
    本身　běnshēn　　　　 pro. itself

3) 拥有　yōngyǒu　　　　v. hold in the arms
    飞驰　fēichí　　　　　v. possess
    抱持　bàochí　　　　　v. speed along

4) 鲜美　xiānměi　　　　 adj. cooked
    涨落　zhǎngluò　　　　adj. fresh and tasty
    熟　　shú　　　　　　 n. (of water) rise and fall

2. Guess the meanings of 如, 与 (yǔ, conj.), and 未 (wèi, adv.) in the following sentences and see how the language is made more formal by them:

1) 他每天都是八点钟到，十年<u>如</u>一日。
    王老师爱校<u>如</u>家。

202

她一到美国就<u>如鱼得水</u>。

2) 这件事，做<u>与</u>不做都可以。

我们的生活离不开学习<u>与</u>工作。

恋爱<u>与</u>结婚不只是年轻人的事。

3) 老师<u>未</u>听说过的事，学生可能听说过。

我父母从<u>未</u>去过中国。

<u>未</u>婚的学生和已婚的学生都可以住在那儿。

3. Work out the meanings of 犹 (yóu, adv.), 仍 (réng, adv.), 仍然 (réngrán, adv.), and 依然 (yīrán, adv.), and judge the stylistic difference between the two sentences in each pair:

1) 新炊却<u>犹</u>未熟。

新做的饭却还没熟。

2) 那些东西，每回翻寻，每回<u>仍</u>在。

那些东西，每次找的时候，每次都还在。

3) 一切<u>仍然</u>会逐渐地过去。

一切还是会一点一点地过去。

4) 那船<u>依然</u>向深幽幽的洞口滑。

那船还是向深幽幽的洞口滑。

4. Mark the following sentences with A or B according to the meaning of 绝 in them:

A. jué, adv., absolutely
B. jué, adj., exhausted

___ 1) 人生<u>绝</u>不是一场梦。

___ 2) 源源 (yuányuán, adv., in a steady flow) 不<u>绝</u>的水从洞里流出来。

___ 3) 这几天，校园里歌声不<u>绝</u>于耳。

___ 4) 我<u>绝</u>不可怜那种人。

III. 课文 🎧

黄粱梦里　席慕容

好多人都喜欢告诉我们，人生不过如一场黄粱梦，在繁复的美丽与曲折的悲欢之后，悠然醒转，新炊却犹未熟。

可是我总是不服气，我总觉得，生命本身应该有一种意义，我们绝不是白白来一场的。在这世间，有些事物是一直在重复着和绵延着的。每回抱我的儿女的时候，就会想到，年轻的母亲曾经怎样温柔地抱持过我。每回在给孩子切洗蔬果的时候，就会想到，母亲当年，曾经怎样一寸一寸地把我们喂养长大。而有一天，我也终于会象今天的母亲一样地老去，那时候，我的女儿也会象今天的我一样，在源源不绝的水龙头下清洗着鲜美的蔬果，再来一寸一寸地把她的孩子喂养长大。所以，谁能说这些都仅仅只是一场黄粱梦而已呢？

而每回闻到草叶的清香，看到潮汐的涨落，就会想到那些我曾经拥有过的幸福时刻。不管时光如何飞驰，景物如何变换，大自然里有些事物却是永远不变的，而我曾经努力生活过的记忆也永远在那里，每回翻寻，每回仍在，这样的生命，你叫我怎能不热爱？

当然，我的朋友们也可以说，不管我如何努力，我仍然是在黄粱梦里：一切仍然会逐渐地过去。

可是，总有一些什么会留下来的吧，我虽然不能很清楚地知道那会是些什么样的事物，我却相信，一切的努力都绝不会是白费的。

在绵延不绝的黄粱梦里，一定也会有喜欢我并且和我有着相同心思的女子吧。当她在千年之后翻阅我的札记时，一定也会欣喜地发现，尽管这么多年已经过去了，尽管世间依然无法避免仇恨和争战，可是只要草叶间依然有清香，潮汐依然按时升落，所有的痛苦就比较容易忍受，而生命仍然是值得信任与值得热爱的吧。

那么，我们还有什么遗憾的呢？

（选自复旦大学出版社１９９６年《千字文阅读与训练》）

繁體字課文

黃粱夢裡　席慕容

好多人都喜歡告訴我們，人生不過如一場黃粱夢，在繁複的美麗與曲折的悲歡之後，悠然醒轉，新炊卻猶未熟。

可是我總是不服氣，我總覺得，生命本身應該有一種意義，我們絕不是白白來一場的。在這世間，有些事物是一直在重覆著和綿延著的。每回抱我的兒女的時候，就會想到，年輕的母親曾經怎樣溫柔地抱持過我。每回在給孩子切洗蔬果的時候，就會想到，母親當年，曾經怎樣一寸一寸地把我們餵養長大。而有一天，我也終於會像今天的母親一樣地老去，那時候，我的女兒也會像今天的我一樣，在源源不絕的水龍頭下清洗著鮮美的蔬果，再來一寸一寸地把她的孩子餵養長大。所以，誰能說這些都僅僅只是一場黃粱夢而已呢

而每回聞到草葉的清香，看到潮汐的漲落，就會想到那些我曾經擁有過的幸福時刻。不管時光如何飛馳，景物如何變換，大自然裡有些事物卻是永遠不變的，而我曾經努力生活過的記憶也永遠在那裡，每回翻尋，每回仍在，這樣的生命，你叫我怎能不熱愛？

當然，我的朋友們也可以說，不管我如何努力，我仍然是在黃粱夢裡：一切仍然會逐漸地過去。

可是，總有一些甚麼會留下來的吧，我雖然不能很清楚地知道那會是些

甚麼樣的事物，我卻相信，一切的努力都絕不會是白費的。

在綿延不絕的黄粱夢裡，一定也會有喜歡我並且和我有著相同心思的女子吧。當她在千年之後翻閱我的札記時，一定也會欣喜地發現，儘管這麼多年已經過去了，儘管世間依然無法避免仇恨和爭戰，可是只要草葉間依然有清香，潮汐依然按時昇落，所有的痛苦就比較容易忍受，而生命仍然是值得信任與值得熱愛的吧。

那麼，我們還有甚麼遺憾的呢？

思考题

作者认为人生不是一场黄粱梦。她为什么这样说？你同意吗？你的看法是什么？

IV. 新词语

黄粱梦	huángliángmèng	n.	"golden millet dream," a Chinese allusion that has several meanings. Here it refers to the quick passage of time and the insignificance of human life.
不过	búguò	adv.	merely
繁复	fánfù	adj.	complicated
曲折	qūzhé	adj.	tortuous
悠然	yōurán	adv.	in a leisurely manner
醒转	xǐngzhuǎn	v.	wake up
炊	chuī	n.	cooking
白白	báibái	adv.	in vain
绵延	miányán	v.	continue
水龙头	shuǐlóngtóu	n.	(water) tap
闻	wén	v.	smell

潮汐	cháoxī	n.	morning and evening tides
如何	rúhé	adv.	how; 怎么
逐渐	zhújiàn	adv.	gradually
翻阅	fānyuè	v.	browse
札记	zhájì	n.	reading notes
尽管	jǐnguǎn	conj.	even though
避免	bìmiǎn	v.	avoid
争战	zhēngzhàn	n.	dispute and war
升落	shēngluò	v.	涨落
信任	xìnrèn	n.	trust

V. 词语与句型

1. 不过 (adv.)　　　　　　　　　　　　　　　人生不过如一场黄粱梦，…

　　Used in this sense, the English equivalents for 不过 are "only" and "merely." Sometimes it takes the form of 只不过…而已 or 只不过…罢了 for emphasis.

　　　她觉得，生活不过是油盐酱醋、锅碗瓢盆，乏味得很。
　　　他只不过是说说而已，不会真的这样做。
　　　你的新居只不过缺少阳光罢了，别的都不错。

2. 服(气) (v.)　　　　　　　　　　　　　　　可是我总是不服气，…

　　服气, sometimes simplified as 服, means "be convinced," "accept with the whole heart," or "accept with resignation."

　　　人家是局长大人的千金，你不服气行吗？
　　　对别人不服气有时候是因为眼红别人的权力和地位。
　　　第三个年轻人被立为新酋长，大家口服心服。

3. 绝(对) (adv.)　　　　　　　　　　　　　　我们绝不是白白来一场的。

This is a word used for emphasis. It means "absolutely" or "definitely."

生活绝不是一场黄粱梦。

眼睛绝不能生在头顶或长在脑后。

我此生此世绝对做不了现代人。

4. 每回/次/当…就…　　　　　　　　每回抱我的儿女的时候，就会想到…

The equivalent structure in English is "each time…, each time…." 就 can be replaced by 便, 都, or 总.

每次"柿把儿"老师在上边说一个"是吧"，学生就在下边学一个。

每回搬家，我们都要换一次沙发。

每当见到上司，他便说"是是是"。

5. 仅仅/只是…(而已)　　　　　谁能说这些都仅仅只是一场黄粱梦而已呢？

In this structure, meaning "only," 仅仅 or 只 has the same function as 不过 (see 1). When 仅仅 and 只 are both used, the statement is further stressed but with some redundancy. 而已 reinforces the statement and makes the sentence sound formal.

瘦子只是木然地望着大河，哑了似地沉默着。

眼睛长在前面，仅仅只是为了向前看吗？

这块陨石，仅仅是一块一般的顽石而已。

6. 不管…，仍然…　　　　　　　不管我如何努力，我仍然是在黄粱梦里，…

This means "no matter what the condition is, the result remains the same." 不管 is followed by an interrogative pronoun such as 谁, 什么, 哪, 怎么, 如何, 多, or a positive-negative structure (such as 是不是, 来不来), and it is usually used in conjunction with 还是, 仍然, 都, 总, and 就 to stress the idea that there is no exception.

不管她怎么安慰我，我还是觉得坐立不安。

不管姑娘说什么，赵老师仍然不想朝政界发展。

不管他回来不回来，我们总要吃饭。

这些人反正是闭上眼睡大觉，<u>不管</u>眼睛长<u>在哪里都</u>行。

7. 如何 (adv.)   不管我<u>如何</u>努力，我仍然是在黄粱梦里，…

It means 怎样 or 怎么, but is more formal.

不管丑石<u>如何</u>丑，它就是一件了不起的东西。

不管权利和地位<u>如何</u>重要，最重要的还是生活本身。

这件事<u>如何</u>是好？

8. 并且 (conj.)   …，一定也会有喜欢我<u>并且</u>和我有着相同心思的女子吧。

并且 is a conjunction, meaning "and" or "moreover." It is sometimes followed by 还 or 也, and it connects verbs, adjectives, verbal constructions, and clauses.

在这世间，有些事物一直在重复着<u>并且</u>绵延着。

你要爱自己，<u>并且</u>还要欣赏自己。

她和她丈夫一起学习汉语，<u>并且</u>水平不相上下。

并且 is sometimes interchangeable with 而且 in a structure where it is preceded by 不但 or 不仅. Together the structure means "not only...but also...":

母鹿<u>不但</u>是小鹿的妈妈，<u>并且</u>是它的朋友。

赵老师又说了一个"是吧"，学生<u>不仅</u>没有学他，<u>并且</u>连笑也没笑。

Sometimes 并且 and 而且 are used in the same sentence to avoid repetition:

天文学家发现了这块丑石。他<u>不但</u>没有嫌弃它，<u>而且</u>还说它美，<u>并且</u>叫来了车，小心翼翼地将它运走了。

9. 当…时   <u>当</u>她在千年之后翻阅我的札记<u>时</u>，…

This is the same as 在…的时候, but more formal. The English equivalents are "when" or "while."

<u>当</u>同学们知道这件事<u>时</u>，他们一个个感动得直流泪。

当瘦子忽然弯下腰向船里一缩<u>时</u>，他是怎么想的呢？

10. <u>尽管</u>…，(<u>可是</u>)…　　　　　　　<u>尽管</u>这么多年已经过去了，…，<u>可是</u>…

"Although" or "though" is the English equivalent.

<u>尽管</u>我老了，我的儿女们还年轻。

<u>尽管</u>他当上了酋长，<u>可是</u>他心中只有 "个人" 被放在天地间的渺小感。

<u>尽管</u>时光飞驰、景物变换，大自然里有些事物<u>却</u>是永远不变的。

11. 那么 (conj.)　　　　　　　　　　　<u>那么</u>，我们还有什么遗憾的呢？

那么, meaning "in that case," introduces a conclusion as a natural result of a foregoing statement. It is often used together with 如果 or 既然 and followed by a pause.

你这么怕热，<u>那么</u>，就去买空调吧。

<u>如果</u>女人爱自己，<u>那么</u>，世界就至少有一半是美好的了。

<u>既然</u>万事万物莫不有理，<u>那么</u>，眼睛的位置怎么能移动呢？

VI. 语言知识与技巧

1. *Allusion: a way to make statements terse and vivid*

Since Lesson Two, we have been introducing four-character expressions, many of which have become set phrases as a result of repeated use. Among such set phrases, many are allusions with reference to historical events, anecdotes, fables, popular tales, etc. The stories they allude to may have been forgotten, but the phrases are actively used by native speakers because of their terseness, vividness, and rich implications. 黄粱梦 or 黄粱一梦, for example, alludes to the story described in a classical tale, "枕中记," by a Tang dynasty writer 沈既济 (Shěn Jìjì, 750-800). Lu, the protagonist, was a poor student who had just failed the civil service examinations. As the innkeeper was cooking millet for dinner, Lu had a dream in which he acquired all the fame and wealth he wanted. When he woke up, the millet over the stove was not ready yet. The phrase 黄粱一梦 was thus coined to mean that illusions or fantasies that have no realistic basis are like transitory dreams. There are many other stock phrases in Chinese that were coined in this manner. The following expressions, for example, all have stories behind them:

自相矛盾　zì xiāng máodùn (use one's spear to attack one's own shield--contradict oneself)

纸上谈兵　zhǐ shàng tán bīng (talk about the strategies of war on paper--engage in idle theorizing)

卷土重来　juǎn tǔ chóng lái (come again in dust--stage a comeback)

四面楚歌　sìmiàn Chǔ gē (be surrounded on all sides by the songs of the Chu state--be besieged on all sides)

刻舟求剑　kè zhōu qiú jiàn (make a notch on the side of a moving boat to show where to look for the sword that has dropped overboard --take measures without regard to changes in circumstances)

Some of these phrases might be of folk origin, but scholars, who used them in their own writings, polished them and thus their folk attributes are no longer evident. However, there are other types of set phrases or expressions in Chinese that were clearly invented by ordinary, illiterate people. These expressions may be based on historical events and anecdotes, but they represent the spontaneous creations of ordinary people to demonstrate a truth of some sort, or to provide a lesson for one to follow. They normally contain more than four characters and are referred to in Chinese as 谚语 (yànyǔ, proverbs):

千里之行, 始于足下　(a thousand-li journey is started with the first step--a great objective can only be achieved by starting to take actions)

雷声大, 雨点小　(loud thunder but small raindrops--much talk, little action)

九牛二虎之力　(the strength of nine bulls and two tigers--tremendous effort)

天下乌鸦一般黑　(all crows under the sun are black--evil people are bad all over the world)

捡了芝麻, 丢了西瓜　(pick up the sesame seeds but throw away the watermelons--concentrate on trivial matters and neglect major ones)

前人种树, 后人乘凉　(one generation plants the trees in whose shade another generation rests--profit by the labor of one's forefathers or sweat for the benefit of future generations)

Native speakers of Chinese use these proverbs frequently, particularly in spoken language. They like to use them because of their vividness and the fact that many of them summarize complicated ideas in a few descriptive words.

2. *The power of rhetorical questions*

Rhetorical questions in Chinese are called 反问句. By asking such a question, the speaker is not attempting to solicit an answer, which he or she already knows, but to affirm or negate what he or she is trying to say. Raising a question is much more effective than a plain statement because it confronts the reader or listener and forces him/her to think more deeply about the speaker's argument. It is for this reason that the author of this essay frequently uses this technique:

所以，谁能说这些都仅仅只是一场黄粱梦而已呢？

这样的生命，你叫我怎能不热爱？

那么，我们还有什么遗憾的呢？

Rhetorical questions can be either positive or negative in form. If positive, the sentence implies a negative meaning, and if negative, it has a positive meaning. In the above examples, the implied meaning of the first sentence is "*nobody* can say that life is only a dream," whereas that of the second sentence is "when life is like this, I *cannot but* thoroughly love it." More examples from the texts we have studied so far in this course are:

你难道在那里一无所见吗？难道连蝴蝶也没有一只吗？

这哪里是条件呀，分明是千载难逢的美事一桩。

眼睛的位置是在脸上，这有什么可说的！

3. *Collocation of words and phrases*

Collocation of words and phrases (词语搭配, *cíyǔ dāpèi*) refers to the arrangement of words and phrases in proper pairs, groups, or units. This is because certain nouns go together with certain verbs, certain adjectives or measure words go together with certain nouns, and so forth. Translated into grammatical relations, such correspondence exists between subject and predicate, predicate and object, subject and object, as well as modifiers (attributive, adverbial, and complementary) and the elements they qualify. In the following are some sentences in which words and phrases are *not* properly paired together.

1) subject vs. predicate

212

*清晨，锻炼身体的<u>人们</u>在路上飞快地<u>奔驰</u>（"gallop"）着。

Note: People run, they do not "gallop."

Correct: 清晨，锻炼身体的<u>人们</u>在路上飞快地<u>奔跑</u>着。

*<u>请帖、贺卡、电话</u>都象雪片一样<u>飞来</u>。

Note: Telephone calls do not "flow in the air like snowflakes," but we can say this for example about cards in a metaphorical sense.

Correct: <u>请帖和贺卡</u>都象雪片一样<u>飞来</u>，<u>电话也响个不停</u>。

2) predicate vs. object

*我们<u>参观</u>了这家公司的先进的<u>管理经验</u>。

Note: Experience can not be "visited."

Correct: 我们<u>参观</u>了<u>这家公司</u>，<u>学习</u>它的先进的<u>管理经验</u>。

*我们应该想办法<u>帮忙</u>他。

Note: 帮忙, as an intransitive verb, cannot take an object.

Correct: 我们应该想办法<u>帮助</u>他。

*每天老师帮助我们<u>纠正和学习发音不对的地方</u>。

Note: Mistakes in pronunciation can be "corrected" but should not be "learned."

Correct: 每天老师帮助我们<u>学习发音</u>，<u>纠正我们发音不对的地方</u>。

3) subject vs. object

*二十岁的<u>人</u>是最好的<u>年龄</u>。

Note: People are not "age."

Correct: <u>二十岁</u>是最好的<u>年龄</u>。

*一些去年就有的<u>问题</u>，现在得到了<u>改变</u>。

Note: Problems are not "changed," but "solved."

Correct: 一些去年就有的<u>问题</u>，现在得到了<u>解决</u>。

4) attributive, adverbial, and complementary modifiers vs. their modifieds

*女孩子那<u>灿烂而深沉</u>的感情打动了周围在座的人。

Note: Affection can be "deep" but not "brilliant."

Correct: 女孩子那<u>热烈而深沉</u>的感情打动了周围在座的人。

*我<u>深深地</u>不同意你的意见。

Note: You can disagree "resolutely" but not "deeply."

Correct: 我<u>坚决</u>不同意你的意见。

*对不起，我们对你们<u>照顾</u>得太不<u>舒服</u>了。

Note: It should be "you," but not what we did ("taking care of you"), that feels "uncomfortable."

Correction: 对不起，我们对你们<u>照顾</u>得不好，让<u>你们</u>不<u>舒服</u>了。

*我们把房子<u>打扫</u>得<u>干干净净、整整齐齐</u>。

Note: A house can be "swept clean," but not "swept tidy."

Correct: 我们把房子<u>打扫</u>得<u>干干净净</u>，<u>安排</u>得<u>整整齐齐</u>。

Proper pairing of words is an important aspect of language use. Competence in this area can be acquired only through long-term exposure to the language under study.

VII. 练习

词语与句型

1. Replace the underlined parts in the following sentences to make them more formal with the words and expressions provided:

如，与，犹未，如何，仍然/依然，倘若/若是，反之

1) 眼睛长在头顶，<u>还是</u>看不见前途，心中缺少把握。

2) 有人认为，人生就<u>象</u>早晨的露水。

3) 旧的稿件<u>还没有</u>看完，新的稿件又堆满了桌子。

4) <u>要是</u>女人都让自己更加可爱，就至少有半个世界是美好的了。

5) 草叶的清香<u>和</u>潮汐的涨落都是人们熟悉的自然现象。

6) 平静和冷清的生活，常常带有一种忧闷的气氛，让人觉得孤独。<u>相反地</u>，充满曲折与悲欢的人生，又给人带来太多的痛苦，也让人没法忍受。

7) 不管周围的人<u>怎么</u>瞧不起她，她的情绪一直很好。

2. Insert the words provided into the proper place in each sentence to make the statements more forceful:

1) 眼睛的位置是不好移动的。（确实）

2) 这块石头太丑了。（是）

3) 因为它不是一般的顽石，所以它不能用来做小玩意儿。（正）

4) 我觉得人生不是一场黄粱梦。（总）

5) 我们的努力不会白费。（决/绝）

6) 她的一辈子是不打折扣的一辈子。（一定/肯定）

7) 赵老师比拿破仑还矮。（肯定）

8) 他谈过不少女朋友。（真的）

3. Fill in the blanks in the following sentences with the monosyllabic verbs:

邀，溢，订，唤，挡，晃，闷，揣，闭，歪

1) 朋友给我 ＿＿＿＿ 好了旅馆的房间，到车站来接我。

2) 鸡 ＿＿＿＿ 着脑袋的样子真难看。

3) 他躺在摇椅里 ＿＿＿＿ 着，一边欣赏音乐。

4) 男人常常 ＿＿＿＿ 在办公室里绞痛眉头，自以为得意。

5) 每天清晨都是阳光把我 ＿＿＿＿ 醒。

6) 新郎脸上 ＿＿＿＿ 出的笑容是如此的灿烂。

7) 现代人用厚厚的窗纱把阳光 ＿＿＿＿ 在窗外。

215

8) 对于 _____ 着眼睛睡大觉的人来说，眼睛长在哪里都一样。

9) 住在楼上的新婚夫妇 _____ 我去他们的新居做客。

10) 我每天在口袋里 _____ 个笔记本，有什么事都记下来。

4. Expand the phrases into sentences by following the examples:

1) 他们<u>只不过</u>失败了一次<u>(而已)</u>，还有成功的机会。
   他们<u>仅仅是</u>失败了一次<u>(而已)</u>，还有成功的机会。

   这位年轻人／有些鲁莽／还是值得信任的
   我爷爷／年纪大了／身体倒还不错
   老人家／觉得孤独／并没有什么别的遗憾
   他的说法／太烦琐／前后并不矛盾

2) <u>每回</u>路过她家，我<u>都</u>会进去看看她。
   <u>每当</u>路过她家<u>(时)</u>，我<u>都</u>会进去看看她。

   跑到终点／小李／落在最后
   做X光胸透／我们／得等很长时间
   收到请帖／她丈夫／自认为很了不起
   听上司说话／他／一个劲儿地点头

3) <u>不管</u>生活如何美好，世界上仍然有仇恨和争战。
   这件事有什么意义／我们／都不可能去做它
   谁来安排今年的麦收／按照传统办事／就错不了
   你的朋友怎么聪明／他／还是做了很多蠢事
   有没有新的情况／我／总得去上海出差一次

4) 这是一种属于情绪<u>并且</u>属于现实的东西。
   我讨厌／痛恨／那些假笑着应付我的人
   他／呆呆地坐着／痴痴地望着我
   这两个人／长期共事／配合得很好

有些人 / 自以为很伟大很神圣 / 不把别人放在眼里

5) 尽管一切都会逐渐地过去，(可是) 总有一些东西会留下来。

　　猎人遇到了好机会 / 他并没有开枪

　　瘦子活了下来 / 谁也不知道他在想什么

　　眼睛长在脸上有利于前进 / 看后方和两旁的情况却不方便

　　他有时候心不在焉 / 他的记忆力却出奇地好

6) (如果) 大家都努力生活，那么，生活就会更有意义。

　　他担心被人小看 / 我们就对他多说好话吧

　　作者很庆幸是个女人 / 她一定要为女人说话

　　大家都讨厌这块石头 / 就让孩子们合伙把它搬走吧

　　离开学校会失去灵感 / 为什么还要离开呢

语言知识与技巧

5. Study the set expressions with the help of their literal translations, and then match them with their extended meanings in the list following:

a. 坐井观天　　(zuò jǐng guān tiān)
　　　　　　　　look at the sky from the bottom of a well

b. 指鹿为马　　(zhǐ lù wéi mǎ)
　　　　　　　　point to a deer, and call it a horse

c. 守株待兔　　(shǒu zhū dài tù)
　　　　　　　　stand by a stump waiting for more hares to come and dash
　　　　　　　　themselves against it

d. 杞人忧天　　(Qí rén yōu tiān)
　　　　　　　　like the man of Qi who feared that the sky might fall

e. 掩耳盗铃　　(yǎn ěr dào líng)
　　　　　　　　plug one's ears while stealing a bell

f. 揠苗助长　　(yà miáo zhù zhǎng)
　　　　　　　　try to help shoots grow by pulling them up

g. 草木皆兵　　(cǎo mù jiē bīng)

every bush and tree looks like an enemy

h. 破镜重圆　　(pòjìng chóng yuán)
　　　　　　　　a broken mirror is joined together

1) (　) deceive oneself

2) (　) spoil things by excessive enthusiasm

3) (　) have a very narrow view

4) (　) a state of extreme nervousness

5) (　) trust to chance and luck

6) (　) reunion of a couple after separation or divorce

7) (　) deliberately misrepresent

8) (　) entertain imagined or groundless fears

6. Study the meanings of the proverbs with the help of their literal translations. Then fill in the blanks in the following sentences:

有奶便是娘: whoever nurses me is my mother

三天打鱼，两天晒网: go fishing for three days and dry the nets for two

井水不犯河水: well water does not intrude into river water

放长线，钓大鱼: throw a long line to catch a big fish

远水救不了近火: distant water won't put out a fire close at hand

冰冻三尺，非一日之寒: it takes more than one cold day for the river to freeze more than three *chi* deep

竹篮打水一场空: nothing is obtained by drawing water with a bamboo basket

种瓜得瓜，种豆得豆: plant melons and you get melons, sow beans and you get beans

好马不吃回头草: a fine horse does not backtrack and graze

只听楼梯响，不见人下来: the stairs creak but no one comes down

前怕狼，后怕虎: fear wolves ahead and tigers behind

木已成舟: the wood is already made into a boat

1) _____，你怎么教育孩子，孩子就会成为怎么样的人。

2) 他的家人都在中国，_____，还是我们来照顾他吧。

3) _____，这么严重的问题，不是今天才开始的。

4) 象你这样_____，有那么多顾虑，怎么会成功呢？

5) 谁出钱我就给谁干，_____嘛！

6) 学外语需要每天下功夫练习，_____是不行的。

7) 她没考上研究生，一年的努力都白费了，真是_____。

8) 这件事你要是早说就好了。现在_____，没法改变了。

9) _____很重要。只看眼前就做不成大事。

10) 他们俩_____，每个人只管做好自己的事。

11) 一直说要在这儿盖一座大楼，可是_____。

12) 我从局长办公室调了出来，就不想再回去了。_____。

7. Using the words and expressions provided, form rhetorical questions to reinforce the same ideas:

1) 人生不是一场黄粱梦。

    a. _____? （真的…吗）

    b. _____? （难道…吗）

    c. _____? （怎么…呢）

    d. _____? （谁能说…呢）

    e. _____? （哪里…呢）

2) 人生是一场黄粱梦。

    a. _____? （真的…吗）

    b. _____? （难道…吗）

    c. _____? （怎么…呢）

    d. _____? （谁能说…呢）

3) 现代人不喜欢阳光。

    a. _____? （真的…吗）

    b. _____? （难道…吗）

    c. _____? （怎么…呢）

    d. _____? （谁能说…呢）

    e. _____? （哪里…呢）

4) 现代人喜欢阳光。

    a. _____? （真的…吗）

    b. _____? （难道…吗）

    c. _____? （怎么…呢）

    d. _____? （谁能说…呢）

8. Identify the item that pairs appropriately with the underlined word or expression in the sentence:

1) 这辆自行车 _____ 不了了。
    a. 开　　b. 骑

2) 休息的时候，他 _____ 了一个故事。
    a. 讲　　b. 告诉

3) 住在那儿的每一个人我都 _____。
    a. 知道　　b. 认识

4) 路上的洼坑太 _____ 了。
    a. 冒险　　b. 危险

5) 昨晚李先生 _____ 大家吃饭。
    a. 请　　b. 问

6) 为了得到 _____ 成绩，我必须努力学习。

　　　　a. 很好的　　b. 很高的

7) 他 ＿＿＿＿ 那是个好主意。

　　　a. 断定　　b. 决定

8) 没有人真正 ＿＿＿＿ 她。

　　　a. 懂　　b. 理解

9) 这些饱经风霜的＿＿＿＿让我终身难忘。

　　　a. 老人　　b. 故事

10) 他们的房子缺少阳光、＿＿＿＿。

　　　a. 坐立不安　　b. 让人坐立不安

11) ＿＿＿＿ 是一年中最美丽的季节。

　　　a. 北京的秋天　　b. 秋天的北京

12) 世上的许多＿＿＿＿都在不断地绵延着。

　　　a. 事物　　b. 人物

活学与活用

9. Using the expressions suggested, discuss the author's attitude toward life:

1) 有人说人生如一场梦，作者为什么总是不服气？

　　总觉得／生命本身／一种意义

　　绝不是／白白来一场

2) 作者用什么例子来说明世上有些事物是一直在重复和绵延着的？

　　当年／母亲／抱过我／一寸一寸／喂养长大

　　现在／我／我的儿女

　　到我老去的时候／我的女儿／她的孩子

3) 她为什么热爱生活？

曾经努力生活过的记忆／曾经拥有过的幸福时刻

永远／在那里

每回翻寻／每回仍在

一切的努力／绝不会白费

4) 她相信千年以后会怎么样？

尽管／仇恨和争战／无法避免

只要／草叶间／清香

只要／潮汐／按时升落

痛苦／就／比较容易忍受

生命／就／值得信任和值得热爱

5) 你同意作者的看法吗？

我认为／作者的意见

人生／黄粱梦

遗憾

10. Using your own words, answer the following questions based on your individual opinions and experiences:

1) 说一说你记得最清楚的一个梦。它当时给了你一种什么样的感觉？

2) 世界上有些事物是一直在重复着和绵延着的。请你举个例子。

3) 在生活中有什么事让你觉得遗憾？你愿意告诉大家吗？

4) 你觉得自己热爱生活吗？为什么？

5) 生命有没有价值？生命的价值是什么？谈谈你的感想。

11. Write an essay or a speech about your understanding of life. You may want to begin with somebody else's argument and refute it by presenting your own views. When appropriate, use rhetorical questions to make your statements more forceful.

VIII. 课文材料对话

A

鬼：你在看的是我的札记。那可是在一千年以前写的。

人：凭你的口气，你一定是担心我会看不懂吧。其实，我很喜欢你，并且和你有着相同的心思。我很欣赏你对生活的热爱。

鬼：这让我很高兴，因为我的努力没有白费。我总算留下了一些有价值的东西。

人：尽管已经过去了这么多年，大自然和人间的许多事物仍然跟你当年在世的时候一样。草叶还在发出清香，潮汐还在按时涨落，甚至仇恨和痛苦也还在继续。

鬼：我一直相信，世上有好些东西是永远不变的。比如，母亲和子女之间的亲情就是代代相传的。

人：我完全同意，所以，我跟你一样，觉得应该信任生命并且热爱生命。我对人生并无遗憾。

B

甲："人生如梦"啊！

乙：看来你的情绪不好。难道有什么不高兴的事吗？

甲："人生一世，草生一秋。"几十年的美丽和悲欢，一晃眼就会过去。怎么高兴得起来？

乙：总有一些什么会留下来的吧。我相信我们的一切努力都不会白费。一个人只要努力生活，就会拥有许多幸福的时刻。越努力，生命就越有意义。

甲：可是不管怎么努力，"人生百岁，总是一死"，一切仍然会逐渐地过去。你没听说过"万事皆空"的说法吗？

乙：对于这样的说法，我总是不服气。"前人种树，后人乘凉。"为后世造福，不就是一种人生的意义吗？

第十课 轻与重

The essay of this lesson also begins with an oppositional argument framed in a statement questioning the value of "self." In reply to this question, the author's own argument constitutes the main body of the essay, and it is sonorous and forceful from beginning to end. In addition to rhetorical questions, the author also resorts to other linguistic and rhetorical devices. In fact, almost all the linguistic and rhetorical devices that can be used to make a statement powerful find their way into this short essay. In the previous nine lessons, we have studied most, if not all, of these powerful devices. Do you remember them? Have you been actively using them? Let us take the opportunity provided by this lesson to review all these devices and techniques that can enforce an argument.

I. 课文导读 ✿

在我心中的世界里珍藏 (zhēncáng, v., collect as a treasure) 着许多以往 (yǐwǎng, adj., past) 的事情，有欢乐的，有悲伤 (bēishāng, adj., sorrowful) 的。它们虽然已经过去，却会永远活在我的心中。

有人认为，宇宙 (yǔzhòu, n., universe) 是无边的，岁月是不变的，而我却只是一个很小很小的粒子 (lìzǐ, n., particle)，我的悲欢一点儿都不重要。他们问我，我这个小小的心灵 (xīnlíng, n., spirit) 世界，到底有什么价值 (jiàzhí, n., worth) 呢？我用一位法国作家的话来回答："是的，对于宇宙，我什么都算不上；可是，对于我自己，我就是一切。"

我怎么会不知道，面对宇宙，我只是一个偶然 (ǒurán, adj., incidental) 的存在 (cúnzài, n., existence)，我确实等于 (děngyú, v., equal) 零。然而，要是我不存在，宇宙对于我来说，不也是等于零吗？要是没有千千万万个自我的存在，宇宙的存在到底有什么意义呢？宇宙本来并没有什么意义，正是一个一个自我对它的估量 (gūliáng, n., appraisal) 才使它获得了意义。

我怎么会不知道，我的故事非常普通 (pǔtōng, adj., ordinary)。然而，我不能不把更多的悲欢加到我的故事里去，因为对于我来说，我自己的经历才是最了不起、最感动人的。如果每个人都看轻自己个人的悲欢，那么，世界上就不会有真正伟大的故事了。

　　我归根到底是我自己。我是我的一切<u>行为</u> (xíngwéi, n., action) 的<u>主体</u> (zhǔtǐ, n., agent)，也是我对世界的一切关系的中心。当然，别人也有别人的自我，我并不想唯我独尊，<u>充当</u> (chōngdāng, v., act as) 世界的中心和别人的中心。

II. 词语导学

1. In each group, match the Chinese words on the left with the English meanings on the right based on the characters you know:

1) 往事　wǎngshì　　　　　　　　n. sufferings
　　波折　bōzhé　　　　　　　　　n. past events
　　苦难　kǔnàn　　　　　　　　　n. sum total
　　生成　shēngchéng　　　　　　n. twists and turns
　　总和　zǒnghé　　　　　　　　n. birth

2) 思考　sīkǎo　　　　　　　　　v. pass by
　　逝去　shìqù　　　　　　　　　v. obtain
　　相伴　xiāngbàn　　　　　　　v. treasure
　　获得　huòdé　　　　　　　　　v. contemplate
　　珍惜　zhēnxī　　　　　　　　v. accompany

2. Study the examples and then match the listed words with their definitions:

1) 无数 (wúshù, <u>not having</u> a number)　-->　innumerable

　　无理　　　　　　　　　　　　priceless
　　无名　　　　　　　　　　　　incomparable
　　无价　　　　　　　　　　　　unreasonable
　　无比　　　　　　　　　　　　nameless
　　无限 (wúxiàn, 限: limit)　　limitless

无穷 (wúqióng, 穷: end)   endless

2) <u>微</u>眯的眼睛 -->   <u>slightly</u> narrowed eyes

   <u>微</u>小 -->   tiny

   微风   gentle breeze

   微笑   meager

   微薄   faint smile

   微粒   particle

3. Guess the meanings of the following four-character expressions. Use your imagination in the cases where extended meanings are used:

1) 化为乌有   （化: huà, v., change; 乌有: wūyǒu, n., nothing）

2) 无影无踪   （踪: zōng, n., footprint）

3) 微不足道   （道: dào, v., talk）

4) 无足轻重

5) 本无意义   （本: běn, adv., originally）

6) 悲欢离合   （合: hé, n., reunion）

7) 惊心动魄   （魄: pò, n., soul）

8) 催人泪下   （催: cuī, v., prompt）

III. 课文 🎧

轻与重   周国平

我活在世上，爱着，感受着，思考着。我心中有一个世界，那里珍藏着许多往事，有欢乐的，也有悲伤的。它们虽已逝去，却将永远活在我心中，与我终身相伴。

一个声音对我说：在无限宇宙的永恒岁月中，你不过是一个顷刻便化为乌有的微粒，这个微粒的悲欢甚至连一丝微风、一缕轻烟都算不上，刹那间就会无影无踪。你如此珍惜的那个小小的心灵世界，究竟有何价值？

我用法国作家辛涅科尔的话回答："是的，对于宇宙，我微不足道；可是，对于我自己，我就是一切。"

我何尝不知道，在宇宙的生成变化中，我只是一个极其偶然的存在，我存在与否完全无足轻重。面对无穷，我确实等于零。然而，我可以用同样的道理回敬这个傲慢的宇宙：倘若我不存在，你对我来说岂不也等于零？倘若没有人类及其众多自我的存在，宇宙的永恒存在究竟有何意义？而每一个自我一旦存在，便不能不从自身出发估量一切，正是这估量的总和使本无意义的宇宙获得了意义。

我何尝不知道，在人类的悲欢离合中，我的故事极其普通。然而，我不能不对自己的故事倾注更多的悲欢。对于我来说，我的爱情波折要比罗密欧更加惊心动魄，我的苦难要比俄狄浦斯更加催人泪下。原因很简单，因为我不是罗密欧，不是俄狄浦斯，而是我自己。事实上，如果人人看轻一己的悲欢，世上就不会有罗密欧和俄狄浦斯了。

我终归是我自己。当我自以为跳出了我自己时，仍然是这个我在跳。我无法不成为我的一切行为的主体，我对世界的一切关系的中心。当然，同时我也知道每个人都有他的自我，我不会狂妄到要充当世界和他人的中心。

（选自长江文艺出版社１９９５年《精美散文 哲理·文化卷》"自我二重奏"之二）

繁體字課文

輕與重　周國平

我活在世上，愛著，感受著，思考著。我心中有一個世界，那裡珍藏著許多往事，有歡樂的，也有悲傷的。它們雖已逝去，卻將永遠活在我心中，與我終身相伴。

一個聲音對我說：在無限宇宙的永恆歲月中，你不過是一個頃刻便化為烏有的微粒，這個微粒的悲歡甚至連一絲微風、一縷輕煙都算不上，剎那間就會無影無蹤。你如此珍惜的那個小小的心靈世界，究竟有何價值？

我用法國作家辛涅科爾的話回答："是的，對於宇宙，我微不足道；可是，對於我自己，我就是一切。"

我何嘗不知道，在宇宙的生成變化中，我只是一個極其偶然的存在，我存在與否完全無足輕重。面對無窮，我確實等於零。然而，我可以用同樣的道理回敬這個傲慢的宇宙：倘若我不存在，你對我來說豈不也等於零？倘若沒有人類及其眾多自我的存在，宇宙的永恆存在究竟有何意義？而每一個自我一旦存在，便不能不從自身出發估量一切，正是這估量的總和使本無意義的宇宙獲得了意義。

我何嘗不知道，在人類的悲歡離合中，我的故事極其普通。然而，我不能不對自己的故事傾注更多的悲歡。對於我來說，我的愛情波折要比羅密歐更加驚心動魄，我的苦難要比俄狄浦斯更加催人淚下。原因很簡單，因為我不是羅密歐，不是俄狄浦斯，而是我自己。事實上，如果人人看輕一己的悲歡，世上就不會有羅密歐和俄狄浦斯了。

我終歸是我自己。當我自以為跳出了我自己時，仍然是這個我在跳。我無法不成為我的一切行為的主體，我對世界的一切關係的中心。當然，同時我也知道每個人都有他的自我，我不會狂妄到要充當世界和他人的中心。

思考題

宇宙永恒无限，可是这位作者说，如果没有"我"，宇宙便失去了意义。你怎么看这个问题？

IV. 新词语

终身	zhōngshēn	adv.	all one's life
永恒	yǒnghéng	adj.	eternal
顷刻	qǐngkè	adv.	instantly
缕	lǚ	m.	(of smoke) wisp
刹那间	chànà jiān	adv.	in an instant
辛涅科尔	Xīnnièkē'ěr	n.	a French writer
何尝	hécháng	adv.	how can; 怎么会
极其	jíqí	adv.	extremely
与否	yǔ fǒu		and not (used to provide a negative alternative for the verb preceding 与)
回敬	huíjìng	v.	do or give sth. in return with respect (being ironic in this context)
傲慢	àomàn	adj.	arrogant
岂	qǐ	adv.	used to ask a rhetorical question; 难道
人类	rénlèi	n.	mankind
及	jí	conj.	and; 和
众多	zhòngduō	adj.	numerous
倾注	qīngzhù	v.	pour into
罗密欧	Luómì'ōu	n.	Romeo, a Shakespearean character
俄狄浦斯	Édípǔsī	n.	Oedipus, a legendary king in Greek mythology
终归	zhōngguī	adv.	after all
狂妄	kuángwàng	adj.	presumptuous

V. 词语与句型

1. 将 (adv.)　　　　　　　　它们虽已逝去，却将永远活在我心中，…

This indicates that something will happen in the future. Less formal variations are (将)会

and (将)要.

　　人生太短。我们的一切都<u>将（会）</u>很快地过去。

　　下个月，我女儿也<u>（将）要</u>做妈妈了。

2. (连…都)算不上　　　　　　这个微粒的悲欢甚<u>至连</u>一丝微风…<u>都算不上</u>，…

　　算, the key word, means "to be regarded as" or "to be counted as." 算不上 (its positive form being 算得上) means "not to be regarded as" and normally suggests a touch of contempt, indignation, or respect on the speaker's part, depending on the context. 算不上 is normally used with the structure 连…都, which further brings out the emotive aspect of the phrase.

　　女人：　"你在我的眼里<u>连</u>一年级的孩子<u>都算不上</u>。"

　　男人：　"如果我<u>连</u>孩子<u>都算不上</u>，怎么有这么多人给我献花呢？"

　　在一些人的心目中，跳下水去求生的胖子<u>算得上</u>一个英雄。

　　他们的语文老师<u>算得上</u>一个作家。

3. 何尝 (adv.)　　　　　　我<u>何尝</u>不知道，…，我只是一个极其偶然的存在，…

The colloquial equivalent is 怎么(会). It is often used in a rhetorical question.

　　我们<u>何尝</u>不知道眼睛的位置应该在脸上！

　　孩子们<u>何尝</u>不想合伙把丑石搬走。

　　猎人<u>何尝</u>愿意错过这个机会，可他就是开不了枪。

4. V 与否　　　　　　　　　　　　　　　　　我存在<u>与否</u>完全无足轻重。

It is a formal way of saying V和不V, where V is often a two-syllable verb. Thus, a more colloquial way of expressing the meaning of the above sentence is 我<u>存在</u>和<u>不存在</u>完全无足轻重. Adj. is also possible in this structure.

　　一个人愚蠢<u>与否</u>不完全是智力的问题。

　　不管你们同意<u>与否</u>，千年之后，草叶将依然清香，潮汐将依然涨落。

　　这些年轻人优秀<u>与否</u>，周围的人都知道。

5. 岂 (adv.)　　　　　　　　　　　　　你对我来说<u>岂</u>不也等于零？

难道 being its colloquial equivalent, 岂 is used in rhetorical questions and adds to the force of affirmation if the question is negative or to the force of negation if the question is positive. In the negative form the question ends with or without 吗; in the positive, the question ends without 吗, and 岂 is often used together with such words as 有, 是, 能, 敢, and 肯.

他<u>岂</u>敢不听上司的话？

如果是后退着走路，<u>岂</u>不是要跌交？

我<u>岂</u>只是我自己，我就是一切！

借钱请客？真是<u>岂</u>有此理！

6. 一旦 (adv.)　　　　　　　　　而每一个自我<u>一旦</u>存在，便不能不…

一旦 is used in a conditional clause and means "once" or "in case." It often occurs in conjunction with 便 or 就 in the main clause.

实在太累的时候，<u>一旦</u>睡着，<u>便</u>醒不过来。

现代人<u>一旦</u>坐在空调的轰鸣声中<u>便</u>不再依恋青山绿水。

眼睛<u>一旦</u>长在头顶上，<u>就</u>只望见天空，看不到周围的一切。

7. 正是 (adv.)　　　　　<u>正是</u>这估量的总和使本无意义的宇宙获得了意义。

Used for emphasis, 正是 can be followed by a wide range of items such as nouns, pronouns, demonstrative pronouns, verbal phrases, prepositional phrases, and sentences. 才 is often used in conjunction with it. The omission of 正 would weaken the force of the statement.

对于这块陨石来说，丑<u>正是</u>它的美。

<u>正是</u>人类的存在使得这个世界有了意义。

<u>正是</u>有了周末的温柔和浪漫，我们的生活<u>才</u>这样美好。

<u>正是</u>因为有阳光和温情，这套房子<u>才</u>让人那么眼红。

8. 对(于)…来说　　　　　　　　　<u>对于</u>我<u>来说</u>，我的爱情波折…

The English equivalents for this are "for," "in terms of, " and "as far as ... is concerned." 来说 is sometimes omitted.

对于我来说，生命是值得信任与热爱的。

作者认为，对于女人来说，最重要的是生活本身。

对于不想自己走路的人来说，眼睛长在哪儿都一样。

9. 事实上　　　　　　　　　　　　事实上，如果人人看轻一己的悲欢，…

It is equivalent to the English phrase "as a matter of fact."

事实上，同学们是喜欢他们的老师的。

你不用去买礼物。事实上，她这个人不喜欢别人送她礼物。

事实上，不管一个人如何努力，他的成功总是有限的。

10. Adj 到/得 V　　　　　　　　　　我不会狂妄到要充当世界和他人的中心。

The structure emphasizes the extent (represented by the verb) to which someone is being a certain way (represented by the adjective).

复习迎考的时候，有的学生忙得没有时间睡觉。

他一天到晚疲倦得睁不开眼睛。

唯我独尊的人常常狂妄到看不起所有的人。

VI. 语言知识与技巧

1. *Images, metaphors, and four-character expressions*

Generally speaking, native speakers of Chinese are fond of using concrete objects or things to express their ideas and feelings. They believe that "suggestion," coming from images and symbols, is much more effective than verbal explanations. This propensity for using concrete objects is clearly reflected in four-character expressions, many of which are concrete and laden with images drawn either from the human body or from the natural world. Look at the following expressions we have learned and note their imagistic characteristics:

无影无踪，无足轻重，惊心动魄，心不在焉，归根到底，一本正经，
油盐酱醋，锅碗瓢盆，青山绿水，风风雨雨，鸟语花香，鸦雀无声，

爱屋及乌，身强体壮，满脸风霜，衣不蔽体，发枯唇燥

In terms of usage, these expressions can be divided into two major categories. The first includes those used mainly for descriptive purposes. Some of the expressions in the above, such as 衣不蔽体, 发枯唇燥, 鸟语花香, and 青山绿水, can be grouped under this category. They depict the appearances or behaviors of things, events, and beings. Conceptual meanings are implied, but they are used more for the literal meanings they stand for. The other type of four-character expressions expresses abstract ideas and notions and is used for their extended meanings. With this type of expression, such as 归根到底, 惊心动魄, 鸦雀无声, and 爱屋及乌 in the above, one must read beyond the words and find their meanings at the metaphorical level based on the concrete pictures they suggest.

It should be pointed out that descriptive expressions are often hyperbolic, and the pictures they convey are by no means objective or factual. Moreover, although they convey physical appearances, the pictures they delineate may sometimes also embody abstract ideas or notions. Take the expression 面红耳赤, for example. It presents a physical appearance, "a face red to the ears." However, it also suggests that in a heated argument someone debates "passionately" with or without a red face. Context decides whether an expression is used metaphorically or for its surface meaning. Hence, you should pay close attention to the context in which an imagistic expression is used and interpret its meaning accordingly.

Regarding the comprehension of these expressions, apart from identifying the words that you already know (as explained in Part VI of Lesson Two), you should focus your attention on the concrete objects reprensented in the expression and draw an association between this object and the idea it suggests. For instance, when coming across the phrase 虎口拔牙, look at 虎 first. Once you figured out its meaning, "tiger," and understood the other words in relation to it, you would probably arrive at the extended meaning of the whole phrase (which suggests the danger of a task). You do, however, need to use imagination in interpreting imagistic expressions like this.

2. Double negation as a way to reinforce statements

It is common knowledge that two negations make an affirmation. However, why does a speaker choose to use "double negation" (双重否定, *shuāngchóng fǒudìng*) instead of presenting his or her statement in a regular positive sentence (肯定句, *kěndìngjù*)? The answer is rather simple: a sentence with double negation carries much more force than a regular positive sentence and thus it is very useful in a situation when you need to emphasize your point. Compare the following sentences:

万事万物<u>莫不</u>有理。(double negative)

万事万物<u>全都</u>有理。(positive)

我<u>不能不</u>对自己的故事倾注更多的悲欢。(double negative)

我<u>只能</u>对自己的故事倾注更多的悲欢。(positive)

我<u>无法不</u>成为我的一切行为的主体。(double negative)

我<u>只能</u>成为我的一切行为的主体。(positive)

眼睛<u>非</u>长在前面<u>不可</u>。(double negative)

眼睛<u>只能</u>长在前面。(positive)

Read these sentences aloud and feel the force of double negation. The following phrases can help you form double negation sentences: 莫不, 没有不, 不能不, 无法不, 没法不, 非⋯不(可/行).

3. *Making statements forceful: a summary*

In this short essay, the author has used a variety of linguistic or rhetorical devices to strengthen his rebuttal of the argument with which he strongly disagrees. We have already learned many of these techniques. Using the examples from this essay alone, they can be summarized as follows:

1) Exaggeration (Lesson 4)

在无限宇宙的永恒岁月中，你不过是一个<u>顷刻</u>便<u>化为乌有</u>的<u>微粒</u>，这个微粒的悲欢甚至连<u>一丝微风</u>、<u>一缕轻烟</u>都算不上，<u>刹那间</u>就会<u>无影无踪</u>。

2) Rhetorical questions (Lesson 9)

倘若我不存在，你对我来说<u>岂不</u>也等于零<u>？</u>倘若没有人类及其众多自我的存在，宇宙的永恒存在<u>究竟有何意义？</u>

3) Enumeration, repetition, and parallelism (Lessons 6 and 7)

我活在世上，*爱着，感受着，思考着*。

原因很简单，因为我不<u>是</u>罗密欧，不<u>是</u>俄狄浦斯，<u>而是</u>我自己。

我的爱情波折<u>要比</u>罗密欧<u>更加</u>惊心动魄，<u>我的</u>苦难<u>要比</u>俄狄浦斯<u>更加</u>催人泪下。

<u>倘若</u>我不存在，你对我来说岂不也等于零？<u>倘若</u>没有人类及其众多自我的存在，宇宙的永恒存在究竟有何意义？

<u>我何尝不知道</u>，<u>在</u>宇宙的生成变化<u>中</u>，我只是一个极其偶然的存在…。<u>然而</u>，<u>我</u>…。<u>我何尝不知道</u>，<u>在</u>人类的悲欢离合<u>中</u>，我的故事极其普通。<u>然而</u>，<u>我</u>…

4) Double negation (Lesson 10)

而每一个自我一旦存在，便<u>不能不</u>从自身出发估量一切。
我<u>无法不</u>成为我的一切行为的主体。

5) Adverbs and certain emphatic structures

Words, particularly adverbs, and certain structures can also be used to reinforce a statement. In this text we repeatedly encounter such emphatic adverbs as 就, 甚至, 究竟, 极其, 完全, 确实. The author also used the following emphatic structures to stress his points:

可是，对于我自己我<u>就</u>是一切。
因为我<u>不是</u>罗密欧，<u>不是</u>俄狄浦斯，<u>而是</u>我自己。
<u>正是</u>这估量的总和使本无意义的宇宙获得了意义。
这个微粒的悲欢<u>甚至</u>连一丝微风、一缕轻烟<u>都</u>算不上。

Other structures that are commonly used for emphasis include 再也(不)…, 再…也…, 怎么…也(都)…, 非…不可, 一 …也没(不):

于是知道自己此生此世<u>再也</u>做不了现代人。
<u>再</u>聪明的男人在女人面前<u>也</u>是个白痴。
（不管）奶奶<u>怎么</u>说，石匠<u>也</u>不愿意用那块丑石。
猎人今天<u>非</u>把妻子接回来<u>不可</u>。
胖子<u>一</u>句话<u>也没</u>说就从船上跳进了水里。

VII. 练习

词语与句型

1. Based on the text, give the Chinese equivalents for the English phrases and then fill them in the blanks in the following sentences:

to be no more than	cannot be counted as
to be equal to zero	in an instant
to always live in our hearts	as a matter of fact
to have no way not to	wouldn't it be

1) 大家都还在等他，但 _____ ，他早就远走高飞了。

2) 千古英雄将 _____ 。

3) 零加上零，还是 _____ 。

4) 我们 _____ 成为社会所需要的人。

5) 在无限的宇宙里，一个人 _____ 一颗微粒。

6) _____ ，小船被吸进了深幽幽的排沙泄流洞。

7) 我连运动员 _____ ，怎么能去参加比赛呢？

8) 要充当世界的中心，_____ 太狂妄了吗？

2. With the expressions given in parentheses, rewrite or restate the following sentences to make them terse, vivid, and more formal:

1) 飞机飞得很快，一下子就看不见了。（无影无踪）

2) 在永恒的岁月中，我们每个人都渺小得不值得一谈。（微不足道）

3) 最近几年世界上发生了几件让人们都受到很大震动的事情。
（惊心动魄）

4) 他在公司里不担任重要的职务，可是大家都喜欢他。（无足轻重）

5) 一部好的小说或电影能让人感动得掉眼泪。（催人泪下）

6) 没有人生的各种遭遇，就不会有优秀的文学作品。（悲欢离合）

7) 听到这个不幸的消息之后，她原先的欣喜顷刻便不见了。（化为乌有）

3. Expand the phrases into sentences by following the examples:

1) 作为父母，我们<u>将</u>把孩子们一寸一寸地喂养长大。

再过二十年 / 我的女儿 / 像我一样成为母亲

在今后的工作中 / 你 / 会发现你自己的价值

有了轰轰烈烈的事业之后 / 你 / 每天在高高的大楼里绞痛眉头

从今以后 / 他们俩 / 终身相伴

2) 这块陨石连墙<u>都</u>垒不成。

你们的苦难 / 三岁小孩 / 能理解

这许多往事 / 我自己 / 忘记了

他的大作 / 三流作品 / 算不上

这么大的响声 / 聋子 / 能听到

3) 我<u>何尝</u>不热爱自己的生命！

姑娘 / 不知道 / 赵老师又矮又丑

堤坝上的人 / 不愿意 / 帮助小船上的人

新婚夫妇 / 不希望 / 新居里充满阳光

女人 / 不会 / 做蠢事

4) 他这个人存在<u>与否</u>都一样。

这把破伞 / 张开 / 都挡不了雨

你对他 / 信任 / 他当然会感到的

一个人 / 努力 / 对他的前途有很大的影响

大家 / 配合 / 完全看你要做什么

5) 我们<u>一旦</u>停止学习，<u>便</u>不再进步。

一个人 / 失去记忆 / 跟白痴一样

眼睛／生在脑后／和腿脚发生了矛盾

孩子们／长大成人／会有他们自己的事业

这个世界／没有了女人／会乏味得不成个世界

6) <u>对于</u>有的女人<u>来说</u>。抢购漂亮衣裙是一件重要的事。

男人／最不爱听的一句话／"象个女人"

一个国家／头等大事／发展教育

天文学家／丑石的丑／它的美

年轻人／爱情波折／难免的

7) 我的故事普通<u>到</u>无人不知。

屋子里的气氛／忧闷／让人坐立不安

我的感受／简单／三分钟就能说完

局长大人的千金／傲慢／瞧不起她的老师

他们的经历／惊心动魄／催人泪下

语言知识与技巧

4. Work out the meanings of the following imagistic expressions, referring to a dictionary if necessary.

    A. Enact the pictures the expressions suggest:

       1) 虎背熊腰　　　2) 贼眉鼠眼

       3) 眼明手快　　　4) 目瞪口呆

       5) 愁眉苦脸　　　6) 甜言蜜语

       7) 有气无力　　　8) 张口结舌

       9) 手舞足蹈　　10) 狼吞虎咽

     11) 冰天雪地　　12) 风雨交加

    B. Imagine the extended meanings based on the pictures the expressions provide:

       1) 如花似玉　　　2) 眼高手低

3) 唇齿相依　　4) 九牛一毛

5) 同床异梦　　6) 石沉大海

7) 细水长流　　8) 举棋不定

9) 雪上加霜　　10) 杀鸡取蛋

11) 过河拆桥　　12) 狗急跳墙

5. Use structures of double negation to rephrase the following statements to make them more forceful:

1) 在场的人全都叫好。（莫不）

2) 万事万物都安排在最好的地方。（没有不…的）

3) 我只能用同样的话来回敬他。（不能不）

4) 我只能从自身出发来估量一切。（没法不）

5) 他只能对上司说"是是是"。（无法不）

6) 他被这么多人欣赏是有道理的。（不是没有）

7) 人生总会有悲欢离合。（不会没有）

8) 这样下去你一定会失败。（非…不可）

6. Exaggerate the following statements using the expressions provided:

1) "柿把儿"老师很长时间说不出一句话。（半天）

2) 他一天到晚被许许多多的稿件压得抬不起头。（没完没了）

3) 他每天坐在空气不好的屋子里假笑着应付客人。（没有空气）

4) 女人全身心都在感受这个世界，不会心不在焉。（有一秒钟）

5) 男人走一小段路就要和人握手。（五米路，三个人）

6) 他们自认为了不起的时候，那种样子就象个孩子。（我上小学一年级的儿子）

7) 女人能马上看透面前的男人。（一眼）

8) 面对无穷的宇宙，我确实什么都算不上。（等于零）：

7. Make the following statements more emphatic,

A. by inserting the words or phrases provided in the appropriate places in the sentences:

1) 我不信人生如梦。（就）

2) 众多自我的存在使宇宙获得了意义。（正是）

3) 他不听使唤，我才训斥他的。（正因为）

4) 我不想成为世界和他人的中心。（绝）

5) 第一个年轻人没有到达山顶，他连山腰也没到。（甚至）

6) 我坐立不安，可是说不出什么地方不对头。（究竟）

7) 小船穿越了几百米隧道，这种事是少有的。（极其）

8) 姑娘是因为喜欢他写的文章而爱屋及乌地喜欢上他的。（完全）

9) 他此生此世不敢冒险。（再也）

10) 我心里不踏实。（怎么也）

B. by inserting the structures provided in the appropriate places in the sentences:

1) 伟大的人物在宇宙面前显得渺小。（再…也）

2) 他跟我说，我不肯迈步。（怎么…都）

3) 一个人，不管是男是女，要欣赏自己。（非…不可）

4) 我买这些东西没打折扣。（一点儿…也）

5) 我不吃不睡，要把这本书看完。（就是…也）

活学与活用

8. Using the expressions provided, talk about the author's views of himself in relation to the universe.

1) 作者心中的世界里珍藏着什么样的往事？

欢乐的／悲伤的

逝去／永远活在心中／终身相伴

2) 这个小小的心灵世界究竟有什么价值？

宇宙／无穷

我 / 无足轻重 / 等于零

宇宙 / 本无意义

众多自我的存在 / 宇宙 / 获得意义

3) 作者怎么看待他自己的故事？

极其普通 / 然而 / 不能不倾注更多的悲欢

爱情波折 / 惊心动魄

苦难 / 催人泪下

4) 他怎么看待自己？

他 / 终归 / 他自己

一切行为 / 主体

一切关系 / 中心

5) 在作者看来，什么"轻"？什么"重"？

宇宙 / 个人

原因 / 简单

9. Using your own words, answer the following questions based on your own opinions and experiences:

1) 介绍一件欢乐的往事，谈谈它为什么让你觉得欢乐。

2) 介绍一件悲伤的往事，谈谈它为什么让你觉得悲伤。

3) 你觉得自己无足轻重吗？你认为你自己的存在对这个世界有什么意义？

4) 你活在世上最看重的是什么东西？

5) 在中国文化和美国文化中有不一样的"轻"和"重"。请你说一下自己的看法。

10. Write an essay on the topic "Self vs. Society." Either party can be 重 or 轻 (depending on your own personal views) as long as you make good arguments. To make your statement

forceful, use double negation and other rhetorical means summarized in this lesson for such a purpose. Also, try to use the type of four-character expressions that convey your ideas through concrete pictures.

VIII. 课文材料对话

A

甲：我活着，爱着，感受着，思考着。我心中的世界里珍藏着许多往事。它们将跟我终身相伴。

乙："心中的世界"。你又来了！难道我们小小的心灵世界有什么价值吗？要知道，宇宙是无限的，岁月是永恒的。相比之下，我们的悲欢连一丝微风都算不上，一眨眼就化为乌有了。

甲：没有必要跟宇宙去比。对于我们自己，我们就是一切。这就够了。

乙：可是我相信，在人类的悲欢离合中，我们的故事一定极其普通。

甲：普通又怎么样？无论如何，这些都是我们自己的故事，我们非要看重它们不可。要是人人都看轻自己的悲欢，世上还会有惊心动魄的爱情波折和催人泪下的人生苦难吗？

乙：这倒也是。我们不可能不成为我们自己行为的主体，也不可能不成为我们一切关系的中心。我们终归是我们自己啊！

B

宇宙：我是至高无上的宇宙，无限而又永恒。在我的面前，一切都显得无足轻重，微不足道。

人：　你这样唯我独尊，目空一切。难道你不觉得自己太狂妄了吗？

宇宙：狂妄又怎么样？在我的眼里，你不过是一个偶然存在的微粒，刹那间就会无影无踪。你不会不知道，面对着我，你只是一个可怜得不能再可怜的零。

人：　　跟无穷相比，我确实是等于零。可是，如果没有我的存在，没有人类的存在，你不也是等于零吗？

宇宙：岂有此理！象我这样的庞然大物怎么会等于零呢？

人：　　如果没有许许多多象我这样的自我，如果这许许多多的自我不是从自身出发来估量一切，那么，你的存在就失去了意义。一件毫无意义的东西，不等于零又等于什么呢？

第十一课　读书人是幸福人

"Those who like to read are happy!" exclaims the author at the beginning of the following essay. Not only this, he continues, but "those who don't or can't read are really unfortunate!" Why is this so? Why, in the author's opinion, does reading make such a difference to how one feels? These are the questions that we, as readers, expect the author to answer, and this is exactly what the author does in the rest of his essay--explain the importance of reading, using various arguments. The author explains his points succinctly and clearly, using short sentences and omitting sentence elements he considers unnecessary. In places where there is a need for him to reveal the steps in his reasoning, the author alternates the short sentences with long ones, using various appropriate sentence connectives. His essay provides us with a good example of how to explain oneself succinctly, accurately, and cohesively. As you read this essay, try to recall the linguistic or rhetorical techniques we have studied in the earlier lessons for achieving this purpose.

I. 课文导读 ✎

读书人除了拥有现实的世界之外，还拥有一个更广大更美好的世界，而这后一个世界只有读书人才有。阅读能力的<u>丧失</u> (sàngshī, n., loss) 是没法<u>补偿</u> (bǔcháng, v., compensate) 的。人们是否具有阅读能力，其实是一种<u>精神</u> (jīngshén, n., spirit) 的不平等。

一个人一生的经历和经验是有限的。然而，通过阅读，人们却能进入不同时空的许多别人的世界。一个人只要能阅读，就等于有了一种<u>超越</u> (chāoyuè, v., transcend) 自己有限生命的无限能力，就能获得无穷无尽的知识。

读书的好处不只是让人增加知识。更重要的是，它还使人受到精神的<u>感化</u> (gǎnhuà, n., persuasion) 和<u>陶冶</u> (táoyě. n., cultivation)。人们从读书学做人，从古今中外的名人<u>著述</u> (zhùshù, n., writings) 学得各种各样的优秀<u>品质</u> (pǐnzhì, n., moral quality)。所以，读书人是很幸运的。

一个有读书<u>嗜好</u> (shìhào, n., hobby) 的人，极其可能具有美好的心灵和<u>崇高</u>

(chónggāo, adj., lofty) 的追求 (zhuīqiú, n., pursuit)。 当然，书并不都是好的。我们说读书，是指读好的书。读好书使人向善 (shàn, n., goodness)，读好书也使人避 (bì, v., avoid) 恶 (è, n., evil)。

　　所以，我说，读书人是幸福人。

II. 词语导学

1. Match each item on the left with an item on the right based on the character(s) you know:

1)　情趣　qíngqù
　　激情　jīqíng
　　同情　tóngqíng

　　n. sympathy
　　n. passion
　　n. temperament and taste

2)　博爱　bó'ài
　　厌恶　yànwù
　　人格　réngé

　　n. moral integrity
　　n. universal love
　　n. resent

3)　财富　cáifù
　　暴力　bàolì
　　抗争　kàngzhēng

　　n. violence
　　n. wealth
　　n. fight

4)　未来　wèilái
　　成人　chéngrén
　　效果　xiàoguǒ

　　n. future
　　n. effect
　　n. adult

5)　闻知　wénzhī
　　饱览　bǎolǎn
　　流传　liúchuán

　　v. spread
　　v. hear
　　v. have a good look at

6)　排除　páichú
　　趋避　qūbì
　　引导　yǐndǎo
　　注定　zhùdìng

　　v. guide
　　v. eliminate
　　v. avoid
　　v. be destined

7)　纯净　chúnjìng
　　高尚　gāoshàng

　　adj. (for abstract things) a good deal of
　　adj. noble

246

诸多　zhūduō　　　　　　　　　　adj. pure

2. Select an appropriate meaning for the underlined word or phrase in each sentence:

  1) 这种做法<u>不仅</u> (bùjǐn, conj.) 避免了波折，而且加快了成功。
      a. not only　　b. not yet　　c. not really

  2) "黄粱梦" 的说法<u>多半</u> (duōbàn, adv.) 是从书上看来的。
      a. definitely　　b. most probably　　c. hardly

  3) 我<u>并非</u> (bìng fēi, adv.) 嫌弃他，我只是不信任他。
      a. never　　b. not　　c. really not

  4) 他们看到缕缕轻烟，<u>由此</u> (yóucǐ, adv.) 认为前边是一个村子。
      a. from this　　b. before long　　c. after that

  5) 这是一个<u>关于</u> (guānyú, prep.) 母爱的故事。
      a. in spite of　　b. for the purpose of　　c. with regard to

  6) 有人说，一本书的价值<u>在于</u> (zàiyú, v.) 它的教育意义。
      a. do well in　　b. lie in　　c. grow in

  7) 夫妇俩<u>无形间</u> (wúxíngjiān, adv.) 闹起了矛盾。
      a. imperceptibly　　b. with no sufficient space　　c. for no reason

  8) 一个敢于冒险的人<u>往往</u> (wǎngwǎng, adv.) 会成功。
      a. rarely　　b. never　　c. often

  9) 冰块放在火上<u>烤</u> (kǎo, v.) 就会变成水。
      a. boil　　b. bake　　c. fry

3. Study the following groups of words, paying attention to how they are formed and used:

  1) 拥有　yōngyǒu　　v. possess　　　　　　　　　拥有土地,拥有财富
     具有　jùyǒu　　v. have as a quality or ability　具有能力,具有正义感
     独有　dúyǒu　　v. have exclusively　　　　　读书人独有的优秀品质

  2) 经历　jīnglì　　n./v. experience; undergo　生活经历;经历很多苦难

247

经验　jīngyàn　　　　n. experience (in the sense of knowledge)

经验丰富, 成功的经验

体验　tǐyàn　　　　　n./v. experience; learn through one's experience

生活体验, 体验生活

3)　亲自　qīnzì　　　adv. in person　亲自闻知, 亲自动手

亲身　qīnshēn　　adj. firsthand　亲身经历, 亲身感受

自身　zìshēn　　　n. one's own　自身的经历, 自身的兴趣

4)　可能　kěnéng　　　　n. possibility

可能性　kěnéngxìng　n. possibility

性　xìng, suffix to designate a quality, property, etc.

e.g., 神秘性, 危险性, 现实性, 时间性, 偶然性

正义　zhèngyì　　　　n. justice

正义感　zhèngyìgǎn　n. sense of justice

感　gǎn, suffix to denote a feeling

e.g., 渺小感, 孤独感, 自豪感, 幸福感, 信任感

弱　ruò　　　adj. weak

弱者　ruòzhě　n. the weak

者　zhě, suffix to indicate a category of people

e.g., 老者, 死者, 勇敢者, 成功者, 居住者, 冒险者

4. Guess the meanings of the following four-character expressions:

1)　草木虫鱼

2)　奇风异俗　　（风: fēng, n., local custom; 异: yì, adj., different; 俗: sú, n., local convention）

3)　往哲先贤　　（哲: zhé, n., wise person; 贤: xián, n., able and virtuous person）

4)　当代才俊　　（俊: jùn, n., person of outstanding talent）

5)　凡书皆好　　（凡（是）: fán, adv. all; 皆: jiē, adv., each and every）

6)　劝善之作　　（劝: quàn, v., persuade）

7) 趋避凡俗　　（凡: fán, n., ordinariness; 俗: sú, n., vulgarity）

III. 课文

读书人是幸福人　谢冕

　　我常想读书人是世间幸福人，因为他除了拥有现实的世界之外，还拥有另一个更为浩瀚也更为丰富的世界。现实的世界是人人都有的，而后一个世界却为读书人所独有，由此我又想，那些失去阅读能力的人和不能阅读的人是多么的不幸，他们的丧失是不可补偿的。世间有诸多的不平等，财富的不平等，权力的不平等，而阅读能力的拥有或丧失却体现为精神的不平等。

　　一个人的一生，只能经历自己拥有的那一份欣悦，那一份苦难，也许再加上一些他亲自闻知的关于自身以外的经历和经验。然而，人们通过阅读，却能进入不同时空的诸多他人的世界。这样，具有阅读能力的人，无形间获得了超越有限生命的无限可能性。阅读不仅使他多识了草木虫鱼之名，而且可以上溯远古下及未来，饱览存在的与非存在的奇风异俗。

　　更为重要的是，读书加惠于人们的不仅是知识的增广，而且还在于精神的感化与陶冶。人们从读书学做人，从那些往哲先贤及当代才俊的著述中学得他们的人格。人们从《论语》中学得智慧的思考，从《史记》中学得严肃的历史精神，从《正气歌》学得人格的刚烈，从马克思学得人世的激情，从鲁迅学得批判的精神，从列夫·托尔斯泰学得道德的执着，从歌德学得睿智的人生，从拜伦学得奋斗的热情。一个读书人，一个有机会拥有超乎个人生命体验的幸运人。

　　一个人一旦与书本结缘，极大的可能是注定与崇高追求和高尚情趣相联系的人。说"极大的可能"，指的是不排除读书人中也有卑鄙和奸诈。况且，并非凡书皆好，在流传的书籍中，并非全是劝善之作，也有无价值的甚而起负面效果的。但我们所指的书，总是以其优好品质得以流传这一类。这类书对人的影响总是良性的。我之所以常感读书幸福，是从喜爱文学书的亲身感受而发。一旦与此种嗜好结缘，人多半向往于崇高。对暴力的厌恶和对弱者的同情，往往使人心灵纯净而富正义感，变得情趣高雅而趋避凡俗。或博爱、或温情、或抗争，大抵总引导人从幼年到成人，一步一步向着人间的美好境界前行。笛卡儿说："读一本好书，就是和许多高尚的人谈话"，这就是读书使人向善；雨果说："各种蠢事，在每天阅读好书的影响下，仿佛烤在火上一样渐渐溶化"，这就是读书使人避恶。

所以，我说，读书人是幸福人。

（选自复旦大学出版社１９９６年《千字文阅读与训练》，有少量改动）

繁體字課文

讀書人是幸福人　　謝冕

我常想讀書人是世間幸福人，因為他除了擁有現實的世界之外，還擁有另一個更為浩瀚也更為豐富的世界。現實的世界是人人都有的，而後一個世界卻為讀書人所獨有，由此我又想，那些失去閱讀能力的人或不能閱讀的人是多麼的不幸，他們的喪失是不可補償的。世間有諸多的不平等，財富的不平等，權力的不平等，而閱讀能力的擁有或喪失卻體現為精神的不平等。

一個人的一生，只能經歷自己擁有的那一份欣悅，那一份苦難，也許再加上一些他親自聞知的關於自身以外的經歷和經驗。然而，人們通過閱讀，卻能進入不同時空的諸多他人的世界。這樣，具有閱讀能力的人，無形間獲得了超越有限生命的無限可能性。閱讀不僅使他多識了草木蟲魚之名，而且可以上溯遠古下及未來，飽覽存在的與非存在的奇風異俗。

更為重要的是，讀書加惠於人們的不僅是知識的增廣，而且還在於精神的感化與陶冶。人們從讀書學做人，從那些往哲先賢以及當代才俊的著述中學得他們的人格。人們從《論語》中學得智慧的思考，從《史記》中學得嚴肅的歷史精神，從《正氣歌》學得人格的剛烈，從馬克思學得人世的激情，從魯迅學得批判精神，從列夫·托爾斯泰學得道德的執著，從歌德學得睿智的人生，從拜倫學得奮鬥的熱情。一個讀書人，一個有機會擁有超乎個人生命體驗的幸運人。

　　一個人一旦與書本結緣，極大的可能是注定與崇高追求和高尚情趣相聯係的人。說"極大的可能"，指的是不排除讀書人中也有卑鄙和奸詐。況且，並非凡書皆好，在流傳的書籍中，並非全是勸善之作，也有無價值的甚而起負面效果的。但我們所指的書，總是以其優好品質得以流傳這一類。這類書對人的影響總是良性的。我之所以常感讀書幸福，是從喜愛文學書的親身感受而發。一旦与此種嗜好結緣，人多半嚮往於崇高。對暴力的厭惡和對弱者的同情，使人心靈純淨而富正義感，人往往變成情趣高雅而趨避凡俗。或博愛、或溫情、或抗爭，大抵總引導人從幼年到成人，一步一步向著人間的美好境界前行。笛卡兒說："讀一本好書，就是和許多高尚的人談話"，這就是讀書使人向善；雨果說："各種蠢事，在每天閱讀好書的影響下，仿彿烤在火上一樣漸漸融化"，這就是讀書使人避惡。

　　所以，我說，讀書人是幸福人。

思考題

　　人间有很多的不平等。作者为什么说"阅读能力的拥有或丧失却体现为精神的不平等"？

IV. 新词语

| 浩瀚 | hàohàn | adj. | vast |

体现	tǐxiàn	v.	reflect
上溯	shàngsù	v.	trace back to the past (lit., go upstream)
下及	xiàjí	v.	extend forward (to the future)
加惠于	jiā huì yú	v.	benefit
增广	zēngguǎng	n.	expansion
《论语》	Lúnyǔ	n.	*The Analects of Confucius*
《史记》	Shǐjì	n.	*Records of the Grand Historian* by 司马迁 (Sīmǎ Qiān, 145 ca. - ? B.C.) of the Han dynasty
严肃	yánsù	adj.	serious
《正气歌》	Zhèngqìgē	n.	a poem by the Song dynasty poet and statesman 文天祥 (Wén Tiānxiáng, 1236-1283)
刚烈	gāngliè	n.	personal quality of being upright and unyielding
马克思	Mǎkèsī	n.	Karl Marx (1818-1883), a German economist and political philosopher
鲁迅	Lǔxùn	n.	real name 周树人 (1881-1931), one of the greatest writers in the May Fourth period
批判	pīpàn	n.	criticism
列夫·托尔斯泰			
	Lièfū · Tuō'ěrsītài	n.	Leo Tolstoy (1828-1910), a great Russian writer
道德	dàodé	n.	morals
执着	zhízhuó	n.	perseverance
歌德	Gēdé	n.	Johann Wolfgang von Goethe (1749-1832), a German poet and playwright
睿智	ruìzhì	adj.	wise and farsighted
拜伦	Bàilún	n.	George Gordon Byron (1785-1859), an English Romantic poet
奋斗	fèndòu	n.	struggle
超乎	chāohū	v.	go beyond; 超出
一旦	yídàn	conj.	once
结缘	jiéyuán	v.	develop an affinity for
卑鄙	bēibǐ	n.	baseness

奸诈	jiānzhà	n.	wickedness
况且	kuàngqiě	conj.	moreover
甚而	shèn'ér	adv.	even; 甚至
起(⋯效果)	qǐ (...xiàoguǒ)	v.	take (effect)
负面	fùmiàn	adj.	negative
得以	déyǐ	v.	be able to
类	lèi	n.	category
影响	yǐngxiǎng	n.	influence
良性	liángxìng	adj.	of good nature
高雅	gāoyǎ	adj.	refined
大抵	dàdǐ	adv.	on the whole
幼年	yòunián	n.	childhood
境界	jìngjiè	n.	realm
笛卡儿	Díkǎ'ér	n.	René Decartes (1596-1650), a French philosopher
雨果	Yǔguǒ	n.	Victor Hugo (1802-1885), a French writer
仿佛	fǎngfú	adv.	as if; 好象; 好似; 犹如
渐渐	jiànjiàn	adv.	gradually; 逐渐
溶化	rónghuà	v.	dissolve

V. 词语与句型

1. 为 N 所 V 　　　　　　现实的世界⋯，而后一个世界却<u>为</u>读书人<u>所</u>独有，⋯

This is a structure of classical Chinese, where the meaning of 为 (wéi, prep.) is similar to 被, introducing the agent that performs the action represented by the verb. 所 can be omitted, but with it, the sentence sounds more formal, forceful, and balanced.

中国的大量古诗至今<u>为</u>人<u>所</u>读，<u>为</u>人<u>所</u>爱。
许多东方的民间艺术<u>为</u>西方人<u>所</u>喜爱。
唯我独尊、自高自大的人<u>为</u>世人<u>所</u>不容("tolerate")。

253

2. 体现为   而阅读能力的拥有或丧失却**体现为**精神的不平等。

Its English equivalent is "to manifest as." 为 (*wéi*, prep.) here means "as" or "into." The phrase is placed after the verb to indicate the state that a person, a thing, or a phenomenon manifests itself as or changes into. Another similar expression is 表现为.

> 丑石的伟大**体现为**多年来的默默忍受。
> 作者认为，女性的特点**体现为**想怎么样就怎么样。

3. 再加上   一个人的一生，只能经历…，也许**再加上**…

The phrase has two related meanings: one is literal, meaning "add," and the other is extended, meaning "moreover," "furthermore," or "besides." The phrase in the above sentence is used in its literal sense.

> 我们家一共有三口人：父亲，母亲，**再加上**我。(literal)
> 今天别出去了，你身体不好，**再加上**天气又太冷。(extended)
> 年轻人又饿又累，**再加上**在山顶一无所见，所以就回来了。(extended)

4. 无形间   具有阅读能力的人，**无形间**获得了…的无限可能性。

The phrase means "without one realizing it" or "before one knows it." This is the same as 无形之中, in which 之, meaning 的, is a relic of classical Chinese.

> 我们从读书学做人，**无形间**明白了很多道理。
> 她们朝夕相处，**无形间**成了好朋友。
> 母亲一寸一寸地把孩子喂养大，自己却**无形之中**老了。

5. 上 V 下 V   阅读不仅使他…，而且可以**上**溯远古**下**及未来，…

This is an idiomatic expression, where 上 and 下 indicate time, with 上 referring to the past and 下 to the future. In different contexts, 上 and 下 can also refer to space, different generations and ranks, etc., with 上 referring to the above, people of an older generation or people of a higher rank, and 下 to their opposites. The two verbs following 上 and 下 can be the same, but often they are different in order to avoid repetition.

母亲常说，她<u>上有</u>老<u>下有</u>小，这一辈子活得很累。

这件事，你一定要做到<u>上不告父母</u>，<u>下不告妻儿</u>。

屈原在诗中<u>上告于天</u>，<u>下诉于地</u>，讲述他的不幸。

6. 更为重要的是　　　　　　<u>更为重要的是</u>，读书加惠于人们的不仅是…

This is a Chinese equivalent to the English phrase "more importantly."

他们的房间没有阳光。<u>更为重要的是</u>，它不能给人一种家的感受。

每个人都有他的自我。<u>更为重要的是</u>，每个人都是自己对世界一切关系的中心。

读书使人增加知识。<u>更为重要的是</u>，读书使人情趣高雅。

7. V 于 N　　　　　　　读书加惠<u>于</u>人们的不仅是知识的增广，而且还…

This is a structure of classical Chinese. The usage of 于 is quite complicated. When used after a verb, it may mean 给, such as in 加惠于, but it may indicate other meanings, some of which are shown in the following examples. Generally speaking, this structure is formal and therefore is used primarily in writing.

人一旦与阅读结缘，多半会向往<u>于</u>崇高。(state to change into, similar to 到)

足球运动开始<u>于</u>两千年前。(time of action, similar to 在)

他们家的孩子都就读<u>于</u>本州的学校。(place of action, similar to 在)

眼睛长在前面利<u>于</u>前进。(what is related to action, similar to 对)

Refer back to Part V.8 of Lesson Three, where you can make a comparison with the structure "Adj 于 V."

8. 在于 (v.)　　　　　　读书加惠于人们的不仅是…，而且还<u>在于</u>…

The phrase means "to lie in." The meaning of 于 here is not very clear. It may be used simply to structure a disyllabic word.

读书的意义<u>在于</u>使人变好。

人类社会的不公平<u>在于</u>很多方面的不平等。

问题不<u>在于</u>读不读书，而<u>在于</u>读什么书。

9. 说 "…"，指的是…　　　　　　　　　<u>说</u> "极大的可能"，<u>指的是</u>…

This structure indicates that the speaker tries to explain or provide further information about what he has previously said. 说 introduces the topic of the explanation, which is to follow 指的是.

<u>说</u> "眼高于顶"，<u>指的是</u>唯我独尊，看不起周围的人。

<u>说</u> "不平等"，<u>指的是</u>财富的不平等，权利的不平等，等等。

<u>说</u> "从读书学做人"，<u>指的是</u>人们可以通过读书使自己变好。

10. 况且 (conj.)　　　　　　　　　　<u>况且</u>，并非凡书皆好，…

This is the same as 何况, meaning "besides," "let alone," or "not to mention." It is somewhat different from 并且 or 而且 ("moreover") in that what follows is normally something obvious, at least in the speaker's eyes.

男人不屑研究女人，<u>况且</u>，他们也弄不懂女人。

丑石没棱角儿，也没平面儿。根本用不上。<u>况且</u>，河滩并不远，随便去掂一块石头回来，哪一块也比它强。

老人自己也曾经年轻，<u>况且</u>，也拥有过许多幸福的时刻，所以他理解年轻人。

11. 并非　　　　　　　　并非凡书皆好，在流传的书籍中，<u>并非</u>全是…

并非 is a formal way of saying 并不是. 非 is an equivalent of 不 in classical Chinese.

<u>并非</u>所有的女人都能一眼看透面前的男人。

一个自我的存在与否<u>并非</u>完全无足轻重。

书的世界跟现实的世界<u>并非</u>毫无关系。

12. 之所以…，是因为…　　　　　我<u>之所以</u>常感读书幸福，<u>是</u>从…而发。

This is a formal fixed structure, meaning "the reason why... is...." 是 is often followed by 因为 or 由于.

> 作者<u>之所以</u>说"读书人是幸福人"，<u>是因为</u>他自己喜欢读书。
>
> 他<u>之所以</u>失败，<u>是因为</u>太自信了。
>
> 我<u>之所以</u>自豪，<u>是因为</u>在无限的宇宙中我并不等于零。

13. 多半　　　　　　　　一旦与此种嗜好结缘，人<u>多半</u>因而向往于崇高一类。

The phase has two meanings: "more than half" and "most likely." The former is literal, and the latter is extended. The phrase in the above sentence is used in its extended meaning.

> 明天的远足，班里<u>多半</u>的人不会去。(literal)
>
> 明天的远足，我<u>多半</u>去不了。(extended)
>
> 看到潮汐的涨落，我<u>多半</u>会想到心中珍藏着的许多往事。(extended)
>
> 眼睛若长在脑后，<u>多半</u>会跟腿脚闹矛盾，走动就不方便了。(extended)

14. 或…，或…　　　　　　　<u>或</u>博爱、<u>或</u>温情、<u>或</u>抗争，大抵总引导人…

This is a structure of classical Chinese marked by an economy of words. 或 is a formal variation of 或者 and means that the case may or may not be so, or sometimes the case is so and sometimes it is otherwise. As a conjunction, it can connect any coordinate elements of a sentence.

> 这些衣裙，<u>或</u>颜色不对，<u>或</u>样子不好，<u>或</u>大小不合，她一件都没买。
>
> <u>或</u>前进，<u>或</u>后退，别的路是没有的。
>
> <u>或</u>早，<u>或</u>晚，<u>或</u>今日，<u>或</u>明日，这个问题非解决不可。

15. 大抵 (adv.)　　　　　　　…，<u>大抵</u>总引导人从幼年到成人，…

This is a formal way of saying "generally," "more or less," or "on the whole." Its colloquial equivalent is 差不多都.

> 作者觉得，男人<u>大抵</u>是热爱事业的，女人<u>大抵</u>是热爱生活的。
>
> 她是个不幸的女人。她心中的记忆，<u>大抵</u>是悲伤的。

世间的事物，<u>大抵</u>在重复着和绵延着。

16. 仿佛…(一样)/(似的)　　　　各种蠢事，…，<u>仿佛</u>烤在火上<u>一样</u>渐渐溶化。

This phrase introduces an analogy, like 犹如. It is more formal and literary than 好象…一样 or 就跟…似的.

读一本好书，<u>仿佛</u>是在同一位先哲谈话。

时光<u>仿佛</u>插了双翅的鸟<u>一样</u>向前飞驰。

宾馆里生活用品应有尽有，住在那儿<u>仿佛</u>在<u>家里似的</u>。

Refer back to Part VI.2 of Lesson Three, where more patterns of comparison are introduced.

VI. 语言知识与技巧

1. *Terse and elegant: using words and structures from classical Chinese*

In Lesson Three when we discussed formal style of language, we touched upon the subject of classical Chinese, and stated that some of its words and structures are still used nowadays. There are several reasons why modern Chinese still retains words and structures from classical Chinese: 1) modern Chinese has directly evolved from its classical counterpart, and thus the appearance of old words and structures in its system is inevitable; 2) classical Chinese is a highly succinct form of language. Its terse but rich expressions provide a desirable means for transmitting knowledge and information in the present-day fast-paced social and technological world; 3) classical Chinese is a rich store from which modern Chinese, in response to the rapid social, economic, and political developments, extracts words and expressions to replenish itself; 4) the continuing use of classical words and structures reflects the nostalgia of the Chinese people for their cultural heritage. Educated speakers are particularly fond of using old words and structures to add a touch of elegance and antiquity to their writings.

The author of this present essay uses many words and structures from classical Chinese. Although modern counterparts are available, he chooses to use old words and expressions to make his text terse and sound elegant. For example, instead of 的, 他/她/它的, 给, and 不, he uses 之, 其, 于, and 非 respectively. The same purpose also motivates his use of classical structures in several places, although less formal or more contemporary ways of saying the same things are available:

现实的世界是人人都有的，而后一个世界却<u>为读书人所独有</u>。

阅读能力的拥有或丧失却<u>体现为</u>精神的不平等。

我<u>之所以</u>常感读书幸福，<u>是</u>从喜爱文学书的亲身感受而发。

<u>或</u>博爱、<u>或</u>温情、<u>或</u>抗争，大抵总引导人从幼年到成人，一步一步向着人间的美好境界前行。

If you paraphrase the last sentence in less formal or colloquial language, you will see how many words the classical structure has saved.

2. *The virtue of brevity: short sentences, omission of the subject, etc.*

The general characteristic of the essay under study is the clarity with which the author explains his viewpoint. Such a stylistic quality has resulted from both the way the author structures his thoughts and his preference for brevity and simplicity reflected in the sentences he uses. In addition to words and structures from classical Chinese, he also uses short sentences and tends to omit any sentence elements that he considers redundant. Some examples of short sentences (discussed in Part VI.2 of Lesson One) in this text are:

说"极大的可能"，指的是不排除读书人中也有卑鄙和奸诈，况且，并非凡书皆好，在流传的书籍中，并非全是劝善之作，也有无价值的甚而起负面效果的。

一旦与此种嗜好结缘，人多半因而向往于崇高。对暴力的厌恶和对弱者的同情，使人心灵纯净而富正义感，人往往变成情趣高雅而趋避凡俗。

或博爱、或温情、或抗争，大抵总引导人从幼年到成人，一步一步向着人间的美好境界前行。

In each of the above examples, we see "sentences within a sentence." In English, such a phenomenon is undesirable because it undermines the grammatical relations in a sentence, and makes it very confusing in terms of meaning. In Chinese, however, sentences are defined not by the punctuation marks but by their self-contained grammatical structures. Short sentences, therefore, provide a means for an author to keep his or her statements short, contributing importantly to the succinctness and clarity of messages.

To obtain clarity by virtue of brevity, the author also avoids repetition of certain sentence elements in the coordinate sentences, as can be seen in the following:

人们从《论语》中学得智慧的思考，从《史记》中学得严肃的历史精神，从《正气歌》学得人格的刚烈，从马克思学得人世的激情，从鲁迅学得批判的精神，从列夫·托尔斯泰学得道德的执著，从歌德学得睿智的人生，从拜伦学得奋斗的热情。

一个人的一生，只能经历自己拥有的那一份欣悦，那一份苦难，也许再加上一些他亲自闻知的关于自身以外的经历和经验。

In the first example, the subject 人们 shared by all the coordinate sentences occurs only once, whereas in the second example, it is the predicate 经历, and the attribute 自己拥有的, that is omitted in the coordinate sentences to avoid repetition. These omissions do not affect the transmission of the message; rather, they enable the author to keep sentences short, resulting not only in a greater degree of clarity but also a greater degree of rhythm and force. The following are more such examples from the texts of the previous lessons, where the items in the parentheses have been omitted:

他又望了一眼依偎在一起的母鹿和小鹿，(他)轻轻地抽回猎枪，(他)离开了树林。(L.1)

我看到繁花夹道，(我看到)流泉淙淙，(我看到)鸟鸣嘤嘤，那地方真不坏啊！(L.2)

你所能看到的，只有你自己，(你所能看到的)只有‘个人’被放在天地间的渺小感，(你所能看到的)只有想起千古英雄的悲激心情。(L.2)

我们这些做孩子的，也讨厌起它来，(我们)曾合伙要搬走它，但力气又不足；(我们)虽时时咒骂它，嫌弃它，(我们)也无可奈何，(我们)只好任它留在那里去了。(L.5)

女人想哭就哭，(女人)想笑就笑，(女人)害怕就害怕，(女人)脆弱就脆弱，(女人)不用担心被人小看。(L.7)

我活在世上，(我)爱着，(我)感受着，(我)思考着。(L.10)

How different the general feeling would be if the omitted items are put back into the sentences!

3. *Making statements cohesive and accurate: a summary*

Being brief is not the only way to achieve clarity. Clarity also results from the coherence and accuracy of a statement. To be coherent and accurate in speech, one must follow clear logical steps in reasoning. In other words, one must connect the individual sentences in a way that clearly reveals the logic of the thought processes. As we have discussed in Lessons One, Five, and Eight, sentence connectives are useful and often indispensable for such a purpose. Certain sentence connectives facilitate the expression of certain thought processes. The nine scenarios we have discussed in the three lessons provide an overall picture of how these sentence connectives are used to cohesively and accurately express one's ideas. Please take the time to review these discussions in the previous three lessons. The following are some passages taken from the essays we have studied. We list them here because they serve as good examples of how, through using various sentence connectives, the authors present their logical steps as they describe, narrate, explain, hypothesize, and argue. In other words, they show us how they make concessions, provide reasons, specify conditions, and anticipate arguments in the successful communication of their thoughts and attitudes.

我常想读书人是世间幸福人，<u>因为</u>他<u>除了</u>拥有现实的世界<u>之外</u>，还拥有另一个更为浩瀚也更为丰富的世界。现实的世界是人人都有的，<u>而</u>后一个世界<u>却</u>为读书人所独有，<u>由此</u>我又想，··· 世间有诸多的不平等，财富的不平等，权力的不平等，<u>而</u>阅读能力的拥有或丧失<u>却</u>体现为精神的不平等。(L.11)

当她在千年之后翻阅我的札记时，一定也会欣喜地发现，<u>尽管</u>这么多年已经过去了，<u>尽管</u>世间依然无法避免仇恨和争战，<u>可是</u><u>只要</u>草叶间依然有清香，潮汐依然按时升落，所有的痛苦<u>就</u>比较容易忍受，<u>而</u>生命仍然是值得信任与值得热爱的吧。(L.9)

<u>就算</u>一个人闷在宾馆里看电视，<u>就算</u>一天到晚被没完没了的稿件压得无法抬头，<u>就算</u>坐在一个没有空气的屋子里假笑着应付客人，<u>就算</u>宴席上周身充满了疲倦和不自在，<u>只要</u>一想到推开那一个小屋的门，<u>便</u>有阳光跳跃着来迎接，<u>便</u>有温柔的清风来照拂，<u>便</u>有花的芬芳草的清香，<u>于是</u>，我的心，<u>便</u>有了慰藉，有了欣悦，有了温情。(L.6)

我们这些做孩子的，也讨厌起它来，曾合伙要搬走它，<u>但</u>力气又不足；<u>虽</u>时时咒骂它，嫌弃它，<u>也</u>无可奈何，<u>只好</u>任它留在那里去了。(L.5)

261

就那一堂课，…他总共说了 180 个 "是吧" …。<u>于是</u>大家暗地里叫他 "是吧" 老师。<u>因</u> "是吧" 与 "柿把" 谐音，<u>而</u>这里多的是柿子，大家<u>就</u>管他叫 "柿把儿" 老师。(L.4)

他掩在粗粗的桦树后面，望着眼前的情景；<u>只要</u>他举起猎枪，一扣扳机，母鹿<u>就</u>会应声倒下。…<u>但</u>不知为什么，这个被村里人认为鲁莽凶狠的汉子，今天一举起猎枪，<u>却</u>感到有一种东西在心里撞击着，牵扯着他的手臂。(L.1)

Read these passages aloud. This will help you better observe and understand the authors' thought processes in their descriptions, explanations, and arguments.

VII. 练习

词语与句型

1. Based on the hints, write out the four-character expressions that you have learned since Lesson Six:

    1) 两个卧房和一个客厅　　　_____

    2) 应该有的全都有了　　　　_____

    3) 用烟和水招待（客人）　　_____

    4) 向周围看去　　　　　　　_____

    5) 这一生一世　　　　　　　_____

    6) 照顾到不同的方面　　　　_____

    7) 一切都很好　　　　　　　_____

    8) 不知道怎么办　　　　　　_____

    9) 应当看成是另一回事　　　_____

   10) 连续不断地（流出来）　　_____

   11) 微小到不值得说起　　　　_____

12) 一点都不重要　　　　＿＿＿＿＿＿＿＿＿

13) 变得什么都没有了　　＿＿＿＿＿＿＿＿＿

14) 永远不变的年月　　　＿＿＿＿＿＿＿＿＿

15) 内心的一块天地　　　＿＿＿＿＿＿＿＿＿

2. Based on the text, translate the English expressions into Chinese and then fill in the blanks in the following sentences:

> cannot be compensated　　　　　unlimited possibilities
> imperceptibly　　　　　　　　　what is more important is
> to develop an affinity for books　to take negative effects
> to learn how to be a human being from reading

1) 阅读给我们带来了获取知识的＿＿＿＿＿＿＿＿＿。

2) 一个人只要＿＿＿＿＿＿＿＿＿，就会向着人间的美好境界前行。

3) 人们生活中的许多损失是＿＿＿＿＿＿＿＿＿的。

4) 读书使人避恶。＿＿＿＿＿＿＿＿＿，读书也使人向善。

5) 世间不断重复和绵延的事物，＿＿＿＿＿＿＿＿＿说明了生命的意义。

6) 我们之所以能＿＿＿＿＿＿＿＿＿，是因为书中充满了人间的智慧和高雅的情趣。

7) 无价值的书往往会＿＿＿＿＿＿＿＿＿。

3. Using the words and expressions provided, replace the underlined words and phrases to make the sentences sound more formal:

> 大抵，诸多，加惠于，向往于，体现为，况且，甚而，因而，得以

1) 世界上存在着许许多多的自我，或男，或女，或老，或少。

2) 宇宙的价值可以由人类对它的估量看出来。

3) 她愿意为此长期等待甚至忍受痛苦。

4) 并非所有的人都希望达到辉煌和灿烂的境界。

5) 他很傲慢，再说，脾气也不好，你还是跟他分手吧。

263

6) 欣赏自己的人常常<u>凭着</u><u>这一点</u>变得浪漫。

7) 阳光<u>给予</u>人类的<u>好处</u>，是它无穷的生命力。

8) 请快把那些稿件送来，让我<u>好</u>拜读他的大作。

9) 他们都是从中国来的，经历<u>基本</u>相同。

4. Expand the phrases into sentences by following the examples. Pay attention to the formal features of many structures:

1) 这样的智力<u>为</u>天才("genius")<u>所</u>独有。

    男人煞有介事的样子 / 女人 / 讨厌

    冒险的故事 / 很多孩子 / 喜欢

    他充满苦难的经历 / 大家 / 同情

    黑黝黝的丑石 / 村子里的人 / 嫌弃

2) 有没有阅读能力<u>体现为</u>精神的不平等。

    一本书好不好 / 是否使人向善

    电影的成功和失败 / 观众反应 ("response") 的好坏

    眼睛位置的正确与否 / 看东西和走路的方便程度 ("degree")

    往事的欢乐和悲伤 / 个人从自我出发的感受

3) 他的教育背景，<u>再加上</u>他的工作经验，使他成了我的上司。

    高尚的情趣 / 崇高的追求 / 使她受到所有人的尊重

    智慧的思考 / 奋斗的热情 / 是他不断成功的原因

    自高自大 / 心不在焉 / 使他什么都听不进去

    他游得不好 / 遇到漩流 / 所以很快就沉了底

4) 读书的好处<u>在于</u>知识的增广和精神的陶冶。

    生命 / 运动

    鲁迅的伟大 / 他的批判精神

    人的善良品质 / 对暴力的厌恶和对弱者的同情

    读书人的幸福 / 有机会超乎个人生命的体验

5) <u>说</u>"幸福人"，<u>指的是</u>因为读书而变得幸福的人。

　　"劝善之作" ／能使人心灵纯净的作品
　　"我就是一切" ／从我自身出发来估量一切
　　"黄粱梦" ／梦里发生了很多事情，但其实梦的时间并不长
　　"现代人" ／不再依恋大自然的现代生活方式（"style"）

6) 不幸的人不只你一个，<u>况且</u>，你还不算太不幸。（你不要太难受了）

　　我跟他本来就不太熟 ／我们有好久没见面了（我实在没法请他帮忙）
　　总是会有失败的 ／失败的原因已经找到了（我们一定会成功）
　　这件事还算简单 ／他有这方面的经验（可以交给他去做）
　　平均分配不是好办法 ／也做不到（还是不要平均分配吧）

7) 请客<u>并非</u>一定要花很多钱。

　　X光胸透 ／什么问题都能发现
　　幸运之神 ／特别喜欢哪一种人
　　做一件事 ／一定要有十分的把握
　　你的顾虑 ／都有道理

8) 他们<u>之所以</u>闹矛盾，<u>是因为</u>两个人都太狂妄。

　　你 ／不努力上进 ／心中缺少目标
　　我们 ／珍惜这个机会 ／这样的机会太难得了
　　女人 ／瞧不起自己 ／没弄清自己需要什么
　　同学们 ／叫他"柿把儿"老师 ／他老爱说"是吧"

9) 奸诈的人<u>多半</u>卑鄙。

　　不前进的人 ／会倒退
　　这个学校的学生 ／会朝政界发展
　　他的关系 ／在教育界
　　太得意了 ／要跌交

10) 一个人在阅读的时候，<u>仿佛</u>进入了不同的时空。

  她／回想起当时的经历／是在梦中

  李老师／一甩教鞭走了出去／真的生气了

  我的同屋／这几天情绪不好／有什么事不对头

  他／每天收一大堆信件、请帖／人人都少不了他

语言知识与技巧

5. Rewrite the following passages using classical words and structures. Refer to the texts we have studied recently for substitutes for the underlined phrases and structures.

1) 万事万物<u>没有一件是没有道理的</u>。(L.8)

2) 两只眼都长在左边不行，<u>反过来</u>，<u>如果</u>两只眼都长在右边，也是一样。 (L.8)

3) 听说有 "<u>眼睛比头顶还高</u>" 的说法，那么，眼睛长在头顶上应当很好。(L.8)

4) 在繁复的美丽<u>和</u>曲折的悲欢之后，悠然醒转，<u>新做的饭</u>却<u>还没熟</u>。(L.9)

5) 不管时光<u>怎么</u>飞驰，景物<u>怎么</u>变化，我努力生活过的记忆却永远在那里。(L.9)

6) 现实的世界是人人都有的，而后一个世界却<u>只有读书人才有</u>。(L.11)

7) 阅读可以<u>向上追溯到遥远的古代</u>，<u>向下涉及到将来</u>，<u>好好地看一看存在的和不存在的奇异的风俗</u>。(L.11)

8) 并<u>不是</u> <u>什么书都好</u>，在流传的书籍中，<u>并不全是劝人向善的作品</u>。(L11)

9) 我们所指的书，总是以<u>它们</u>的优好品质<u>能得到</u>流传这一类。(L.11)

6. Cross out any redundant elements in the following sentences:

1) 他们住在中国已经很多年，他们完全习惯了那儿的生活，他们也交了很多朋友。

266

2) 这种治病的方法起源于古代，它经过不断的发展，它一直流传到现在。

3) 二十四岁，我走上了讲台，我当时没什么特别的感受，我只是觉得：我得有一份工作活着。

4) 回到我的家以后，我吃我的饭，我做我的功课，我给我的朋友打电话。

5) 两年来，小黄熟悉了那一带的山山水水，小黄熟悉了那一带的村村落落，小黄熟悉了那一带的男男女女，小黄熟悉了那一带的的老老少少。

6) 眼睛长在前面便于远望，眼睛长在前面便于近看，眼睛长在前面利于迈步，眼睛长在前面利于前进。

7) 家的感觉指的是温柔与浪漫，家的感觉指的是慰籍与欣悦，家的感觉指的是一种属于情绪的东西。

8) 读书人情趣高雅而趋避凡俗，读书人心灵纯净而富正义感，读书人一步一步向着人间的美好境界前行。

7. Modeling the examples, create sentences by following the logical steps suggested by the words and phrases in parentheses.

1) 每回抱我的儿女的时候，就会想到当年母亲曾经温柔地抱持过我。而有一天，我也会象今天的母亲一样地老去，那时候，我的女儿也会象今天的我一样，一寸一寸地把她的孩子喂养长大。(L.9)

　（每回…，就会…，而…，…也会…，那时候，…）

2) 尽管这么多年已经过去了，尽管世间依然无法避免仇恨和争战，可是只要草叶间依然有清香，潮汐依然按时升落，所有的痛苦就比较容易忍受，而生命仍然是值得信任与值得热爱的吧。(L.9)

　（尽管…，尽管…，可是只要…，…就…，而…）

3) 面对无穷，我确实等于零。然而，我可以用同样的道理回敬这个傲慢

的宇宙：倘若我不存在，你对我来说岂不也等于零？(L.10)

（…确实…。然而，…：倘若…，…岂不…？）

4) 倘若没有人类及其众多自我的存在，宇宙的永恒存在究竟有何意义？而每一个自我一旦存在，便只能从自身出发估量一切，正是这估量的总和使本无意义的宇宙获得了意义。(L.10)

（倘若…，…究竟…？而…一旦…，便只能…，正是…使…）

5) 对于我来说，我的爱情波折要比罗密欧更加惊心动魄。原因很简单，因为我不是罗密欧而是我自己。事实上，如果人人看轻一己的悲欢，就不会有罗密欧了。(L.10)

（对于我来说，…。原因很简单，因为…。事实上，如果…，就…）

6) 一个人只能经历自己的一份欣悦和苦难，也许再加上一些他亲自闻知的别人的经历和经验。然而，人们通过阅读却能进入不同时空的的世界。这样，具有阅读能力的人就获得了超越有限生命的无限可能性。(L.11)

（…只能…，也许再…。然而，…却…。这样，…就…）

7) 说"极大的可能"，指的是读书人中也有卑鄙和奸诈。…。但我们所指的书，总是以其优好品质得以流传这一类。(L.11)

（说…，指的是…。但我们所指的…，总是…）

8) 我之所以常感读书幸福，是因为有喜爱文学书的亲身感受。一旦与此种嗜好结缘，人多半就会向往于崇高。(L.11)

（…之所以…，是因为…。一旦…，…就…）

活学与活用

8. Talk about the author's views of reading using the expressions suggested.

1) 在作者看来，读书人拥有什么样的两个世界？

现实的世界／人人都有

精神的世界／读书人独有／更浩瀚更丰富

世间幸福人

2) 读书怎么使人增广知识？

除了／自身的悲欢／亲自见闻的东西

能进入／不同时空／众多他人的世界

具有／无限的可能性

超越／有限的生命

3) 读书怎么使人获得精神的的感化和陶冶？

从读书学做人

往哲先贤／当代才俊／人格

超越个人生命体验／幸运

4) 一个跟好书结缘的人很可能怎么样？

受到良性的影响

崇高的追求／高尚的情趣

5) 作者喜爱文学书，这为什么会使他感到读书幸福？

有这种嗜好的人／多半／向往于崇高

厌恶暴力／同情弱者／心灵纯净／富有正义感

道德高尚／趋避凡俗

6) 作者最后引用了什么人的什么话？他用这些话说明什么？

笛卡儿／读好书／和高尚的人谈话

雨果／读好书／蠢事／烤在火上渐渐溶化

向善／避恶

9. Using your own words, answer the following questions based on your individual opinions and experiences:

1) 你喜欢读书吗？你觉得读书有什么意义？

2) 你常常在什么时候什么地方读书？你喜欢读什么样的书？

3) 介绍一本你读过的好书。你为什么觉得它是一本好书？

4) 你读过没有价值甚至有负面效果的书吗？说一下那是一本什么样的书？

5) 人们不只是通过读书学做人。回想一下，你自己是怎么学做人的？

10. Write an essay on either of the following two topics: 1) your disagreement with the author's views of reading; 2) your own views of a happy person. Use words and structures from classical Chinese to make your writing terse, formal, and elegant. Also, make sure to use appropriate sentence connectives to reveal the logical steps of your reasoning.

VIII. 课文材料对话 ✎

A

甲：读书人是幸福人。作者说得真好，一针见血。

乙：什么"一针见血"！这么简单的道理，也让他费了半天口舌。说来说去，结果还不是这一句话吗？

甲：这"说来说去"，就是他的高明之处了。不这么苦口婆心，能让人明白读书人为什么幸福吗？

乙：其实，这个道理不言自明。象你我这样有读书嗜好的人，何尝不知道读书使人幸福呢？作者大谈特谈，未免多此一举。

甲：世上还有许多不爱读书的人呢。对于他们来说，这篇文章算得上是劝善之作吧。

乙：不爱读书的人，难道会看到这篇文章吗？就算看到，又有几个人能看懂其中的语言呢？这不是对牛弹琴又是什么？

B

笛卡儿：　读书使人向善。读一本好书，就是和许多高尚的人谈话。

雨　果：　读书也使人避恶。在每天阅读好书的影响下，各种蠢事就象烤在火上一样，会一点一点地溶化。

笛卡儿：　如果避恶仅仅是让人不做蠢事而已，那么，不做蠢事的人，未必心灵纯洁，未必向往于崇高。我认为，阅读的真正意义还是在于向善。

雨　果：　向善固然是目标。可是，如果离开了避恶，向善岂不成了一句空话？之所以要避恶，正是因为只有避恶的人才可能向善。

笛卡儿：　反过来也一样。只有向善的人才可能真正避恶，甚至避凡，避俗。

雨　果：　看来，向善和避恶是同一事物的两个方面，是不可分离的。

第十二课　《茶经》与"茶神"

With the following two lessons, we enter the fourth unit of this course devoted to studying 说明文 or "expository essays." Essays of this type are intended to impart knowledge about things, matters, or facts. Explanation is typical of the writing style, and the author is most concerned with the clarity in the way the information is presented.

The first essay in this unit introduces 《茶经》(*The Book of Tea*) and its author 陆羽 (Lù Yǔ, fl. 766). 《茶经》is the first classic document on tea in China, and yet, despite China's long-standing "culture of tea" (茶文化), not all tea-drinkers in China know about it. The author describes the content of this book step by step in a systematic manner. The essay is marked by the same formal features that characterize the one we have just finished. If the author of the previous essay writes formally and elegantly because he is a 读书人, the author of this present essay, by intending a general atmosphere of formality and elegance, finds in it an ideal means to introduce a document written in as early as the eighth century. We have by now studied all the linguistic techniques for writing formally. Because all these techniques are used by the author in this present essay, we shall take the opportunity to review these important language strategies.

I. 课文导读

陆羽生活在唐朝 (tángcháo, n., Tang dynasty, 618-904)。他之所以被后人奉为 "茶神"，是因为他对茶很有研究，而且留下了一部伟大的茶学著作《茶经》。为了写《茶经》，他去许多地方采访 (cǎifǎng, v., visit and interview)，专心研究十二年，才终于在 775 年写完。

《茶经》这部书分成上、中、下三卷 (juàn, n., volume)。书中的内容 (nèiróng, n., content) 有：茶是怎么开始有的，采 (cǎi, v., pick) 茶和制 (zhì, v., make) 茶用什么工具和方法，制成的茶叶有哪些类别，煮 (zhǔ, v., brew) 茶和饮茶用什么样的茶具，怎么比较唐代各地瓷茶具的好坏，用什么方法煮茶，怎么看水的品第 (pǐndì, n., grade)，饮茶有哪些风俗，饮茶有怎样的历史，唐代的名茶产地在哪儿，如何比较名茶品质的高低，等等。这些内容都跟茶有关系，里面的有些知识一直到今天还很有用。

陆羽在《茶经》中指出：茶叶具有很多有利于健康的<u>功效</u> (gōngxiào, n., function and effect)，长期饮用，可以使人身体好，精神好，思考问题的效果好。而且，茶叶还可以入药治病，确实具有<u>疗效</u> (liáoxiào, n., curing effect)。

《茶经》中介绍的煮茶方法，对怎么用水及怎么用火都作了<u>规定</u> (guīdìng, n., regulation)。用山水煮茶最好，用江水差一些，用井水就更差了。在煮茶的<u>过程</u> (guòchéng, n., process) 中，水要煮<u>沸</u> (fèi, adj., boiling) 三次，每次水沸的时候，都要按照规定做不同的事情。做完以后，茶就可以饮用了。用这种方法煮出来的茶，颜色、香气和味道确实要比用沸水<u>冲泡</u> (chōngpào, v., pour boiling water on tea and leave the tea to steep) 出来的茶更好。当然，现在一般家庭大多还是采用沸水冲泡茶叶的饮茶法。这可能是因为陆羽的煮茶<u>要求</u> (yāoqiú, n., requirement) 比较高，做起来也太<u>繁难</u> (fánnán, adj., troublesome)。不过，在过节、放假或有喜事的时侯，<u>偶尔</u> (ǒu'ěr, adv., occasionally) 试一下煮茶，也自然会有不少乐趣。陆羽被尊奉为"神"，<u>毕竟</u> (bìjìng, adv., after all) 是有道理的啊！

II. 词语导学

1. Match each item on the left with an item on the right based on the radicals and the character(s) you know:

1) 产地　chǎndì　　　　　　n. place of production
　　各地　gè dì　　　　　　　n. origin
　　起源　qǐyuán　　　　　　n. finished product
　　成品　chéngpǐn　　　　　n. different places

2) 药方　yàofāng　　　　　　n. statuette
　　医药　yīyào　　　　　　　n. prescription
　　巨著　jùzhù　　　　　　　n. monumental work
　　偶人　ǒurén　　　　　　　n. medicine

3) 时代　shídài　　　　　　　n. times
　　现代　xiàndài　　　　　　n. later generations

后世	hòushì	n. contemporary times

4) 检验　jiǎnyàn　　　　　　n. test
　　角度　jiǎodù　　　　　　n. duration and degree of heating
　　火候　huǒhòu　　　　　　n. angle; perspective

5) 撰写　zhuànxiě　　　　　　v. retain
　　保留　bǎoliú　　　　　　v. record
　　记载　jìzǎi　　　　　　　v. write

6) 选择　xuǎnzé　　　　　　n. refreshment of mind
　　提神　tíshén　　　　　　n. choice
　　醒酒　xǐngjiǔ　　　　　　n. relief from the effects of alcohol

7) 奇妙　qímiào　　　　　　n. pleasure
　　过度　guòdù　　　　　　adv. excessively
　　乐趣　lèqù　　　　　　　adj. marvellous

2. Select an appropriate meaning for the underlined word or phrase in each sentence:

1) 孩子太小，去医院看病要到<u>小儿</u> (xiǎo'ér, n.) 科。
　　　a. little son　　b. little boy　　c. children

2) <u>由于</u> (yóuyú, conj.) 读书人拥有一个精神世界，他们是幸福人。
　　　a. because　　b. if only　　c. unless

3) 他在北京的学习<u>历时</u> (lìshí, v.) 五个月。
　　　a. last　　b. be scheduled as　　c. requires

4) 教材的<u>优劣</u> (yōuliè, n.) 对教学有很大的影响。
　　　a. quality　　b. superiority　　c. inferiority

5) 我买了许多跟中国<u>有关</u> (yǒuguān, v.) 的书籍。
　　　a. have fun　　b. have something to do with　　c. have interest

6) 她到过很多地方，<u>其中</u> (qízhōng, adv.) 她最喜欢的是黄石公园。
　　　a. other than these　　b. among which　　c. moreover

7) <u>无故</u> (wúgù, adv.) 不到学校上课总是不好的吧。

274

a. without a story   b. without a procedure   c. without a reason

8) 病人应该在规定的时间<u>服</u> (fú, v.) 药。
    a. buy   b. take   c. change

9) 邮局九点种才开门，不要去得<u>过</u> (guò, adv.) 早。
    a. too   b. relatively   c. obviously

10) 这件事，<u>待</u> (dài, v.) 我们的上司回来再说吧。
    a. look for   b. call for   c. wait until

3. Mark the following phrases and sentences with A, B, or C according to the meanings of 以 and 为 in them:

1) 以: yǐ

    A. prep., with or by means of; 用, 拿
    B. conj., in order to; 为了; 为的是
    C. 以…为…: regard... as...; 把…作为…; 把…当作…
    （such as in 以丑为美）

    ____ 1) <u>以</u>热茶洗脸
    ____ 2) <u>以</u>高山上的茶为最好
    ____ 3) 要多喝茶<u>以</u>利于提神。
    ____ 4) 那儿的人饮茶<u>以</u>煮为主要的方法。
    ____ 5) 陆羽<u>以</u>他的《茶经》使自己成为"神"。

2) 为: wéi

    A. prep., as (as in 以丑为美 and 体现为)
    B. v., stand for or be regarded as
    C. prep., by; 被

    ____ 1) 茶<u>为</u>世人所喜爱。
    ____ 2) 在所有的茶叶中，以高山上的茶<u>为</u>最好。
    ____ 3) 水煮到微微有声的时候<u>为</u>第一沸。

___ 4) 那儿的人饮茶以<u>煮</u>为主要的方法。

___ 5) 煮出来的茶确实比用沸水冲泡出来的茶<u>为</u>佳。

___ 6) 茶神陆羽<u>为</u>后世所尊崇。

4. Guess the meanings of the following expressions:

A. 1) 天资聪明 （天资: tiānzī, n., natural talent）

 2) 学习勤奋 （勤奋: qínfèn, adj., diligent）

 3) 广采博访 （广: guǎng, adv., broadly; 博: bó, adv., widely）

 4) 潜心研究 （潜心: qiǎnxīn, adv., with great concentration）

 5) 长期饮用 （长期: chángqī, adv., for a long time）

 6) 入药治病 （入药: rùyào, v., be used as medicine）

 7) 腾波鼓浪 （腾: téng, v., prance; 波: bō, n. wave;, 鼓: gǔ, v., rouse; 浪: làng, n., wave）

 8) 以煮为主 （主: zhǔ, adj., primary）

B. 1) 解热渴 （解: jiě, v., relieve）

 2) 驱凝闷 （驱: qū, v., expel; 凝: níng, adj., stagnant）

 3) 缓脑痛 （缓: huǎn, v., relieve）

 4) 明眼目 （明: míng, v., make clear）

 5) 息烦劳 （息: xī, v., cease; 烦劳: fánláo, n., agitation）

 6) 荡昏寐 （荡: dàng, v., clear away; 昏寐: hūnmèi, n., lethargy）

III. 课文 🎧

《茶经》与"茶神" 郗志群

　　自唐朝以后，我国各地茶肆中大多供奉一个瓷制偶人，这个偶人就是陆羽。由于陆羽对茶很有研究，而且撰写了我国第一部茶学巨著—《茶经》，所以后世尊奉他为"茶神"。

陆羽生活在盛唐时代,他天资聪明,学习勤奋,为了撰写《茶经》,他广采博访,潜心研究,历时十二载,终于在唐代宗大历十年(775年)完成。

《茶经》全书分上、中、下三卷,十节,内容包括:茶的起源;采茶、制茶所使用的十五种工具;茶叶的采制方法及成品茶的几种类别;煮饮茶所用的二十五种茶具及唐代各地瓷茶具的优劣;煮茶的方法及各种水的品第;饮茶的风俗;唐以前饮茶的历史;唐代全国名茶产地及品质的高下等等。这些内容,基本包括了与茶有关的知识的各个方面。其中所谈饮茶的功效和茶的煮法,直到今天,无论是从科学的角度、还是从日常生活的观点看,仍使我们感到非常亲切。

陆羽在《茶经》中指出:茶叶具有解热渴,驱凝闷,缓脑痛,明眼目,息烦劳,荡昏寐,提神,醒酒等功效,长期饮用,可以"有力悦志","增益思考"。而且,茶叶还可以入药治病。如说:"疗小儿无故惊厥,以苦茶,葱须煮服之。"这剂药方,据现代医药检验,确实具有疗效。

《茶经》中所记载的一套煮茶法,对用水及火候的掌握都有严格规定:"其水,用山水上,江水中,井水下",而山水又以"乳泉"为最好;"其沸,如鱼目,微有声,为一沸;缘边如涌泉连球,为二沸;腾波鼓浪为三沸"。具体的煮茶过程是:水在一沸时,加入一点食盐调味,但不可以过咸。当水二沸时,先舀出一碗水备用,然后将茶叶从沸水中心投下。至三沸时,再将备用的那碗水倒回,使沸水暂缓,以防煮茶过度,待水面出现汤花(茶汤表面上的沫)时就可以饮用了。

现在,我国一般家庭大多采用沸水冲泡茶叶的饮茶法,只有在广东、福建某些地方还保留有一种以煮为主称作为"功夫茶"的饮茶习惯,保存了一些《茶经》中所介绍的煮茶方法。据说,用"功夫茶"方法煮出的茶,其色泽、香气、味道确实要比沸水冲泡出的茶为佳。

陆羽的煮茶法，在用水的选择上及火候的掌握上，要求都很高，程序也显得繁难；不过节假喜庆之时，偶尔一试，也自有不少乐趣。陆羽以他奇妙的《茶经》，由人而进入"神"的行列，毕竟不是没有道理的啊！

（选自复旦大学出版社１９９６年《千字文阅读与训练》）

繁體字課文

《茶經》與"茶神" 郗志群

自唐朝以後，我國各地茶肆中大多供奉一個瓷製偶人，這個偶人就是陸羽。由於陸羽對茶很有研究，而且撰寫了我國第一部茶學巨著 —《茶經》，所以後世尊奉他為"茶神"。

陸羽生活在盛唐時代，他天資聰明，學習勤奮，為了撰寫《茶經》，他廣採博訪，潛心研究，歷時十二載，終於在唐代宗大歷十年（775 年）完成。

《茶經》全書分上、中、下三卷，十節，內容包括：茶的起源；採茶、製茶所使用的十五種工具；茶葉的採製方法及成品茶的幾種類別；煮飲茶所用的二十五種茶具及唐代各地瓷茶具的優劣；煮茶的方法及各種水的品第；飲茶的風俗；唐以前飲茶的歷史；唐代全國名茶產地及品質的高下等等。這些內容，基本包括了與茶有關的知識的各個方面。其中所談飲茶的功效和茶的煮法，直到今天，無論是從科學的角度、還是從日常生活的觀點看，仍使我們感到非常親切。

陸羽在《茶經》中指出：茶葉具有解熱渴，驅凝悶，緩腦痛，明眼目，息煩勞，蕩昏寐，提神，醒酒等功效，長期飲用，可以"有力悅志"，"增益思考"。而且，茶葉還可以入藥治病。如說："療小兒無故驚厥，以苦茶，蔥鬚煮服之。"這劑藥方，據現代醫藥檢驗，確實具有療效。

　　《茶經》中所記載的一套煮茶法，對用水及火候的掌握都有嚴格規定："其水，用山水上，江水中，井水下"，而山水又以"乳泉"為最好；"其沸，如魚目，微有聲，為一沸；緣邊如湧泉連球，為二沸；騰波鼓浪為三沸"。具體的煮茶過程是：水在一沸時，加入一點食鹽調味，但不可過鹹。當水二沸時，先舀出一碗水備用，然後將茶葉從沸水中心投下。至三沸時，再將備用的那碗水倒回，使沸水暫緩，以防煮茶過度，待水面出現湯花（茶湯表面上的沫）時就可以飲用了。

　　現在，我國一般家庭大多採用沸水沖泡茶葉的飲茶法，只有在廣東、福建某些地方還保留有一種以煮為主稱作為"功夫茶"的飲茶習慣，保存了一些《茶經》中所介紹的煮茶方法。據說，用"功夫茶"方法煮出來的茶，其色澤、香氣、味道確實要比沸水沖泡出的茶為佳。

　　陸羽的煮茶法，在用水的選擇上及火候的掌握上，要求都很高，程序也顯得繁難；不過節假喜慶之時，偶爾一試，也自有不少樂趣。陸羽以他奇妙的《茶經》，由人而進入"神"的行列，畢竟不是沒有道理的啊！

思考題

　　《茶经》是一本什么样的书？茶叶有什么功效？《茶经》所记载的一套煮茶法是什么？

IV. 新词语

茶肆	chásì	n.	teahouse; 茶馆; 茶楼
供奉	gòngfèng	v.	enshrine and worship
盛(唐)	shèng (táng)	adj.	prosperous (age of the Tang dynasty)
唐代宗	tángdàizōng	n.	10th Tang dynasty emperor (762-780)
节	jié	n.	section (of a book)

唐代	tángdài	n.	same as 唐朝
包括	bāokuò	v.	include
基本	jīběn	adv.	basically; 基本上
悦	yuè	v.	please
志	zhì	n.	will
增益	zēngyì.	v.	facilitate
惊厥	jīngjué	n.	convulsion
葱须	cōngxū	n.	root of green onion
剂	jì	m.	dose (for herbal medicine)
据	jù	prep.	according to
掌握	zhǎngwò	n.	control
乳泉	rǔquán	n.	milk-like spring water
缘边	yuánbiān	n.	edge; 边缘
具体	jùtǐ	adj.	specific
食盐	shíyán	n.	salt; 盐
舀出	yǎochū	v.	ladle out
投下	tóuxià	v.	drop
暂	zàn	adv.	temporarily; 暂时
防	fáng	v.	guard against
沫	mò	n.	foam
某些	mǒuxiē	adj.	certain
称作为	chēngzuò wéi	v.	be called as; 称作; 称为; 叫做
功夫	gōngfu	n.	skill or art
保存	bǎocún	v.	preserve; 保留
佳	jiā	adj.	good
程序	chéngxù	n.	procedure
显得	xiǎnde	v.	appear
行列	hángliè	n.	rank

V. 词语与句型

1. 对…有研究　　　　　　　　　　由于陆羽对茶很有研究，…

This phrase means "to know something very well" or "to be an expert on a certain subject."

广东人对饮茶很有研究。

我对歌德和拜伦都没有研究。只看过他们的一些诗歌。

2. 所 V 的 N　　　　　　　　采茶、制茶所用的十五种工具；…

所 is used before the verb of a subject-predicate structure to turn the phrase into an attributive phrase. Semantically, 所 can be dispensed of without affecting the meaning. However, because 所 is a relic of classical Chinese, its presence makes the sentence sound more formal.

陆羽所撰写的《茶经》是中国第一部茶学巨著。

《茶经》所介绍的煮茶法，直到今天人们还在使用。

书所带来的幸福只有读书人才知道。

我所经历的欢乐与悲伤将与我终身相伴。

3. 等等 (aug.)　　　　　内容包括：…唐代全国名茶产地及品质的高下等等。

Like 等, 等等 also means "and so on" or "etc.." However, although 等 is used after either a complete or an incomplete list of items, 等等 is normally used to indicate that the list of the items can go on (i.e., the list is incomplete).

等等：

王老师的爱好很多，比如看书、写文章、听音乐等等。(incomplete)
茶叶的功效有解热渴、驱凝闷、缓脑痛、明眼目等等。(incomplete)

等：

中国有很多大河，如长江、黄河、黑龙江、珠江等。(incomplete)
长江、黄河、黑龙江、珠江等四大河流都是由西向东流的。(complete)

中国、日本和韩国<u>等</u>许多亚洲国家参加了这次会议。(incomplete)

美国总统访问了中国、日本和韩国<u>等</u>三个亚洲国家。(complete)

4. 与…有关   这些内容，基本包括了<u>与茶有关</u>的知识的各个方面。

This means 跟…有关系 ("to be related to" or "to have something to do with"). Its opposite form is 与…无关.

一个人的知识面<u>与</u>阅读能力<u>有关</u>。

一般来说，女人喜欢<u>与</u>家庭、子女<u>有关</u>的话题。

你说的这个问题<u>与</u>我完全<u>无关</u>。

5. 无论(是)… 还是…   <u>无论是</u>从科学角度、<u>还是</u>从日常生活的观点看，…

The structure is the same as 不管(是)… 还是…, but a little more formal. It indicates that no matter what the circumstances, the result would remain the same. 都 is often used in the main sentence.

一个人<u>无论是</u>读书<u>还是</u>写书，<u>都</u>得有一个丰富的内心世界。

眼睛<u>无论是</u>长在左边<u>还是</u>右边<u>都</u>不行。

<u>无论是</u>在用水上<u>还是</u>在火候上，"功夫茶"的要求<u>都</u>很高。

6. 之   疗小儿无故惊厥，以苦茶、葱须煮服<u>之</u>。

之 is a relic of classical Chinese and has a literary flavor. We have encountered it in the previous lesson, where it serves its widely known function as an equivalent of 的 in modern Chinese (e.g., 草木虫鱼之名, 劝善之作). Here 之 serves as a pronoun, meaning "it" (and in other contexts, "him," "her," and "them").

我的悲欢永远留在我的记忆里，每回寻<u>之</u>，每回仍在。

对这件事，只能听<u>之</u>任<u>之</u>。

古人认为，"学而时习<u>之</u>"是一件快乐的事情。

7. 过 (adv.)   加入一点食盐调味，但不可<u>过</u>咸。

As an adverb, 过 modifies monosyllabic adjectives only, meaning "too" or "overly." Its more formal variant is 过于, which modifies disyllabic or polysyllabic words or phrases. Both 过 and 过于 can be replaced by 太, which sounds better in spoken language.

> 书读得过快会影响效果。
> 一个人追求的目标过多，就会觉得力不从心。
> 有些人过于脆弱，经不起大风大浪。
> 这件事显得过于繁难，大家都不想插手。

8. 以 V　　　　　　　　　　　　　　　使沸水暂缓，以防煮茶过度，…

以 here means "so as to" and occurs at the head of a second clause to introduce a purpose. The verb that follows 以 is often monosyllabic.

> 请留下姓名和地址，以便今后联系。
> 你们得早一点儿回来，以免大家担心。
> 我们要多运动，以利身体健康。

9. 待…时　　　　　　　　　　　待水面出现汤花（茶汤表面上的沫）时就…

This is a more formal way of saying 等到…的时(候).

> 待飞机飞得无影无踪时，孩子们才让我继续讲故事。
> 待世界上不再有仇恨和争战时，人类社会就进入了一个美好的境界。
> 待毕业时，他们将去海外继续学习。

10. 某　　　　　　　　　　　　　　只有在广东、福建某些地方还…

某, meaning "certain," is used before a noun (or a measure word plus a noun) when the speaker either has no sufficient knowledge about what he or she is referring to or does not want to give more details.

> 在那儿的许多树上，刻满了"某人某年某月某日到此一游"。
> 某些草木虫鱼之名在普通的词典里是找不到的。
> 某位先贤说过："活到老，学到老；学到老，学不了。"

某某, which has the same meaning, cannot be followed by a measure word, but instead has to be followed immediately by a noun.

<u>某某</u>人在<u>某某</u>书中写道:"对于我自己,我就是一切。"

11. 据说   <u>据说</u>,用"功夫茶"方法煮出来的茶,…

The English equivalent is "it is said" or "according to someone (not specified)."

<u>据说</u>,读书人中也有卑鄙和奸诈。
<u>据说</u>,喜爱文学的人多半心灵纯洁。

12. 以 N 而 V   陆羽<u>以</u>他奇妙的《茶经》,由人<u>而</u>进入…

以 is equivalent to 因, and here indicates the cause of the action represented by the verb, which is normally preceded by 而.

好书总是<u>以</u>它们优好的品质<u>而</u>使人避恶向善。
《史记》<u>以</u>其严肃的历史精神<u>而</u>流传至今。
我们<u>以</u>通过阅读进入他人的世界<u>而</u>超越自己有限的生命。

13. 由 N 而 V   陆羽…,<u>由</u>人而进入"神"的行列,…

由, a preposition, is a more formal equivalent of 从, indicating a starting point in time or space. It can also indicate a change from one state to another.

每一个自我一旦存在,便只能<u>由</u>自身出发估量一切。
好书引导着我们<u>由</u>幼年到成年,一步一步向着美好的境界前行。
烤在火上的东西<u>由</u>水珠变成一缕缕轻烟,再<u>由</u>轻烟化为乌有。

由 can be followed by a person, who is the agent of the action represented by the verb.

这个问题<u>由</u>你来回答。
一个人结婚与否,应该<u>由</u>这个人自己决定。

14. 毕竟   陆羽…,<u>毕竟</u>不是没有道理的啊!

The English equivalent of the phrase is "after all" or "in the final analysis."

虽然不是凡书皆好，书<u>毕竟</u>还是好的多。

尽管人生充满了曲折的悲欢，生命<u>毕竟</u>是值得热爱的。

面对无限永恒的宇宙，个人<u>毕竟</u>是渺小的。

VI. 语言知识与技巧

1. *Making statements formal and elegant: a summary*

The text of this lesson is written in typical formal language. Previously, in Lessons Two, Three, and Four, we discussed the features of formal language and the various techniques to write formally and elegantly. There are more such techniques that we have studied elsewhere, and most, if not all, of these techniques are present in this essay, and contribute to the formal and elegant atmosphere of the essay:

1) Formal words (Lesson 3)

One tendency of modern Chinese is to use disyllabic words, which normally sound more formal than monosyllabic words. The author of this essay either uses disyllabic words in places where monosyllabic words would serve the purpose, or adopts disyllabic expressions that are more formal than those used in colloquial language:

Formal or More Formal	Less Formal or Casual
供奉	供
撰写	写
尊奉（…为…）	（把…）当作（…）
品第	等级
具有	有
饮用	喝
记载	记
加入	加
食盐	盐

采用	用
由于	因为
历时	经历（的时间）
据说	听说
色泽	颜色
偶尔	有时

2) One word instead of two

Contrary to its modern counterpart, classical Chinese is characterized by a heavy use of monosyllabic words. Because being succinct and terse is a hallmark of classical Chinese, omitting a character from a disyllabic word evokes a sense of classical elegance and therefore makes the sentence more formal. In the following, the expressions without the words in the parentheses are more formal than the ones with them:

自（从）唐朝以后，

唐（朝）以前饮茶的历史

（消）解热渴

驱（除）凝闷

缓（和）脑痛

明（亮）眼目

（止）息烦劳

荡（平）昏寐

（治）疗小儿无故惊厥

（根）据现代医药检验

水在一沸（的）时（候）

但（是）不可（以）过（分）咸

以（便）防（止）煮茶过度

也自（然）有不少乐趣

3) Short forms (Lesson 5)

286

The concise nature of the short forms lends an air of formality, which the unabridged versions of the phrases expressing the same ideas do not have. This text is full of such short forms, most of which are used on formal occasions:

各地	各个地方	巨著	巨篇的著作
后世	后代的世人	采制	采集和制作
优劣	优良和低劣	产地	生产的地点
品质	物品的质量	高下	高低上下
功效	功用和效果	疗效	治疗的效果
备用	准备采用	暂缓	暂时缓解
繁难	繁复和困难		

4) Four-character expressions (Lessons 2 and 10)

Like short forms, four-character expressions are terse because they embody rich implications in only four characters. The author has used the following four-character expressions in the essay, some of which are put together by himself:

瓷制偶人，茶学巨著，盛唐时代，天资聪明，学习勤奋，广采博访，
潜心研究，采制方法，名茶产地，现代医药，严格规定，涌泉连球，
腾波鼓浪，饮茶习惯，煮茶方法，节假喜庆

5) Words and sentence structures from classical Chinese (Lesson 11)

This essay is littered with quotations taken directly from the classical text of 《茶经》. In addition, the author consciously uses words and structures from classical Chinese, resulting in an increased feeling of refinement and quaintness:

后世尊奉他<u>为</u> "茶神"

历时十二<u>载</u>

茶叶的采制方法<u>及</u>成品茶的几种类别

<u>以</u>苦茶，葱须煮服<u>之</u>

<u>而</u>山水又<u>以</u> "乳泉" <u>为</u>最好

<u>至</u>三沸时，再<u>将</u>备用的那碗水倒回，使沸水暂缓，<u>以</u>防煮茶过度

待水面出现汤花

以煮为主

其色泽、香气、味道确实要比沸水冲泡出的茶为佳。

不过节假喜庆之时，偶尔一试，也自有不少乐趣。

陆羽以他奇妙的《茶经》，由人而进入"神"的行列。

The above represents the factors that account for the formal chracteristics of this essay. Are there any other techniques for writing formally and elegantly that you have learned and that the author has not used in this text?

2. *Speaking with humility: being circumspect (1)*

Ever since the establishment of Confucianism more than two thousand years ago, humility has been considered one of the most important virtues that anyone in Chinese society should aim to incorporate into his or her way of thinking and behaving. Arrogance and assertion are regarded as obstacles to one's moral improvement, whereas modesty and circumspection are believed to facilitate such moral progress. Even if a person is a master of a trade or an expert on a certain subject, he or she is still supposed to be humble, at least outwardly if not in his or her heart. This explains the common behavior in Chinese culture of humbling oneself before giving a speech or making a statement about a certain topic, saying something to the effect that he or she knows very little about the subject. For example, in the essay of Lesson Eight, the author expresses his opinion about the importance of having the eyes grow on the front of the head. We know that he is not really talking about the eyes, which he only uses as a metaphor, and that he is a sophisticated thinker and eloquent speaker, but he begins his essay with quotes from other great thinkers, saying that he knows nothing about philosophy:

眼睛的位置是在脸上，这有什么可说的！不过我听说古代中国有位哲学家朱熹说过：万事万物莫不有理。又听说古代外国有位哲学家莱布尼茨说过：一切事物都安排在最好的地方。我不懂哲学，但凭常识想，眼睛的位置确是不好移动。(L.8)

The phrase 听说 and the acknowledgment of 不懂哲学 and 凭常识想 all demonstrate the author's sense of humility, whether it is sincere or feigned.

Another method frequently used by Chinese to show humility is to use words that suggest a sense of uncertainty on the part of the speaker. 听说 in the above passage is a good example. The author must have studied the renowned Chinese Song dynasty philosopher 朱熹 and the great German philosopher 莱布尼茨. However, he chooses to use the word 听说 to "downplay" the extent of his knowledge, thereby to impress the reader with his humility. Other frequently used words for such a purpose are: 可能, 也许, 好象是, 说不定, 多半, 据说, 有(的)人, 某(些), 一定的(时候). Study the following examples and see how these phrases are used:

听说有"眼高于顶"的说法，那么，眼睛长在头顶上应当很好。(L.8)

可是前后左右 都不知道，一抬步，说不定会掉进泥坑。(L.8)

一个人的一生，只能经历自己拥有的那一份欣悦，那一份苦难，也许再加上他亲自闻知的那一些关于自身以外的经历和经验。(L.11)

一旦与此种嗜好结缘，人多半因而向往于崇高一类。(L.11)

这剂药方，据现代医药检验，确实具有疗效。(L.12)

现在，我国一般家庭大多采用沸水冲泡茶叶的饮茶法，只有在广东、福建某些地方还保留有一种以煮为主称作为"功夫茶"的饮茶习惯。(L.12)

据说，用"功夫茶"方法煮出来的茶，其色泽、香气、味道确实要比沸水冲泡出的茶为佳。(L.12)

3. Punctuation marks (2)

Let us continue our discusson on punctuation marks that we began in Lesson Six.

1) Comma

A comma indicates a break inside a sentence. Its usage is both extensive and complicated. Some of its uses resemble those of a comma in English, but others are unique to the Chinese language, as specified in the following:

a) Occurring between the subject and the predicate (if the subject is long, a pause is needed before the predicate; if it is short, the pause dictated by the comma helps highlight and emphasize the subject):

稍稍能安慰我们的，是在那石上有一个不大不小的坑凹儿。(L.5)
死神，正向它们走近。

b) Occurring after the verb before a long object (such an object is normally a subject-predicate structure):

岸上的人都看见了，胖子忽然跃起身，坚决地从船上跳进了水里。(L.3)

c) Occurring between coordinate words, expressions, or sentences:

我看到繁花夹道，流泉淙淙，鸟鸣嘤嘤，那地方真不坏啊！(L.2)
我看到高大肃穆的松树林，我看到秃鹰盘旋，那是一个好地方。(L.2)

d) Occurring between short sentences:

它静静地卧在那里，院边的槐荫没有庇覆它，花儿也不在它身边生长。(L.5)

常常雨过三天了，地上已经干燥，那石凹里水儿还有，鸡儿便去那里喝饮。(L.5)

e) Occurring before or after the inserted items, or between the inverted sentence elements:

我嘛，就这副尊容，是吧！(L.4)
真的，是太丑了。
多寂静啊，今天的山林！

2) Slight-pause mark

Like the comma, the slight-pause mark is also used to indicate a pause inside a sentence. Unlike the comma, however, it is used only to set off short coordinate items (one to four characters) in a series, and the pause is shorter than that represented by a comma. Between the last two coordinated items, it is customary that 和, 以及, or 等(等) is normally used:

目前让许多广州人眼红的居住条件：地毯、空调、墙纸、组合家具和高级音响，应该是应有尽有了。(L.6)

《茶经》全书分上、中、下三卷，十节。(L.12)

茶叶具有解热渴、驱凝闷、缓脑痛、明眼目、息烦劳、荡昏寐、提神、醒酒等功效。(L.12)

When using the slight-pause mark, a distinction should be made with pauses made at different levels. In other words, discretion should be used as to when to use the slight-pause mark and when to use a comma. In the following sentence, for example, the second and the fourth slight-pause marks should be changed to commas because the sentence includes coordination at two different levels:

人们从《论语》、《庄子》中学得智慧的思考__从《史记》、《汉书》中学得严肃的历史精神__从《正气歌》、《满江红》学得人格的刚烈。

3) Semicolon

As in English, the semicolon is used for a pause as well as for distinguishing sentence structures. The break represented by the semicolon is longer than that of a comma, but shorter than that of a period. The semicolon is mainly used between two separate sentences whose semantic connection does not warrant a period. In Chinese, however, because of the "sentences within a sentence," what takes a semicolon in English takes a comma in Chinese:

其沸，如鱼目，微有声，为一沸；缘边如涌泉连球，为二沸；腾波鼓浪为三沸。(L.12)

是的，对于宇宙，我微不足道；可是，对于我自己，我就是一切。(L.10)

我的爱情波折要比罗密欧更加惊心动魄，我的苦难要比俄狄浦斯更加催人泪下。(L.10)

In the third sentence, the comma would be a semicolon in English. In Chinese, a comma is used because the two coordinate sentences are structurally simple and similar, and because this is the only comma used in the entire sentence. Even if there are more than two coordinate sentences, a comma rather than a semicolon should be used between them This is exemplified by the following:

女人想哭就哭，想笑就笑，害怕就害怕，脆弱就脆弱。(L.7)
没有山的伟岸，没有海的飘然，没有风的轻柔也没有雨的忧烦。(L.6)

In these sentences, a semicolon would unnecessarily separate the semantically closely related short sentences and, what is more, cause confusion on the part of the reader as far as the sentence structures are concerned.

VII. 练习

词语与句型

1. Based on the text give the Chinese equivalents for the English phrases and then fill in the blanks of the following sentences:

A. to worship as

to be an expert on language acquisition (语言习得)

to relate to literature

to last a few years (数载)

to basically include

to look from the perspective of science

to take U.S.-made as the best

to take chinaware (瓷器) as primary

to preserve an old habit

to have strict regulations about how to take a medicine (药的服法)

1) 中国的餐具是 _____ 的。

2) 在现代社会，_____ 常常是难而又难。

3) 天文学家对这块陨石的全面研究 _____ 。

4) 在学生中流传的好书，_____ 当代和历代的名人著作。

5) 我的汉语老师 _____ 。

6) 美国的医院 _____ 。

7) _____，外星人是有可能存在的。

8) 这一类运动鞋，_____ 。

9) 他家里的藏书都 _____ 。

10) 那座大山被村里人 _____ "圣山"。

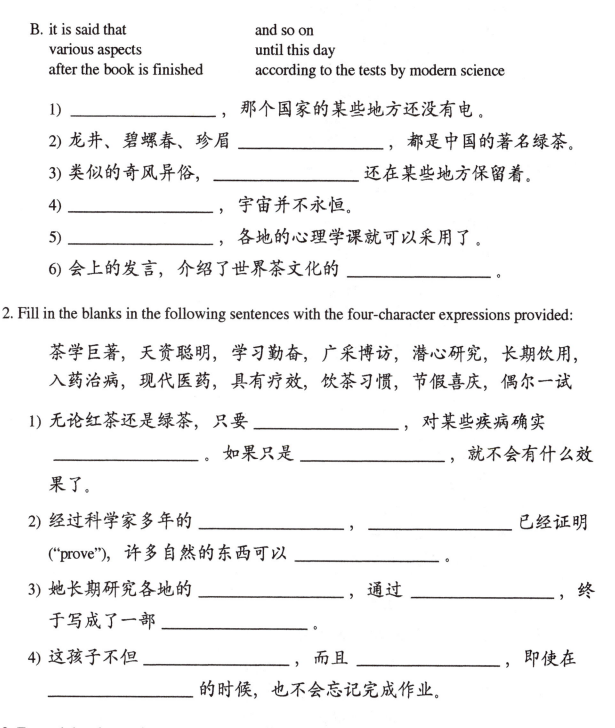

B. it is said that   and so on
   various aspects   until this day
   after the book is finished   according to the tests by modern science

1) ＿＿＿＿＿＿＿＿ ，那个国家的某些地方还没有电。

2) 龙井、碧螺春、珍眉 ＿＿＿＿＿＿＿＿ ，都是中国的著名绿茶。

3) 类似的奇风异俗，＿＿＿＿＿＿＿＿ 还在某些地方保留着。

4) ＿＿＿＿＿＿＿＿ ，宇宙并不永恒。

5) ＿＿＿＿＿＿＿＿ ，各地的心理学课就可以采用了。

6) 会上的发言，介绍了世界茶文化的 ＿＿＿＿＿＿＿＿ 。

2. Fill in the blanks in the following sentences with the four-character expressions provided:

茶学巨著，天资聪明，学习勤奋，广采博访，潜心研究，长期饮用，入药治病，现代医药，具有疗效，饮茶习惯，节假喜庆，偶尔一试

1) 无论红茶还是绿茶，只要 ＿＿＿＿＿＿＿＿ ，对某些疾病确实 ＿＿＿＿＿＿＿＿ 。如果只是 ＿＿＿＿＿＿＿＿ ，就不会有什么效果了。

2) 经过科学家多年的 ＿＿＿＿＿＿＿＿ ，＿＿＿＿＿＿＿＿ 已经证明（"prove"），许多自然的东西可以 ＿＿＿＿＿＿＿＿ 。

3) 她长期研究各地的 ＿＿＿＿＿＿＿＿ ，通过 ＿＿＿＿＿＿＿＿ ，终于写成了一部 ＿＿＿＿＿＿＿＿ 。

4) 这孩子不但 ＿＿＿＿＿＿＿＿ ，而且 ＿＿＿＿＿＿＿＿ ，即使在 ＿＿＿＿＿＿＿＿ 的时候，也不会忘记完成作业。

3. Expand the phrases into sentences by following the examples:

1) 他们<u>所用</u>的某些工具是从国外进口的。

赵老师 / 做 / 选择 / 是留在学校保持他的灵感

学校 / 做 / 规定 / 非常具体

少数人 / 拥有 / 财富 / 超越了多数人的财富

大家 / 担心 / 情况 / 终于发生了

2) <u>无论（是）</u>亚洲人<u>还是</u>欧洲人<u>都</u>喜欢喝茶。

煮的茶 / 冲泡的茶 / 能提神、醒酒

前进 / 后退 / 没有出路

成品 / 半成品 / 可以留作备用

早晨 / 黄昏 / 要往湖中投食喂鱼

3) 这部共三卷的书<u>以</u>第二卷<u>为</u>最好。

中国绿茶 / 杭州的龙井茶 / 佳

我校的亚洲学生 / 中国学生 / 多

幼年时的小朋友 / 我的同桌同学 / 幸运

教学效果 / 张老师的课 / 明显

4) 今天的菜做得<u>过</u>咸。

他身上的衣服 / 显得 / 长

有些规定 / 掌握得 / 严

这本成人教材 / 看上去 / 难

"功夫茶"的煮法 / 听上去 / 繁

5) 新泡的茶要放一会儿再喝，<u>以防</u>烫嘴。

蔬菜和水果 / 洗过以后再吃 / 利 / 健康

用完的工具 / 放回原处 / 便 / 下次使用

买东西时 / 看清产品的优劣 / 免 / 上当 ("be fooled")

这个姑娘的遭遇 / 让周围的人知道 / 期 / 得到大家的同情和帮助

6) 新茶的色泽、香气和味道比陈茶<u>为</u>好。

电视的效果 / 广播 / 佳

醋的醒酒功效 / 茶 / 好

用山水煮茶 / 用井水 / 好

住在海边 / 住在山上 / 佳

7) 陆羽<u>由</u>人<u>而</u>进入"神"的行列。

日本 / 落后 / 变成 / 先进

瘦子 / 懦夫 / 加入到 / 勇士的的行列

他们 / 小公司 / 发展成 / 五百强之一

她 / 普通工人 / 登上 / 世界小姐的宝座

8) 他成为"茶神"<u>毕竟</u>是有道理<u>的</u>。

个人 / 无足轻重

读书人中 / 有卑鄙小人

学生对赵老师的热爱 / 很感动人

对于他的傲慢 / 不能不回敬

<u>语言知识与技巧</u>

4. Rewrite the following passages to make them more formal. Substitutes for the underlined phrases can be found in the texts after Lesson Six.

1) <u>到（水）第三次沸腾</u>的时侯，再把备用的那碗水倒回，使<u>沸腾的水暂时</u>缓和，<u>用这样的办法来</u>防止煮茶过度，<u>等到</u>水面出现汤花（茶汤表面上的沫）<u>的时侯</u>就可以饮用了。(L.12)

2) <u>再说</u>，并<u>不</u>是<u>不管什么书</u>都好，在流传的书籍中，<u>并不全是劝人向善的</u>作品，也有<u>没</u>价值的<u>甚至</u>起负面效果的。但我们所指的书，总是以<u>书的</u>优好品质<u>能得到</u>流传这一类。这类书对人的影响总是良性的。(L.11)

3) 我<u>怎么</u>不知道，在宇宙的生成变化中，我只是一个<u>非</u>常偶然的存在，我存在<u>和</u>不存在完全<u>没</u>有影响。面对无穷，我确实等于零。<u>但是</u>，我

可以用同样的道理回敬这个傲慢的宇宙：<u>如果</u>我不存在，你对我来说<u>难道</u>不也等于零？(L.10)

4) 听说有"<u>眼睛比头顶高</u>"的说法，那么，眼睛长在头顶上应当很好。只望见天空，看不见周围一切，<u>只有我一个人最了不起</u>。(L.8)

5) 都市的人不<u>再舍不得离开</u>自然环境，相反地，他们<u>把</u>自然用厚厚的纱挡住，<u>情愿</u> <u>一天到晚</u>坐在空调的<u>巨大响声</u>中。(L.6)

5. Following is the beginning of a speech by Professor Wang, an expert on classical Chinese literature whose writings have greatly influenced the field both in China and abroad. He is talking to a group of students from the Chinese department at a certain university. Underline the words and expressions that show his sense of humility despite his fame:

今天有机会在这里跟大家见面，我感到很荣幸。我跟大家一样，是学习中国古代文学的，多年来也写过一些不象样的东西，我自己觉得在各方面都很肤浅，更谈不上有什么重要的贡献。相反，最近我看到一些年轻学者的论著，包括在座的林宇同先生的大作，觉得深受启发，得益非浅。有人说，后生可畏；可是我说，后生可敬可佩。我们这代人已经老了，不中用了。我们现在所能做的，也是我们应该做的，就是要向年轻人学习，向在座的各位学习。今天，我就是来学习的。

下面我要谈的是中国古代文学的浪漫主义色彩问题。这个问题，林宇同先生有深入、独到的研究，本来应该由林先生来谈。我的发言不过是就教于林先生，就教于各位，也可以说是抛砖引玉吧。发言中的错误不当之处，还得请大家多多批评指正。

6. Using what is provided in the parentheses, rewrite the following sentences to show humility or circumspection on the part of the speaker:

1) 月球向着地球的一面永远向着地球。（我不太懂天文学，只知道…）
2) 男人和女人的智力是一样的。（凭常识想，…应该…）
3) 老师说的是以丑为美。（我可能听错了，可是…好象…）
4) 用山水泡茶效果最好。（据说）

5) 宇宙不是无限的，岁月不是永恒的。（也许）

6) 最欣赏他的是他自己。（说不定）

7) 仇恨会演变成暴力。（多半）

8) 寂寞是不可避免的。（在某些时候）

7. Apply punctuation marks to the following passages, and then check if you are correct by referring back to the relevant texts:

1) 一对新婚夫妇的两房一厅＿＿目前让许多广州人眼红的居住条件＿＿地毯＿＿空调＿＿墙纸＿＿组合家具和高级音响＿＿应该是应有尽有了＿＿ (L.6)

2) 一个声音对我说＿＿在无限宇宙的永恒岁月中＿＿你不过是一个顷刻便化为乌有的微粒＿＿这个微粒的悲欢甚至连一丝微风＿＿一缕轻烟都算不上＿＿刹那间就会无影无踪＿＿你如此珍惜的那个小小的心灵世界＿＿究竟有何价值＿＿ (L.10)

3) 它不象汉白玉那样的细腻＿＿可以凿下刻字雕花＿＿也不象大青石那样的光滑＿＿可以供来浣纱捶布＿＿它静静地卧在那里＿＿院边的槐荫没有庇覆它＿＿花儿也不在它身边生长＿＿荒草便繁衍出来＿＿枝蔓上下＿＿慢慢地＿＿竟锈上了绿苔＿＿黑斑＿＿我们这些做孩子的＿＿也讨厌起它来＿＿曾合伙要搬走它＿＿但力气又不足＿＿虽时时咒骂它＿＿嫌弃它＿＿也无可奈何＿＿只好任它留在那里去了＿＿ (L.5)

4) 现在＿＿我国一般家庭大多采用沸水冲泡茶叶的饮茶法＿＿只有在广东＿＿福建某些地方还保留有一种以煮为主称作为＿＿功夫茶＿＿的饮茶习惯，保存了一些＿＿茶经＿＿中所介绍的煮茶方法＿＿据说＿＿用＿＿功夫茶＿＿方法煮出的茶＿＿其色泽＿＿香气＿＿味道确实要比沸水冲泡出的茶为佳＿＿ (L.12)

活学与活用

8. Answer the following questions using the expressions provided:

1) 陆羽是谁？

　　盛唐时代／对茶很有研究
　　第一部茶学巨著《茶经》／被尊奉为"茶神"
　　天资聪明／学习勤奋
　　撰写《茶经》／历时十二载

2) 你怎么简单介绍《茶经》？

　　上、中、下三卷／十节
　　内容／与茶有关的知识／各个方面
　　今天／从科学的角度／从日常生活的观点／非常亲切

3)《茶经》中怎么介绍茶的功效？

　　去除内热和烦闷／缓解头痛和疲劳
　　改进视力／消除困倦／提神／醒酒
　　长期饮用／身心愉快／思路敏捷
　　入药治病／具有疗效

4)《茶经》中怎么介绍煮茶法？

　　用水／火候／有严格的规定
　　井水／江水／山水（"乳泉"）
　　一沸／加盐
　　二沸／舀出一碗水备用／投下茶叶
　　三沸／将备用的水倒回
　　水面出现泡沫／可以饮用

5) 现在中国家庭怎么饮茶？

　　一般家庭／用沸水冲泡

在广东、福建某些地方 ／ "功夫茶" ／以煮为主

据说 ／ "功夫茶" 的色泽、香气、味道

6) 你觉得煮茶法怎么样？

用水和火候 ／ 要求很高 ／ 程序繁难

节假喜庆的时候 ／ 偶尔一试 ／ 不少乐趣

9. Using your own words, answer the following questions based on your individual opinions and experiences:

1) 介绍一下饮料的种类。你最爱喝什么饮料？为什么？

2) 你喜欢喝茶还是喝咖啡？为什么？

3) 你觉得什么饮料最有助于健康？你为什么这样认为？

4) 一个人喜欢喝什么样的饮料跟他（或她）是什么样的人有关系吗？请你至少举两个例子来说明。

5) 中国人喝的饮料跟美国人喝的饮料有什么不同？

10. You have been asked to make a presentation on a research project you have recently finished. As you prepare for the presentation, make sure that, first, the speech sounds formal using the techniques summarized in this lesson, and secondly, words and expressions are used in a way that demonstrates your sense of humility (even though you are an expert on the topic!). The presentation should be in an expository style.

VIII. 课文材料对话

A

顾　客　这儿的茶不错，色、香、味俱全。我从来没喝过这么好的茶。

服务员：先生，您可是说对了。我们 "仙茶楼" 是老字号的茶馆儿，名气大着呢。从外地来的人，没有不上这儿喝茶的。

顾　客：真是名不虚传。今日来此，终生难忘。

服务员：那先生您就请多光顾吧。我们这儿各地名茶应有尽有，就近取山水冲泡。我们老板对煮茶法也很有研究，据说他还是陆羽的后代呢。

顾　客：陆羽？就是写了《茶经》的那位"茶神爷"？

服务员：对呀，先生您看，那儿不是供着他的瓷像吗？

B

朋友甲：每逢节假喜庆，你都要煮茶，这有什么特别的意义吗？

朋友乙：倒是没什么特别的意义。之所以煮茶，不过是为了乐趣罢了。

朋友甲：程序如此繁难，有何乐趣可言？

朋友乙：正是因为程序繁难，才乐在其中啊。再说，也算不上太繁难。况且也不是非要煮茶不可。想煮才煮，其乐无穷。

朋友甲：可是对于我来说，这样的煮茶法实在是过于繁难了。我宁可躺在摇椅里，一边晃着一边喝可乐。

朋友乙：喝可乐就喝可乐，只要自得其乐就行。万一想喝茶，请随时光临寒舍好了。能为足下煮茶，将是我的荣幸。

第十三课　幽默感从何处来？

Expository essays cover a wide range of topics from explanation of concrete things to elucidation of abstract ideas. While the previous essay introduces a classic document hardly known to present-day tea-drinkers, the essay of this lesson focuses on one aspect of human behavior (sense of humor) conducive to enhancing personal image or interpersonal relations in social situations. Although both essays share the same purpose, that is, to explain or clarify things, the two authors have adopted different approaches: the author of the former essay writes in a straightforward manner introducing the *Book of Tea* point by point, whereas the author of this present essay achieves his goal by telling stories or citing self-explanatory examples. Not only do these stories and examples speak by analogy, but the author also draws analogies, such as "调味剂" and "味精," in his speech. If, as the author argues, possessing a sense of humor "enhances the taste" of one's routine life, drawing analogies in one's speech undoubtedly enhances what otherwise could be a boring conversation or explanation. In this lesson we will also review all the linguistic and rhetorical devices that we have studied in this course to help us speak and write in a vivid and effective manner.

I. 课文导读 🎧

人们多半希望自己变得<u>幽默</u> (yōumò, adj., humorous) 一点。说幽默，指的是以<u>巧妙</u> (qiǎomiào, adj., ingenious) 的语言来<u>表达</u> (biǎodá, v., express) 说话的主题。那么，一个人如何才能有幽默感呢？要做到这一点，有许多方式可以<u>借鉴</u> (jièjiàn, v., use for reference)。

<u>自嘲</u> (zìcháo, n., self-ridicule) 可以带来幽默，使陌生的心灵变得亲近。有一次，一位黑人<u>律师</u> (lùshī, n., lawyer) 对很多人讲话，听的人大部分是白人，而且<u>普遍</u> (pǔbiàn, adv., generally) 不喜欢黑人。于是这位律师一开头就说："女士们，先生们，我到这里来，是给这个地方<u>增添</u> (zēngtiān, v., add) 一点'颜色'。"听的人"哄"地笑成一片，全场的气氛就此变得很<u>融洽</u> (róngqià, adj., harmonious)。

<u>调侃</u> (tiáokǎn, n., ridicule) 也能带来幽默，使普通的事情变得充满情趣。有

301

一个人非常喜欢下棋 (xiàqí, n., playing chess)，但是下得不好，每次下棋总是输 (shū, v., lose) 给别人。有人问他比赛的情况，他回答说："第一盘 (pán, m., game) 我没赢 (yíng, v., win)，第二盘他没输，第三盘我说和 (hé, v., end in a draw) 了吧，他不肯！"这样的调侃很好笑，却并不讨厌，反而让人觉得有点儿可爱。

比喻产生的幽默能引起丰富的联想 (liánxiǎng, n., association in the mind)。一位读者给一位大作家打电话，希望见他。作家回答道："如果你吃了鸡蛋觉得味道不错，为什么一定想去认识一下那只下蛋的母鸡呢？"

有时幽默也以对抗 (duìkàng, n., confrontation) 的方式出现。一位大诗人在小路上遇到一位反对 (fǎnduì, v., oppose) 他的批评家 (pīpíngjiā, n., critic)。批评家说："我从来不给傻瓜 (shǎguā, n., fool) 让路。"大诗人却说："而我正好相反。"说完就给批评家让路，让他走了过去。

带有悬念 (xuánniàn, n., suspense) 的幽默更加浪漫。一对恋人分别了好久又见面了。男的说："我现在又爱上了一个女朋友，并准备马上结婚。"女的听后哑了似地沉默着。男的又接着说："你看，这里有她的照片。"这时他递给女的一面镜子。女的接过镜子看到自己的脸，顿时 (dùnshí, adv., immediately) 喜笑颜开。

有人说，幽默是生活的味精 (wèijīng, n., MSG)，它使人在笑声中明白很多道理。希望幽默走进我们的生活，成为我们人生的一部分。

II. 词语导学

1. Match each item on the left with an item on the right based on the character(s) you know:

1) 思想　sīxiǎng　　　　　　　n. thought
　　思绪　sīxù　　　　　　　　n. affection
　　感情　gǎnqíng　　　　　　　n. taste (in life)

情调　qíngdiào　　　　　　　n. train of thought

2) 能力　nénglì　　　　　　　　n. behavior
   行为　xíngwéi　　　　　　　 n. ability
   修养　xiūyǎng　　　　　　　 n. impressive style or manner
   气派　qìpài　　　　　　　　　n. cultivation

3) 作用　zuòyòng　　　　　　　n. interaction
   力度　lìdù　　　　　　　　　 n. role
   交往　jiāowǎng　　　　　　　n. dynamics

4) 听众　tīngzhòng　　　　　　n. meeting place
   敌意　díyì　　　　　　　　　 n. audience
   会场　huìchǎng　　　　　　　n. result of a battle
   战果　zhànguǒ　　　　　　　n. hostility

5) 求见　qiújiàn　　　　　　　v. give up
   注意　zhùyì　　　　　　　　 v. ask to see
   体会　tǐhuì　　　　　　　　　v. pay attention to
   放弃　fàngqì　　　　　　　　v. realize

6) 培养　péiyǎng　　　　　　　v. foster
   感受　gǎnshòu　　　　　　　v. accompany
   发表　fābiǎo　　　　　　　　v. feel
   伴随　bànsuí　　　　　　　　v. deliver (a formal speech)

7) 增强　zēngqiáng　　　　　　v. disperse
   沟通　gōutōng　　　　　　　v. reinforce
   驱散　qūsàn　　　　　　　　v. communicate

8) 著名　zhùmíng　　　　　　　adj. antagonistic
   平凡　píngfán　　　　　　　 adj. ordinary
   呆板　dāibǎn　　　　　　　　adj. famous
   对立　duìlì　　　　　　　　　adj. dull

2. Study the following chess language:

1) 棋　　qí　　　n. chess　　　　2) 下棋　xiàqí　 v. play chess
   棋盘　qípán　n. chessboard　　　　杀　　shā　　 v. fight

棋子	qízi	n. chessman	让	ràng	v. give ground
棋谱	qípǔ	n. chess manual	赢	yíng	v. win
棋艺	qíyì	n. skill in playing chess	输	shū	v. lose
棋迷	qímí	n. chess fan	和	hé	v. end in a draw

3. Guess the meanings of the following expressions:

1) 开场白　　　（白: bái, n., statement）

2) 调味剂　　　（调: tiáo, v., adjust）

3) 恋棋如命　　（compare: 爱财如命, 嗜酒如命）

4) 屡战屡败　　（屡: lǚ, adv., repeatedly）

5) 耐人寻味　　（耐: nài, v., be able to bear or endure）

6) 情笃意切　　（笃: dǔ, adj., sincere; 切: qiè, adj., passionate）

7) 久别重逢　　（重: chóng, adv., again）

8) 喜上眉梢　　（眉梢: méishāo, n., tip of an eyebrow）

III. 课文

幽默感从何处来？　　杨东鲁

在人际交往中，人们大都希望自己变得幽默一点。那么，如何才能具有幽默感呢？这就要求具有一定的文化知识和思想修养，在人际交往中要尽量让自己轻松、洒脱，平时要注意培养自己生动活泼的表达能力。

精彩的幽默，不在于语言的多少和行为的气派，而在于是否以巧妙的方式表达了主题。要做到这一点，有许多方式可以借鉴——

自嘲式的幽默让人感受到谦逊和豁达，能使紧张的气氛变得轻松，能使陌生的心灵变得亲近。美国著名黑人律师约翰·马克在发表《要解放黑人奴隶》时，听众大部分是白人，且普遍对黑人怀有敌意。于是，他放弃了原来的"开场白"，讲道："女士们，先生们：我到这里来，与其说是发表讲话，倒不如说是给这场合增添点'颜色'。"听众大笑，对立情绪被笑声驱散，此后的几个小时，会场秩序很好。这里，幽默起了沟通感情、融洽气氛的作用。

调侃式的幽默使平凡的事情变得富有情趣，是呆板生活中的调味剂。一位棋迷，棋艺不高，但恋棋如命，与人下棋屡战屡败，但屡败屡战。有人问他战果，答曰："第一盘我没赢，第二盘他没输，第三盘我没有让他，杀得十分激烈，最后，我说和了算了，他还不肯！"这死爱面子的调侃让人捧腹，却并不讨厌，言语中透出一股调皮的可爱。

比喻式的幽默能让人体会到学识的渊博，联想的丰富，把你的思绪带到一个广阔的空间。一位读者打电话求见《围城》的作者钱钟书老先生。钱老回答道："假如你吃了鸡蛋觉得味道不错，何必想去认识一下那只下蛋的母鸡呢？"

对抗式的幽默体现出机智与敏捷。一天，德国大诗人歌德在公园里散步，在一条狭窄的小路上遇到了一位反对他的批评家。这位傲慢无礼的批评家说："你知道吗？我这个人从来不给傻瓜让路。"哥德却说："而我恰恰相反。"说完闪身让批评家走过去。这种对抗性的幽默耐人寻味，且增强了对抗的力度。

悬念式的幽默更富有生活的情调与浪漫。马克思与夫人燕妮恋爱时就情笃意切。久别重逢，马克思异常高兴。他想给燕妮一个悬念，却说："我现在又爱上了个女友，并准备马上结婚。"燕妮听后沉默不语。马克思继续说："你看，这里有她的照片。"说着，马克思递给燕妮一面镜子："照片在这上面。"燕妮接过镜子，不见照片，却透过镜面见到了自己的芳容，顿时喜上眉梢。

有人说，幽默是生活的味精。幽默使人在笑声中得到启迪。愿幽默走进我们的生活，伴随我们的人生。

（选自《人民日报》（海外版）１９９６年８月２３日）

繁體字課文

幽默感從何處來？　　楊東魯

　　在人際交往中，人們大都希望自己變得幽默一點。那麼，如何才能具有幽默感呢？這就要求具有一定的文化知識和思想修養，在人際交往中要盡量讓自己輕鬆、灑脫，平時要注意培養自己生動活潑的表達能力。

　　精彩的幽默，不在於語言的多少和行為的氣派，而在於是否以巧妙的方式表達了主題。要做到這一點，有許多方式可以借鑒——

　　自嘲式的幽默讓人感受到謙遜和豁達，能使緊張的氣氛變得輕鬆，能使陌生的心靈變得親近。美國著名黑人律師約翰・馬克在發表《要解放黑人奴隸》時，聽眾大部份是白人，且普遍對黑人懷有敵意。於是，他放棄了原來的“開場白”，講道：“女士們，先生們：我到這裡來，與其說是發表講話，倒不如說是給這場合增添點‘顏色’。”聽眾大笑，對立情緒被笑聲驅散，此後的幾個小時，會場秩序很好。這裡，幽默起了溝通感情、融洽氣氛的作用。

　　調侃式的幽默使平凡的事情變得富有情趣，是呆板生活中的調味劑。一位棋迷，棋藝不高，但戀棋如命，與人下棋屢戰屢敗，但屢敗屢戰。有人問他戰果，答曰：“第一盤我沒贏，第二盤他沒輸，第三盤我沒有讓他，殺得十分激烈，最後，我說和了算了，他還不肯！”這死愛面子的調侃讓人捧腹，卻並不討厭，言語中透出一股調皮的可愛。

　　比喻式的幽默能讓人體會到學識的淵博，聯想的豐富，把你的思緒帶到一個廣闊的空間。一位讀者打電話求見《圍城》的作者錢鍾書老先生。錢老回答道："假如你吃了雞蛋覺得味道不錯，何必想去認識一下那隻下蛋的母雞呢？"

　　對抗式的幽默體現出機智與敏捷。一天，德國大詩人歌德在公園裡散步，在一條狹窄的小路上遇到了一位反對他的批評家。這位傲慢無禮的批評家說："你知道嗎？我這個人從來不給傻瓜讓路。"哥德卻說："而我恰恰相反。"說完閃身讓批評家走過去。這種對抗性的幽默耐人尋味，且增強了對抗的力度。

　　懸念式的幽默更富有生活的情調與浪漫。馬克思與夫人燕妮戀愛時就情篤意切。久別重逢，馬克思異常高興。他想給燕妮一個懸念，卻說："我現在又愛上了個女友，並準備馬上結婚。"燕妮聽後沉默不語。馬克思繼續說："你看，這裡有她的照片。"說著，馬克思遞給燕妮一面鏡子："照片在這上面。"燕妮接過鏡子，不見照片，卻透過鏡面見到了自己的芳容，頓時喜上眉梢。

　　有人說，幽默是生活的味精。幽默使人在笑聲中得到啟迪。願幽默走進我們的生活，伴隨我們的人生。

思考題

　　幽默感从何处来？有哪些"巧妙的方式"能使你变得幽默而具有吸引力？

IV.新词语

人际	rénjì	adj.	interpersonal
大都	dàdū	adv.	mostly
尽量	jìnliàng	adv.	as much as possible
轻松	qīngsōng	adj.	relaxed

洒脱	sǎtuō	adj.	unrestrained
活泼	huópō	adj.	lively
精彩	jīngcǎi	adj.	brilliant
谦逊	qiānxùn	n.	modesty
豁达	huòdá	n.	open-mindedness
紧张	jǐnzhāng	adj.	tense
约翰·马克	Yuēhàn·Mǎkè	n.	John Mark, an American lawyer
解放	jiěfàng	v.	liberate
奴隶	núlì	n.	slave
怀有	huáiyǒu	v.	maintain
与其	yǔqí	conj.	(see Part V.6)
场合	chǎnghé	n.	occasion
秩序	zhìxù	n.	order
富有	fùyǒu	v.	be rich in
曰	yuē	v.	say; 说
激烈	jīliè	adj.	vehement
捧腹	pěngfù	v.	split one's sides laughing
透	tòu	v.	reveal
股	gǔ	m.	as in 一股泉水, 一股香味
调皮	tiáopí	adj.	mischievous
渊博	yuānbó	n.	erudition
广阔	guǎngkuò	adj.	vast
《围城》	Wéichéng	n.	*Fortress Beseiged* by 钱钟书
钱钟书	Qián Zhōngshū	n.	a contemporary Chinese writer and scholar (1910-1998)
何必	hébì	adv.	why (see Part V.10)
机智	jīzhì	n.	quick-wittedness
敏捷	mǐnjié	n.	quick-mindedness

狭窄	xiázhǎi	adj.	narrow
无礼	wúlǐ	adj.	rude
恰恰	qiàqià	adv.	exactly
闪身	shǎnshēn	v.	dodge
燕妮	Yànní	n.	Jenny von Westphalen, Karl Marx's wife
异常	yìcháng	adv.	unusually
芳容	fāngróng	n.	beautiful face (honorific)
启迪	qǐdí	n.	inspiration

V. 词语与句型

1. 不在于···，而在于···　　　　　精彩的幽默，<u>不在于</u>语言的···，<u>而在于</u>是否···

在于 means "to lie in" or "because of." Placed within the framework of 不···，而···, the whole structure means that something (indicated by the subject) "does not lie in..., but lies in...," or something happens "not because of..., but because of...." What follows 不在于 and 而在于 respectively is an alternative-question structure.

一个人幸福与否<u>不在于</u>有多少财富，<u>而在于</u>精神世界丰富不丰富。

生命的意义<u>不在于</u>我们自己通过努力获得了什么，<u>而在于</u>我们的努力为后世留下了什么。

醉翁 ("a drunk man") 之意<u>不在（于）</u>酒，<u>而在（于）</u>山水之间。

2. 要 V　　　　　　　　　　　　　<u>要</u>做到这一点，有许多方式可以借鉴。

要 introduces a verbal phrase and together they indicate a purpose to be achieved. The phrase is followed by a pause indicated by a comma.

<u>要</u>体验饮茶的乐趣，最好试一试"功夫茶"。
<u>要</u>提高自己的思想修养，一个人必须多读书、多思考。
<u>要</u>使世界充满意义，人人都得看重自己的悲欢。

3. 使 Obj V　　　　　　　　　　自嘲式的幽默…，能使紧张的气氛变得轻松…

Translated into English, this structure means "to make somebody do something" or "to cause something to happen." In this sense, 使 can be replaced by its less formal equivalent 让 or more formal equivalent 令.

《茶经》使陆羽成为 "茶神"。

读书使我们避恶而向善。

虚心("modesty")使人进步，骄傲("arrogance")使人落后。

4. V 有 N　　　　　　　　　　听众大部分是白人，且普遍对黑人怀有敌意。

The verb before 有 can be omitted without changing the basic meaning of the phrase. However, with it the phrase sounds more formal and has further connotations depending on the verb.

人生只能经历自己拥有的那一份欣悦和苦难。　(own)

对于 "柿把儿" 老师，学生们心中都怀有一份敬意。　(cherish)

茶叶具有提神、醒酒等许多功效。　(possess)

An "Adj 有 N" phrase is also possible. For example:

幽默使人变得富有情趣。　(be rich in)

5. 与其…,(倒/还)不如…　　　　…，与其说是发表讲话，倒不如说是…

This is a rather formal expression, used to indicate one's choice after weighing the pros and the cons of an option. What follows 与其 is the option rejected or negated by the speaker, who opts for the option introduced by 倒不如 or 还不如.

与其读坏书,还不如不读书。

与其两只眼睛都长在左边, 倒不如一只长在左边, 一只长在右边, 以便左右兼顾。

与其在没有空气的屋子里绞痛眉头,不如到绿水青山中去享受生活。

6. 大 V　　　　　　　　　　听众大笑, 对立情绪被笑声驱散, …

310

大 here serves as an adverb, modifying the action indicated by the verb. It means that one does something free from restraint. The verbs it modifies are typically monosyllabic, such as 哭, 笑, 吃, 喝, 谈, 唱, etc.

听到这个不幸的消息，她顿时放声大哭起来。

在这篇文章里，作者大谈宇宙的生成和变化。

大吃大喝对健康有害。

7. 起(…的)作用　　　　　　　这里，幽默起了沟通感情、融洽气氛的作用。

In English the phrase means "to play a role (in)."

我的话对他不起作用，还是你去跟他说吧。

一本好书可以起劝善的作用。

父母在孩子成长的过程中起很大的作用。

8. 算了　　　　　　　　　　最后，我说和了算了，他还不肯！

算 by itself means "to count" or "to reckon." 算了 here indicates that the speaker has decided to let the matter rest.

算了，不跟你多说了。

让那块丑石留在我家门前算了。

煮茶太繁难，泡茶算了。

9. 死(不) V　　　　　　　　这死爱面子的调侃让人捧腹，…

The adverb 死 here indicates the extent to which one is determined to do or not to do something represented by the verb. It stresses the degree of the determination and has actually little to do with its original meaning of "death."

有的人借钱请客，真是死要面子活受罪。

瘦子躲在船上，抓住船桨死不放手。

姑娘来打探结果，没想到赵老师死不开口。

311

10. 何必…呢？　　　　　　　假如…，何必想去认识一下那只下蛋的母鸡呢？

This is a rhetorical question meaning that there is no need to do something.

这本书错误百出，何必读它呢？

你何必跟她开这样的玩笑呢？万一她误解了怎么办？

有人对我说：何必如此珍惜你那个小小的心灵世界呢？

11. 从来不/没 V　　　　　　　　　　　我这个人从来不给傻瓜让路。

从来 means "always" or "at all times," and therefore 从来不 and 从来没 means "never" or "never in the past." The phrase in both its positive and negative forms implies a strong sense of will on the part of the subject of the sentence.

女人想哭就哭，想笑就笑，从来不怕被人小看。

我从来没想过要充当世界和他人的中心。

我们的努力从来没有白费，也永远不会白费。

12. 恰恰 (adv.)　　　　　　　　　哥德却说："而我恰恰相反。"

This means "just" or "exactly," and its colloquial versions are 正好 and 刚好.

参加演讲会的，恰恰是一百人。

医药检验恰恰证明这剂药方具有疗效。

事实恰恰相反。如果没有人的存在，宇宙便失去了意义。

13. 愿…　　　　　　　　　愿幽默走进我们的生活，伴随我们的人生。

愿 means "to be willing to" or "to prefer," as in "我愿为这一事业努力工作" and "我不愿跟那个人谈话。" Used at the beginning of a sentence, however, it introduces a wish or a longing. In this sense it is used in the same way as "may" in English.

愿我们今后的生活更加美好！

愿中美两国人民的友谊 ("friendship") 万古长存。

VI.语言知识与技巧

1. Same word, double meaning

In this essay, the author cites five different stories to show the effect of humor at social occasions. One of these stories concerns John Mark, whose opening remarks in a speech to a somewhat hostile audience were filled with humor:

> 女士们，先生们：我到这里来，与其说是发表讲话，倒不如说给这场合增添点"<u>颜色</u>"。

The word 颜色 here has a double meaning. It is what Chinese speakers call 双关语 (*shuāngguānyǔ*, n., pun), with one reference to its literal meaning, "color," and the other reference to its extended meaning, John's dark skin. The use of pun helps John to achieve a humorous or even sarcastic effect. By deliberately referring to his presence as "adding color," he seemingly "pokes fun" at himself. In reality, however, he intends to produce laughter among the audience and by doing so sets up a rapport with the people in the crowd.

There are two types of 双关语: one plays on meaning, as is the case with John Mark's example, and the other plays on pronunciation. The great number of homophones in Chinese makes it very easy to "pun" on a word. Many of what are called 歇后语 (*xiēhòuyǔ*, n., a two-part allegorical saying in which the first part normally simulates a riddle, and the second part provides an answer to this riddle) are the result of this rhetorical device. In the following examples, the underlined part represents the speaker's real meaning:

> 泥菩萨过河—自身难保。（punning on meaning）
> "A Buddha of mud wades through the river--<u>he can hardly protect himself</u>."

> 山顶滚石头—实打实（石打石）。（punning on pronunciation）
> "Rocks fall over the hill--<u>real stuff</u> (piling up one layer of rocks after another)."

> 老虎拉车—谁敢（谁赶）？（punning on pronunciation）
> "The cart is pulled by a tiger--<u>who dares</u> (who steers it)?"

> 飞机上挂水壶—高水平（高水瓶）。（punning on pronunciation）
> "A water bottle hangs in an airplane--<u>high standard</u> (a high water bottle)."

Do you like this component of the Chinese language?

2. Making statements vivid: a summary

The best way to make a statement vivid is through conjuring up mental images in the minds of the listeners. One should limit one's words to a minimum and simply rely on the concrete pictures to convey what one actually wants to say. This belief in the power of suggestion accounts for the extensive use of metaphors and other figurative expressions by native speakers of Chinese. They are used at the text level, as is exemplified by the texts of Lesson Five (seemingly about the "ugly stone") and Lesson Eight (seemingly about the "position of the eyes"). They are also used extensively at the word and syntactic levels by means of some or all of the following techniques that we have studied in this course.

1) Drawing analogies (Lesson 3)

In drawing analogies, the comparison between the "vehicle" and the "tenor" can be either suggested or openly indicated. According to some scholars, the second type of analogies are more suggestive than the first because, without such designative words as 如, 像, 似, 若, and 仿佛, they leave more room for the creative imagination of the listener or the reader. However, it seems that native speakers of Chinese show no preference for one way or the other and use all types of analogies widely and frequently. The following are some examples from the texts we have studied in the second half of this course:

倘若是两只眼都长在左边，那就只好<u>像螃蟹一样横行</u>，一个劲儿向左跨大步。 (L.8)

那么，我一只眼长在右边，一只眼长在左边，平均分配，左右兼顾，<u>像鸟一样</u>，该是万事大吉了吧？ (L.8)

在绵延不绝的<u>黄粱梦</u>里，一定也会有喜欢我并且和我有着相同心思的女子吧。 (L.9)

在无限宇宙的永恒岁月中，你不过<u>是</u>一个顷刻便化为乌有的<u>微粒</u>。 (L.10)

假如你吃了<u>鸡蛋</u>觉得味道不错，何必想去认识一下那只下蛋的<u>母鸡</u>呢？ (L.13)

调侃式的幽默使平凡的事情变得富有情趣，<u>是</u>呆板生活中的<u>调味剂</u>。 (L.13)

幽默<u>是</u>生活的<u>味精</u>。 (L.13)

314

2) Personification (Lesson 3)

Personification also represents an effective way for one to express oneself suggestively and vividly. By investing things with human characteristics, personification brings about vivid pictures in the reader/listener's mind.

不管<u>时光</u>如何<u>飞驰</u>, …, 大自然里有些事物却是永远不变的。 (L.9)

只要一想到推开那一个小屋的门, 便有<u>阳光跳跃着</u>来<u>迎接</u>, …, 我的心,便有了慰藉。 (L.6)

我常常遗憾我家门前的那块丑石呢: <u>它</u>黑黝黝地<u>卧</u>在那里, 牛似的模样(L.5)

我怨恨<u>它（丑石）</u>这么多年竟会<u>默默</u>地<u>忍受着</u>这一切? (L.5)

3) Exaggeration (Lesson 4)

Exaggeration is often interwoven with analogy. In other words, exaggeration is often reflected in the analogy made by the speaker.

<u>男人走五米路同三个人握手</u>, 随时准备对上司说: "是是是"。 (L.7)

有一半男人自以为得意地在高高的大楼里<u>绞痛眉头</u>, 其实干的都是些谁也不需要的蠢事。 (L.7)

而且女人能<u>一眼看透</u>面前的男人, <u>如X光胸透那样</u>简单明了。 (L.7)

你不过是一个<u>顷刻便化为乌有</u>的<u>微粒</u>, 这个微粒的悲欢甚至连<u>一丝微风、一缕轻烟都算不上</u>, 刹那间就会<u>无影无踪</u>。 (L.10)

4) Use of numbers (Lesson 7)

Numbers can make things more concrete, and thus can create vivid pictures in the mind of the listener or reader. Take the phrase 三心二意 for example. There is only "one heart" in a human body, and normally a person has only "one will" when he or she sets his/her mind on (doing) something. By saying that one has "three hearts" and "two wills," the speaker vividly expresses the idea that this individual is indecisive and/or irresponsible.

5) Onomatopoeia (Lesson 2)

Onomatopoeic words imitate the natural sounds of things, beings, and actions in the natural world. The whole point of using onomatopoeia is to present things as they are, to shorten or eliminate the distance between the observer and the observed so that the former can see things clearly and vividly.

3. *Speaking courteously: being circumspect (2)*

The Chinese people attach great importance to proper social etiquette. The long-standing assumption is that each individual must behave according to his or her role (i.e., 名, such as parent, child, boss, employee, friend, etc.), which is hierarchical in nature and a key factor for the social inequities still prevalent in contemporary China. This being the case, one must speak appropriately to elders and one's superiors at work by using polite language that honors the listener and humbles the speaker. In addition to age and hierarchy in work relations, the fame of the individual one talks to or about in public also commands respect. For example, Qian Zhongshu is a world-famous literary scholar in China. Therefore, in the essay under study, the author refers to him as "钱老" (老 as in 老前辈, a nomenclature used to address an individual who has made great contributions in an academic field or to a noble human cause). The same is true with Karl Marx, still an idol in the minds of the Chinese people. Out of respect for Marx, the author refers to his wife's beauty as "芳容." Polite language is particularly expected to be used on formal social and professional occasions. At such times, formality is maintained, and the courtesy demonstrated by both parties in a conversation helps them gain respect and trust for each other.

There is a set of words and expressions commonly used by native speakers to elevate others and humble oneself. Referred to as 敬辞 (*jìngcí*, term of respect) and 谦辞 (*qiāncí*, humble word), they are so popularly used that they have almost become *clichés* (客套话, *kètàohuà*). Review Part VI.3 and Exercise 7 of Lesson Four for some of these formulaic sayings. Other such expressions are:

敬辞:　　贵姓，尊姓大名
　　　　　贵国，贵公司
　　　　　令尊，令堂
　　　　　见教，有请
　　　　　请问，保重

谦辞:　　敝人，敝处
　　　　　恕我冒昧，献丑，见笑

316

过奖，不敢当

VII. 练习

词语与句型

1. Write out the four-character expressions based on the text:

    1) cultural knowledge   _____

    2) ideological cultivation   _____

    3) interpersonal contact   _____

    4) ability for expression   _____

    5) antagonistic feeling   _____

    6) arrogant and rude   _____

    7) be rich in feelings and taste   _____

    8) love playing chess as one loves one's life   _____

    9) exactly the opposite   _____

   10) be able to bear thought (afford food for thought)   _____

   11) sincere and passionate affection   _____

   12) reunite after a long separation   _____

   13) keep silent (without saying anything)   _____

   14) joy climbing to the tips of the eyebrows
       (be radiant with joy)   _____

2. Complete the sentences with the designated expressions:

    1) 幽默在呆板的生活中 (to play the role of condiment)。

    2) 不能让 (to maintain hostility against the U.S.) 的人进入美国。

    3) 精彩的幽默常常 (to make people split their sides laughing)。

4) 那位著名的律师一下车，大家就都 (to make way for him) 。

5) 轻松的言语 (to make strange hearts become intimately close)。

6) 小男孩调皮的笑容 (to let people feel his quick-wittedness)。

7) 现代社会要求我们 (to foster the ability of interacting with people)。

8) 笑声可以 (to disperse antagonistic feelings)，使气氛变得融洽。

3. Expand the phrases into sentences by following the examples:

1) 问题<u>不在于</u>你看不看书，<u>而在于</u>你看什么样的书。

　　生命的意义 / 现实的世界 / 精神的世界

　　生活的乐趣 / 权力和地位 / 生活本身

　　读书人的幸福 / 读书本身 / 读书所起的正面效果

　　煮茶的乐趣 / 茶的色香味 / 煮茶过程的奇妙

2) <u>要</u>利于前进，眼睛只能长在脸上。

　　有家的感受 / 屋子里 / 少不了阳光

　　活得有意义 / 我们 / 不能不热爱生命

　　学好汉语 / 大家 / 应该重视声调

　　使自己情趣高雅 / 你 / 就得趋避凡俗

3) 读书<u>使</u>人变得幸福。

　　饮茶 / 人 / 变得健康

　　眼睛长在脑后 / 前进 / 变得困难

　　人类 / 宇宙的存在 / 获得了意义

　　坏天气 / 人们 / 为她的安危担心

4) 幽默感具<u>有</u>改善气氛的作用。

　　茶叶 / 具 / 很多功效

　　那儿的人 / 对我们 / 怀 / 敌意

　　这些学生 / 持 / 英国护照

具 / 阅读能力的人 / 拥 / 两个世界

5) 我们<u>与其</u>闷在家里，<u>倒不如</u>出去享受风雨和阳光。

　　石匠 / 用这块丑石 / 去河滩捎一块石头回来

　　赵老师 / 朝政界发展 / 留在学校教书

　　胖子 / 跳入水中 / 留在船上

　　有空的人 / 干些谁也不需要的蠢事 / 读几本好书

6) 姑娘对他<u>大</u>喝一声："去你的'是吧'吧！"

　　她一个人关在屋子里 / 哭 / 喊

　　一大批陌生人在院子里 / 吵 / 闹

　　你们 / 可不必为我担心

　　他喝醉了酒 / 出洋相

7) 茶叶起缓解疲劳<u>的作用</u>。

　　好书 / 使人向善

　　陆羽 / 茶学研究引路人

　　人造卫星上天 / 推动科学发展

　　阳光 / 促使（"prompt"）万物生长

8) 那块丑石太重没法搬，让它留在我家门前<u>算了</u>。

　　这份稿件不能用 / 退还给作者

　　你做不了现代人 / 还是不做

　　他自认为很伟大很了不起 / 就让他去得意

　　让我们只留下美好的回忆 / 把痛苦都忘了

9) 他明知自己错了，却<u>死</u>不认错。

　　她很丑 / 却 / 爱打扮

　　他们没钱请客 / 但又 / 要面子

　　这些人走错了路 / 可还是 / 不回头

　　他知道姑娘来打探结果 / 可就是 / 不开口

10) 这种药没有疗效，<u>何必</u>再服用<u>呢</u>？

　　那<u>些</u>人如此卑鄙奸诈 / 跟他们打交道

　　你自己已经够忙了 / 多管闲事

　　这本书只要翻阅一下就可以了 / 花很多时间去看

　　冰块自己会溶化 / 把它们放在火上烤

11) 她<u>从来不</u>喜欢这儿的天气。

　　我 / 同意 / 人生如梦的说法

　　心灵纯洁的人 / 和暴力结缘

　　她<u>从来没</u>喜欢<u>过</u>这儿的天气。

　　许多人的不幸 / 得到 / 补偿

　　这<u>些</u>外国人 / 见识 / 中国的饮茶风俗

12) 您的大作很多人不知道，<u>而</u>我<u>恰恰</u>拜读过。

　　煮茶法对用水和火候有严格的的规定 / 而 / 我 / 都学过

　　刚才你谈到鲁迅的批判精神 / 而 / 这 / 也是我想说的话

　　闭着眼说瞎话的人应该不多 / 但 / 这样的人 / 不少

　　有人认为这方面的研究缺少价值 / 但 / 事实 / 相反

13) <u>愿</u>世界变得更美好。

　　你 / 早日康复 ("get well")

　　地球 / 不再变暖

　　我们的事业 / 越来越兴旺 ("flourishing")

　　美中两国人民 / 世世代代友好相处

<u>语言知识与技巧</u>

4. Match the first part of an allegorical saying in the left column with its second part in the right column:

A. Pay attention to how the description in the first part contributes to the idea in the second part:

1) 画上的苹果　　　　　____　a. 说变就变

2) 老虎打架　　　　　　____　b. 纸上谈兵

3) 孩子的脸　　　　　　____　c. 好看不好吃

4) 长了三只手　　　　　____　d. 嘴硬心软

5) 棋盘上的英雄　　　　____　e. 有去无回

6) 跳进黄河洗不清　　　____　f. 劝不得

7) 火车上放电影　　　　____　g. 痛的是自己的脚

8) 生气踢石头　　　　　____　h. 爱偷

9) 肉包子打狗　　　　　____　i. 小题大作

10) 做梦娶媳妇　　　　　____　j. 是非难分

11) 刀子嘴豆腐心　　　　____　k. 走着瞧

12) 杀鸡用牛刀　　　　　____　l. 一场空欢喜

B. Do the same with the following phrases as for A, but also note how the puns play on pronunciation:

1) 出太阳下雨　　　　　____　a. 老实（老十）

2) 苍蝇飞进花园里　　　____　b. 不用他了（不用踏了）

3) 老九的兄弟　　　　　____　c. 忘光了（望光了）

4) 石头人开口　　　　　____　d. 假情（假晴）

5) 油画里卷国画　　　　____　e. 装疯（装蜂）

6) 和尚的脑袋　　　　　____　f. 慌啦（荒啦）

7) 自行车下坡　　　　　____　g. 话中有话（画中有画）

8) 夜里看电灯　　　　　____　h. 没法（没发）

9) 澡堂搬家　　　　　　____　i. 说实话（说石话）

10) 心里头长草　　　　　____　j. 不让人喜（不让人洗）

5. Complete the sentences by

A. drawing different analogies:

1) 他凶狠地盯着我，眼光象<u>两把刀</u>。

他凶狠地盯着我，眼光象 ＿＿＿＿＿＿＿＿＿＿＿＿。

2) 山没有水，好比<u>人没有眼睛</u>。

山没有水，好比 ＿＿＿＿＿＿＿＿＿＿＿＿＿＿。

3) 平静的湖面犹如<u>一张摊开的饼</u>。

平静的湖面犹如 ＿＿＿＿＿＿＿＿＿＿＿＿＿。

4) 好书使蠢事仿佛<u>冰块烤在火上一样渐渐溶化</u>。

好书使蠢事仿佛 ＿＿＿＿＿＿＿＿＿＿＿＿＿＿。

5) 教师是<u>一支蜡烛，牺牲自己，却照亮了学生</u>。

教师是 ＿＿＿＿＿＿＿＿＿＿＿＿＿＿＿＿。

6) 十六岁的她，成了<u>一朵花</u>。

十六岁的她，成了 ＿＿＿＿＿＿＿＿＿＿＿。

7) 姑娘<u>心灵的窗户一下子打开了</u>，她不再感到痛苦。

姑娘 ＿＿＿＿＿＿＿＿＿＿＿＿＿，她不再感到痛苦。

8) 一个只敢<u>在澡盆里学游泳</u>的人，永远也体验不到奋斗的乐趣。

一个 ＿＿＿＿＿＿＿＿＿＿＿的人，永远也体验不到奋斗的乐趣。

B. using different personifications:

1) 这些<u>稿件</u>在桌子上一<u>躺</u>就是三个月。

这本书 ＿＿＿＿＿＿＿＿＿＿＿＿＿＿＿＿＿。

2) 这台<u>石磨</u>已经转了一天一夜，它<u>太累了</u>，真想<u>停下来歇口气</u>。

这座屋子＿＿＿＿＿＿＿＿＿＿＿＿＿＿＿＿。

3) 山腰的<u>松树一棵棵站得笔直</u>，似乎永远也<u>不知道疲倦</u>。

　　路旁的鲜花 _____。

4) 他心中的<u>遗憾一天天长大</u>，<u>压得他喘不过气来</u>。

　　她心中的寂寞 _____。

C. exaggerating:

1) 那条路<u>长得没个完</u>，好象<u>永远也走不到头</u>。

　　那座山 _____。

2) 这两个棋迷只要一坐下来，就能<u>三天三夜不吃饭不睡觉</u>。

　　这两个影迷 _____。

3) 猎人掩在大树后面，<u>满身是眼睛</u>，<u>满身是耳朵</u>。

　　批评家 _____。

4) 他那宽广的胸怀里<u>装得下五湖四海</u>，<u>装得下千军万马</u>。

　　她那机智的头脑里 _____。

6. Fill in the blanks

A. with appropriate sound words from the list given:

叽叽，沙沙，砰砰，呜呜，哗哗，呼呼，嗒嗒嗒，汪汪汪，喀嚓喀嚓
丁冬丁冬，丁零丁零，啪嗒啪嗒，轰隆轰隆

1) 楼上传来一阵 _____ 的笑声。

2) 门外吹着 _____ 的北风，到处是一片白色的世界。

3) _____ 的雨声让我很快进入了梦乡。

4) 一阵 _____ 的敲门声把我吵醒。

5) 小鸟在鸟巢里发出 _____ 的叫声。

6) 随着 _____ 的叫声，火车 _____ 地开进了车站。

7) 他们手中的照相机 ＿＿＿＿＿＿＿＿ 地响着。

8) 满街都是自行车 ＿＿＿＿＿＿＿ 的铃声。

9) 门铃 ＿＿＿＿＿＿＿ 地响起来，客人到了。

10) 她穿着拖鞋 ＿＿＿＿＿＿＿＿ 地走过来。

11) 在电脑房里只听到一片 ＿＿＿＿＿＿＿＿ 敲打键盘的声音。

12) 周围的狗都 ＿＿＿＿＿＿＿＿ 地叫了起来。

B. with appropriate numerals:

1) 他＿＿心想赢棋，所以下得很认真。

2) 这件事，你得＿＿思而行。

3) 张律师的演说＿＿分成功。

4) 她放下镜子，＿＿话不说，走了出去。

5) 这件事，＿＿言＿＿语说不清楚。

6) 同学们来自＿＿面＿＿方。

7) 人太多，＿＿手＿＿脚做不好事。

8) 这些＿＿颜＿＿色的药片究竟能治什么病？

9) 他们经历了＿＿死＿＿生，终于从外层空间回到地球。

10) 象他这样优秀的人才，真是＿＿里挑＿＿。

11) 这盘棋，我＿＿ ＿＿没想到会输给你。

12) 你一定要＿＿方＿＿计地找到这位大诗人。

7. Underline the words and phrases that honor others or humble oneself:

1) A: 请问您贵姓？
   B: 免贵姓王。

2) A. 知道您贵体欠安，大家都说要来看望。

B:不敢当。我过几天就回去上班了，还是不要惊动大家吧。

3) A:有请令尊令堂在方便的时候光临寒舍。

B:多谢。家父家母早有此意，一定会来贵府拜访。

4) A:最近拜读您的大作，受益非浅。

B:见笑，见笑。拙文一定有不少疏漏，还请多多指教。

5) A:恕我冒昧，令郎学习钢琴多久了？

B:小儿从六岁就开始学琴，今天在这里献丑，就是为了见教于各位。

6) A:贵公司在上海大展宏图，听说近来有不少建树。

B:过奖了。敝公司根基浅薄，最近只是小有进展而已。

活学与活用

8. Answer the following questions using the expressions provided:

1) 怎样才能具有幽默感？

文化知识／思想修养

在人际交往中／轻松、洒脱

平时／注意培养／生动活泼的表达能力

2) 精彩的幽默靠什么来实现？

不在于／语言的多少／行为的气派

而在于／以巧妙的方式／表达主题

3) 黑人律师约翰·马克如何对白人听众运用幽默？

我到这里来

与其说是／发表讲话

倒不如说是／增添点"颜色"

4) 钱钟书老先生如何对一位读者运用他的幽默感？

假如／吃了鸡蛋／味道不错

何必／认识／下蛋的母鸡

5) 幽默有什么用处？

生活／味精（调味剂）

笑声／启迪

9. Using your own words, answer the following questions based on your own opinions and experiences:

1) 我们为什么必须具有人际交往的能力？你觉得在人际交往中最重要的是什么？

2) 你经历过紧张的气氛和对立的情绪吗？说一下当时的情况，并说明最后问题是怎么解决的。

3) 你会下棋吗？你喜欢下哪种棋？下得好不好？你经常跟什么人下棋？

4) 你喜欢有幽默感的人吗？你知道中国式的幽默和美国式的幽默有什么不同吗？

5) 有人说中国人爱面子，你同意吗？请举例说明。你觉得美国人爱面子吗？也请举例说明。

10. Write an essay on a human characteristic that you do not have but you would like to acquire. Explain the benefits of having this human characteristic point by point. You may want to cite stories about people who do have this characteristic to make your explanation concrete. You may also want to use the rhetorical techniques summarized in this lesson to make your stories vivid.

VIII. 课文材料对话 🎧

A

学生：老师，我很希望自己变得幽默一点。我该如何努力才能具有幽默感呢？

老师：要我回答你的问题，你得先告诉我什么是幽默。

学生：有人说："幽默是生活的调味品。"幽默不就是"有趣、好笑"吗？

老师：与其说幽默是"有趣、好笑"，还不如说幽默是通过生动活泼的语言来达到人际交往中的一种目的。精彩的幽默在于以巧妙的方式来表达说话的主题，而不在于语言的多少和行为的气派。

学生：那么，老师，我怎么才能学会这些巧妙的方式，让自己的谈话显得轻松、洒脱呢？

老师：这就要求一定的文化知识和思想修养，也需要在平时注意培养自己生动活泼的表达能力。

B

甲：这件事，我看你是"做梦吃西瓜——心里想得美"。王思国怎么会肯帮你的忙呢？

乙：他现在大做生意大发财。我从来没找过他，可他总该记得我这个老同学吧。

甲：谁都知道，王思国是"铁公鸡——一毛不拔"。他要是肯帮忙，那可真是"公鸡下蛋——怪事"。

乙：你的意思我懂。我想让他帮忙，也是因为没有别的办法。

甲：反正他这个人"哑巴看书——心里毒（读）"。你得小心，别让他害了。

乙：既然你这么说，我何必还去找他呢？看来我还是不找他算了。

第十四课　长城

This last unit of the course introduces you to a style of writing termed 抒情文 or "lyrical essays," the main purpose of which is to express one's feelings about a person, an object, a place, or indeed life in general. The author may openly describe how he or she feels; or the author may embody his or her feelings in a concrete object or scene. The essay in this lesson exemplifies this second type of lyrical essays. The aim of the author is to express his thoughts and feelings toward the antiquity and vitality of China as a nation. However, he does so by focusing his attention on the Great Wall, a symbol of China or Chinese history in the eyes of both the Chinese people and the peoples all over the world.

In writing a lyrical essay, the author's primary concern lies in how to convey his/her emotions vividly and provocatively. To achieve such a purpose, the author resorts to all the linguistic and rhetorical tools at his/her disposal, the most common of which is personification. Other linguistic devices the author frequently uses in writing a lyrical essay are exaggeration, repetition, drawing analogies, comparison and contrast, and so on. Particularly, the author takes full advantage of the nature of the Chinese language (i.e., one character stands for one sound and normally one meaning), choosing words carefully so that the sentence produces rhythm, adding to the force and contagiousness of his/her expression. Because the author of this present essay employs all these linguistic and rhetorical techniques, let us review them as a summary of this course.

I. 课文导读 🎧

　　我在傍晚下山的路上，看见你被落日照着，被西风吹着，四周是一片深秋的景色，鸦雀无声。然而我在抬头望天的时候，却看到了云间从北方飞回的鸿雁 (hóngyàn, n., swan goose)。它们让我想起了历史上的一些故事。

　　我在想象中把鸿雁当作了历史的见证 (jiànzhèng, n., witness)。仿佛就在不久以前，你这里还是一片战场，刀光剑影 (dāoguāng-jiànyǐng, n., the glint and flash of daggers and swords)，死尸 (sǐshī, n., corpse) 满地。所以我说，你是一卷凄惋 (qīwǎn, adj., dreary) 的历史，长城！

　　人们幻想 (huànxiǎng, v., fantasize) 着自我保护 (bǎohù, n., protection)，于是你被

建造出来。墙高六七米，墙厚四五米，随着山坡蜿蜒 (wānyán, v., zigzag) 达六千七百公里，非常险峻 (xiǎnjùn, adj., precipitous)。你使得途中的商人因为交通不便而皱眉 (zhòu méi, v., frown)，却又使一代又一代的皇帝 (huángdì, n., emperor) 心中安泰 (āntài, adj., peaceful)。但幻想毕竟是幻想，封闭 (fēngbì, n., closure) 终于失败了。于是你变得可笑，在风沙的剥蚀 (bōshí, n., denudation) 下过早地衰老 (shuāilǎo, v., become old and feeble) 了。所以我说，你是一个文化愚钝 (yúdùn, n., stupidity) 的标志 (biāozhì, n., mark)，长城！

现在你敞开 (chǎngkāi, v., open wide) 胸怀，迎接着来自四面八方的无数游客。他们之中有各种各样的人。他们的到来使你显得十分开放而又充满自信。可是我不知道你对这一切有什么感想。你受得了历史的再冲荡 (chōngdàng, n., rinse-out) 和新世纪 (shìjì, n., century) 的胎动 (tāidòng, n., movement of the fetus) 吗？

我没有听到回答。我只知道，从外层空间看地球，你是所能看到的唯一 (wéiyī, adj., sole) 的人工痕迹 (hénjì, n., vestige) 呵，长城！

II. 词语导学

1. Match each item on the left to an item on the right based on the radicals and the character(s) you know:

1) 外宾　wàibīn　　　　　n. traveling merchant
   商旅　shānglǚ　　　　 n. group of mountains
   民族　mínzú　　　　　　n. nation
   群山　qúnshān　　　　 n. foreign guest

2) 躯体　qūtǐ　　　　　　 n. key (to a lock)
   咽喉　yānhóu　　　　　 n. mind (lit., front of a garment)
   胸襟　xiōngjīn　　　　 n. throat
   锁钥　suǒyuè　　　　　 n. human body

3)　嘲弄　cháonòng　　　n. all-absorbing thought
　　凝思　níngsī　　　　n. mockery
　　平衡　pínghéng　　　n. pinnacle
　　顶端　dǐngduān　　　n. balance

4)　想象　xiǎngxiàng　　v. quiet down
　　沉寂　chénjì　　　　v. swallow
　　淹没　yānmò　　　　v. imagine
　　接待　jiēdài　　　　v. receive
　　吞噬　tūnshì　　　　v. be drowned by

5)　摧　　cuī　　　　　v. tread
　　折　　zhé　　　　　v. break
　　冻　　dòng　　　　v. destroy
　　踏　　tà　　　　　v. freeze

6)　砖　　zhuān　　　　n. (insect) cry
　　缝　　fèng　　　　n. blade
　　刃　　rèn　　　　　n. brick
　　基　　jī　　　　　n. crack
　　吟　　yín　　　　　n. foundation

2. Guess the meanings suggested by the numerals:

　　1)　这件事<u>一年半载</u>做不完。
　　　　电影院里只有<u>五六</u>个人。
　　　　学生们<u>三三两两</u>地从图书馆走出来。
　　　　最近<u>七七八八</u>的事把我弄得很忙。

　　2)　她回来了让我<u>十分</u>高兴。
　　　　他一开口说话我心里就明白了<u>三分</u>。
　　　　做这件事只有<u>五分</u>的把握。

　　3)　我一共收到<u>二十多</u>封信。
　　　　这里有<u>数百</u>家商店。
　　　　听他讲话的有<u>好几千</u>人。

每年有<u>成千上万</u>的人到这里参观。

长城迎来了<u>亿万</u>游人。

3. Guess the meanings of the following four-character expressions:

   1)　如火嫣红　　（嫣红: yānhóng, adj., bright red）

   2)　西风扑剌　　（扑剌: pūlā, onm., sound of wind）

   3)　仰天一瞥　　（瞥: piē, v., take a glance）

   4)　悠悠岁月　　（悠悠: yōuyōu, adj., long-drawn-out）

   5)　黑云掩月　　（掩: yǎn, v., cover）

   6)　雨雪纷纷　　（纷纷: fēnfēn, adj., profuse）

   7)　旌旗横倒　　（旌旗: jīngqí, n., banners and flags）

   8)　死尸相撑　　（相撑: xiāng chēng, v., support each other）

   9)　随山就坡　　（随: suí, v. go along with; 就: jiù, v., accommodate to）

 10)　险峻万状　　（状: zhuàng, n., form）

 11)　固若金汤　　（固: gù, adj., strongly fortified; 金汤: jīntāng, n., short for 金城汤池, ramparts of metal and a moat of boiling water--an impregnable fortress）

 12)　无求于人

 13)　万寿无疆　　（寿: shòu, n., longevity; 疆: jiāng, n., boundary）

 14)　毫不羞怯　　（羞怯: xiūqiè, adj., shy and timid）

 15)　四面八方

 16)　作何感想

 17)　异国他乡

III. 课文 ☙

长城　　鲍昌

   因为深秋的季节已至，下山的时间已晚，我看见落日照得你如火嫣红。在西风扑剌下，砖缝间的野草开始黄枯，基石下的酸枣变了颜色。这时，听不见秋虫之低吟，却在仰天一瞥时，看到了黄云间的归鸿。

那不是沿着昭君出塞的老路吗？那不是飞向苏武牧羊的北海吗？在凝思中，我想象那飞鸿乃是悠悠岁月的见证。曾几何时，黑云掩月，雨雪纷纷，狼烟在山头升起，矢刃在石间摧折；当旌旗横倒，死尸相撑，战场上的一切声音沉寂之后，只有红了眼睛的野犬在吞噬谁家的"春闺梦里人"了。

所以我不能不说，你是一卷凄惋的历史，长城！

于是，在人们的一种幻想里，你被建造出来。那是自我保护、自我心理平衡的幻想。墙高六七米，墙厚四五米，随山就坡，险峻万状，蜿蜒竟达六千七百公里。你用一座座雄关，卡住咽喉古道，构成北门锁钥。这使得途中的商旅为之皱眉，却又使历代的皇帝心中安泰，他们自以为统治下的"中央之国"，固若金汤，无求于人，万寿无疆。

所以我不能不说，你是一种民族封闭的象征，长城！

但幻想毕竟是幻想，封闭终不能封闭。几多寒霜冻硬的弓弦，射出了断喉的利箭。城门被踏平，边关被摧垮。由是人们发现：边墙不再是屏障。它变得可笑，仿佛受尽了时间与空间的嘲弄。在风沙剥蚀下，它过早地衰老了。

所以我不能不说，你又是一个文化愚钝的标志，长城！

正因为如此吧，现在你敞开胸襟了。你毫不羞怯地迎来了四面八方的亿万游人。他们之中有总统，有商人，有教师，有学生，也有开心的演员与体育明星。照相机咔嚓咔嚓响着，但又被哗哗的笑声淹没。我不知道他们各自的目的，但是他们来了，来了。他们的来，使你显得十分开放，而又充满自信。我看到一位外宾，踏上烽火台的顶端，高举双臂，做成一个V字，仿佛向着美好的未来，发出爽朗的笑声。

哦，长城！我不知道你对此作何感想。你那虽然古老但仍坚固的躯体，愿意接待来自异国他乡的杂色人流吗？你能承受住历史的再冲荡和新世纪的胎动吗？

你不语。你扎根的群山不语，晴洁的长天也不语。

但人们告诉我：从外层空间能看到的地球上唯一的人工痕迹，就是你呵，长城！

（选自漓江出版社１９９１年《当代中国散文擂台赛作品选》，有较多删节和改动）

繁體字課文

長城　鮑昌

因為深秋的季節已至，下山的時間已晚，我看見落日照得你如火嫣紅。在西風撲剌下，磚縫間的野草開始黃枯，基石下的酸棗變了顏色。這時，聽不見秋蟲之低吟，卻在仰天一瞥時，看到了黃雲間的歸鴻。

那不是沿著昭君出塞的老路嗎？那不是飛向蘇武牧羊的北海嗎？在凝思中，我想像那飛鴻乃是悠悠歲月的見證。曾幾何時，黑雲掩月，雨雪紛紛，狼煙在山頭昇起，矢刃在石間摧折；當旌旗橫倒，死屍相撐，戰場上的一切聲音沉寂之後，只有紅了眼睛的野犬在吞噬誰家的"春閨夢裡人"了。

所以我不能不說，你是一卷淒惋的歷史，長城！

於是，在人們的一種幻想裡，你被建造出來。那是自我保護、自我心理平衡的幻想。牆高六七米，牆厚四五米，隨山就坡，險峻萬狀，蜿蜒竟達六千七百公里。你用一座座雄關，卡住咽喉古道，構成北門鎖鑰。這使得途中的商旅為之皺眉，卻又使歷代的皇帝心中安泰，他們自以為統治下的"中央之國"，固若金湯，無求於人，萬壽無疆。

所以我不能不說，你是一種民族封閉的像徵，長城！

但幻想畢竟是幻想，封閉終不能封閉。幾多寒霜凍硬的弓弦，射出了斷喉的利箭。城門被踏平，邊關被摧垮。由是人們發現：邊牆不再是屏障。它變得可笑，彷彿受盡了時間與空間的嘲弄。在風沙剝蝕下，它過早地衰老了。

所以我不能不說，你又是一個文化愚鈍的標誌，長城！

正因為如此吧，現在你敞開胸襟了。你毫不羞怯地迎來了四面八方的億萬遊人。他們之中有總統，有商人，有教師，有學生，也有開心的演員與體育明星。照相機喀嚓喀嚓響著，但又被嘩嘩的笑聲淹沒。我不知道他們各自的目的，但是他們來了，來了。他們的來，使你顯得十分開放，而又充滿自信。我看到一位外賓，踏上烽火台的頂端，高舉雙臂，做成一個V字，彷彿向著美好的未來，發出爽朗的笑聲。

哦，長城！我不知道你對此作何感想。你那雖然古老但仍堅固的軀體，願意接待異國他鄉的雜色人流嗎？你能承受住歷史的再沖蕩和新世紀的胎動嗎？

你不語。你扎根的群山不語，晴潔的長天也不語。

但人們告訴我：從外層空間能看到的地球上唯一的人工痕跡，就是你呵，長城！

思考題

作者为什么说长城是"一个文化愚钝的标志"？文中最后说："但人们告诉我：从外层空间能看到的地球上唯一的人工痕迹，就是你呵，长城！"作者在这里抒发了他对长城（中国）的一种什么感情？

IV. 新词语

基石	jīshí	n.	foundation stone
酸枣	suānzǎo	n.	wild jujube

鸿	hóng	n.	swan goose; 鸿雁
昭君出塞	Zhāojūn chū sài		an allusion concerning Wáng Qiáng (王嫱, whose styled name was 王昭君), a palace lady in the Han dynasty. For diplomatic purposes, she was offered by Emperor Yuan as bride to a Khan of the Tartars occupying the northern borders of China.
塞	sài	n.	north of the Great Wall
苏武牧羊	Sū Wǔ mù yáng		an allusion referring to 苏武, whose styled name was Zǐqīng (子卿). A famous general in the Han dynasty, he was captured in a battle with the Tartars and exiled to the wilderness known as 北海, where he survived the ordeal as a shepherd.
牧	mù	v.	herd
乃	nǎi	adv.	就
几何	jǐhé	adj.	多少
狼烟	lángyān	n.	the smoke of wolves' dung burnt at border posts to signal alarm in ancient China
升	shēng	v.	rise
矢刃	shǐrèn	n	arrows and swords (ancient weapons)
犬	quǎn	n.	狗
春闺梦里人			referring to husbands who fought the invaders on the borders but appeared in the dreams of their wives at home
闺	guī	n.	lady's chamber
公里	gōnglǐ	n.	kilometer
雄关	xióngguān	n.	impregnable pass
卡	qiǎ	v.	have in a stranglehold
构成	gòuchéng	v.	form
北门锁钥	běimén suǒyuè	n.	strategic gateway to the North Gate (the north gate of an old fort at the Badaling section of the Great Wall northwest of Beijing)

统治	tǒngzhì	v.	rule
中央	zhōngyāng	n.	center, 中心
象征	xiàngzhēng	n.	symbol
寒	hán	adj.	冷
弓弦	gōngxián	n.	bowstring
利	lì	adj.	sharp
箭	jiàn	n.	arrow
垮	kuǎ	adj.	collapsed
由是	yóushì	conj.	于是
屏障	píngzhàng	n.	natural defense (lit., protective screen)
总统	zǒngtǒng	n.	president of a country
演员	yǎnyuán	n.	actor or actress
体育	tǐyù	n.	sports
目的	mùdì	n.	purpose
烽火台	fēnghuǒtái	n.	beacon tower
爽朗	shuǎnglǎng	adj.	clear and loud
坚固	jiāngù	adj.	strong
承受	chéngshòu	v.	endure
扎根	zhāgēn	v.	take root

V. 词语与句型

1. 沿着 (prep.)　　　　　　　　　那不是<u>沿着</u>昭君出塞的老路吗？

This is the same as 顺着, meaning "along."

<u>沿着</u>这条小路就能一直走到树林。
大人们<u>沿着</u>海岸寻找走失的小孩。
小船<u>顺着</u>堤坝向岸边的山崖滑去。

2. 乃 (adv.)   我想象那飞鸿乃是悠悠岁月的见证。

This is the same as 就. It is a word of classical Chinese, indicating that the fact is so, and nothing more. It often modifies 是 for emphasis.

陆羽乃是中国人所尊奉的"茶神"。

幽默乃是呆板生活的润滑剂 ("lubricant")。

汉语乃是汉民族的共同语言。

3. 曾几何时   曾几何时，黑云掩月，雨雪纷纷，…

曾 is short for 曾经. 几何 here means "how much." This is a structure of classical Chinese, meaning (那只是)不久以前(的事) or 没过多久. Although in a question form, it is not used to ask a question about time, but to call attention to what is introduced next. Therefore, a sentence beginning with this expression (normally separated from the rest of the sentence by a comma) is much more emphatic than the one without it.

曾几何时，美国的许多黑人还只是奴隶。

他现在批评我写的文章，曾几何时，他还是我的学生呢！

他对她说尽了好话，但曾几何时，就爱上了别的女人。

4. 随 N / 就 N   墙高六七米，墙厚四五米，随山就坡，险峻万状，…

Both 随 and 就 are used as verbs here. Depending on the context, they can have a variety of meanings and are not usually interchangeable.

很多人在生活中随大流。 (to go along with)

你哪天去都可以，随你的高兴。 (to depend on)

不能随地大小便。 (not to be selective with)

我什么时候都有空，就你的时间开会吧。 (to accomodate to)

就我所知，他们学校今年不放春假。 (to be based on)

对这个问题我们只能就事论事。 (to be limited to)

5. 达 (v.)   …，蜿蜒竟达六千七百公里。

Here 达 means "to reach" in the sense of "amounting to" a certain number. This usage often occurs in written language.

> 该校学生达三万多人。
>
> 中国的人口多达十二亿。
>
> 长城长达六千七百公里。
>
> 那座大山高达一千多米。

6. 几多 (adj.)　　　　　　　　　　几多寒霜冻硬的弓弦，射出了断喉的利箭。

几多 is dialectal, meaning 多少. It is not recommended for use in your own speech.

> 你们班有几多学生？
>
> 几多听众在听完讲话后问了问题？

7. 毫不/毫无　　　　　　　　　　你毫不羞怯地迎来了四面八方的亿万游人。

Used with 不 or 无, 毫 means "(not) in the least" or "(not) at all" with a strong sense of negation. Colloquial equivalents are 一点儿也不 and 一点儿也没有.

> 她说出这样的话来毫不奇怪。
>
> 我毫不遗憾做了这个决定。
>
> 恶人对弱者毫无同情感。

8. 显得 (v.)　　　　　　　　　　他们的来，使你显得十分开放，…

显得 means "appear (to be)." It is the same as 看上去 or 看起来, but sounds more formal. Compare:

> 他刚从考场出来，显得十分轻松。
>
> 他刚从考场出来，看上去很轻松。

> 幽默使平凡的事情显得富有情趣。
>
> 幽默使平凡的事情看上去很有情趣。

煮茶的程序<u>显得</u>过繁。

煮茶的程序看起来太繁。

9. 唯一 (adj.)   从外层空间能看到的地球上<u>唯一</u>的人工痕迹，…

唯一, meaning "only" or "sole," sounds a little formal.

她是我们认识的<u>唯一</u>的韩国学生。

Compare: 我们只认识她这一个韩国学生。

自嘲并非幽默的<u>唯一</u>方式。

Compare: 幽默并不是只有自嘲这一种方式。

VI. 语言知识与修辞技巧

1. *Making statements succinct: a summary*

Throughout this course, we have been emphasizing succinctness as a stylistic goal one should aim for in speaking and writing. Succinctness is considered a sign of effective speech in many cultures. Chinese discourse is particularly marked by such a quality because of the nature of the language. Native speakers of Chinese consciously pursue succinctness through the following means:

1) Short sentences

In Lessons One and Eleven we have discussed "short sentences" as a distinctive feature of Chinese and a linguistic means that writers actively employ to keep their statements terse and succinct. Short sentences are a hallmark of all the essays we have studied in this course.

曾几何时，黑云掩月，雨雪纷纷，狼烟在山头升起，矢刃在石间摧折。(L.14)

我活在世上，爱着，感受着，思考着。我心中有一个世界，那里珍藏着许多往事，有欢乐的，也有悲伤的。它们虽已逝去，却将永远活在我心中，与我终身相伴。(L.10)

女人想哭就哭，想笑就笑，害怕就害怕，脆弱就脆弱，不用担心被人小看。(L.7)

它补过天，在天上发过热，闪过光，我们的先祖或许仰望过它，它给了他们光明，向往，憧憬。(L.5)

我还是爱我的学生，我不能离开我的学生，离开他们，我就失去灵感了。(L.4)

2) Omission of sentence elements

Omission of sentence elements (primarily subjects and predicates) is also a typical characteristic of Chinese, and has been practiced by all the authors of the essays in this textbook in order to keep their statements brief and succinct. Look at the sentences above, for example. In most of them the subject is omitted. If you reread the essays of this textbook carefully, you will notice that this omission of the subject is fairly common. Study the sentences in the above examples and see where a subject is omitted and what this omitted subject would be.

3) Analogies

In the previous lesson, we discussed drawing analogies as a means to help one speak and write vividly. In addition to this function, drawing analogies can also help one express ideas succinctly through the use of an image or metaphor. Explanation becomes unnecessary, reducing the words the speaker would otherwise have to use in order to make things clear. Look at the following examples, and imagine how much verbal explanation would be needed if the idea in each of the sentences were not expressed through an analogy:

你用一座座雄关，卡住咽喉古道，构成北门锁钥。(L.14)

幽默是生活的味精。(L.13)

笛卡尔说：“读一本好书，就是和许多高尚的人谈话。”(L.11)

雨果说：“各种蠢事，在每天阅读好书的影响下，仿佛烤在火上一样渐渐溶化”。(L.11)

4) Four-character expressions

Native speakers of Chinese are fond of using four-character expressions, particularly in writing. Many four-character expressions are set phrases, formed through a repeated use of what originally were impromptu creations. Many others, however, are temporarily put together by a speaker or a writer to achieve a rhetorical effect. Four-character expressions render language terse and succinct by incorporating rich content in a few words. Moreover, many four-character expressions involve the use of analogy, which further condense what the speaker has to say. As a result, what takes one, two, or more sentences to express is embodied in the vivid picture of an analogy. Some typical expressions from the essays of this textbook are:

爱屋及乌， 惊心动魄， 鸟语花香， 腾波鼓浪， 亭亭玉立， 无影无踪

鸦雀无声， 黑云掩月， 雨雪纷纷， 固若金汤， 油盐酱醋， 锅碗瓢盆

Succinctness is also the hallmark of "short forms" in Chinese. Please refer to Part VI.4 of Lesson Five for a review.

5) Allusions

Many of the four-character expressions are also allusions, as we have discussed in Lesson Nine. The main reason for using allusions is to express a meaning as briefly as possible simply by referring to a story. Understanding allusions requires knowledge of Chinese history and literary writings (as in the cases of 昭君出塞 and 苏武牧羊 referred to in the text of this lesson). However, many allusions have become standard modes of expression (such as 自相矛盾, 四面楚歌, and 纸上谈兵), and therefore one can use these allusions for the meanings they suggest without knowing the stories behind them.

6) Words and structures of classical Chinese

As we discussed in Lessons Three and Eleven respectively, using words and structures of classical Chinese can effect an air of formality and elegance in writing. Another purpose of using classical Chinese is to reduce verbiage because brevity was a marked feature of Chinese in the classical periods. Many two-syllable words in modern Chinese (such as 曾经, 如果, and 因为) appear in classical Chinese as monosyllabic words (such as 曾, 如, and 因). There are other reasons why classical Chinese is more terse than its modern counterpart, but for our purposes here, suffice it to say that using words and structures from classical Chinese provides a means for one to speak and write succinctly.

2. *Intention and strategy: a summary of the course*

In this lyrical essay seemingly about the Great Wall, the author resorts to almost all the rhetorical and syntectic devices to express his strong emotions toward China both as an ancient and a modern nation. The most striking technique he uses is "personification." The Great Wall is referred to as an animate being throughout the text: the author talks to it, speaks through it, and, in short, treats it as a human being who can think, feel, and communicate feelings. As he proceeds, the author also uses many other linguistic devices to express his feelings succinctly, vividly, cohesively, and forcefully. The following is a list of all the rhetorical and syntactic techniques the author has used. Because it is so comprehensive, this list can serve as a summary of most of the advanced language skills taught in this course.

1) Personification (Lesson 3)

你用一座座雄关，卡住咽喉古道，构成北门锁钥。

边墙不再是屏障。它变得可笑，仿佛受尽了时间与空间的嘲弄。在风沙剥蚀下，它过早地衰老了。

现在你敞开胸怀了。你毫不羞怯地迎来了四面八方的亿万游人。

你那虽然古老但仍坚固的躯体，愿意接待来自异国他乡的杂色人流吗？

2) Exaggeration (Lesson 4)

因为深秋的季节已至，下山的时间已晚，我看见落日照得你如火嫣红。

他们自以为统治下的"中央之国"，固若金汤，无求于人，万寿无疆。

3) Drawing analogies (Lesson 3)

你用一座座雄关，卡住咽喉古道，构成北门锁钥。
你能承受住历史的再冲荡和新世界的胎动吗？

4) Enumeration (Lesson 6)

他们自以为统治下的"中央之国"，固若金汤，无求于人，万寿无疆。

他们之中有总统，有商人，有教师，有学生，也有开心的演员与体育明星。

5) Repetition (Lesson 7)

但<u>幻想</u>毕竟是<u>幻想</u>，<u>封闭</u>终不能<u>封闭</u>。

我不知道他们各自的目的，但是他们<u>来了</u>，<u>来了</u>。他们的<u>来</u>，使你显得十分开放，而又充满自信。

你<u>不语</u>。你扎根的群山<u>不语</u>，晴洁的长天也<u>不语</u>。

6) Parallel structures (Lesson 7)

在西风扑剌下，<u>砖缝间的野草开始黄枯</u>，<u>基石下的酸枣变了颜色</u>。
<u>黑云掩月</u>，<u>雨雪纷纷</u>，<u>狼烟在山头升起</u>，<u>矢刃在石间摧折</u>。
<u>墙高六七米</u>，<u>墙厚四五米</u>，<u>随山就坡</u>，<u>险峻万状</u>。
<u>城门被踏平</u>，<u>边关被摧垮</u>。

7) Comparison and contrast (Lesson 8)

这时，<u>听不见秋虫之低吟</u>，<u>却</u>在仰天一瞥时，<u>看到了黄云间的归鸿</u>。
这使得途中的商旅<u>为之皱眉</u>，<u>却</u>又使历代的皇帝<u>心中安泰</u>。

8) Allusions (Lessons 9 and 14)

那不是沿着<u>昭君出塞</u>的老路吗？那不是飞向<u>苏武牧羊</u>的北海吗？

9) Numbers (Lesson 7)

墙高<u>六七</u>米，墙厚<u>四五</u>米，随山就坡，险峻万状，蜿蜒竟达<u>六千七百</u>公里。

你毫不羞怯地迎来了<u>四面八方</u>的<u>亿万</u>游人。

10) Onomatopoeia (Lesson 2)

在西风<u>扑剌</u>下，砖缝间的野草开始黄枯，基石下的酸枣变了颜色。
照相机<u>咔嚓咔嚓</u>响着，但又被<u>哗哗</u>的笑声淹没。

11) Tones (Lessons 4 and 5)

但幻想<u>毕竟</u>是幻想，封闭<u>终</u>不能封闭。<u>几多</u>寒霜冻硬的弓弦，射出了断喉的利箭。

但人们告诉我：外层空间能看到地球上唯一的人工痕迹，<u>就是你呵，长城</u>！

12) Rhetorical questions (Lesson 9)

那<u>不是</u>沿着昭君出塞的老路<u>吗</u>？ 那<u>不是</u>飞向苏武牧羊的北海<u>吗</u>？

13) Double negation (Lesson 10)

所以我<u>不能不</u>说，你是一卷凄惋的历史，长城！
所以我<u>不能不</u>说，你是一个文化愚钝的标志，长城！

14) Short sentences (Lessons 1 and 11)

这时，听不见秋虫之低吟，却在仰天一瞥时，看到了黄云间的归鸿。

曾几何时，黑云掩月，雨雪纷纷，狼烟在山头升起，矢刃在石间摧折。

由是人们发现：边墙不再是屏障。它变得可笑，仿佛受尽了时间与空间的嘲弄。在风沙剥蚀下，它过早地衰老了。

15) Omission (Lesson 11)

墙高六七米，墙厚四五米，（墙）随山就坡，险峻万状，（墙）蜿蜒竟达六千七百公里。

我看到一位外宾，（他）踏上烽火台的顶端，高举（他的）双臂，做成一个V字，（他）仿佛向着美好的未来，发出爽朗的笑声。

16) Sentence connectives (Lessons 1, 5, and 8)

…。<u>所以我不能不说</u>，你是一卷凄惋的历史，长城！

…。<u>于是</u>，在人们的一种幻想里，你被建造出来。

…。<u>正因为</u>如此吧，现在你敞开胸怀了。

我不知道他们各自的目的，<u>但是</u>他们来了，来了。

17) Classical Chinese (Lessons 3 and 11)

这时，听不见秋虫<u>之</u>低吟，却在<u>仰天一瞥</u>时，看到了黄云间的<u>归鸿</u>。

在独立的凝思中，我想象那飞鸿<u>乃</u>是悠悠岁月的见证。

<u>曾几何时</u>，黑云掩月，雨雪纷纷，狼烟在山头升起，矢刃在石间摧折。

这使得途中的商旅为<u>之</u>皱眉，却又使历代的皇帝心中安泰。

哦，长城！我不知道你对<u>此</u>作何感想。

18) Four-character expressions (Lessons 2, 9, and 10)

如火嫣红，仰天一瞥，悠悠岁月，曾几何时，黑云掩月，雨雪纷纷
旌旗横倒，死尸相撑，自我保护，随山就坡，险峻万状，固若金汤
无求于人，万寿无疆，敞开胸怀，毫不羞怯，四面八方，充满自信
高举双臂，作何感想，异国他乡，杂色人流

Please review these linguistic and rhetorical techniques in the relevant lessons (indicated in the parentheses). Make a point of using them in your own speech and writing whenever you can.

VII. 练习

词语与句型

1. In each section, fill the blanks with two-syllable words and then tell what common feature in word formation that group of words shares (refer to Part VI.3 of Lesson Three if necessary):

A. 建造，保护，吞噬，承受，封闭，旌旗，标志，颜色，痕迹，躯体
愚钝，安泰，坚固

1) swallow _____   2) strong _____

3) human body _____   4) endure _____

5) color _____   6) vestige _____

7) build _____   8) stupidity _____

9) peaceful _____   10) protection _____

11) banners and flags _____   12) closure _____

13) mark _____

B. 接待，开放，凄惋，古老，险峻，爽朗，嘲弄，咽喉，锁钥，屏障

1) precipitous _____   2) receive _____

3) mockery _____   4) dreary _____

5) key (to a lock) _____   6) ancient _____

7) throat _____   8) clear and loud _____

9) open _____   10) natural defense (lit., protective screen)
_____

C. 深秋，外宾，野犬，古道，明星，边墙，利箭，杂色，幻想，寒霜
群山，顶端，落日，归鸿，胎动，低吟，凝思

1) ancient path _____   2) foreign guest _____

3) sharp arrow _____   4) (occupational) star _____

5) chilling frost _____   6) wall on the border _____

7) late fall _____   8) (insect) cry in a low voice _____

9) wild dog _____   10) all-absorbing thought _____

11) setting sun _____   12) returning swan goose _____

13) fantasy _____   14) movement of a fetus _____

15) pinnacle _____   16) group of mountains _____

17) multicolored _____

D. 踏平，催垮，冻硬，淹没，充满，发现，升起，构成，敞开

1) be filled with	_____	2) smash	_____
3) open wide	_____	4) be drowned by	_____
5) rise up	_____	6) trample	_____
7) form	_____	8) be frozen hard	_____
9) discover	_____		

2. Write out the four-character expressions based on the text:

1) have nothing to ask other people for _____

2) all directions _____

3) be not at all shy and timid _____

4) foreign countries and lands _____

5) strongly fortified as an impregnable fortress _____

6) what to think of _____

7) everlasting longevity _____

8) precipitous in various forms _____

9) not a long time ago _____

10) long-drawn-out years _____

11) look up and take a glance at the sky _____

12) rain and snow profusely _____

13) self-protection _____

14) go along with mountains and slopes _____

3. Complete the sentences with the designated expressions:

1) 山山水水 (to be all witnesses of history)。

2) 面对怀有敌意的听众，讲话的人 (to be full of self-confidence)。

3) 美国 (to open wide one's mind) 迎来了世界各地的移民。

4) 那位傲慢无礼的批评家 (to be mocked by Goethe, a great poet)。

5) 燕妮从镜子里看到自己，顿时 (to burst into a clear and loud laughter)。

6) 这死爱面子的棋迷 (to think oneself) 每个人都喜欢跟他下棋。

7) 你如果让他走过去，(isn't that making way for a fool)？

8) 钱老的学识非常渊博，(exactly because of this)，他的谈吐十分幽默。

4. Expand the phrases into sentences by following the examples:

1) 小船<u>沿着</u>堤坝在水面上漂。

    大雁 / 老路 / 飞回南方

    鹿群 / 小道 / 一闪而过

    猎人 / 河岸 / 寻找猎物

    游人们 / 狭窄的街道 / 走向博物馆

2) 古代的中国人通常<u>随</u>山建造长城。

    他总是 / 处 / 乱放东西

    你们可以 / 时 / 来找我

    我们都会 / 手 / 关门

    没有人会 / 意 / 把这里的书拿走

3) 结婚以后她<u>就此</u>不再工作。

    他出去时 / 手 / 把门关上了

    我到上海后 / 地 / 买了一些礼物

    他们出发前 / 近 / 给汽车加满了油

    哥哥到中国出差时 / 便 / 去看了中医

4) 长城长<u>达</u> 6,700 公里。

    目前的世界人口 / 多 / 50 亿

    山坡上的那口井 / 深 / 10 米

世界上最高的山峰 / 高 / 8,800 多公尺

新发现的那块陨石 / 重 / 1,400 多公斤

5) 听众<u>毫不在意地</u>听完了他的讲话。

那位黑人律师 / 动摇 / 站在台上

老师 / 厌烦 / 给我们解释课文

听众<u>对</u>他的讲话<u>毫不在意</u>。

有能力的人 / 找工作 / 担心

大家 / 她的遭遇 / 同情

6) 陆羽的煮茶法<u>显得</u>过于繁难。

有幽默感的人 / 轻松和洒脱

你说的那位棋迷 / 又调皮又可爱

喜爱文学的人 / 情趣高雅

今天的中国 / 十分开放

7) 他是到过山顶的<u>唯一的</u>年轻人。

Compare: 他是<u>唯一</u>到过山顶的年轻人。

陆羽 / 是 / 生活在唐代的 / 茶学家

汤姆 / 是 / 能在这里找到的 / 中文翻译

他 / 不是 / 给钱老打电话的 / 读者

幽默 / 不是 / 表达主题的 / 方式

语言知识与技巧

5. Explain the underlined words and note how they contribute to the tersity of the expression:

A. 恋棋如<u>命</u> _____   固<u>若</u>金汤 _____

久别重<u>逢</u> _____   作<u>何</u>感想 _____

上<u>溯</u>远古 _____   下<u>及</u>未来 _____

凡书<u>皆</u>好 ＿＿＿＿＿＿＿＿＿＿   <u>唯</u>我独尊 ＿＿＿＿＿＿＿＿＿

绵延<u>不绝</u> ＿＿＿＿＿＿＿＿＿   应有<u>尽</u>有 ＿＿＿＿＿＿＿＿＿

又当<u>别</u>论 ＿＿＿＿＿＿＿＿＿   左右<u>兼</u>顾 ＿＿＿＿＿＿＿＿＿

险峻万<u>状</u> ＿＿＿＿＿＿＿＿＿   <u>终</u>有一日 ＿＿＿＿＿＿＿＿＿

B. <u>饱览</u> ＿＿＿＿＿＿＿＿＿   <u>相伴</u> ＿＿＿＿＿＿＿＿＿

    <u>闪身</u> ＿＿＿＿＿＿＿＿＿   <u>前行</u> ＿＿＿＿＿＿＿＿＿

    <u>暂缓</u> ＿＿＿＿＿＿＿＿＿   <u>倾注</u> ＿＿＿＿＿＿＿＿＿

    <u>芳容</u> ＿＿＿＿＿＿＿＿＿   <u>本无</u> ＿＿＿＿＿＿＿＿＿

C. 1) <u>非</u> <u>请</u> <u>莫</u> <u>入</u>。

    非 ＿＿＿＿ 请 ＿＿＿＿ 莫 ＿＿＿＿ 入 ＿＿＿＿

2) 回校<u>后</u>请<u>即</u> <u>来电</u>。

    后 ＿＿＿＿ 即 ＿＿＿＿ 来电 ＿＿＿＿

3) <u>因</u>有急事<u>相商</u>, 请<u>暂</u> <u>勿</u>外出。

    因 ＿＿＿＿ 相商 ＿＿＿＿ 暂 ＿＿＿＿ 勿 ＿＿＿＿

4) 我<u>与</u>他<u>虽</u> <u>曾</u>同学, <u>但</u>已<u>久</u>未 <u>晤面</u>。

    与 ＿＿＿＿ 虽 ＿＿＿＿ 曾 ＿＿＿＿ 但 ＿＿＿＿ 已 ＿＿＿＿

    久 ＿＿＿＿ 未 ＿＿＿＿ 晤面 ＿＿＿＿

5) 你<u>是否</u>心情不<u>佳</u>? <u>为何</u> <u>一言不发</u>?

    是否 ＿＿＿＿ 佳 ＿＿＿＿ 为何 ＿＿＿＿ 一言不发 ＿＿＿＿

6) 我<u>何尝</u>不<u>思</u>上进? 只是 <u>力不从心</u>而已。

    何尝 ＿＿＿＿ 思 ＿＿＿＿ 力不从心 ＿＿＿＿

7) <u>自</u><u>此</u>之后, 他<u>常</u> <u>感</u>人生<u>过</u>短。

    自 ＿＿＿＿ 此 ＿＿＿＿ 常 ＿＿＿＿ 感 ＿＿＿＿ 过 ＿＿＿＿

8) <u>该</u> 处交通<u>极</u>其不<u>便</u>, <u>确实</u> <u>无法</u> <u>居住</u>。

该 _____　　处 _____　　极其 _____　　便 _____　　确实 _____

无法 _____　　居住 _____

9) 我对<u>此</u>事所<u>知</u> <u>甚</u> <u>微</u>, <u>无</u> <u>可</u> <u>奉告</u>。

此 _____　　知 _____　　甚 _____　　微 _____　　无 _____

可 _____　　奉告 _____

10) <u>若</u> <u>数人</u> <u>同</u> <u>往</u>, <u>则</u> <u>万无一失</u>。

若 _____　　数人 _____　　同 _____　　往 _____　　则 _____

万无一失 _____

6. Following the examples, complete the sentences by

A. using comparison and contrast:

1) 绿茶<u>暖胃</u>, 而红茶<u>明目</u>。

坏书 _____, 而好书 _____。

2) 你<u>每次都赢</u>, 可我<u>每次都输</u>。

听众 _____, 可说话的人自己 _____。

3) 长城<u>衰老了</u>, 却又<u>在开放中显得年轻了</u>。

中国 _____, 却又 _____。

4) 你要找的人<u>远在天边</u>, <u>近在眼前</u>。

我说的这个人 _____。

B. using enumeration:

1) 他们之中<u>有</u>总统, <u>有</u>商人, <u>有</u>教师, <u>也有</u>学生。

我去过的国家, _____。

2) 我活在世上，<u>爱着</u>，感受<u>着</u>，思考<u>着</u>。

孩子们在小湖边，_____。

3) 世间有诸多的<u>不平等</u>：财富的<u>不平等</u>，权力的<u>不平等</u>，智慧的<u>不平等</u>，精神的<u>不平等</u>，等等。

幽默有诸多的<u>方式</u>：_____

_____。

4) 他的棋艺，跳棋<u>上</u>，象棋<u>中</u>，围棋<u>下</u>。

煮茶用的水，_____。

C. using repetition:

1) 他们<u>来了</u>，<u>来了</u>。他们的<u>来</u>，使你充满自信。

春天 _____，_____。春天的 _____，使我们 _____。

2) <u>宇宙</u>毕竟是<u>宇宙</u>，<u>个人</u>不过是<u>个人</u>。

生活现实 _____，黄梁梦 _____。

3) 他下棋<u>屡战屡败</u>，但<u>屡败屡战</u>。

我打乒乓球 _____。

4) 老师<u>一遍一遍地</u>领读生词，又<u>一遍一遍地</u>领读课文。

母亲 _____，又 _____。

7. What follows are excerpts from a lyrical essay singing the praises of Chinese characters. This author, unlike the author of the text in this lesson, expresses his feelings in a direct way. Study these paragraphs and identify cases of 1) four-character expressions, 2) rhetorical questions, 3) enumeration, 4) personification, 5) analogy, and 6) exaggeration.

　　我常常为我面前这一个个方块字而动情。它们像一群活泼可爱的孩子在纸上玩笑嬉戏，像一朵朵美丽多姿的鲜花愉悦你的眼睛。这时，我真不忍将它们框在方格里，真想叫它们离开格子去舒展，去不受拘束地享受自己的欢乐。

真的，它们可不是僵硬的符号，而是有着独特性格的精灵。……这些有影无形的图画，这些横竖勾勒的奇妙组合，同人的气质多么相近。它们在瞬间走进想象，然后又从想象流出，只在记忆中留下无穷的回味。这是一些多么可爱的小精灵呵！

而在书法家的笔下，它们更能生发出无穷无尽的变化，或挺拔如峰，或清亮如溪，或浩瀚如海，或凝滑如脂。它们自身就有一种智慧的力量，一个想象的天地，任你尽情飞翔与驰骋。在人类古老的长河中，有哪一个民族能像中华民族拥有这么丰富的书法瑰宝？

唉，像徜徉在夏天夜晚的星空下，为那壮丽的景色而迷醉，我真的是无限钟情我赖以思维和交往的中国汉字，并震惊于它的再生活力和奇特魅力。我想，在人类历史的长河中，这种文字将越来越被世人所珍惜和喜爱。

我的使用汉字的同胞们朋友们，请去发展它丰富它吧！历史和文明正向我们投来新的目光！

(摘自漓江出版社１９９１年《当代中国散文擂台赛作品选》；刘湛秋:
"我爱你，中国的汉字"；有删改)

活学与活用

8. Answer the following questions using the expressions provided.

1) 作者在深秋下山的时候看到了什么？

落日／照／长城／火红火红
野草／黄枯
酸枣／变了颜色
黄云间／飞向南方的大雁

2) 大雁让作者想起什么？

昭君出塞／苏武牧羊
历史上的争战

凄惋的历史

3) 作者为什么说长城是一个愚钝的标志？

　　幻想／自我保护／自我心理平衡

　　民族封闭的象征

　　但是／不能封闭／不是屏障

　　可笑／受尽了嘲弄／过早地衰老

4) 现在长城怎么了？

　　敞开胸襟／亿万游人

　　十分开放／充满自信

5) 作者的什么问题没有得到回答？

　　愿意／接待／来自四方的杂色人流

　　能／承受／历史的再冲荡／新世纪的胎动

6) 作者最后说什么？你觉得他为什么这样说？

　　外层空间／地球

　　唯一的人工痕迹

　　我觉得／⋯⋯

9. Using your own words, answer the following questions based on your own opinions and experiences:

1) 你去过中国的长城吗？“不到长城非好汉”是什么意思？

2) 你学过中国历史吗？请你谈谈为什么长城代表了中国和中国文化。

3) 介绍一个能代表美国的地方或建筑物。

4) 古老的中国和年轻的美国有什么相同和不同的地方？

5) 幻想和理想有什么不同？你的理想是什么？你有过什么样的幻想？

10. Write an essay on an important place or landmark in the United States. To a great extent, this place or landmark should reflect the history and national character of the American people. Try

to write the essay in a lyrical style expressing your feelings toward the subject of your description. Use as many linguistic and rhetorical skills as possible to make your essay terse, elegant, vivid, cohesive, and forceful.

VIII. 课文材料对话 🎧

A

甲：你不觉得那落日下的长城显得有几分凄婉吗？

乙：怎么会不觉得呢。它让我想起了历史上的无数争战。从北方来的敌人踏平了多少城门，摧垮了多少边关。在这座墙的周围又留下了多少人的白骨啊！

甲：可笑的是，历代的皇帝总以为这一座座雄关固若金汤，总以为"中央之国"在长城的保护下可以高枕无忧，万寿无疆。

乙：这不过是他们的幻想而已。事实上，尽管有了这一座屏障，封闭却从来没有真正实现过。

甲：但是不管怎么说，长城是为了封闭而建造的。它完全是一个文化愚钝的标志。

乙：就因为是文化愚钝的标志吧，它受尽了时间和空间的嘲弄而过早地衰老，也真是难为它了。

B

学生：哦，长城，你是中华民族的骄傲。"不到长城非好汉"这句话，表达了千古英雄的共同追求。可是现在有人说，你变得可笑了。

长城：我的伟大，原来就存在于人们的幻想之中。以现代的眼光来看，我不过是一个文化愚钝的标志而已。我的存在究竟还有什么价值吗？

学生：你是历史的最好见证。再说，你现在敞开胸怀，迎接着来自地球各个角落的人们。他们的到来，使你显得十分开放，也使你的存在获得了新的意义。

长城：照你这么说，我应该充满自信才对。其实，面对这些来自四面八方的人流，我也确实怀有一种对美好未来的向往。

学生：正因为如此，你就一定能承受住历史的再冲荡。古老的长城啊，愿你在开放中获得新生。

长城：谢谢。这也正是我自己的心愿。

Glossary of Words and Expressions

词语表

Some words and expressions that students may have learned before are treated as "new" items in this course for two reasons. First, students taking this course may have used different lower-level textbooks; some items that have appeared in one textbook may not have appeared in another. Second, although students have studied these words and expressions, they may not have retained every one of them, and therefore reinforcement is necessary.

The English definition of a word or expression is given based on the *context* in which this word or expression *first* occurs in this course (as specified by the lesson number at the end of an entry). The same word or expression involving a different meaning in a different text is listed as a separate entry.

Since in Chinese a word functions differently in different contexts, it is often difficult to determine the part of speech of an isolated word. In this course, the part of speech of a word is defined according to the *context* in which it *first* occurs. If this word occurs again in a later text as a different part of speech, it is not listed for a second time.

A

碍	ài	v.	be in the way of	5
爱情	àiqíng	n.	love	4
安排	ānpái	v.	arrange	8
安泰	āntài	adj.	peaceful	14
安危	ānwēi	n.	safety	2
安慰	ānwèi	v.	comfort	5
岸	àn	n.	bank	3
暗地里	àndìli	adv.	secretly	4
按照	ànzhào	prep.	in accordance with	2
傲慢	àomàn	adj.	arrogant	10

B

把握	bǎwò	n.	certainty	8
坝	bà	n.	dam	3
白白	báibái	adv.	in vain	9

白痴	báichī	n.	idiot	7
白费	báifèi	v.	waste	9
拜读	bàidú	v.	read with respect	4
拜伦	Bàilún	n.	George Gordon Byron (1785-1859), an English Romantic poet	11
斑	bān	n.	spot	5
般	bān	part.	just like	3
扳机	bānjī	n.	trigger	1
斑斓	bānlán	adj.	multicolored	1
搬运	bānyùn	v.	transport	5
伴随	bànsuí	v.	accompany	13
包括	bāokuò	v.	include	12
保存	bǎocún	v.	preserve; 保留	12
保护	bǎohù	n.	protection	14
饱览	bǎolǎn	v.	have a good look at	11
保留(有)	bǎoliú yǒu	v.	retain; 保存	12
抱持	bàochí	v.	hold in the arms	9
暴力	bàolì	v.	violence	11
悲	bēi	adv.	sorrowfully	2
卑鄙	bēibǐ	n.	baseness	11
悲欢	bēihuān	n.	sorrows and joys	9
悲激	bēijī	adj.	solemn and indignant	2
悲伤	bēishāng	adj.	sorrowful	10
北门锁钥	běimén suǒyuè	n.	strategic gateway to the North Gate (the north gate of an old fort at the Badaling section of the Great Wall northwest of Beijing)	14
背影	bèiyǐng	n.	back viewed from behind	4
本	běn	adv.	originally; 本来	10
本身	běnshēn	pro.	itself	9
迸	bèng	v.	burst forth	4
鼻尖	bíjiān	n.	tip of the nose	4
鼻孔	bíkǒng	n.	nostril	3

彼时	bǐ shí	adv.	at that time	3
闭	bì	v.	close	8
蔽	bì	v.	cover	2
避	bì	v.	avoid	11
庇覆	bìfù	v.	protect and cover	5
毕竟	bìjìng	adv.	after all	12
避免	bìmiǎn	v.	avoid	9
标志	biāozhì	n.	mark	14
表达	biǎodá	v.	express	13
并非	bìng fēi	adv	really not	11
病危	bìngwēi	v.	be dying of illness	2
波浪	bō	n.	wave	12
剥蚀	bōshí	n.	denudation	14
波折	bōzhé	n.	twists and turns	10
博	bó	adv.	widely	12
博爱	bó'ài	n.	universal love	11
伯父	bófù	n.	father's elder brother	5
不过	búguò	conj.	but	2
不过	búguò	adv.	merely	9
不屑	búxiè	v.	disdain to do sth.	7
补偿	bǔcháng	v.	compensate	11
补天	bǔtiān	v.	mend the sky (alluding to the story of Nǚ Wā, a mythical figure who is said to have fixed the collapsed sky with the colorful stones she smelted)	5
不仅	bùjǐn	conj.	not only	11
不屈于	bùqū yú	v.	not yield to	5
不然	bùrán		不是这样	8
不时	bùshí	adv.	often	1

C

| 才 | cái | n. | capable person | 11 |

财富	cáifù	n.	wealth	11
采	cǎi	v.	pick (tea)	12
采访	cǎifǎng	v.	visit and interview	12
采用	cǎiyòng	v.	select and use	5
灿烂	cànlàn	n.	brilliance	6
沧桑	cāngsāng	n.	沧海桑田, a Chinese allusion referring to the quick passage of time as is seen in the change of seas into mulberry fields and vice versa	6
苍蝇	cāngying	n.	fly	3
草丛	cǎocóng	n.	clusters of tall grass	1
蹭	cèng	v.	move slowly	2
茶肆	chásì	n.	teahouse; 茶馆; 茶楼	12
刹那间	chànà jiān	adv	in an instant	10
产地	chǎndì	n.	place of production	12
颤动	chàndòng	v.	shake	3
长期	chángqī	adv.	for a long time	12
常识	chángshí	n.	common sense	8
长途	chángtú	n.	long distance	2
场合	chǎnghé	n.	occasion	13
敞开	chǎngkāi	v.	open wide	14
超乎	chāohū	v.	go beyond; 超出	11
超越	chāoyuè	v.	transcend	11
朝	cháo	prep.	in the direction of; 往	4
嘲弄	cháonòng	n.	mockery	14
潮汐	cháoxī	n.	morning and evening tides	9
沉	chén	v.	sink	3
晨	chén	n.	morning	1
沉寂	chénjì	v.	quiet down	14
沉默	chénmò	v.	be silent	3
撑	chēng	v.	maintain	7
称作为	chēngzuò wéi	v.	be called as; 称作; 称为; 叫做	12
成功	chénggōng	adj.	success	7

盛满	chéng mǎn	v.	fill (a container with sth.)	5
成品	chéngpǐn	n.	finished product	12
澄清	chéngqīng	v.	(of liquid) become clear	3
成人	chéngrén	n.	adult	11
承受	chéngshòu	v.	endure	14
程序	chéngxù	n.	procedure	12
痴痴地	chīchīde	adv.	dumbfoundedly	4
尺	chǐ	m.	traditional unit of length, equal to one-third of a meter	7
翅膀	chìbǎng	n.	wing	8
充当	chōngdāng	v.	act as	10
冲荡	chōngdàng	n.	rinse-out	14
充满	chōngmǎn	v.	fill	6
冲泡	chōngpào	v.	pour boiling water on tea and leave the tea to steep	12
憧憬	chōngjǐng	n.	yearning for	5
重	chóng	adv.	again	13
重复	chóngfù	v.	repeat	9
崇高	chónggāo	adj.	lofty	11
抽	chōu	v.	draw back (a gun)	1
仇恨	chóuhèn	n.	hatred	9
丑	chǒu	adj.	ugly	5
出奇	chūqí	adv.	extraordinarily	4
矗立	chùlì	v.	stand tall and upright	3
揣	chuāi	v.	carry in one's hand or pocket	7
穿越	chuānyuè	v.	pass through	3
传统	chuántǒng	n.	tradition	2
船头	chuántóu	n.	front end of a boat	3
炊	chuī	n.	cooking	9
垂	chuí	v.	hang down	2
捶布	chuíbù	v.	beat cloth (i.e., wash cloth)	5
春闺梦里人			referring to husbands who fought invaders on the borders but appeared in the dreams of their wives at home	14

唇	chún	n.	lips	2
纯净	chúnjìng	adj.	pure	11
蠢事	chǔnshì	n.	stupid thing	7
葱须	cōngxū	n.	root of green onion	12
淙淙	cóngcóng	onm.	gurgling of flowing water	2
醋	cù	n.	vinegar	7
摧	cuī	v.	destroy	14
催	cuī	v.	prompt	10
脆弱	cuìruò	adj.	fragile	7
存在	cúnzài	n.	existence	10

D

打湿	dǎshī	v.	wet	1
打探	dǎtàn	v.	inquire about	4
大抵	dàdǐ	adv.	on the whole	11
大都	dàdū	adv.	mostly	13
大人	dàrén	n.	official (old way of addressing, honorific)	4
大作	dàzuò	n.	your great writing (honorific)	4
呆板	dāibǎn	adj.	dull	13
呆呆地	dāidāide	adv.	dully	3
待	dài	v.	wait until	12
担心	dānxīn	v.	feel worried	2
当	dāng	v.	should	8
当代	dāngdài	adj.	contemporary	11
当年	dāngnián	adv.	in those years	2
挡	dǎng	v.	block	6
荡	dàng	v.	clear away	12
道	dào	v.	talk	10
到达	dàodá	v.	arrive	2
道德	dàodé	n.	morals	11
道理	dàolǐ	n.	reason	8
得以	déyǐ	v.	be able to	11

得意	déyì	adj.	complacent	7
蹬蹬蹬	dēngdēngdēng	onm.	sound of a person's heavy footsteps	4
等于	děngyú	v.	equal	10
堤坝	dībà	n.	dam	3
笛卡儿	Díkǎ'ér	n.	René Decartes (1596-1650), a French philosopher	11
敌意	díyì	n.	hostility	13
递	dì	v.	pass over	6
地面	dìmiàn	n.	surface of the ground	5
地毯	dìtǎn	n.	carpet	6
地位	dìwèi	n.	social position	7
地狱	dìyù	n.	hell	3
雕花	diāohuā	v.	carve patterns or designs	5
调	diào	v.	transfer	4
跌交	diējiāo	v.	stumble and fall	8
顶端	dǐngduān	n.	pinnacle	14
冻	dòng	v.	freeze	14
抖动	dǒudòng	v.	tremble	4
独有	dúyǒu	v	have exclusively	11
肚	dù	n.	abdomen	1
段	duàn	n.	length of distance	3
堆	duī	m.	pile	7
对抗	duìkàng	n.	confrontation	13
对立	duìlì	adj.	antagonistic	13
对头	duìtóu	adj.	correct	6
顿时	dùnshí	adv.	immediately	13
多半	duōbàn	adv.	most probably	11
躲	duǒ	v.	hide	3

E

俄狄浦斯	Édípǔsī	n.	Oedipus, a legendary king in Greek mythology	10

恶	è	n.	evil	11
遏	è	v.	check	3

F

发表	fābiǎo	v.	deliver (a formal speech)	13
发喊	fāhǎn	v.	shout out	3
发火	fāhuǒ	v.	lose one's temper	4
发热	fārè	v.	emit heat	5
发现	fāxiàn	v.	discover	5
发作	fāzuò	v.	flare up	4
乏味	fáwèi	adj.	boring	7
翻寻	fānxún	v.	search	9
翻阅	fānyuè	v.	browse	9
凡	fán	adv.	all	11
凡	fán	n.	ordinariness	11
繁复	fánfù	adj.	complicated	9
繁花	fánhuā	n.	flowers of all kinds and colors	2
烦劳	fánláo	n.	agitation	12
繁难	fánnán	adj.	troublesome	12
烦琐	fánsuǒ	n.	trifles	7
繁衍	fányǎn	v.	increase gradually in number or quantity	5
反对	fǎnduì	v.	oppose	13
反正	fǎnzhèng	adv.	in any case	8
饭量	fànliàng	n.	appetite	7
芳容	fāngróng	n.	beautiful face (honorific)	13
防	fáng	v.	guard against	12
仿佛	fǎngfú	adv.	as if; 好象; 好似; 犹如	11
放弃	fàngqì	v.	give up	13
飞驰	fēichí	v.	speed along	9
沸	fèi	adj.	boiling	12
芬芳	fēnfāng	n.	fragrance	6
纷纷	fēnfēn	adj.	profuse	14

分明	fēnmíng	adv.	obviously	4
分配	fēnpèi	v.	distribute	8
份	fèn	m.	used after 这 or 那 for certain abstract things	7
奋斗	fèndòu	n.	struggle	11
封闭	fēngbì	v.	seal	6
封闭	fēngbì	n.	closure	14
烽火台	fēnghuǒtái	n.	beacon tower	14
风	fēng	n.	local custom	11
逢	féng	v.	come across	4
奉	fèng	v.	revere	2
缝	fèng	n.	crack	14
服	fú	v.	take (medicine)	12
浮标	fúbiāo	n.	buoy	3
服气	fúqì	v.	be convinced	9
富	fù	v.	(same as 富于) be rich in	11
副	fù	m.	pair (of glasses)	4
负面	fùmiàn	adj.	negative	11
富有	fùyǒu	v.	be rich in	13

G

盖房	gài fáng	v.	build a house	5
干燥	gānzào	adj.	dry	5
敢	gǎn	v.	dare	3
感	gǎn	n.	suffix to denote a feeling	11
感化	gǎnhuà	n.	persuasion	11
感情	gǎnqíng	n.	affection	13
感受	gǎnshòu	v.	feel	13
感叹	gǎntàn	v.	sigh with feeling	3
刚烈	gānglià	n.	personal quality of being upright and unyielding	11
高处	gāochù	n.	high place	1

高级	gāojí	adj.	top-grade	6
高尚	gāoshàng	adj.	noble	11
高雅	gāoyǎ	adj.	refined	11
稿件	gǎojiàn	n.	manuscripts	6
告别	gàobié	v.	say "good-bye"	4
歌德	Gēdé	n.	Johann Wolfgang von Goethe (1749-1832), a German poet and playwright	11
各地	gè dì	n.	different places	12
根	gēn	n.	root	8
供	gōng	v.	provide	5
功夫	gōngfu	n.	skill or art	12
公里	gōnglǐ	n.	kilometer	14
弓弦	gōngxián	n.	bowstring	14
功效	gōngxiào	n.	function and effect	12
拱	gǒng	v.	push with one's shoulders or head	1
供奉	gòngfèng	v.	enshrine and worship	12
钩	gōu	n.	hook	3
沟通	gōutōng	v.	communicate	13
构成	gòuchéng	v.	form	14
孤单	gūdān	adj.	lonely	2
孤独	gūdú	adj.	lonely	6
估量	gūliáng	n.	appraisal	10
鼓	gǔ	v.	rouse	12
股	gǔ	m.	as in 一股泉水, 一股香味	13
鼓翅	gǔ chì	v.	pluck wings	3
固	gù	adj.	strongly fortified	14
顾	gù	v.	attend to	8
顾虑	gùlǜ	n.	worry	7
怪异	guàiyì	adj.	strange	3
关于	guānyú	prep.	with regard to	11
光滑	guānghuá	adj.	smooth	5
光明	guāngmíng	n.	brightness	5
光鲜	guāngxiān	adj.	bright and new	2

广	guǎng	adv.	broadly	12
广阔	guǎngkuò	adj.	vast	13
闺	guī	n.	lady's chamber	14
归	guī	v.	return	8
规定	guīdìng	n.	regulation	12
规则	guīzé	adj.	regular	5
滚出去	gǔn chūqu	v.	get out	4
锅	guō	n.	pot	7
果然	guǒrán	adv.	sure enough	5
过	guò	v.	surpass	2
过	guò	adv.	too	12
过程	guòchéng	n.	process	12
过度	guòdù	adv.	excessively	12

H

寒	hán	adj.	冷	14
寒舍	hánshè	n.	my humble home (humble)	4
汉白玉	hànbáiyù	n.	white marble	5
汗珠	hànzhū	n.	bead of sweat	4
汉子	hànzi	n.	fellow	1
行列	hángliè	n.	rank	12
好似	hǎosì	v.	好象	3
好心人	hǎoxīn rén	n	kindhearted person	4
浩瀚	hàohàn	adj.	vast	11
喝饮	hēyǐn	v.	drink	5
何	hé	adj.	what	2
合	hé	n.	reunion; 聚会	10
和	hé	v.	(of a chess game) end in a draw	13
何必	hébì	adv.	why (see Part V.10)	13
何尝	hécháng	adv.	how can; 怎么会	10
河道	hédào	n.	river course	3
河滩	hétān	n.	riverside	5

合伙	héhuǒ	v.	join forces to do sth.	5
喝	hè	v.	shout loudly	4
黑黝黝	hēiyǒuyǒu	adj.	jet-black	5
痕迹	hénjì	n.	vestige	14
横(着走)	héng(zhe zǒu)	v.	move sideways	8
轰轰烈烈	hōnghōnglièliè	adj.	on a grand and spectacular scale	7
轰鸣	hōngmíng	n.	roar	6
鸿	hóng	n.	swan goose; 鸿雁	14
鸿雁	hóngyàn	n.	swan goose	14
哄	hōng	onm.	sound of a group of people's sudden laughter	4
后世	hòushì	n.	later generations	12
忽	hū	onm.	sound of a bird's sudden flight	1
蝴蝶	húdié	n.	butterfly	2
胡子	húzi	n.	moustache	4
花茎	huājīng	n.	flower stem	4
滑	huá	v.	slide	3
化	huà	v.	change; 变	10
桦树	huàshù	n.	birch	1
槐荫	huáiyīn	n.	shade of a Chinese scholartree	5
怀有	huáiyǒu	v.	maintain	13
环顾	huángù	v.	look around	6
缓	huǎn	v.	relieve	12
唤起	huànqǐ	v.	arouse	6
浣纱	huànshā	v.	wash yarn	5
幻想	huànxiǎng	v.	fantasize	14
荒草	huāngcǎo	n.	weeds on a piece of desolate land	5
皇帝	huángdì	n.	emperor	14
黄昏	huánghūn	adv.	at dusk	6
黄梁梦	huángliángmèng	n.	"golden millet dream," a Chinese allusion that has several meanings. Here it refers to the quick passage of time and the insignificance of human life.	9

晃	huàng	v.	rock	6
辉煌	huīhuáng	n.	splendor	6
回敬	huíjìng	v.	do or give sth. in return with respect (being ironic in this context)	10
会场	huìchǎng	n.	meeting place	13
会员	huìyuán	n.	member of an organization	4
昏寐	hūnmèi	n.	lethargy	12
混浊	hùnzhuó	adj.	muddy	3
活泼	huópō	adj.	lively	13
火候	huǒhòu	n.	duration and degree of heating	12
豁达	huòdá	n.	open-mindedness	13
获得	huòdé	v.	obtain	10

J

基	jī	n.	foundation	14
基本	jīběn	adv.	basically; 基本上	12
饥饿	jī'è	adj.	hungry	1
讥讽	jīfěng	n.	ridicule	5
激烈	jīliè	adj.	vehement	13
激情	jīqíng	n.	intense emotion	11
基石	jīshí	n.	foundation stone	14
机智	jīzhì	n.	quick-wittedness	13
吉	jí	adj.	auspicious	8
及	jí	v.	reach	4
及	jí	conj.	and	10
极其	jíqí	adv.	extremely	10
几何	jǐhé	adj.	多少	14
剂	jì	m.	dose (for herbal medicine)	12
系	jì	v.	fasten	4
寂静	jìjìng	adj.	quiet	1
寂寞	jìmò	n.	loneliness	5
继续	jìxù	v.	continue	9

记忆	jìyì	n.	memory	9
记载	jìzǎi	v.	record	12
佳	jiā	adj.	good	12
夹道	jiādào	v.	line up at both sides of a road	2
加惠于	jiā hùi yú	v.	benefit	11
家具	jiājù	n.	furniture	6
价值	jiàzhí	n.	worth	10
兼	jiān	adv.	concurrently	8
坚固	jiāngù	adj.	strong	14
坚决地	jiānjuéde	adv.	resolutely	3
奸诈	jiānzhà	n.	wickedness	11
检验	jiǎnyàn	n.	test	12
箭	jiàn	n.	arrow	14
渐渐	jiànjiàn	adv.	gradually; 逐渐	11
见闻	jiànwén	n.	what one sees and hears	2
见证	jiànzhèng	n.	witness	14
将	jiāng	prep.	把	3
疆	jiāng	n.	boundary	14
桨	jiǎng	n.	oar	3
讲桌	jiǎngzhuō	n.	podium	4
酱	jiàng	n.	soy sauce	7
交往	jiāowǎng	n.	interaction	13
绞	jiǎo	v.	twist	7
搅	jiǎo	v.	stir	3
角度	jiǎodù	n.	angle; perspective	12
脚跟	jiǎogēn	n.	heel	8
角落	jiǎoluò	n.	corner	4
侥幸地	jiǎoxìngde	adv.	by luck	3
教鞭	jiàobiān	n.	pointer	4
皆	jiē	adv.	each and every	11
接待	jiēdài	v.	receive	14
节	jié	n.	section (of a book)	12
截断	jiéduàn	v.	cut off	3

结果	jiéguǒ	n.	result	4
孑然	jiérán	adj.	alone	4
结缘	jiéyuán	v.	develop an affinity for	11
解	jiě	v.	relieve	12
解放	jiěfàng	v.	liberate	13
借鉴	jièjiàn	v.	use for reference	13
禁不住	jīnbuzhù	v.	can not help (doing)	3
今晨	jīnchén	n.	this morning	1
金汤	jīntāng	n.	short for 金城汤池, ramparts of metal and a moat of boiling water--an impregnable fortress	14
尽管	jǐnguǎn	conj.	even though	9
仅仅	jǐnjǐn	adv.	merely	9
紧张	jǐnzhāng	adj.	tense	13
尽	jìn	v.	exhaust	2
尽	jìn	adv.	all	4
尽量	jìnliàng	adv.	as much as possible	13
近日	jìnrì	adv.	recently	4
近视镜	jìnshìjìng	n.	nearsighted eyeglasses; 近视眼镜	4
经	jīng	n.	scripture	7
精彩	jīngcǎi	adj.	brilliant	13
惊厥	jīngjué	n.	convulsion	12
经历	jīnglì	n./v.	experience; undergo	11
惊奇	jīngqí	adj.	surprised	5
旌旗	jīngqí	n.	banners and flags	14
精神	jīngshén	n.	spirit	11
经验	jīngyàn	n.	experience (in the sense of knowledge)	11
景物	jǐngwù	n.	scenes and things	9
竟	jìng	adv.	unexpectedly; 竟然	4
境界	jìngjiè	n.	realm	11
静静的	jìngjìngde	adj	quiet	1
静悄悄	jìngqiāoqiāo	adj.	quiet	4
敬意	jìngyì	n.	respect	4

究竟	jiūjìng	adv.	after all	8
就	jiù	v.	accomodate to	14
居住	jūzhù	n.	living	6
局长	júzhǎng	n.	head of a government bureau	4
举起来	jǔ qǐlai	v.	lift up	1
据	jù	prep.	according to	12
距离	jùlí	n.	distance	1
剧烈地	jùliède	adv.	rapidly	4
巨兽	jùshòu	n.	giant beast	3
具体	jùtǐ	adj.	specific	12
具有	jùyǒu	v.	have as a quality or ability	11
巨著	jùzhù	n.	monumental work	12
卷	juàn	n.	volume	12
绝	jué	adj.	exhausted	9
绝	jué	adv.	absolutely	9
俊	jùn	adj.	pretty	4
俊	jùn	n.	person of outstanding talent	11

K

开场白	kāichǎngbái	n.	opening remarks	13
开枪	kāiqiāng	v.	shoot (with a gun)	1
看来	kànlái	adv.	it seems	8
抗争	kàngzhēng	v.	fight	11
烤	kǎo	v.	bake	11
考虑	kǎolǜ	v.	consider	4
磕破	kē pò	v.	hit (sth. hard) and break	5
可耻	kěchǐ	adj.	shameful	5
可怜	kělián	adj.	pitiable	7
可能	kěnéng	n.	possibility	11
可能性	kěnéngxìng	n.	possibility	11
可惜	kěxī	adv.	regrettably	2
刻字	kèzì	v.	carve or engrave characters	5

肯定	kěndìng	adv.	definitely	4
坑凹	kēng'āo	n.	hole	5
空地	kòngdì	n.	open ground	1
口袋	kǒudài	n.	pocket	7
扣	kòu	v.	pull (a trigger)	1
枯	kū	adj.	dry; withered	2
苦	kǔ	n.	hardships	2
苦难	kǔnàn	n.	sufferings	10
垮	kuǎ	adj.	collapsed	14
跨	kuà	v.	stride	8
狂	kuáng	adj.	mad	3
狂吼	kuánghǒu	n.	wild roar	3
狂妄	kuángwàng	adj.	presumptuous	10
况且	kuàngqiě	conj.	moreover	11
愧恨	kuìhèn	n.	remorse	1
困难	kùnnan	n.	difficulty	2

L

拉直	lā zhí	v.	pull (sth.) straight	5
菜布尼茨	Láibùnící	n.	Gottfried Wilhelm Leibniz (1646-1719), a German philosopher	8
懒得	lǎnde	v.	not feel like (doing sth.)	5
狼烟	lángyān	n.	the smoke of wolves' dung burnt at border posts to signal alarm in ancient China	14
浪	làng	n.	wave	12
浪漫	làngmàn	adj.	romantic	6
老实	lǎoshí	adj.	honest	4
老鹰	lǎoyīng	n.	eagle	2
乐趣	lèqù	n.	pleasure	12
垒	lěi	v.	build by piling up (stones, etc.)	5
类	lèi	n.	category	11
泪水	lèishuǐ	n.	tears	1

棱角	léngjiǎo	n.	edges and corners	5
冷漠地	lěngmòde	adv.	indifferently	3
理	lǐ	n.	same as 道理	8
理会	lǐhuì	v.	pay attention to	5
立	lì	v.	appoint	2
利	lì	adj.	sharp	14
力度	lìdù	n.	dynamics	13
立即	lìjí	adv	immediately	5
历时	lìshí	v.	last	12
利于	lìyú	v.	be of advantage to, 有利于	8
粒子	lìzǐ	n.	particle	10
联想	liánxiǎng	n.	association in the mind	13
恋	liàn	n.	love	6
凉	liáng	adj.	chilly	1
凉丝丝	liángsīsī	adj.	slightly cool	1
良性	liángxìng	adj.	of good nature	11
两	liǎng	m.	unit of weight, equal to one-twentieth of a kilogram	7
两旁	liǎngpáng	n.	both sides	8
亮晶晶	liàngjīngjīng	adj.	sparkling	1
疗效	liáoxiào	n.	curing effect	12
了不起	liǎobuqǐ	adj.	extraordinary	2
料	liào	v.	expect	4
列夫·托尔斯泰	Lièfū · Tuō'ěrsītài	n.	Leo Tolstoy (1828-1910), a great Russian writer	11
猎枪	lièqiāng	n.	hunting gun	1
猎人	lièrén	n.	hunter	1
林间	línjiān	n.	clearing in a wood	1
铃	líng	n.	bell	4
灵动	língdòng	adj.	quick and nimble	4
灵感	línggǎn	n	inspiration	4
凌越	língyuè	adj.	paramount	2
流传	liúchuán	v.	spread	11

流露	liúlù	v.	reveal	1
流失	liúshī	v.	flow away	6
鲁莽	lǔmǎng	adj.	crude and rash	1
鲁迅	Lǔxùn	n.	real name 周树人 (1881-1931), one of the greatest writers in the May Fourth period	11
屡	lǚ	adv.	repeatedly	13
缕	lǚ	m.	(of smoke) wisp	10
鹿	lù	n.	deer	1
露珠	lùzhū	n.	dewdrops	1
律师	lǜshī	n.	lawyer	13
《论语》	Lúnyǔ	n.	*The Analects of Confucius*	11
罗密欧	Luómì'ōu	n.	Romeo, a Shakespearean character	10
落	luò	v.	fall	1
落寞	luòmò	n.	despondence	6

M

马克思	Mǎkèsī	n.	Karl Marx (1818-1883), a German economist and political philosopher	11
迈步	màibù	v.	take steps	8
麦收	màishōu	n.	wheat harvest (wheat, 麦子)	5
满脸	mǎnliǎn	n.	the whole face	2
满月	mǎnyuè	n.	full moon	5
漫天	màntiān	adj.	all over the sky	3
矛盾	máodùn	n.	contradiction	8
冒险	màoxiǎn	adj.	risky	8
眉头	méitóu	n.	eyebrows	7
眉梢	méishāo	n.	tip of an eyebrow	13
美事	měishì	n.	wonderful thing	4
闷	mēn	v.	shut oneself indoors	6
眯	mī	v.	narrow (one's eyes)	1
米	mǐ	n.	meter	1
绵延	miányán	v.	continue	9

瞄准	miáozhǔn	v.	aim at	1
渺小	miǎoxiǎo	adj.	insignificant	2
民族	mínzú	n.	nation	14
敏捷	mǐnjié	n.	quick-mindedness	13
明	míng	v.	make clear	12
鸣	míng	n.	calling of birds	2
明了	míngliǎo	adj.	clear	7
沫	mò	n.	foam	12
莫	mò	adv.	not	8
漠	mò	n.	desert; 沙漠	3
莫非	mòfēi	adv.	can it be that	3
某些	mǒuxiē	adj.	certain	12
模样	múyàng	n.	appearance	5
牧	mù	v.	herd	14
目标	mùbiāo	n.	target	8
目的	mùdì	n.	purpose	14
木然	mùrán	adv.	stupefiedly	3
沐浴	mùyù	v.	bathe	6

N

拿破仑	Nápòlún	n.	Napoleon Bonaparte	4
乃	nǎi	adv.	就	14
耐	nài	v.	be able to bear or endure	13
难为	nánwéi	v.	be a tough job to	2
脑袋	nǎodai	n.	head	8
闹不清(楚)	nàobuqīng(chu)	v.	cannot tell	8
内容	nèiróng	n.	content	12
能力	nénglì	n.	ability	13
年华	niánhuá	n.	(of human life) years	6
鸟巢	niǎocháo	n.	bird's nest	1
凝	níng	adj.	stagnant	12
凝思	níngsī	n.	all-absorbing thought	14

宁愿	nìngyuàn	adv.	would rather	6
扭头	niǔtóu	v.	turn around one's head	8
奴隶	núlì	n.	slave	13
怒	nù	n.	anger	3
懦夫	nuòfū	n.	coward	3

O

偶尔	ǒu'ěr	adv.	occasionally	12
偶然	ǒurán	adj.	incidental	10
偶人	ǒurén	n.	statuette	12

P

爬	pá	v.	climb (a mountain)	2
排除	páichú	v.	eliminate	11
排沙	páishād	n.	sand-discharging	3
攀登	pāndēng	v.	limb	2
盘	pán	m.	game (of chess)	13
盘旋	pánxuán	v.	circle	2
盼	pàn	v.	long for	5
螃蟹	pángxiè	n.	crab	8
胖	pàng	adj.	fat	3
抛却	pāoquè	v.	cast away	6
培养	péiyǎng	v.	foster	13
配合	pèihé	v.	coordinate	8
喷	pēn	v.	spurt	3
盆	pén	n.	plate	7
捧腹	pěngfù	v.	split one's sides laughing	13
批判	pīpàn	n.	criticism	11
批评家	pīpíngjiā	n.	critic	13
疲倦	píjuàn	adj.	weary	2
漂	piāo	v.	drift (in water)	3

飘	piāo	v.	drift (in the air)	4
飘然	piāorán	n.	gracefulness	6
瓢	piáo	n.	ladle	7
撇	piě	m.	strand (of moustache)	4
瞥	piē	v.	take a glance	14
拼命	pīnmìng	adv.	with all one's might	3
品第	pǐndì	n.	grade	12
品质	pǐnzhì	n.	moral quality	11
凭	píng	prep.	on the basis of	8
平凡	píngfán	adj.	ordinary	13
平衡	pínghéng	n.	balance	14
平静	píngjìng	adj.	calm	3
平均	píngjūn	adv.	at an average of	4
平面	píngmiàn	n.	flat surface	5
平时	píngshí	n.	ordinary times	1
屏障	píngzhàng	n.	natural defense (lit., protective screen)	14
魄	pò	n.	soul	10
破开	pò kāi	v.	break (sth.) into parts	5
铺	pū	v.	spread	6
扑剌	pūlā	onm.	sound of wind	14
普遍	pǔbiàn	adv.	generally	13
普通	pǔtōng	adj.	ordinary	10

Q

萋萋	qīqī	adj.	lush	1
凄婉	qīwǎn	adj.	dreary	14
其	qí	pro.	your (his, her, its, their)	2
棋	qí	n.	chess	13
奇迹	qíjì	n.	miracle	3
棋迷	qímí	n.	chess fan	13
奇妙	qímiào	adj.	marvellous	12
棋盘	qípán	n.	chessboard	13

棋谱	qípǔ	n.	chess manual	13
其实	qíshí	adv.	as a matter of fact	7
棋艺	qíyì	n.	skill in playing chess	13
其中	qízhōng	adv.	among which	12
棋子	qízi	n.	chessman	13
岂	qǐ	adv.	used to ask a rhetorical question; 难道	10
启迪	qǐdí	n.	inspiration	13
起(…效果)	qǐ (...xiàoguǒ)	v.	take (effect)	11
起源	qǐyuán	n.	origin	12
气氛	qìfēn	n.	atmosphere	6
气派	qìpài	n.	impressive style or manner	13
卡	qiǎ	v.	have in a stranglehold	14
恰恰	qiàqià	adv.	exactly	13
牵扯	qiānchě	v.	tug	1
千古	qiāngǔ	adj.	of all ages	2
千金	qiānjīn	n.	someone's daughter (honorific)	4
谦逊	qiānxùn	n.	modesty	13
掮	qián	v.	carry on the shoulder	5
前途	qiántú	n.	future	4
钱钟书	Qián Zhōngshū	n.	a contemporary Chinese writer and scholar (1910-1998)	13
浅	qiǎn	adj.	shallow; superficial	4
潜心	qiǎnxīn	adv.	with great concentration	12
强	qiáng	adj.	better	5
强	qiáng	adj.	strong	2
抢购	qiǎnggòu	v.	rush to purchase	7
瞧	qiáo	v.	look	8
瞧不起	qiáobuqǐ	v.	look down upon	7
巧妙	qiǎomiào	adj.	ingenious	13
翘	qiào	v.	tilt up	3
翘望	qiàowàng	v.	look up at	5
切洗	qiēxǐ	v.	cut and wash	9
怯懦	qiènuò	adj.	timid and scared	3

亲	qīn	v.	kiss	4
亲身	qīnshēn	adj.	firsthand	11
亲自	qīnzì	adv.	in person	11
勤奋	qínfèn	adj.	diligent	12
青春豆	qīngchūndòu	n.	pimple; 青春痘	4
清炯	qīngjiǒng	adj.	(of eyes) clear, bright, and piercing	2
青年	qīngnián	n.	young person	4
轻柔	qīngróu	n.	lightness and gentleness	6
轻松	qīngsōng	adj.	relaxed	13
倾注	qīngzhù	v.	pour into	10
情调	qíngdiào	n.	taste (in life)	13
情景	qíngjǐng	n.	scene	1
情况	qíngkuàng	n.	situation	8
情趣	qíngqù	n.	temperament and taste	11
情绪	qíngxù	n.	mood	6
顷刻	qǐngkè	adv.	instantly	10
请帖	qǐngtiē	n.	invitation card	7
庆幸	qìngxìng	v.	feel happy because things could be worse	7
求见	qiújiàn	v.	ask to see	13
求生	qiúshēng	n.	seeking survival	3
酋长	qíuzhǎng	n.	chief of a tribe	2
驱	qū	v.	expel	12
屈	qū	v.	bend	1
趋避	qūbì	v.	avoid	11
驱散	qūsàn	v.	disperse	13
躯体	qūtǐ	n.	human body	14
曲折	qūzhé	adj.	tortuous	9
权力	quánlì	n.	power	7
全身	quánshēn	n.	the whole body	2
泉水	quánshuǐ	n.	spring water	2
犬	quǎn	n.	狗	14
劝	quàn	v.	persuade	11
雀	què	n.	sparrow	4

确	què	adv.	really; 确实	8
确实	quèshí	adv.	indeed	4
群山	qúnshān	n.	group of mountains	14

R

让	ràng	v.	give ground	13
人格	réngé	n.	moral integrity	11
人际	rénjì	adj.	interpersonal	13
人家	rénjia,	pron.	others	8
人类	rénlèi	n.	mankind	10
人造	rénzào	adj.	manmade	8
忍受	rěnshòu	v.	endure	5
刃	rèn	n.	blade	14
任	rèn	v.	allow	5
仍	réng	adv.	still; 还; 仍然	9
仍然	réng	adv.	still; 还; 仍	9
溶化	rónghuà	v.	dissolve	11
融洽	róngqià	adj.	harmonious	13
如此	rúcǐ	adv.	so; 这么; 这样	6
如何	rúhé	adv.	how; 怎么; 怎样	9
乳泉	rǔquán	n.	milk-like spring water	12
入药	rùyào	v.	be used as medicine	12
睿智	ruìzhì	adj.	wise and farsighted	11
弱	ruò	adj.	weak	11
弱者	ruòzhě	n.	the weak	11

S

洒	sǎ	v.	shed (light)	1
洒脱	sǎtuō	adj.	unrestrained	13
塞	sài	n.	a place of strategic importance	14
丧失	sàngshī	n.	loss	11

沙	shā	n.	sand	3
杀	shā	v.	fight (in a chess game)	13
傻	shǎ	adj.	stupid	7
傻瓜	shǎguā	n.	fool	13
啥	shà	pro.	what; 什么	4
山顶	shāndǐng	n.	mountain top	2
山林	shānlín	n.	wood in a mountain	1
山麓	shānlù	n.	foot of a mountain	2
山墙	shānqiáng	n.	gable	5
山崖	shānyá	n.	cliff	3
闪动	shǎndòng	v.	gleam	1
闪光	shǎnguāng	v.	glitter	5
闪身	shǎnshēn	v.	dodge	13
善	shàn	n.	goodness	11
伤痕	shānghén	n.	wound	2
商旅	shānglǚ	n.	traveling merchant	14
上司	shàngsī	n.	boss	7
上溯	shàngsù	v.	trace back to the past (lit., go upstream)	11
上游	shàngyóu	n.	upper reaches of a river	3
稍稍	shāoshāo	adv.	a little bit	5
设想	shèxiǎng	v.	imagine	8
深幽幽	shēnyōuyōu	adj.	deep and dark	3
神秘	shénmì	adj.	mysterious	1
神情	shénqíng	n.	facial expression	2
神色	shénsè	n.	look	1
神圣	shénshèng	adj.	sacred	2
甚而	shèn'ér	adv.	even; 甚至	11
甚至	shènzhì	conj.	so much so that	4
升	shēng	v.	rise	14
生成	shēngchéng	n.	birth	10
生存	shēngcún	v.	survive	5
升落	shēngluò	v.	涨落	9
生长	shēngzhǎng	v.	grow	5

省得	shěngde	conj.	so as (for sth.) not (to happen)	5
盛(唐)	shèng (táng)	adj.	prosperous (age of the Tang dynasty)	12
剩下	shèngxia	v.	be left with	2
失败	shībài	adj.	failed	4
失去	shīqù	v.	lose	4
时代	shídài	n.	times	12
时光	shíguāng	n.	time	9
石匠	shíjiàng	n.	stonemason	5
时节	shíjié	n.	season (for a certain agricultural activity)	5
石磨	shímò	n.	millstones	5
食盐	shíyán	n.	salt; 盐	12
实在	shízài	adj.	down-to-earth	7
食指	shízhǐ	n.	index finger	1
使唤	shǐhuàn	n.	order	8
《史记》	Shǐjì	n.	*Records of the Grand Historian* by 司马迁 (Sīmǎ Qiān, 145 ca. - ? B.C.) of the Han dynasty	11
矢刃	shǐrèn	n	arrows and swords (ancient weapons)	14
柿把	shìbà	n.	persimmon stem	4
适从	shìcóng	v.	follow	8
嗜好	shìhào	n.	hobby	11
世纪	shìjì	n.	century	14
逝去	shìqù	v.	pass by	10
世俗	shìsú	n.	worldly convention	5
事业	shìyè	n.	career	7
寿	shòu	n.	longevity	14
瘦弱	shòuruò	adj.	thin and weak	1
输	shū	v.	lose	13
蔬菜	shūcài	n.	vegetables	9
熟	shú	adj.	cooked	9
熟路	shúlù	n.	familiar road (or route)	8
属于	shǔyú	v.	belong to	6
树枝	shùzhī	n.	twig	1

摔	shuāi	v.	fall	5
衰老	shuāilǎo	v.	become old and feeble	14
甩	shuǎi	v.	toss	4
霜	shuāng	n.	frost	2
爽朗	shuǎnglǎng	adj.	clear and loud	14
水龙头	shuǐlóngtóu	n.	(water) tap	9
水平	shuǐpíng	n.	level	4
顺着	shùnzhe	prep.	along; 沿着	3
说不定	shuōbudìng	adv.	maybe	8
说法	shuōfǎ	n.	argument	8
思考	sīkǎo	v.	contemplate	10
思想	sīxiǎng	n.	thought	13
思绪	sīxù	n.	train of thought	13
死神	sǐshén	n.	Death (personified)	1
死尸	sǐshī	n.	corpse	14
似乎	sìhū	adv.	as if; 好象	3
松树	sōngshù	n.	pine tree	2
苏武牧羊	Sū Wǔ mù yáng		an allusion referring to 苏武, whose styled name was Zǐqīng (子卿). A famous general in the Han dynasty, he was captured in a battle with the Tartars and exiled to the wilderness called 北海, where he survived the ordeal as a shepherd.	14
俗	sú	n.	local convention (as in 风俗)	11
俗	sú	n.	vulgarity (as in 凡俗)	11
肃穆	sùmù	adj.	solemn and quiet	2
酸枣	suānzǎo	adv.	wild jujube	14
随	suí	v.	go along with	14
隧道	suìdào	n.	tunnel	3
岁月	suìyuè	n.	(of human life) years	6
缩	suō	v.	(of body) huddle up	3
锁钥	suǒyuè	n.	strategic gateway (lit., key to a lock)	14

T

踏实	tāshi	adj.	free from anxiety	8
踏	tà	v.	tread	14
胎动	tāidòng	n.	movement of the fetus	14
苔	tái	n.	moss	5
抬步	táibù	v.	take steps	8
台阶	táijiē	n.	steps	5
摊开	tānkāi	v.	spread out	3
谈(朋友)	tán (péngyou)	v.	date	4
弹射	tánshè	v.	shoot off (as with a catapult)	3
堂	táng	m.	(of a class) period	4
唐朝	tángcháo	n.	Tang dynasty (618-904)	12
唐代	tángdài	n.	same as 唐朝	12
唐代宗	tángdàizōng	n.	10th Tang dynasty emperor (762-780)	12
倘若	tǎngruò	conj.	if	8
躺下	tǎngxia	v.	lie down	1
讨厌	tǎoyàn	v.	dislike	5
陶冶	táoyě	n.	cultivation	11
腾	téng	v.	prance	12
提神	tíshén	n.	refreshment of mind	12
体会	tǐhuì	v.	realize	13
体现	tǐxiàn	v.	reflect	11
体验	tǐyàn	n./v.	experience; learn through one's experience	11
体育	tǐyù	n.	sports	14
替	tì	prep.	for	7
天文学家	tiānwénxuéjiā	n.	astronomer	5
天意	tiānyì	n.	the will of Heaven	2
天资	tiānzī	n.	natural talent	12
调侃	tiáokǎn	n.	ridicule	13
调皮	tiáopí	adj.	mischievous	13
调味剂	tiǎowèijì	n.	condiment; 调味品	13
跳跃	tiàoyuè	v.	jump	1

贴	tiē	v.	keep close to	1
听众	tīngzhòng	n.	audience	13
艇	tǐng	n.	light boat	3
挺(胸)	tǐng (xiōng)	v.	throw out (one's chest)	7
通路	tōnglù	n.	open road	3
同情	tóngqíng	n.	sympathy	11
统计	tǒngjì	n.	count	4
统治	tǒngzhì	v.	rule	14
痛苦	tòngkǔ	n.	sufferings	9
偷偷	tōutōu	adv.	secretly	7
头顶	tóudǐng	adj.	the top of the head	1
投下	tóuxià	v.	drop	12
透	tòu	v.	penetrate	1
透	tòu	v.	reveal	13
凸(肚)	tū (dù)	v.	protrude (one's belly)	7
秃鹰	tūyīng	n.	vulture	2
吞	tūn	v.	swallow	3
吞噬	tūnshì	v.	swallow	14

W

洼坑	wākēng	n.	holes in the ground	8
歪	wāi	v.	tilt (to one side)	8
外宾	wàibīn	n.	foreign guest	14
弯	wān	v.	bend	3
蜿蜒	wānyán	v.	zigzag	14
完全	wánquán	adj.	complete	4
顽石	wánshí	n.	hard rock	5
碗	wǎn	n.	bowl	7
往事	wǎngshì	n.	past events	10
往往	wǎngwǎng	adv.	often	11
望	wàng	v.	look into the distance	1
微	wēi	adj.	tiny	10

微	wēi	adv.	slightly	1
微粒	wēilì	n.	particle	10
为	wéi		see Part II.3 of Lesson 12	
唯	wéi	adv.	only	8
《围城》	Wéichéng	n.	*Fortress Beseiged* by 钱钟书	13
唯一	wéiyī	adj.	sole	14
尾	wěi	n.	tail	3
伟岸	wěi'àn	n.	magnificence	6
未	wèi	adv.	did not; 没	9
慰藉	wèijiè	n.	comfort	6
味精	wèijīng	n.	MSG	13
未来	wèilái	n.	future	11
卫星	wèixīng	n.	satellite	8
喂养	wèiyǎng	v.	feed and raise	9
位置	wèizhi	n.	location	8
温暖	wēnnuǎn	adj.	warm (sunlight)	1
温情	wēnqíng	n.	tender feeling	6
温热	wēnrè	adj.	warm (water)	1
温柔	wēnróu	adj.	gentle and soft	6
闻	wén	v.	smell	9
闻知	wénzhī	v.	hear	11
卧	wò	v.	(of animal) crouch	1
握手	wòshǒu	v.	shake hands	7
污土	wūtǔ	n.	filthy dirt	5
乌(鸦)	wū(yā)	n.	crow	4
乌有	wūyǒu	n.	nothing	10
无	wú	n.	nothing	2
无	wú	adj.	not having	10
无故	wúgù	adv.	without a reason	12
无礼	wúlǐ	adj.	rude	13
无穷	wúqióng	n.	endlessness	10
无限	wúxiàn	adj.	limitless	10
无形间	wúxíngjiān	adv.	imperceptibly	11

| 雾 | wù | n. | fog | 3 |
| 误解 | wùjiě | n. | misunderstanding | 5 |

X

X光	X guāng	n.	X-ray	7
吸	xī	v.	suck	3
息	xī	v.	cease	12
膝盖	xīgài	n.	knee	5
嘻嘻哈哈	xīxī hāhā	onm.	sound of laughter	4
嬉戏	xīxì	v.	play	1
洗	xǐ	v.	make (millstones)	5
细腻	xìnì	adj.	fine and smooth	5
狭窄	xiázhǎi	adj.	narrow	13
下及	xiàjí	v.	extend forward (to the future)	11
下课铃	xiàkè líng	n.	class-dismissing bell	4
下棋	xiàqí	n.	playing chess	13
下游	xiàyóu	n.	lower reaches of a river	3
鲜美	xiānměi	adj.	fresh and tasty	9
鲜艳	xiānyàn	adj.	bright-colored	4
先祖	xiānzǔ	n.	ancestors	5
嫌	xián	v.	complain	5
贤	xián	n.	able and virtuous person	11
衔	xián	v.	hold in the mouth	1
嫌弃	xiánqì	v.	dislike	5
显得	xiǎnde	v.	appear	12
险峻	xiǎnjùn	adj.	precipitous	14
现代	xiàndài	n.	contemporary times	12
献花	xiànhuā	v.	present flowers	7
现实	xiànshí	n.	reality	6
香	xiāng	v.	give forth fragrance	2
相撑	xiāng chēng	v.	support each other	14
相伴	xiāngbàn	v.	accompany	10

相反	xiāngfǎn	adv.	on the contrary	6
响	xiǎng	v.	(of a bell) ring	4
想象	xiǎngxiàng	v.	imagine	14
向往	xiàngwǎng	n.	longing	5
象征	xiàngzhēng	n.	symbol	14
小儿	xiǎo'ér	n.	children	12
小玩意儿	xiǎowányìr	n.	ornamental knickknack	5
效果	xiàoguǒ	n.	effect	11
笑容	xiàoróng	n.	smile	6
笑盈盈	xiàoyíngyíng	v.	be all smiles	4
斜视	xiéshì	v.	look sideways	7
谐音	xiéyīn	v.	be a homophone with	4
写作	xiězuò	n.	writing	4
泄流孔	xièliúkǒng	n.	water-discharging hole; outlet	3
新居	xīnjū	n.	new residence	6
新郎	xīnláng	n.	bridegroom	6
心灵	xīnlíng	n.	spirit	10
新娘	xīnniáng	n.	bride	6
辛涅科尔	Xīnnièkē'ěr	n.	a French writer	10
心情	xīnqíng	n.	mood	2
欣赏	xīnshǎng	v.	appreciate	7
心思	xīnsī	n.	thought	9
欣悦	xīnyuè	n.	joy	6
信任	xìnrèn	n.	trust	9
行为	xíngwéi	n.	action	10
行为	xíngwéi	n.	behavior	13
醒酒	xǐngjiǔ	n.	relief from the effects of alcohol	12
醒转	xǐngzhuǎn	v.	wake up	9
性	xìng	n.	suffix to designate a quality, property, etc.	11
胸	xiōng	n.	chest	1
凶狠	xiōnghěn	adj.	fierce	1
胸襟	xiōngjīn	n.	mind (lit., front of a garment)	14
胸透	xiōngtòu	n.	X-ray examination of chest; 胸部透视	7

雄关	xióngguān	n.	impregnable pass	14
羞怯	xiūqiè	adj.	shy and timid	14
修养	xiūyǎng	n.	cultivation	13
锈	xiù	v.	be stained with	5
蓄	xù	v.	grow (moustache)	4
旋	xuán	v.	see 盘旋	2
漩流	xuánliú	n.	eddy	3
悬念	xuánniàn	n.	suspense	13
选择	xuǎnzé	n.	choice	12
询问	xúnwèn	v.	inquire	3
训斥	xùnchì	v.	reprimand	4

Y

鸦	yā	n.	crow	4
压铺	yāpū	v.	hold and lay down	5
哑	yǎ	adj.	mute	3
焉	yān	pron.	this	7
嫣红	yānhóng	adj.	bright red	14
咽喉	yānhóu	n.	throat	14
淹没	yānmò	v.	be drowned by	14
盐	yán	n.	salt	7
严肃	yánsù	adj.	serious	11
沿着	yánzhe	prep.	along	3
掩	yǎn	v.	hide	1
掩	yǎn	v.	cover	14
眼光	yǎnguāng	n.	sight	5
眼红	yǎnhóng	v.	envy	6
眼眶	yǎnkuàng	n.	eye socket	4
眼泪	yǎnlèi	n.	tears	1
眼神	yǎnshén	n.	expression in the eyes	2
演员	yǎnyuán	n.	actor or actress	14
咽	yàn	v.	swallow	7

艳福	yànfú	n.	amorous fortune	4
燕妮	Yànní	n.	Jenny von Westphalen, Karl Marx's wife	13
厌恶	yànwù	n.	resent	11
宴席	yànxí	n.	banquet	6
扬眉	yáng méi	v.	raise one's eyebrows	7
仰望	yǎngwàng	v.	look up at	5
邀	yāo	v.	invite	6
要求	yāoqiú	n.	requirement	12
腰围	yāowéi	n.	waist measurement	7
摇头	yáotóu	v.	shake one's head	5
舀出	yǎochū	v.	ladle out	12
药方	yàofāng	n.	prescription	12
野	yě	adj.	wild	4
靥	yè	n.	dimple	2
夜晚	yèwǎn	n.	night	5
依旧	yījiù	adv.	as before	3
依恋	yīliàn	v.	be emotionally attached to	6
衣履	yīlǚ	n.	clothes and shoes	2
依然	yīrán	adv.	still; 还是; 依旧	3
依偎	yīwēi	v.	lean closely on	1
医药	yīyào	n.	medicine	12
一辈子	yíbèizi	n.	one's whole life	7
一刹那	yíchànà	adv.	in an instant	6
一旦	yídàn	conj.	once	11
移动	yídòng	v.	move	1
一个劲儿	yígejìnr	adv.	persistently	8
遗憾	yíhàn	v.	regret	5
一切	yíqiè	n.	everything	5
一向	yíxiàng	adv.	all along	2
以	yǐ		(see Part II.3)	12
以往	yǐwǎng	adj.	past	10
溢	yì	v.	overflow	6
异	yì	adj.	different	11

一般	yìbān	adj.	ordinary	5
异常	yìcháng	adv.	unusually	13
一如	yìrú	prep.	just like	7
殷勤	yīnqín	adv.	hospitably	6
音响	yīnxiǎng	n.	stereo system	6
吟	yín	n.	hum	14
引导	yǐndǎo	v.	guide	11
英雄	yīngxióng	n.	hero	2
嘤嘤	yīngyīng	onm.	chirping of a bird or birds	2
赢	yíng	v.	win	13
迎接	yíngjiē	v.	greet	6
影响	yǐngxiǎng	n.	influence	11
应付	yìngfù	v.	deal with	6
应声	yìngshēng	v.	respond to a sound	1
拥有	yōngyǒu	v.	possess	9
涌	yǒng	v.	surge	1
勇敢	yǒnggǎn	adj.	brave	3
永恒	yǒnghéng	adj.	eternal	10
用不着	yòngbuzháo	v.	not need	8
忧烦	yōufán	n.	worry	6
优劣	yōuliè	n.	quality (lit., good or bad)	12
忧闷	yōumèn	adj.	depressive	6
幽默	yōumò,	adj.	humorous	13
悠然	yōurán	adv.	in a leisurely manner	9
优秀	yōuxiù	adj.	outstanding	2
悠悠	yōuyōu	adj.	long-drawn-out	14
犹	yóu	adv.	still; 还	9
油	yóu	n.	oil	7
由此	yóucǐ	adv.	from this	11
犹如	yóurú	v.	好像	3
由是	yóushì	conj.	于是	14
由于	yóuyú	conj.	because; 因为	12
有关	yǒuguān	v.	have something to do with	12

有心	yǒuxīn	adj.	with a mind set to do something	4
幼年	yòunián	n.	childhood	11
愚蠢	yúchǔn	adj.	stupid	7
愚钝	yúdùn	n.	stupidity	14
于是	yúshì	conj.	so	5
与	yǔ	conj.	and; 和; 跟	9
与否	yǔ fǒu		and not (used to provide a negative alternative for the verb preceding 与)	10
雨果	Yǔguǒ	n.	Victor Hugo (1802-1885), a French writer	11
与其	yǔqí	conj.	(see Part V.6)	13
语文	yǔwén	n.	language and literature	4
宇宙	yǔzhòu	n.	universe	10
愈	yù	adv.	愈…愈…: the more... the more...	2
遇到	yùdào	v.	run into	1
渊博	yuānbó	n.	erudition	13
缘边	yuánbiān	n.	edge; 边缘	12
原来	yuánlái	adv.	as it turns out	5
源源	yuányuán	adv.	in a steady flow	9
怨恨	yuànhèn	v.	have a grudge against	5
曰	yuē	v.	say; 说	13
约翰·马克	Yuēhàn · Mǎkè	n.	John Mark, an American lawyer	13
悦	yuè	v.	please	12
陨石	yǔnshí	n.	stony meteorite	5
运	yùn	v.	transport	5
运气	yùnqi	n.	luck	3

Z

载	zǎi	n.	year	4
载	zài	v.	carry	3
在于	zàiyú	v.	lie in	11
暂	zàn	adv.	temporarily; 暂时	12

鏨	zàn	n.	chisel	5
赞叹	zàntàn	v.	praise highly	3
糟	zāo	adj.	poor	4
遭到	zāodào	v.	suffer from	5
凿	záo	v.	chisel	5
燥	zào	adj.	dry	2
增广	zēngguǎng	n.	expansion	11
增强	zēngqiáng	v.	reinforce	13
增添	zēngtiān	v.	add	13
增益	zēngyì.	v.	facilitate	12
赠	zèng	v.	bestow	2
扎根	zhāgēn	v.	take root	14
札记	zhájì	n.	reading notes	9
眨	zhǎ	v.	blink	4
粘	zhān	v.	glue	3
占	zhàn	v.	occupy	5
战果	zhànguǒ	n.	result of a battle	13
张开	zhāngkāi	v.	open (one's mouth)	4
涨落	zhǎngluò	n.	(of water) rise and fall	9
掌握	zhǎngwò	n.	control	12
昭君出塞	Zhāojūn chū sài		an allusion concerning Wáng Qiáng (王嫱, whose styled name was 王昭君), a palace lady in the Han dynasty. For diplomatic purposes, she was offered by Emperor Yuan as bride to a Khan of the Tartars occupying the nothern borders of China	14
罩	zhào	v.	cover	4
照拂	zhàofú	v.	attend to	6
哲	zhé	n.	wise person	11
折	zhé	v.	turn back	2
折	zhé	v.	break	14
折扣	zhékòu	n.	discount	7
哲学家	zhéxuéjiā	n.	philosopher	8

者	zhě	n.	suffix to indicate a category of people	11
珍藏	zhēncáng	v.	collect as a treasure	10
真切	zhēnqiè	adj.	vivid	2
珍惜	zhēnxī	v.	treasure	10
镇住	zhènzhù	v.	bring under control	4
争战	zhēngzhàn	n.	dispute and war	9
正	zhèng	adj.	standard	7
政界	zhèngjiè	n.	political circle	4
《正气歌》 Zhèngqìgē		n.	a poem by the Song dynasty poet and statesman 文天祥 (Wén Tiānxiáng, 1236-1283)	11
挣腿	zhèng tuǐ	v.	struggle to get legs free	3
正义	zhèngyì	n.	justice	11
正义感	zhèngyìgǎn	n.	sense of justice	11
枝蔓	zhīmàn	v.	(of branches and tendrils) grow	5
枝桠	zhīyā	n.	branch	1
值得	zhíde	v.	be worth	9
执着	zhízhuó	n.	perseverance	11
只管	zhǐguǎn	adv.	by all means	8
纸条	zhǐtiáo	n.	slip of paper	4
志	zhì	n.	will	12
制	zhì	v.	make	12
质	zhì	n.	texture	5
智慧	zhìhuì	n.	intelligence	2
智力	zhìlì	n.	intelligence	7
至少	zhìshǎo	adv.	at least	7
秩序	zhìxù	n.	order	13
终	zhōng	adv.	eventually	5
终点	zhōngdiǎn	n.	destination	8
终归	zhōngguī	adv.	after all	10
终日	zhōngrì	adv.	all day long	6
终身	zhōngshēn	adv.	all one's life	10
中央	zhōngyāng	n.	center, 中心	14

终于	zhōngyú	adv.	finally	2
众多	zhòngduō	adj.	numerous	10
周	zhōu	n.	week	2
周身	zhōushēn	adv.	all over the body; 全身	6
周围	zhōuwéi	n.	surrounding area	1
咒骂	zhòumà	v.	curse	5
皱眉	zhòu méi	v.	frown	14
诸多	zhūduō	adj.	(for abstract things) a good deal of	11
朱熹	Zhū Xī	n.	a Song dynasty philosopher, 1130-1200	8
逐渐	zhújiàn	adv.	gradually	9
主	zhǔ	adj.	primary	12
煮	zhǔ	v.	brew (tea)	12
主体	zhǔtǐ	n.	agent	10
注定	zhùdìng	v.	be destined	11
祝福	zhùfú	v.	bless	2
著名	zhùmíng	adj.	famous	13
著述	zhùshù	n.	writings	11
注意	zhùyì	v.	pay attention to	13
砖	zhuān	n.	brick	14
转身	zhuǎnshēn	v.	turn around	4
撰写	zhuànxiě	v.	write	12
装	zhuāng	v.	fill with	4
壮	zhuàng	adj.	strong	2
状	zhuàng	n.	form	14
撞击	zhuàngjī	v.	clash	1
追求	zhuīqiú	n.	pursuit	11
追踪	zhuīzōng	v.	trace	8
坠	zhuì	v.	hang down	3
着	zhuó	v.	wear	6
自嘲	zìcháo	n.	self-ridicule	13

自豪	zìháo	n.	pride in oneself	6
自然	zìrán	n.	nature	6
自身	zìshēn	n.	one's own	11
自在	zìzài	n.	comfort	6
踪	zōng	n.	footprint	10
总和	zǒnghé	n.	sum total	10
总统	zǒngtǒng	n.	president of a country	14
走廊	zǒuláng	n.	corridor	6
足	zú	adj.	sufficient; 够	5
组合	zǔhé	n.	combination	6
钻	zuān	v.	make one's way into	1
嘴唇	zuǐchún	n.	lips	2
醉	zuì	adj.	drunk	7
尊	zūn	v.	honor	8
尊容	zūnróng	n.	distinguished face (note the ironic tone in the text)	4
作协	zuòxié	n.	writers' society; 作家协会	4
作用	zuòyòng	n.	role	13

Glossary of Four-Character Expressions

四字词语表

爱屋及乌	ài wū jí wū	love for a person extends even to the crows on the roof	4
傲慢无礼	àomàn wúlǐ	arrogant and rude	13
报刊杂志	bàokān-zázhì	newspapers and magazines	4
悲欢离合	bēi-huān-lí-hé	vicissitudes of life	10
本无意义	běn wú yìyì	be originally meaningless	10
不大不小	búdà-bùxiǎo	be neither big nor small	5
草木虫鱼	cǎo-mù-chóng-yú	a variety of plants and little pets	11
曾几何时	céng jǐhé shí	not a long time ago	14
敞开胸襟	chǎngkāi xiōngjìn	open one's mind wide	14
沉默不语	chénmò bù yǔ	keep silent (without saying anything)	13
矗立而起	chùlì ér qǐ	stand up tall	3
催人泪下	cuī rén lèi xià	move people to tears	10
当代才俊	dāngdài cáijùn	contemporary talents	11
刀光剑影	dāoguāng-jiànyǐng	the glint and flash of daggers and swords	14
发枯唇燥	fàkū-chúnzào	with dried hair and lips	2
繁花夹道	fánhuā jiā dào	roads are lined with flowers of all kinds and colors	4
凡书皆好	fán shū jiē hǎo	all books are good	11
风风雨雨	fēngfēng-yǔyǔ	hardships in life	6
固若金汤	gù ruò jīn tāng	strongly fortified as an impregnable fortress	14
广采博访	guǎngcǎi-bófǎng	collect (tea) and visit (people) everywhere	12
归根到底	guīgēn-dàodǐ	in the final analysis	8
锅碗瓢盆	guō-wǎn-piáo-pén	kichen utensils	4
毫不羞怯	háo bù xiūqiè	be not at all shy and timid	14
黑云掩月	hēi yún yǎn yuè	dark clouds cover the moon	14
轰轰烈烈	hōnghōnglièliè	on a grand and spectacular scale	7
花草树木	huācǎo-shù mù	plants such as flowers and trees	7

化为乌有	huà wéi wūyǒu	vanish	10
环顾四周	huángù sìzhōu	look around	6
孑然一身	jiérán yì shēn	be all alone in the world	4
旌旗横倒	jīngqí héng dǎo	banners and flags fall down to the ground	14
惊心动魄	jīngxīn-dòngpò	soul-stirring; profoundly affecting	10
久别重逢	jiǔ bié chóngféng	reunite after a long separation	13
蓝天四垂	lán tiān sì chuí	a blue sky hangs down on all sides	4
恋棋如命	liàn qí rú mìng	love playing chess as one loves one's life	13
流泉淙淙	liú quán cóngcóng	flowing springs gurgle	2
屡战屡败	lǚzhàn-lǚbài	fight repeatedly but lose repeatedly	13
绿草萋萋	lǜ cǎo qīqī	green grass is lush	1
满脸风霜	mǎnliǎn fēngshuāng	with hardships (represented by wind and frost) shown on the face	4
没完没了	méiwán-méiliǎo	without an end	6
绵延不绝	miányán bù jué	stretch long and unbroken	9
莫不有理	mò bù yǒulǐ	there is nothing that is not reasonable	8
目不斜视	mù bù xiéshì	not look sideways	7
耐人寻味	nài rén xúnwèi	be able to bear thought (afford food for thought)	13
鸟鸣嘤嘤	niǎo míng yīngyīng	birds call	2
鸟语花香	niǎoyǔ-huāxiāng	birds sing and flowers send forth fragrance	2
怒不可遏	nù bù kě è	be in an uncontrollable rage	3
奇风异俗	qífēng-yìsú	exotic customs and conventions	11
千古英雄	qiāngǔ yīngxióng	people who remain heroes through the ages	2
千载难逢	qiān zǎi nán féng	not occur once in a thousand years	4
潜心研究	qiánxīn yányōu	study with great concentration	12
青山绿水	qīngshān-lǜshuǐ	a natural environment with green hills and clear waters	6
情笃意切	qíngdǔ-yìqiè	sincere and passionate affection	13
趋避凡俗	qūbì fánsú	avoid being commonplace and vulgar	11
劝善之作	quàn shàn zhī zuò	works that persuade people to be good	11

人际交往	rénjì jiāowǎng	interpersonal contact	13
如火嫣红	rú huǒ yānhóng	bright red like fire	14
入药治病	rùyào-zhìbìng	be used as medicine to cure diseases	12
煞有介事	shà yǒu jiè shì	with a show of being serious	7
身强体壮	shēnqiáng-tǐzhuàng	(of a person) strong and sturdy	2
声声发喊	shēngshēng fāhǎn	shout continuously	3
死尸相撑	sǐshī xiāng chēng	dead bodies pile up	14
四面八方	sìmiàn-bāfāng	all directions	14
送烟递水	sòngyān-dìshuǐ	serve cigarettes and drinks	6
随山就坡	suíshān-jiùpō	go along with mountains and slopes	14
岁月沧桑	suìyuè cāngsāng	time brings about great changes	6
弹射而出	tánshè ér chū	shoot out	3
腾波鼓浪	téngbō-gǔlàng	waves prancing and rousing	12
天资聪明	tiānzī cōngming	gifted	12
亭亭玉立	tíngtíng yù lì	(of a young woman) slim and graceful	4
挺胸凸肚	tǐngxiōng-tūdù	put up an air of importance	7
万事大吉	wàn shì dàjí	everything is just fine	8
万事万物	wànshì-wànwù	everything	8
万寿无疆	wànshòu wú jiāng	everlasting longevity	14
往哲先贤	wǎngzhé-xiānxián	past outstanding people	11
微不足道	wēi bùzú dào	too trivial or insignificant to mention	10
唯我独尊	wéi wǒ dú zūn	extremely conceited	8
无可奈何	wúkě nàihé	have no alternative	5
无求于人	wú qiúyú rén	have nothing to ask other people for	14
无所适从	wú suǒ shì cóng	not know what to do	8
无影无踪	wúyǐng-wúzōng	without a trace	10
无足轻重	wú zú qīng-zhòng	of little importance or consequence	10
西风扑剌	xīfēng pūlà	west wind causing "pūlà" sounds	14
喜上眉梢	xǐ shàng méishāo	joy climbing to the tips of the eyebrows (be radiant with joy)	13

险峻万状	xiǎnjùn wàn zhuàng	precipitous in various forms	14
小心翼翼	xiǎoxīn yìyì	very cautiously	5
笑成一片	xiào chéng yí piàn	break into laughter	4
笑生双靥	xiào shēng shuāng yè	smile showing two dimples	2
心不在焉	xīn bú zài yān	absentminded	7
鸦雀无声	yā-què wú shēng	all being quiet	4
艳福不浅	yànfú bù qiǎn	(of a man) have a lot of good fortune in love affairs	4
仰天一瞥	yǎngtiān yì piē	look up and take a glance at the sky	14
衣不蔽体	yī bù bì tǐ	with clothes hardly covering the body	2
衣履光鲜	yīlǚ guāngxiān	be dressed in bright and new clothes and shoes	2
一步一蹭	yíbù-yícèng	drag on slowly with difficulty at every step	2
一胖一瘦	yípàng-yíshòu	one who is fat and one who is thin	3
以丑为美	yǐ chǒu wéi měi	use ugliness as a proof of beauty	5
一本正经	yì běn zhèngjīng	put up an air of complete seriousness	7
异国他乡	yìguó-tāxiāng	foreign countries and lands	14
一无所见	yì wú suǒjiàn	see not even one thing	2
以煮为主	yǐ zhǔ wéi zhǔ	take boiling as the primary means	12
应有尽有	yīngyǒu-jìnyǒu	have everything that one can wish for	6
悠悠岁月	yōuyōu suìyuè	long-drawn-out years	14
油盐酱醋	yóu-yán-jiàng-cù	condiments; seasonings	7
又当别论	yòu dāng biélùn	should be regarded as a different matter	8
又怪又丑	yòuguài-yòuchǒu	both odd and ugly	5
雨雪纷纷	yǔ xuě fēnfēn	rain and snow profusely	14
源源不绝	yuányuán bù jué	in an endless stream	9
智慧过人	zhìhuì guòrén	excel in wisdom	2
自我保护	zìwǒ bǎohù	self-protection	14
自我介绍	zìwǒ jièshào	introduce oneself; self-introduction	4
左右兼顾	zuǒ-yòu jiān gù	attend to two different aspects of something concurrently	8

| 作何感想 | zuò hé gǎnxiǎng | what to think of | 14 |
| 坐立不安 | zuò-lì bù ān | feel uneasy whether sitting or standing | 6 |

Index of Explained Words, Expressions, and Sentence Patterns
词语句型学习索引

过 (adv.)	加入一点食盐调味，但不可过咸。	12.7

H

还…呢！	可他的写作水平却出奇的好。还是市作协的会员呢！	4.11
还是 (adv.)	没长翅膀不能飞，还是不要学习鸟…	8.10
还是 (conj.)	母鹿的身体有些瘦弱，皮毛还是很漂亮的。	1.2
毫不/毫无		14.7
(好像/仿佛) Adj 似的	他却哑了似的沉默著，…	3.11
何必…呢？	假如…，何必想去认识一下那只下蛋的母鸡呢？	13.10
何尝 (adv.)	我何尝不知道，…，我只是一个极其偶然的存在，…	10.3
何所 V / 一无所 V	真英雄何所遇？	2.9
或…，或…	或博爱、或温情、或抗争，大抵总引导人…	11.14

J

几多 (adj.)	几多寒霜冻硬的弓弦，射出了断喉的利箭。	14.6
将 (adv.)	它们虽已逝去，却将永远活在我心中，…	10.1
禁不住 V	坝上和崖边的人见了，禁不住声声发喊，"快回！"	3.7
尽管…，(可是)…	尽管这么多年已经过去了，…，可是…	9.10
仅仅/只 …(而已)	谁能说这些都仅仅只是一场黄粱梦而已呢？	9.5
竟，竟然 (adv.)	新郎脸上溢出的笑容竟是如此的灿烂…	6.1
究竟 (adv.)	可是看得清前面新路怎么走，…究竟是比…强。	8.12
Adj / V 就 Adj / V	害怕就害怕，脆弱就脆弱，…	7.2
(就是) V1 也 V2	借钱也要请客，醉死也要喝酒。	7.4
就算…，(也/还是) …	就算一个人闷在宾馆里看电视…	6.7
据说	据说，用"功夫茶"方法煮出来的茶，…	12.11
绝(对) (adv.)	我们绝不是白白来一场的。	9.3

K

看来 (conj.)	<u>看来</u>没长翅膀，不能向上飞。	8.9
可怜	<u>可怜</u>那份热闹跟我们抢购漂亮衣裙时差不多，…	7.6
况且 (conj.)	<u>况且</u>，并非凡书皆好，…	11.10

L

老实说	<u>老实说</u>，在同学们心中某个角落，还装着…	4.12
V Adj 了 N	姑娘气红<u>了</u>脸，大喝一声…	4.15
连 N 都 V	周围的山林静静的，<u>连</u>鸟的叫声<u>都</u>听不见，…	1.4
(连…都)算不上	这个微粒的悲欢甚至<u>连</u>一丝微风…<u>都算不上</u>，…	10.2

M

每回/次/当…就…	<u>每回</u>抱我的儿女的时候，<u>就</u>会想到…	9.4
莫非…？	水底<u>莫非</u>有一条吞了钩的大鱼<u>？</u>	3.6
某	只有在广东、福建<u>某</u>些地方还…	12.10

N

哪里是…，分明是…	这<u>哪里是</u>条件呀，<u>分明是</u>美事一桩。	4.13
哪一 M N…也/都	随便去搡一块回来，<u>哪一</u>块<u>也</u>比它强。	5.4
那 (pron.)	…，截断了它<u>那</u>大漠狂沙般的黄色的热情。	3.2
那么 (adv.)	不知道什么地方，总有<u>那么</u>一点点不对头…	6.2
那么 (conj.)	<u>那么</u>，我们还有什么遗憾的呢？	9.11
乃 (adv.)	我想象那飞鸿<u>乃</u>是悠悠岁月的见证。	14.2
难道…(吗)？	你<u>难道</u>在那里一无所见<u>吗</u>？	2.7
难为(了)N	不过，也<u>难为了</u>你，你回去吧！	2.6
宁愿 (adv.)	他们将自然挡住，<u>宁愿</u>终日坐在空调的轰鸣中。	6.5

P

凭 (prep.)	我不懂哲学，但<u>凭</u>常识想，眼睛的位置确是不好移动。	8.1

Q

R

S

Z

Supplementary Readings
补充阅读材料

1. 死的？活的？　　张晓风

在一个小村庄的尽头，住着一位老人，他被公认为历经世故，长于回答各种问题。

这村庄的村尾有一个刁钻顽皮的小男孩，知道了这件事便想去为难一下老人，他活捉了一只小鸟，偷偷握在掌心里，急急地跑到老人面前：

"老公公，听说你是这个村子里最聪明的人哪！你能回答这个问题吗？你知道我手里的鸟是活的还是死的？"

老人微笑地注视着小男孩跑得汗湿而发红的小脸，以及他慧黠而捣鬼的眼神，心中立刻了然，如果他回答是死的，孩子就会张开手让小鸟飞掉。如果他回答是活的，孩子就会暗加一把劲把小鸟捏死。他于是轻轻地拍了拍小男孩的肩膀，说：

"孩子，答案是这样的：'这只鸟一方面既不是活的，也不是死的，另一方面呢，它既是活的也是死的。至于它到底是活的还是死的—既然小鸟捏在你的手里，那就全看你了！'"

其实世间万事岂不皆可作如此观，一个人的学业是否有成，婚姻能否美满，乃至于一项公营事业会盈会亏，都可以用老人的那句话回答：

"它，既然在你的手里，是死是活，那就全看你了。"

（选自中国人民大学出版社１９９１年《中国当代名家小品精选》）

繁體字材料

死的？活的？　　張曉風

在一個小村莊的盡頭，住著一位老人，他被公認為歷經世故，長於回答各種問題。

這村莊的村尾有一個刁鑽頑皮的小男孩，知道了這件事便想去為難一下老人，他活捉了一隻小鳥，偷偷握在掌心裡，急急地跑到老人面前：

"老公公，聽說你是這個村子裡最聰明的人哪！你能回答這個問題嗎？你知道我手裡的鳥是活的還是死的？"

老人微笑地注視著小男孩跑得汗濕而發紅的小臉，以及他慧黠而搞鬼的眼神，心中立刻了然，如果他回答是死的，孩子就會張開手讓小鳥飛掉。如果他回答是活的，孩子就會暗加一把勁把小鳥捏死。他於是輕輕地拍了拍小男孩的肩膀，說：

"孩子，答案是這樣的：'這隻鳥一方面既不是活的，也不是死的，另一方面呢，它既是活的也是死的。至於它到底是活的還是死的——既然小鳥捏在你的手裡，那就全看你了！'"

其實世間萬事豈不皆可作如此觀，一個人的學業是否有成，婚姻能否美滿，乃至於一項公營事業會盈會虧，都可以用老人的那句話回答：

"它，既然在你的手裡，是死是活，那就全看你了。"

    *   *   *   *   *   *

回答下列问题

1. 你觉得这位老人长于回答问题吗？为什么？

2. 作者讲这样一个故事是为了说明什么？你同意他的看法吗？

3. 这篇短文的语言又简洁又典雅。这种效果是怎么造成的？

2. 修行与洗澡　林清玄

有 16 个兄弟一起到深山里修行，希望通过不断思维静坐，开发内心，达到最高的智慧境界。16 个兄弟苦心地在森林中打坐，他们风餐露宿，一言不发，夜里也不休息。他们面无表情，冷漠肃然，一如林中的枯木。他们双目紧闭，吃得很少，才过了几天就已经形容枯槁了。

有一天，最小的弟弟实在受不了，他张开眼睛说："我想去洗个澡。"

15 个哥哥从定中出来，用非常惊讶冷漠的眼睛看着弟弟，以为自己的耳朵听错了。

兄弟们纷纷斥责他，但是小弟依然坚持说："不管啦！我现在一定要去洗澡，现在对我最重要、最能让我喜悦的事就是，让我去洗澡！"

大哥看到小弟有点失控，就说："先去洗个澡，再回来思维人生，也不会怎么样吧！何况我们真的已经很久没有洗澡了。"

既然大哥已经开口，大家也都觉得洗个澡是一件愉快的事，并异口同声地说："那我们去洗个澡吧！"

当时是盛夏，在走向森林边瀑布下的水塘时，一路上都有着美妙的蝉声，使他们的耳朵灵敏异常；路的两旁开满了各种颜色的野花，花上彩蝶飞舞，使他们的眼睛非常明亮；森林到处飘送着花香和草香，使他们的鼻子都变得深邃而宁静；偶然张开嘴巴，舌头尝到了林中香甜的水气，美好得说不出话来；他们的身体被林中黄昏的雾气弥漫，感到无比的清凉和欢喜……

16 个兄弟终于漫步到水塘，非常舒坦地走入水塘洗澡，呀！那水的甘洌、清凉、爽利，刹那间深入了全身的细胞，使他们的身心进入完美和圆满的境界。

（选自２０００年８月９日人民日报海外版）

修行與洗澡　　林清玄

有 16 個兄弟一起到深山裡修行，希望通過不斷思維靜坐，開發內心，達到最高的智慧境界。16 個兄弟苦心地在森林中打坐，他們風餐露宿，一言不發，夜裡也不休息。他們面無表情，冷漠蕭然，一如林中的枯木。他們雙目緊閉，吃得很少，才過了幾天就已經形容枯槁了。

有一天，最小的弟弟實在受不了，他張開眼睛說："我想去洗個澡。"

15 個哥哥從定中出來，用非常驚訝冷漠的眼睛看著弟弟，以為自己的耳朵聽錯了。

兄弟們紛紛斥責他，但是小弟依然堅持說："不管啦！我現在一定要去洗澡，現在對我最重要、最能讓我喜悅的事就是，讓我去洗澡！"

大哥看到小弟有點失控，就說："先去洗個澡，再回來思維人生，也不會怎麼樣吧！何況我們真的已經很久沒有洗澡了。"

既然大哥已經開口，大家也都覺得洗個澡是一件愉快的事，並異口同聲地說："那我們去洗個澡吧！"

當時是盛夏，在走向森林邊瀑布下的水塘時，一路上都有著美妙的蟬聲，使他們的耳朵靈敏異常；路的兩旁開滿了各種顏色的野花，花上彩蝶飛舞，使他們的眼睛非常明亮；森林到處飄送著花香和草香，使他們的鼻子都變得深邃而寧靜；偶然張開嘴巴，舌頭嚐到了林中香甜的水氣，美好得說不出話來；他們的身體被林中黃昏的霧氣彌漫，感到無比的清涼和歡喜……

16 個兄弟終於漫步到水塘，非常舒坦地走入水塘洗澡，呀！那水的甘冽、清涼、爽利，剎那間深入了全身的細胞，使他們的身心進入完美和圓滿的境界。

*　　　　*　　　　*　　　　*　　　　*　　　　*

回答下列問題

1. 这 16 个兄弟是怎样在深山里打坐修行的？作者用了哪些四字词语描述他们？

2. 兄弟们在去水塘洗澡的路上听到了什么？看到了什么？他们又闻到了什么？尝到了什么？这一切使他们的身心发生了什么变化？

3. 这个故事要说明一个什么道理？

4. 作者在文章的两个地方用了"排比"(parallelism)。找出这两个排比，想一想它们为什么用在这些地方，并看看它们带来了什么样的效果。

3. 兄弟俩 郑国雄

你哥哥比你大几岁？噢，大5岁。

我呢？我跟我哥哥一样—都是13岁。

你一定会感到奇怪：哥哥怎么会跟弟弟同岁？同岁怎么算得上是哥哥？

哈哈，这是因为我跟哥哥是孪生兄弟。严格地讲，我哥哥的年龄才比我大一分钟！

我跟我哥哥简直长得一模一样：一样的脸，一样的高矮，一样的胖瘦。平常又穿一样的衣服，一样的鞋子，一样的袜子。就连头发的长短和式样也一模一样。

爸爸妈妈给我们俩取了两个非常有趣的名字：哥哥叫小土，我叫小士—写起来只差那么一点儿。

我们兄弟俩不论在里弄里、在学校里，都非常出名，几乎没有人不认识我们。因为只要我们俩手挽手在街上一走，就非常引人注目—咦，怎么长得一个模样？

我跟哥哥总是在一起。不过有的时候，我们俩不得不暂时分开，于是闹出了许许多多笑话。

比如说，我跟哥哥升中学了，要发学生证，学生证上要贴一张本人的一寸照片。在照相的时候，我们俩不得不暂时分开。我先拍，我一拍完，哥哥就去拍。照相师弄糊涂了，喊道："你怎么啦？不是刚拍过吗？怎么还要拍？拍出瘾头啦？"等弄清楚了是怎么回事，他一手抚摩着哥哥的头顶，一手抚摩着我的头顶，笑着说："你们俩差不多呀，长得太象了！其实，你们俩拍一张照片也就够了，反正长得一模一样。"

有一次，我们学校跟另一个学校进行篮球比赛。我们俩都是校队队员。哥哥先上场，我在场下作准备，兄弟俩又不得不暂时分开了。球赛进行了一会儿，我哥哥就犯了五次规，领队叫他下场，让我上场。我一进篮球场，裁判就喊起来了："你怎么啦？才罚下去怎么又上场啦？快下去！快下去！"直到他仔细看了我背心上的号码—6号，才知道我不是犯了规的队员—我哥哥是5号。

这样的笑话，真是举不胜举，三天三夜也说不完。

正因为我跟我哥哥长得特别象，不论是爸爸、妈妈、叔叔、阿姨，还是老师、同学，大家都非常喜欢我们俩。

（选自华语教学出版社１９９４年《序列短文阅读４》）

繁體字材料

兄弟倆 鄭國雄

你哥哥比你大幾歲？噢，大5歲。

我呢？我跟我哥哥一樣—都是13歲。

你一定會感到奇怪：哥哥怎麼會跟弟弟同歲？同歲怎麼算得上是哥哥？

哈哈，這是因為我跟哥哥是孿生兄弟。嚴格地講，我哥哥的年齡才比我大一分鐘！

我跟我哥哥簡直長得一模一樣：一樣的臉，一樣的高矮，一樣的胖瘦。平常又穿一樣的衣服，一樣的鞋子，一樣的襪子。就連頭髮的長短和式樣也一模一樣。

爸爸媽媽給我們倆取了兩個非常有趣的名字：哥哥叫小土，我叫小士—寫起來只差那麼一點兒。

我們兄弟倆不論在里弄裡、在學校裡，都非常出名，幾乎沒有人不認識我們。因為只要我們倆手挽手在街上一走，就非常引人注目—咦，怎麼長得一個模樣？

我跟哥哥總是在一起。不過有的時候，我們倆不得不暫時分開，於是鬧出了許許多多笑話。

比如說，我跟哥哥升中學了，要發學生證，學生證上要貼一張本人的一寸照片。在照相的時候，我們倆不得不暫時分開。我先拍，我一拍完，哥哥就去拍。照相師弄糊塗了，喊道："你怎麼啦？不是剛拍過嗎？怎麼還要拍？拍出癮頭啦？"等弄清楚了是怎麼回事，他一手撫摩著哥哥的頭頂，一手撫摩著我的頭頂，笑著說："你們倆差不多呀，長得太像了！其實，你們倆拍一張照片也就夠了，反正長得一模一樣。"

有一次，我們學校跟另一個學校進行籃球比賽。我們倆都是校隊隊員。哥哥先上場，我在場下作準備，兄弟倆又不得不暫時分開了。球賽進行了一會兒，我哥哥就犯了五次規，領隊叫他下場，讓我上場。我一進籃球場，裁判就喊起來了："你怎麼啦？才罰下去怎麼又上場啦？快下去！快下去！"直到他仔細看了我背心上的號碼—6號，才知道我不是犯了規的隊員—我哥哥是5號。

這樣的笑話，真是舉不勝舉，三天三夜也說不完。

正因為我跟我哥哥長得特別像，不論是爸爸、媽媽、叔叔、阿姨，還是老師、同學，大家都非常喜歡我們倆。

*　　　*　　　*　　　*　　　*　　　*

回答下列問題

1. 读这篇文章，我们觉得这"兄弟俩"非常可爱。为什么？这跟作者讲这个故事的方法有关系吗？？

2. 这篇文章是用口语体的书面语写的。口语体的主要特征是什么？你能用这篇文章做例子谈一谈吗？

3. 谈谈这篇文章的语气。找出文章中的语气词、象声词、标点符号及其它表达这种语气的因素。

4. 骑自行车的中国人　林希

她是我们中间的一个，一个骑自行车的中国人。

我从来没有看见过她的面容，是清秀、是俊美，或者是妩媚生动；她总是从我的背后缓缓地跟上来，漫过我的肩侧，又从容地蹬车而去。我因看到坐在她自行车后架上不足三四岁的女儿，断定她多不过三十岁的年纪。她身材消瘦，高高的个子，本来似曾有过一身使不完的劲，但终究劳累了，她的背影显出疲惫。

清晨，从来是沉浸着紧迫的气氛，整个城市的每一条街道都似一根根绷紧的琴弦，车辆、行人如音符般跳跃而过，生活的节奏似欢快、热烈的快板。她骑着车子，沿着每天上班下班必经的熟悉道路奔驰而去。鼓鼓滚圆的书包挎在车把上，一个尼龙网兜里装着大小两个饭盒，这大概和我们每一个人一样，大饭盒里是米饭、小饭盒里是素菜。

她蹬着车子，目光凝视着远方，头昂着，上身向前倾斜。有一次我看见她一面蹬车一面吃早点，今早该是太匆忙了，她还想着身后的女儿，不时地从衣兜里掏出饼干回手向背后送去。她还轻声地吟唱着儿歌，那是托儿所阿姨教孩子们唱的儿歌，女儿听着儿歌自然乖多了，向妈妈保证今天不淘气。

我目送她向前驶去，我知道还有一天的劳累等着她：她是一个女工，她要去开动机器；她是一位会计，还要和枯燥的数字共度过八小时的时光；也许她是位炊事员，要去为千百人烧饭；或者是位护士，要为病人减轻痛苦。但此刻她是一个骑自行车的中国人，时间追赶着她，她的家庭，大半就在这辆自行车上，缓慢地，沉重地，疲惫地行进着。可惜她行进的里程只能在同一的距离内无数次重复，否则纪录世界之最的书籍会发现她是世界上背负着一个家庭行路最长的女人，她将成为一位明星。

外国人说中国是自行车的王国，但他们无法理解骑自行车的中国人在创建着怎样的生活。我们辛劳，有时几乎是疲于奔命，生活有些艰难，大家又苦于总也没有想出更好的办法。但骑自行车的中国人依然在前进，而且在相互提示不要忘记自己肩负的社会责任。如果说中国文化曾在"净"与"静"的境界中探索人性，那么中国人创建的自行车文化却是在前进与辛劳中拥抱世界与未来。

她是我们中间的一个，一个骑自行车的中国人。

（选自漓江出版社１９９１年《当代中国散文擂台赛作品选》，有删改）

<u>繁體字材料</u>

騎自行車的中國人　　林希

她是我們中間的一個，一個騎自行車的中國人。

我從來沒有看見過她的面容，是清秀、是俊美，或者是嫵媚生動；她總是從我的背後緩緩地跟上來，漫過我的肩側，又從容地蹬車而去。我因看到坐在她自行車後架上不足三四歲的女兒，斷定她多不過三十歲的年紀。她身材消瘦，高高的個子，本來似曾有過一身使不完的勁，但終究勞累了，她的背影顯出疲憊。

清晨，從來是沉浸著緊迫的氣氛，整個城市的每一條街道都似一根根繃緊的琴弦，車輛、行人如音符般跳躍而過，生活的節奏似歡快、熱烈的快板。她騎著車子，沿著每天上班下班必經的熟悉道路奔馳而去。鼓鼓滾圓的書包挎在車把上，一個尼龍網兜裡裝著大小兩個飯盒，這大概和我們每一個人一樣，大飯盒裡是米飯、小飯盒裡是素菜。

她蹬著車子，目光凝視著遠方，頭昂著，上身向前傾斜。有一次我看見她一面蹬車一面吃早點，今早該是太匆忙了，她還想著身後的女兒，不時地從衣兜裡掏出餅乾回手向背後送去。她還輕聲地吟唱著兒歌，那是托兒所阿姨教孩子們唱的兒歌，女兒聽著兒歌自然乖多了，向媽媽保證今天不淘氣。

我目送她向前駛去，我知道還有一天的勞累等著她：她是一個女工，她要去開動機器；她是一位會計，還要和枯燥的數字共度過八小時的時光；也許她是位炊事員，要去為千百人燒飯；或者是位護士，要為病人減輕痛苦。但此刻她是一個騎自行車的中國人，時間追趕著她，他的家庭，大半就在這輛自行車上，緩慢地，沉重地，疲憊地行進著。可惜她行進的里程只能在同一的距離內無數次重復，否則紀錄世界之最的書籍會發現她是世界上背負著一個家庭行路最長的女人，她將成為一位明星。

外國人說中國是自行車的王國，但他們無法理解騎自行車的中國人在創建著怎樣的生活。我們辛勞，有時幾乎是疲於奔命，生活有些艱難，大家又苦於總也沒有想出更好的辦法。但騎自行車的中國人依然在前進，而且在相互提示不要忘記自己肩負的社會責任。如果說中國文化曾在"淨"與"靜"的境界中探索人性，那麼中國人創建的自行車文化卻是在前進與辛勞中擁抱世界與未來。

她是我們中間的一個，一個騎自行車的中國人。

*　　　*　　　*　　　*　　　*　　　*

回答下列问题

1. "她"是一个怎样的"骑自行车的中国人"？作者是怎样描写她的长相和行动的？

2. 谈谈你所知道的"中国自行车文化"。

3. 在谈到"她"的职业时，作者的猜想是怎样表达出来的？

4. 这篇文章的主题虽然简单，语言却正式、典雅(elegant)、整齐。这些语言特点是什么原因造成的？

5. 雾城·山城·江城·文化城　李秋生

重庆是什么样的呢？

重庆是一座雾城。清晨，浓浓的晨雾笼罩住这座山城，整座城市仿佛是位美丽而又害羞的姑娘。当太阳轻轻地揭开雾纱，她那娇美的面容便展示在人们面前。

重庆又是一座典型的山城。群山环抱、岗巅起伏，城市的立体感极强。高楼大厦一层一层地矗立在山坡上，高耸入云。市内道路一会儿冲上去，一会儿滑下来，一会儿向前走，一会儿急转弯。正是因为这种行路如登山的特点，所以在重庆市区内很难见到一辆自行车。在重庆观光，还要经常钻隧道，不少道路穿山而过，充满情趣。

重庆还是一座江城。滔滔长江和嘉陵江穿城而过，把重庆市分割成三块。重庆拥有起伏的群山，还拥有两条穿城而过的美丽的江，真正是得天独厚，美不胜收。

重庆的文化业，尤其是报业相当发达。饭店商场、大街小巷，报贩到处可见。

重庆的夜景令人难忘。登上城市的最高点俯瞰山城夜景，只见群山与江面上灯火万盏，长江大桥和嘉陵江大桥的金色灯光，恍如两条金龙跃过江面，给人们以"疑是银河落九天"的感觉。

重庆，作为一座具有悠久历史的文化名城，正吸引着越来越多的中外游客。

（选自１９９９年３月５日人民日报海外版，有删改）

繁體字材料

霧城．山城．江城．文化城　李秋生

重慶是甚麼樣的呢？

重慶是一座霧城。清晨，濃濃的晨霧籠罩住這座山城，整座城市彷彿是位美麗而又害羞的姑娘。當太陽輕輕地揭開霧紗，她那嬌美的面容便展示在人們面前。

重慶又是一座典型的山城。群山環抱、崗巒起伏，城市的立體感極強。高樓大廈一層一層地矗立在山坡上，高聳入雲。市內道路一會兒沖上去，一會兒滑下來，一會兒向前走，一會兒急轉彎。正是因為這種行路如登山的特點，所以在重慶市區內很難見到一輛自行車。在重慶觀光，還要經常鑽隧道，不少道路穿山而過，充滿情趣。

重慶還是一座江城。滔滔長江和嘉陵江穿城而過，把重慶市分割成三塊。重慶擁有起伏的群山，還擁有兩條穿城而過的美麗的江，真正是得天獨厚，美不勝收。

重慶的文化業，尤其是報業相當發達。飯店商場、大街小巷，報販到處可見。

重慶的夜景令人難忘。登上城市的最高點俯瞰山城夜景，只見群山與江面上燈火萬盞，長江大橋和嘉陵江大橋的金色燈光，恍如兩條金龍躍過江面，給人們以"疑是銀河落九天"的感覺。

重慶，作為一座具有悠久歷史的文化名城，正吸引著越來越多的中外遊客。

    *   *   *   *   *   *

回答下列問題

1, 重庆是怎样的一个城市？作者用了一个什么样的句子结构 (sentence structure) 来一一介绍重庆的特点？

2. 作者是怎样描写这个城市的？在描写的过程中，作者特别用了哪些修辞技巧 (rhetorical skills)？

3. 找出文中用 "拟人" (personification) 手法的句子。

6. 野草　夏衍

有这样一个故事。

有人问：世界上什么东西的气力最大？回答纷纭得很，有的说"象"，有的说"狮"，有人开玩笑似地说是"金刚"。金刚有多少气力，当然大家全不知道。

结果，这一切答案完全不对，世界上气力最大的，是植物的种子。一粒种子所可以显现出来的力，简直是超越一切，这儿又是一个故事。

人的头盖骨，结合得非常致密与坚固，生理学家和解剖学者用尽了一切的方法，要把它完整地分出来，都没有这种力气，后来忽然有人发明了一个方法，就是把一些植物的种子放在要剖析的头盖骨里，给它以温度与湿度，使它发芽，一发芽，这些种子便以可怕的力量，将一切机械力所不能分开的骨骼，完整地分开了，植物种子力量之大，如此如此。

这，也许特殊了一点，常人不容易理解。那么，你看见过笋的成长吗？你看见过被压在瓦砾和石块下面的一颗小草的生成吗？它为着向往阳光，为着达成它的生之意志，不管上面的石块如何重，石块与石块之间如何狭，它必定要曲曲折折地，但是顽强不屈地透到地面上来。它的根往土壤钻，它的芽往地面挺，这是一种不可抗的力，阻止它的石块，结果也被它掀翻，一粒种子的力量之大，如此如此。

没有一个人将小草叫做"大力士"，但是它的力量之大，的确是世界无比。这种力，是一般人看不见的生命力，只要生命存在，这种力就要显现，上面的石块，丝毫不足以阻挡，因为它是一种"长期抗战"的力，有弹性，能屈能伸的力，有韧性，不达目的不止的力。

种子不落在肥土而落在瓦砾中，有生命力的种子决不会悲观和叹气，因为有了阻力才有磨练。生命开始的一瞬间就带了斗志而来的草，才是坚韧的草，也只有这种草，才可以傲然地对那些玻璃棚中养育着的盆花嗤笑。

（选自复旦大学出版社１９９６年《千字文阅读与训练》）

繁體字材料

野草　夏衍

有這樣一個故事。

有人問：世界上甚麼東西的氣力最大？回答紛紜得很，有的說"象"，有的說"獅"，有人開玩笑似地說是"金剛"。金剛有多少氣力，當然大家全不知道。

結果，這一切答案完全不對，世界上氣力最大的，是植物的種子。一粒種子所可以顯現出來的力，簡直是超越一切，這兒又是一個故事。

人的頭蓋骨，結合得非常緻密與堅固，生理學家和解剖學者用盡了一切的方法，要把它完整地分出來，都沒有這種力氣，後來忽然有人發明了一個方法，就是把一些植物的種子放在要剖析的頭蓋骨裡，給它以溫度與濕度，使它發芽，一發芽，這些種子便以可怕的力量，將一切機械力所不能分開的骨骼，完整地分開了，植物種子力量之大，如此如此。

這，也許特殊了一點，常人不容易理解。那麼，你看見過筍的成長嗎？你看見過被壓在瓦礫和石塊下面的一顆小草的生成嗎？它為著嚮往陽光，為著達成它的生之意志，不管上面的石塊如何重，石塊與石塊之間如何狹，它必定要曲曲折折地，但是頑強不屈地透到地面上來。它的根往土壤鑽，它的芽望地面挺，這是一種不可抗的力，阻止它的石塊，結果也被它掀翻，一粒種子的力量之大，如此如此。

沒有一個人將小草叫做"大力士"，但是它的力量之大，的確是世界無比。這種力，是一般人看不見的生命力，只要生命存在，這種力就要顯現，上面的石塊，絲毫不足以阻擋，因為它是一種"長期抗戰"的力，有彈性，能屈能伸的力，有韌性，不達目的不止的力。

種子不落在肥土而落在瓦礫中，有生命力的種子決不會悲觀和嘆氣，因為有了阻力才有磨練。生命開始的一瞬間就帶了鬥志而來的草，才是堅韌的草，也只有這種草，才可以傲然地對那些玻璃棚中養育著的盆花嗤笑。

*   *   *   *   *   *

回答下列问题

1. 作者讲了一个什么样的故事来说明种子的力量之大？

2. 被压在瓦砾和石块之下的小草是怎样生长出来的？作者对此是怎样进行描述的？

3. 在这篇短文中，"长在瓦砾中的草"和"玻璃棚中的盆花"分别代表了什么？作者通过它们想要说明的道理是什么？

4. "短句"是这篇文章的主要特点之一。运用短句产生了什么样的效果？

7. 苍蝇　　白墨

我虽然并不喜欢苍蝇，然而我却羡慕苍蝇，佩服苍蝇；理由是我愿意有苍蝇的本领而不能。

苍蝇有不可及的厚脸皮，无论对于怎样厌恶着它的人或畜类，从来没有一时一刻会因了挫折而灰心泄气：那种驱之不走，打之不去，不到惨死不甘心的追求生活的精神和毅力，恐怕世界上再不容易找到第二类东西！

苍蝇还有随"寓"而安的本领，不论是高楼，不论是厕所，也不论是火热的厨房，也不论是清凉的饮冰室……；苟得其门而入，皆优居之。

苍蝇也有什么都能吃的福气，中餐，西餐，香片，龙井，脓血，大粪……无往而不吃：而吃着又似乎无往而不适口。

苍蝇更有"明哲保身"的长处，它的身上具有一种毒质；除却鸡或鸭子可以拿之当作食品外，至于人类，虽然喜欢喝血吃肉；但是下饭馆子的，指名要一碟"五香苍蝇"的，尚未曾见。所以在"只须向人家揩油，不须人家向自己借光"的一点上说，生在如今的世道上，苍蝇是有厚望焉的！

能人之所不能，苍蝇才真正是万物之灵呢，我岂敢"吹"乎哉？

（选自群言出版社1994年《20世纪中国杂文精粹百篇》，有个别改动）

繁體字材料

蒼蠅　　白墨

我雖然並不喜歡蒼蠅，然而我卻羨慕蒼蠅，佩服蒼蠅；理由是我願意有蒼蠅的本領而不能。

蒼蠅有不可及的厚臉皮，無論對於怎樣厭惡著它的人或畜類，從來沒有一時一刻會因了挫折而灰心洩氣：那種驅之不走，打之不去，不到慘死不甘心的追求生活的精神和毅力，恐怕世界上再不容易找到第二類東西！

蒼蠅還有隨"寓"而安的本領，不論是高樓，不論是廁所，也不論是火熱的廚房，也不論是清涼的飲冰室……；苟得其門而入，皆優居之。

蒼蠅也有甚麼都能吃的福氣，中餐，西餐，香片，龍井，膿血，大糞……無往而不吃；而吃著又似乎無往而不適口。

蒼蠅更有"明哲保身"的長處，它的身上具有一種毒質；除卻雞或鴨子可以拿之當作食品外，至於人類，雖然喜歡喝血吃肉；但是下飯館子的，指名要一碟"五香蒼蠅"的，尚未曾見。所以在"只須向人家揩油，不須人家向自己借光"的一點上說，生在如今的世道上，蒼蠅是有厚望焉的！

能人之所不能，蒼蠅才真正是萬物之靈呢，我豈敢"吹"乎哉？

    ＊   ＊   ＊   ＊   ＊   ＊

回答下列问题

1. 作者不喜欢苍蝇，却"美慕"苍蝇、"佩服"苍蝇，为什么？

2. 苍蝇只是一个比喻，作者真正要讲的意思是什么？为什么作者说"生在如今的世道上，苍蝇是有厚望焉的"？

3. 作者是用什么语气来"赞美"苍蝇的？这种语气有什么效果？

4. 注意古汉语在这篇短文中的运用。古汉语的主要特征及效果是什么？

5. 从文中找出运用"对偶"（parallel structures）的句子。

8. 不一样的自由 龙应台

她那个打扮实在古怪，而且难看。头发狠狠的束在左耳边，翘起来那么短短的一把，脸蛋儿又肥，看起来就像个横摆着的白萝卜。腿很短，偏又穿松松肥肥的裤子，上衣再长长的罩下来，盖过膝盖，矮矮的人好像撑在面粉袋里作活动广告。她昂着头、甩着头发，春风得意的自我面前走过。

她实在难看，但我微笑的看她走过了，欣赏她有勇气穿跟别人不太一样的衣服。

这个学生站起来，大声说他不同意我的看法。他举了一个例子，一个逻辑完全错误的例子。比手划脚的把话说完，坐下。全班静静的，斜眼看着他，觉得他很猖狂，爱自我炫耀，极不稳重。

他的论点非常偏颇，但我微笑的听他说话，欣赏他有勇气说别人不敢说的话。

朋友发了两百张喜帖，下星期就要结婚了。可是又发觉这实在不是个理想的结合——两百个客人怎么办？他硬生生的取消了婚宴。

他的决定实在下得太晚了一点，但我微笑的撕掉那张喜帖，欣赏他有勇气做一般人不敢做的事，上了车，还有下车的勇气。

简陋的讲台上，披着红条子的候选人讲得声嘶力竭。穿制服的警察、着便衣的监选员，紧张的站在群众堆里。候选人口沫横飞的，把平常报纸绝对不会刊登的言论大声大嚷的说出来。

他举的例子谬误百出，他的用语粗糙而低级，可是我站在榕树荫里，耐心的听他说完，欣赏他有勇气主张与大众不同的意见。

那个萝卜头也许很幼稚，只是为了与别人不同而不同。我的学生也许很肤浅，站起来说话只是为了出锋头。取消婚宴的朋友或许有朝三暮四的个性，极不可靠。使警察紧张的候选人或许知识和格调都很低，对民主的真义只有很浅薄的了解。

可是，我想，他们有与我不一样的自由，也有与你不一样的自由。

（选自中国人民大学出版社１９９１年《中国当代名家小品精选》）

繁體字材料

不一樣的自由　　龍應台

她那個打扮實在古怪，而且難看。頭髮狠狠的束在左耳邊，翹起來那麼短短的一把，臉蛋兒又肥，看起來就像個橫擺著的白蘿蔔。腿很短，偏又穿鬆鬆肥肥的褲子，上衣再長長地罩下來，蓋過膝蓋，矮矮的人好像撐在面粉袋裡作活動廣告。她昂著頭、甩著頭髮，春風得意地自我面前走過。

她實在難看，但我微笑地看她走過了，欣賞她有勇氣穿跟別人不太一樣的衣服。

這個學生站起來，大聲說他不同意我的看法。他舉了一個例子，一個邏輯完全錯誤的例子。比手劃腳地把話說完，坐下。全班靜靜地，斜眼看著他，覺得他很猖狂，愛自我炫耀，極不穩重。

他的論點非常偏頗，但我微笑地聽他說話，欣賞他有勇氣說別人不敢說的話。

朋友發了兩百張喜帖，下星期就要結婚了。可是又發覺這實在不是個理想的結合——兩百個客人怎麼辦？他硬生生地取消了婚宴。

他的決定實在下得太晚了一點，但我微笑地撕掉那張喜帖，欣賞他有勇氣做一般人不敢做的事，上了車，還有下車的勇氣。

簡陋的講台上，披著紅條子的候選人講得聲嘶力竭。穿制服的警察、著便衣的監選員，緊張地站在群眾堆裡。候選人口沫橫飛地，把平常報紙絕對不會刊登的言論大聲大嚷地說出來。

他舉的例子謬誤百出，他的用語粗糙而低級，可是我站在榕樹蔭裡，耐心地聽他說完，欣賞他有勇氣主張與大眾不同的意見。

那個蘿蔔頭也許很幼稚，只是為了與別人不同而不同。我的學生也許很膚淺，站起來說話只是為了出鋒頭。取消婚宴的朋友或許有朝三暮四的個性，極不可靠。使警察緊張的候選人或許知識和格調都很低，對民主的真義只有很淺薄的了解。

可是，我想，他們有與我不一樣的自由，也有與你不一樣的自由。

 *   *   *   *   *   *

回答下列问题

1. 这是一篇边叙事边议论的"议论文"。通过四个小故事，作者想要说明一个什么道理？

2. 分别谈谈故事里的四个人与众不同的地方。

3. 就象故事里的那些人物，作者在看问题的方法上也跟一般人不一样。作者的态度极为鲜明。她是用了哪些 connectives 来清楚地、准确地表达她的观点的？

4. 找出文中的words of reduplication，并体会它们做修饰语的修辞效果。

9. 送礼物　　刘健威

节日送礼物，是很伤脑筋的事。

曾经试过一个月内要送几份生日礼物，朋友警告说：不要送相同的礼物，否则收礼的人恨死你。每隔几天就要构思出一份别具心思的礼物，真有人情紧过债的感觉。

送礼物是一种考验，考验你对收礼者认识的程度——他（她）喜欢的是什么？不喜欢的是什么？除此，送礼物也是一种对话，在考虑对方喜好之余，也要藉礼物来呈现自己的个性。送礼轻重又要考究——交浅"礼"深，很容易给人非奸即盗的印象。

常常收到一些礼物，明知价值不少，却不合自己的意，很为送礼的人肉痛。

投其所好，也不一定正确，因为"好"是很深入细微的——假如你与对方认识不深，那就千万不要给一个收藏家送书画艺术品——收到品味不合的东西，丢掉不是，好象对朋友不尊；陈列在家中，又跟别的东西不协调，很是尴尬。

最讨厌的礼物是——送礼的人明知所送未必为你所喜，还是送了——他也是收回来的，借花敬佛，做个顺水人情。像过年的蓝罐曲奇，A送给B，B又送给C，很有荒诞感。

也许很多人都喜欢贵重的礼物，但我认为，最高级的礼物应该是送给对方你的智慧，想象或幽默感。有人曾给朋友寄过一个空瓶子，只附了一句话：巴黎的空气。

一个空瓶一句话，包含了多少智慧和想象，还写入了艺术史。

曾经效颦，在纽约中央公园捡了片红叶寄给朋友，也是一句话：天上来的明信片。

这话后来成了一张唱片的标题。

送礼物，应该是创作。

（选自《书城》１９９９年第２期）

繁體字材料

送禮物　　劉健威

節日送禮物，是很傷腦筋的事。

曾經試過一個月內要送幾份生日禮物，朋友警告說：不要送相同的禮物，否則收禮的人恨死你。每隔幾天就要構思出一份別具心思的禮物，真有人情緊過債的感覺。

送禮物是一種考驗，考驗你對收禮者認識的程度——他（她）喜歡的是甚麼？不喜歡的是甚麼？除此，送禮物也是一種對話，在考慮對方喜好之餘，也要藉禮物來呈現自己的個性。送禮輕重又要考究——交淺"禮"深，很容易給人非奸即盜的印像。

常常收到一些禮物，明知價值不少，卻不合自己的意，很為送禮的人肉痛。

投其所好，也不一定正確，因為"好"是很深入細微的——假如你與對方認識不深，那就千萬不要給一個收藏家送書畫藝術品——收到品味不合的東西，丟掉不是，好像對朋友不尊；陳列在家中，又跟別的東西不協調，很是尷尬。

最討厭的禮物是——送禮的人明知所送未必為你所喜，還是送了——他也是收回來的，借花敬佛，做個順水人情。像過年的藍罐曲奇，A送給B，B又送給C，很有荒誕感。

也許很多人都喜歡貴重的禮物，但我認為，最高級的禮物應該是送給對方你的智慧，想像或幽默感。有人曾給朋友寄過一個空瓶子，只附了一句話：巴黎的空氣。

一個空瓶一句話，包含了多少智慧和想像，還寫入了藝術史。

曾經效顰，在紐約中央公園撿了片紅葉寄給朋友，也是一句話：天上來的明信片。

這話後來成了一張唱片的標題。

送禮物，應該是創作。

      *   *   *   *   *   *

回答下列问题

1. 作者的论点是：送礼物是件伤脑筋的事。他的论据是什么？

2. 你同意作者说的"最高级的礼物应该是送给对方你的智慧、想象或幽默感"吗？为什么？

3. 这篇短文用了许多四字词语。从文中找出这些四字词语，并说明它们哪些是固定的、哪些是作者为达到简洁、有力的效果而自己临时组成的？

10. 饮料与人生　尤金

饮料与人生，有着不可分割的密切关系。

少年多喜欢汽水。它甜，它变化多，少年不识愁滋味，人生的甜酸苦辣，他独独只尝到甜味。世界在他眼中，犹如味道各异的汽水，缤纷多彩。

进入青春期，他工作了，他恋爱了。这时，他的口味已由汽水转向了咖啡。咖啡亦苦亦甜，也香也涩，有一种成熟的刺激感，符合了他复杂多变的心境。这时期，山和水在他眼中，非山亦非水。他有奋斗的野心和理想，他有成家的需要和欲望；但是，事业和爱情，都可能带给他一些小挫折；他有时在笑里流泪，有时却又破涕为笑。他患得患失，却又乐在其中。

中年以后，多爱中国茶。中国茶那股若有若无的幽香，是深藏不露的，它恬淡而隽永，沉实而深刻。它绝不肤浅地刺激你的味觉。然而，喝了，缠在舌上的清香，却叫你回味无穷。江山已定的中年人，这时，见山又是山，见水又是水。对生活，他再也没有不切实际的憧憬，然而，他充分领略夕阳的绚烂在黄昏难以久留的道理，所以，他珍惜生活里的每一寸光阴。他的每一个日子，都包裹在一个平淡而又平实的快乐里。

老年人，喝白开水。白开水，不含糖精，没有咖啡因，更无茶碱。它极淡极淡，但若细细啜饮，却也能尝出一丁点儿的甜味来。人生的大风大浪，他看过了；人生的惊涛骇浪，他经历过了；成败得失，都成了过眼烟云。此刻，他安恬地坐在摇椅里，回首前尘，一切的一切，都淡淡如水、如水……

（选自中国人民大学出版社１９９１年《中国当代名家小品精选》）

繁體字材料

飲料與人生　尤金

飲料與人生，有著不可分割的密切關係。

少年多喜歡汽水。它甜，它變化多，少年不識愁滋味，人生的甜酸苦辣，他獨獨只嘗到甜味。世界在他眼中，猶如味道各異的汽水，繽紛多彩。

進入青春期，他工作了，他戀愛了。這時，他的口味已由汽水轉向了咖啡。咖啡亦苦亦甜，也香也澀，有一種成熟的刺激感，符合了他復雜多變的心境。這時期，山和水在他眼中，非山亦非水。他有奮鬥的野心和理想，他有成家的需要和欲望；但是，事業和愛情，都可能帶給他一些小挫折；他有時在笑裡流淚，有時卻又破涕為笑。他患得患失，卻又樂在其中。

中年以後，多愛中國茶。中國茶那股若有若無的幽香，是深藏不露的，它恬淡而雋永，沉實而深刻。它絕不膚淺地刺激你的味覺。然而，喝了，纏在舌上的清香，卻叫你回味無窮。江山已定的中年人，這時，見山又是山，見水又是水。對生活，他再也沒有不切實際的憧憬，然而，他充分領略夕陽的絢爛在黃昏難以久留的道理，所以，他珍惜生活裡的每一寸光陰。他的每一個日子，都包裹在一個平淡而又平實的快樂裡。

老年人，喝白開水。白開水，不含糖精，沒有咖啡因，更無茶鹼。它極淡極淡，但若細細啜飲，卻也能嘗出一丁點兒的甜味來。人生的大風大浪，他看過了；人生的驚濤駭浪，他經歷過了；成敗得失，都成了過眼煙雲。此刻，他安恬地坐在搖椅里，回首前塵，一切的一切，都淡淡如水、如水……

       *   *   *   *   *   *

回答下列问题

1. 为什么作者说"饮料与人生，有着不可分割的密切关系"？

2. 青春期，山和水在一个人眼中"非山亦非水"。而进入中年以后，他"见山又是山，见水又是水"。这是为什么？

3. 这篇议论文简洁有力。短句是造成这个效果的主要原因之一。大声朗读这篇文章，随着标点符号做相应的停顿，并仔细体会语言的抑扬顿挫 (cadence)。

4. 除了短句以外，作者还用对偶来取得简洁有力的效果。找出这些对偶的句子，看一看作者是怎样根据需要来增加或减少字数的。

11. 只在乎曾经拥有　　亦然

小时侯，曾相信那一个美丽的童话，多少次多少次，想抓住流星许一个愿：但愿人长久，但愿人长久。

然而每一次，流星都在一个完整的愿望出口之前便一闪即逝，每一次，都留了一个愿望在嘴边，留了一份遗憾在心底。

于是人生的旅途上，便是不断的相送与相别，于是生命的客栈里，永远扮一位匆匆的过客，来不及留恋和回味，就象来不及在流星消失前许一个愿。

来不及享受那学生时代的无忧无虑，高考的重压便如一座沉重的山压在背上。

来不及享受工作后的那一份自由与轻松，便不得不背负一个沉重的家。

初恋的甜言蜜语还未在耳边温热，却已经天涯地角形同陌路。

什么是地老天荒？

什么是天长地久？

花落才有花开，有散才能有聚，若没了那一份遗憾，又何来狂喜？若没了那一份无奈，又怎么懂得珍惜？

我们总是不遗余力地追求那一个天长地久，我们总是千方百计去留住那一个结果，却不知天有老时地有荒，这世上哪有不变的情？却不知如果曾经拥有过美，便不须再去强求什么结果。

这世界许多东西没有永恒，这世界许多事情没有结果，而美丽依旧美丽，辉煌照样辉煌，又何必斤斤计较时间的长短，又何必兜兜转转寻求因与果。

离别时，如果我们可以执手相互道珍重，又何必一定要留在一起重复那许多琐碎的岁月？分开时，如果我们可以轻轻松松挥挥手，又何必无谓地去翻找昔日的海誓山盟？花儿落了，明日还会再开；流星虽逝，美好的愿望依旧在心底。

于是所有的日子都轻松，于是所有的负重都甜美，于是不会再后悔后悔又后悔，于是不会再遗憾未了又遗憾，于是过去了的成回忆，于是今天拥有的不会再无奈。

拥有过的，永远不会失去，没得到的，亦无须苦苦追求。是你的，迟早都是你的，不是你的，永远都不会属于你。只要你，不为天长地久而苦恼，不必为失去的而遗憾，不必留恋昨天。

只在乎曾经拥有。

（选自陕西旅游出版社１９９２年《散文诗精品》）

繁體字材料

只在乎曾經擁有　　　亦然

小時侯，曾相信那一個美麗的童話，多少次多少次，想抓住流星許一個願：但願人長久，但願人長久。

然而每一次，流星都在一個完整的願望出口之前便一閃即逝，每一次，都留了一個願望在嘴邊，留了一份遺憾在心底。

於是人生的旅途上，便是不斷的相送與相別，於是生命的客棧裡，永遠扮一位匆匆的過客，來不及留戀和回味，就像來不及在流星消失前許一個願。

來不及享受那學生時代的無憂無慮，高考的重壓便如一座沉重的山壓在背上。

來不及享受工作後的那一份自由與輕鬆，便不得不背負一個沉重的家。

初戀的甜言蜜語還未在耳邊溫熱，卻已經天涯地角形同陌路。

甚麼是地老天荒？

甚麼是天長地久？

花落才有花開，有散才能有聚，若沒了那一份遺憾，又何來狂喜？若沒了那一份無奈，又怎麼懂得珍惜？

我們總是不遺餘力地追求那一個天長地久，我們總是千方百計去留住那一個結果，卻不知天有老時地有荒，這世上哪有不變的情？卻不知如果曾經擁有過美，便不須再去強求甚麼結果。

這世界許多東西沒有永恆，這世界許多事情沒有結果，而美麗依舊美麗，輝煌照樣輝煌，又何必斤斤計較時間的長短，又何必兜兜轉轉尋求因與果。

離別時，如果我們可以執手相互道珍重，又何必一定要留在一起重覆那許多瑣碎的歲月？分開時，如果我們可以輕輕鬆鬆揮揮手，又何必無謂地去翻找昔日的海誓山盟？花兒落了，明日還會再開；流星雖逝，美好的願望依舊在心底。

於是所有的日子都輕鬆，於是所有的負重都甜美，於是不會再後悔後悔又後悔，於是不會再遺憾未了又遺憾，於是過去了的成回憶，於是今天擁有的不會再無奈。

擁有過的，永遠不會失去，沒得到的，亦無須苦苦追求。是你的，遲早都是你的，不是你的，永遠都不會屬於你。只要你，不為天長地久而苦惱，不必為失去的而遺憾，不必留戀昨天。

只在乎曾經擁有。

*   *   *   *   *   *

回答下列问题

1. 这篇文章的主要意思是什么？"花落才有花开，有散才能有聚"是什么意思？

2. 作者说："是你的，迟早都是你的，不是你的，永远都不会属于你，"苦苦追求是没有必要的。你同意这个观点吗？

3. 作者在很多地方反复使用同一个词或句子（如"来不及"，"于是"等）。这种"重复"的技巧使文章产生了什么效果？

4. 在这篇文章里有许多问句。这些问句都需要回答吗？如果不是都需要回答，那么作者采用"反问句"的意图是什么？

5. 找出文中运用"排比"的例子。

12. 我说男人　王锋

很庆幸是个男人。

男人挺拔伟岸，男人顶天立地，男人走路生风。男人有力量把女人轻松地举过头顶。男人吻女人从不用踮脚。只要愿意，男人张开双臂，便可以乐呵呵地把整个女人拥在怀里。

很庆幸是个男人。男人洒脱豪放，爽朗通达。男儿下雪也不打伞，见沟坎一跃而过从不左顾右盼。男儿可以趿拉着拖鞋四处乱逛，可以让衣服被烟烬烧上几个小洞也不在乎，还可以在走廊里旁若无人地唱歌而不被蔑视为神经病。男儿们今天晚上破口大骂拳脚相加而明天早上就可以前嫌尽弃握手言欢。男人在餐馆可以体验到"派酒"的快感，或者上舞场去挑选别人而不是等着被人挑选。

男人们个性鲜明坦坦荡荡。他们从来不会围在一起窸窸窣窣：不会为一个问题争来吵去半天而毫无结果不知所云；也不会当面夸奖你而在背后却把你贬斥得有失分寸。男人们爱憎分明，从不掩饰自己内心的热爱和厌恶。他爱你就天翻地覆排山倒海，他厌恶你则不会多看你哪怕半眼。找几个哥们儿围坐一圈，男人们几杯清茶、几包香烟便可以上天入地神侃逍遥。男人们向往的便是这样眼观八路四面来风广交宾朋有滋有味的生活。

男人独立自主意志刚强。女人受了委屈就会来找男人，而男人痛苦了只去点燃一支香烟。男儿尊严神圣，有泪不轻弹，让血流在心里，男儿可杀不可辱。

男人的美是气质是力量。是逼你后退的高山，是将你倾没的骇浪。男人扬扬头轻轻抖落身上的尘土，而从不去抹奥琪、华姿、海飞丝……

男人们往往很强横自信，哪怕这种强横过分得令人讨厌，甚至这种自信也没有多少基础。不过也正是这种品质，男人成其为真正的男人，其余的都不重要了。

女人们一辈子寻求解放，争先恐后地去竞选女强人，可男人从不。他知道男人本身就意味着解放，他本身就是坚强。我想，只有这个世界无须再用"三八"妇女节来提醒人们尊重女人时，女人才获得了真正意义上的解放。

我发现"妇女"们对男人有误解，也发现男人对女人有误解。这没办法，看来我朋友的一句话不幸而言中了：男人和女人是两种完全不同的动物，永远不可能完全一致。

不过谁知道呢？这殊异也许是上帝最杰出的安排。

（选自陕西旅游出版社１９９２年《散文诗精品》）

<u>繁體字材料</u>

我說男人　　王鋒

很慶幸是個男人。

男人挺拔偉岸，男人頂天立地，男人走路生風。男人有力量把女人輕鬆地舉過頭頂。男人吻女人從不用踮腳。只要願意，男人張開雙臂，便可以樂呵呵地把整個女人擁在懷裡。

很慶幸是個男人。男人灑脫豪放，爽朗通達。男兒下雪也不打傘，見溝坎一躍而過從不左顧右盼。男兒可以趿拉著拖鞋四處亂逛，可以讓衣服被煙爐燒上幾個小洞也不在乎，還可以在走廊裡旁若無人地唱歌而不被蔑視為神經病。男兒們今天晚上破口大罵拳腳相加而明天早上就可以前嫌盡棄握手言歡。男人在餐館可以體驗到"派酒"的快感，或者上舞場去挑選別人而不是等著被人挑選。

男人們個性鮮明坦坦蕩蕩。他們從來不會圍在一起窸窸窣窣：不會為一個問題爭來吵去半天而毫無結果不知所雲；也不會當面誇獎你而在背後卻把你貶斥得有失分寸。男人們愛憎分明，從不掩飾自己內心的熱愛和厭惡。他愛你就天翻地覆排山倒海，他厭惡你則不會多看你哪怕半眼。找幾個哥們兒圍坐一圈，男人們幾杯清茶、幾包香煙便可以上天入地神侃逍遙。男人們嚮往的便是這樣眼觀八路四面來風廣交賓朋有滋有味的生活。

男人獨立自主意志剛強。女人受了委屈就會來找男人，而男人痛苦了只去點燃一支香煙。男兒尊嚴神聖，有淚不輕彈，讓血流在心裡，男兒可殺不可辱。

男人的美是氣質是力量。是逼你後退的高山，是將你傾沒的駭浪。男人揚揚頭輕輕抖落身上的塵土，而從不去抹奧琪、華姿、海飛絲……

男人們往往很強橫自信，哪怕這種強橫過分得令人討厭，甚至這種自信也沒有多少基礎。不過也正是這種品質，男人成其為真正的男人，其餘的都不重要了。

女人們一輩子尋求解放，爭先恐後地去競選女強人，可男人從不。他知道男人本身就意味著解放，他本身就是堅強。我想，只有這個世界無須再用"三八"婦女節來提醒人們尊重女人時，女人才獲得了真正意義上的解放。

我發現"婦女"們對男人有誤解，也發現男人對女人有誤解。這沒辦法，看來我朋友的一句話不幸而言中了：男人和女人是兩種完全不同的動物，永遠不可能完全一致。

不過誰知道呢？這殊異也許是上帝最傑出的安排。

*　　　*　　　*　　　*　　　*　　　*

回答下列问题

1. 作者为什么庆幸自己是个男人？

2. 你同意作者关于男人的看法吗？你怎么看男人？

3. 作者在这篇文章里大量采用四字词语，如"顶天立地"，"走路生风"，"一跃而过"，"左顾右盼"，"破口大骂"，"拳脚相加"等等。这些四字词语都需要查字典吗？

4. 作者在谈男人的时候也谈到了女人。他为什么采用这种"对比"的手法？

5. 找出文中具有"夸张"(exaggeration)特点的词组与句子。

13. 书的味道　　徐立和

书不是名花，也不是美酒，但书的味道却又在花、酒之外。时常有人这样说：这本书真有味。是什么味呢？我谓：食有五味，书亦有五味。

酸

书的酸，不是指人们常说的穷酸的酸，此酸非彼酸也。书的酸，是让你眼为之酸，鼻为之酸的一种味道。电影电视令人泪下不算真本事，读一册书，能让人鼻酸才为真能耐。譬如我吧，我承认我已经很久没有哭过了，前几天读蔡志恒的《第一次亲密接触》，当那只蝴蝶翩然而去时，我的鼻端便充满了久违的酸涩……这就是我们常说的以情感人，书的酸味就是真情的味道。

甜

犹太人的孩子，对书的第一印象应该是甜的，因为每个犹太家庭都会在孩子小的时候在书上滴上蜂蜜，让他去闻。我不知道这究竟有没有结果，但这种做法却十分令人赞赏，不过话又说回来，虽然我们的孩子从未像犹太人的孩子一般闻过书本，但我相信，若问他们书是什么味道，回答准是：甜的。书里优美的散文，精巧的童话，还有一个个动听的故事，无不让人唇齿留香。高尔基说过：我扑在书上，就像饥饿的人扑在面包上。这是对书的甜所作的绝妙的注解。

苦

书自然是苦的。否则怎会有"苦读"一说。书的苦涩厚味，也只有苦读方能体味得到。书里的历史变迁，社会改革，国家兴亡，一幅幅宏伟的长卷所散发的是一股带有火焦气味的苦涩。千年的时间，沉淀的一切都在书中。细细嚼来，如一枚枚青橄榄，一股淡淡的、清清的苦味绕在舌间。

辣

书不仅仅是文化的载体，思想的航船，不仅仅是休闲的工具，它也能成为匕首。读一读鲁迅的杂文，真如醇酒一般辛辣。所以，当我们从书中品出辣味来时，一定要注意……

咸

一本真正的好书，它身上的每一条皱纹都应是泪水的凝结。书让人笑，让人哭，让人喜极而泣，让人悲痛而哭，浸透了无数人的眼泪，这薄薄的一本书，自然而然地便透出一丝咸涩。

书有五味，但一味地哀伤便落入俗套，都成苦涩便失之于机械，只顾辛辣就显得过分偏激。一本好书，应如高明的厨师所调出的佳肴，品一口则百味变幻，层出不穷，亦如雨后彩虹，七彩纷呈。更要在百味过后，留一股清甜的香味，让人回味无穷，唇齿留香。

且找一本好书，品一品看，如何？

（选自２００１年６月２４日《中国商报社会周刊》）

繁體字材料

書的味道　　徐立和

書不是名花，也不是美酒，但書的味道卻又在花、酒之外。時常有人這樣說：這本書真有味。是甚麼味呢？我謂：食有五味，書亦有五味。

酸

書的酸，不是指人們常說的窮酸的酸，此酸非彼酸也。書的酸，是讓你眼為之酸，鼻為之酸的一種味道。電影電視令人淚下不算真本事，讀一冊書，能讓人鼻酸才為真能耐。譬如我吧，我承認我已經很久沒有哭過了，前幾天讀蔡智恆的《第一次親密接觸》，當那隻蝴蝶翩然而去時，我的鼻端便充滿了久違的酸澀……這就是我們常說的以情感人，書的酸味就是真情的味道。

甜

猶太人的孩子，對書的第一印象應該是甜的，因為每個猶太家庭都會在孩子小的時候在書上滴上蜂蜜，讓他去聞。我不知道這究竟有沒有結果，但這種做法卻十分令人贊賞，不過話又說回來，雖然我們的孩子從未像猶太人的孩子一般聞過書本，但我相信，若問他們書是甚麼味道，回答準是：甜的。書裡優美的散文，精巧的童話，還有一個個動聽的故事，無不讓人唇齒留香。高爾基說過：我撲在書上，就像飢餓的人撲在面包上。這是對書的甜所作的絕妙的注解。

苦

書自然是苦的。否則怎會有"苦讀"一說。書的苦澀厚味，也只有苦讀方能體味得到。書裡的歷史變遷，社會改革，國家興亡，一幅幅宏偉的長卷所散發的是一股帶有火焦氣味的苦澀。千年的時間，沉澱的一切都在書中。細細嚼來，如一枚枚青橄欖，一股淡淡的、清清的苦味繞在舌間。

辣

書不僅僅是文化的載體，思想的航船，不僅僅是休閒的工具，它也能成為匕首。讀一讀魯迅的雜文，真如醇酒一般辛辣。所以，當我們從書中品出辣味來時，一定要注意……

鹹

一本真正的好書，它身上的每一條皺紋都應是淚水的凝結。書讓人笑，讓人哭，讓人喜極而泣，讓人悲痛而哭，浸透了無數人的眼淚，這薄薄的一本書，自然而然地便透出一絲鹹澀。

書有五味，但一味地哀傷便落入俗套，都成苦澀便失之于機械，只顧辛辣就顯得過分偏激。一本好書，應如高明的廚師所調出的佳肴，品一口則百味變幻，層出不窮，亦如雨後彩虹，七彩紛呈。更要在百味過後，留一股清甜的香味，讓人回味無窮，脣齒留香。

且找一本好書，品一品看，如何？

*　　　*　　　*　　　*　　　*　　　*

回答下列问题

1. 用“味”来形容文学作品是中国文学批评的一个传统。对于作者来说，书有几种味道？是什么味道？

2. 作者认为，一本好书应该是一本怎样的书？只有一种味道的书是好书吗？

3. 这篇文章处处使用“比喻”(analogies)。这些比喻有些是明喻，有些是暗喻。从文章中找出这些使用比喻的地方，并想一想在相同的情况下英文也用比喻吗？英文中的比喻与中文有什么不一样？

4. 作者的议论典雅、古朴，很明显他是一个学者。从文中找出古汉语的成分，并想一想如果不用这些词汇或句式，同样的意思应该怎样表达？

14. 敦煌石窟   泳汀

敦煌石窟，包括今甘肃省敦煌市境内的莫高窟、西千佛洞，安西县境内的榆林窟、东千佛洞，肃北蒙古族自治县境内的五个庙石窟等。在古代，上述石窟都在敦煌郡境内，其内容及艺术风格亦同属一脉，因此，我们总称之为敦煌石窟。

敦煌石窟是佛徒修行、礼拜和进行法事的石窟寺。窟内有塑绘佛像和壁画。塑像包括佛、菩萨、弟子、天王、力士、地祇、高僧等形象。壁画包括佛像画、经义画、佛本生故事画、佛传故事画、佛教史迹画、汉族神话故事画、供养画（供养人画和出行图）、装饰图案画等内容。

莫高窟位于敦煌市东南 25 公里，开凿在砾石层的断崖上，背靠鸣沙山，面对三危峰，前临岩泉，窟区全长 1600 米，现存洞窟 49 个，洞窟大小不一，上下错落，密布崖面，如蜂窝状。莫高窟始建于前秦建元二年（366年），历经北魏、西魏、北周、隋、唐、五代、宋、西夏、元等朝代，在武周时期，洞窟已多达千余，由于历史变迁，自然的和人为的损毁，前秦始建的洞窟已不可考。在现存的洞窟中，有壁画 45000 平方米，塑像 2300 余身，最大塑像高 33 米，最大壁画约 50 平方米。这些壁画，塑像，在不同程度上反映了我国从 4 世纪到 14 世纪，上下延续千年的不同时代的社会生产、生活、交通、建筑、艺术、民情风俗、宗教信仰、思想变化、民族关系、中外交往等情况。在我国现存的石窟中，莫高窟是开凿时期最早、延续时间最长、规模最大、内容最丰富的石窟群，在世界文化史上也具有珍贵的价值，有"人类文化珍藏"、"形象历史博物馆"、"世界画廊"之称。1960 年，我国国务院确定莫高窟为"全国文物重点保护单位"，1987 年联合国教科文组织将莫高窟列为"人类珍贵文化遗产"。

榆林窟位于安西县踏实乡境内，开凿在榆林河峡谷两岸的砾石崖断崖上，现存北魏至元代的洞窟 42 个，最高塑像 20 余米，吐蕃统治初期（敦煌石窟分期为中唐）所凿建的第 25 窟，艺术价值颇高，在整个敦煌石窟中也属佼佼者。西夏时期凿建的第二、三窟，无论在内容还是艺术上都独树一帜，并弥补了莫高窟西夏石窟艺术之不足。窟中的水月观音和文殊菩萨出行图，均为脍炙人口的佳作。1961 年被国务院确定为"全国文物重点保护单位"。

西千佛洞现存 16 窟，保存完好，1961 年国务院确定为"全国文物重点保护单位"。东千佛洞现存 23 窟，密宗题材壁画尤多。五个庙石窟现存 22 窟。这几处石窟都可以作为莫高、榆林两窟群之参证和补阙。

（选自复旦大学出版社１９９６年《千字文阅读与训练》）

繁體字材料

敦煌石窟　　泳汀

敦煌石窟，包括今甘肅省敦煌市境內的莫高窟、西千佛洞，安西縣境內的榆林窟、東千佛洞，肅北蒙古族自治縣境內的五個廟石窟等。在古代，上述石窟都在敦煌郡境內，其內容及藝術風格亦同屬一脈，因此，我們總稱之為敦煌石窟。

敦煌石窟是佛徒修行、禮拜和進行法事的石窟寺。窟內有塑繪佛像和壁畫。塑像包括佛、菩薩、弟子、天王、力士、地祇、高僧等形像。壁畫包括佛像畫、經義畫、佛本生故事畫、佛傳故事畫、佛教史跡畫、漢族神話故事畫、供養畫（供養人畫和出行圖）、裝飾圖案畫等內容。

莫高窟位於敦煌市東南 25 公里，開鑿在礫石層的斷崖上，背靠鳴沙山，面對三危峰，前臨巖泉，窟區全長 1600 米，現存洞窟 49 個，洞窟大小不一，上下錯落，密布崖面，如蜂窩狀。莫高窟始建於前秦建元二年（366 年），歷經北魏、西魏、北周、隋、唐、五代、宋、西夏、元等朝代，在武周時期，洞窟已多達千餘，由於歷史變遷，自然的和人為的損毀，前秦始建的洞窟已不可考。在現存的洞窟中，有壁畫 45000 平方米，塑像 2300 餘身，最大塑像高 33 米，最大壁畫約 50 平方米。這些壁畫，塑像，在不同程度上反映了我國從 4 世紀到 14 世紀，上下延續千年的不同時代的社會生產、生活、交通、建築、藝術、民情風俗、宗教信仰、思想變化、民族關係、中外交往等情況。在我國現存的石窟中，莫高窟是開鑿時期最早、延續時間最長、規模最大、內容最豐富的石窟群，在世界文化史上也具有珍貴的價值，有"人類文化珍藏"、"形象歷史博物館"、"世界畫廊"之稱。1960 年，我國國務院確定莫高窟為"全國文物重點保護單位"，1987 年聯合國教科文組織將莫高窟列為"人類珍貴文化遺產"。

　　榆林窟位于安西縣踏實鄉境內，開鑿在榆林河峽谷兩岸的礫石崖斷崖上，現存北魏至元代的洞窟 42 個，最高塑像 20 餘米，吐蕃統治初期（敦煌石窟分期為中唐）所鑿建的第 25 窟，藝術價值頗高，在整個敦煌石窟中也屬佼佼者。西夏時期鑿建的第二、三窟，無論在內容還是藝術上都獨樹一幟，並彌補了莫高窟西夏石窟藝術之不足。窟中的水月觀音和文殊菩薩出行圖，均為膾炙人口的佳作。1961 年被國務院確定為"全國文物重點保護單位"。

　　西千佛洞現存 16 窟，保存完好，1961 年國務院確定為"全國文物重點保護單位"。東千佛洞現存 23 窟，密宗題材壁畫尤多。無個廟石窟現存 22 窟。這幾處石窟都可以作為莫高、榆林兩窟群之參證和補闕。

　　　　*　　　　*　　　　*　　　　*　　　　*　　　　*

回答下列問題

　1. 敦煌石窟位于何处？它们是什么时候开凿的？

　2. 为什么联合国教科文组织将莫高窟列为"人类珍贵文化遗产"？

　3. 作者在这篇文章里把敦煌石窟介绍得清清楚楚。他是怎样达到这个目的的？

　4. "长句"是这篇"说明文"的主要特点之一。找出文中的长句，并想一想在说明文中用长句有什么优势。

15. 汉语可以治病　　晓来

两年前美国费城的心理学家公布了一例用学汉语的方法治病的实验，引起了医学界、心理学界、语言学界乃至信息科学界的广泛注意。

美国费城有一少年，聪明好学，深得老师的喜爱。但一天不幸的事情发生了：他父亲叫他看报上的天气预报，他一看，报上的字一个都不认识，他痛苦地告诉父亲，说看不懂。已读小学五年级的他怎么连天气预报也看不懂呢？他父亲不相信，带他去看医生，医生经过测试证实这是真的，并说孩子患了一种叫"失读症"的病。

我们知道，人的大脑皮层有一个语言中枢，是人类语言能力的生理基础，它的作用就是调控人类的语言行为，例如听懂别人说话的意思，正确表达自己的思想。这个中枢一旦因脑外伤受损或因脑血管供血障碍，则人的语言行为便出现障碍，常见的有"失语症"。这种患者常常不能用语言正确表达自己的思想，说起话来颠三倒四，复杂一些的内容他们就说不出来，严重的甚至完全不能使用语言。"失读症"是失语症中的一种。这个美国少年怎么会患上这种病呢？追查的结果，证实是脑外伤造成的。

传统的看法是，人脑的语言中枢在大脑左半球，按这个观点推论，只要在左半球的这个中枢受损，就可能发生失语症或失读症，不管他是哪个国家、哪个地区的人。但事实却不全是这样。

科学家经过调查发现，中国和日本患失读症的人要比欧美少得多。这是为什么？经过多次实验，发现了一个基本的、却是简单的事实：中国和日本都使用汉字。循着这条线索，科学家进一步实验、探索，发现欧美人使用的是拼音文字，他们记认字音和字义使用的是大脑左半球，而且仅仅是左半球。但中国人、日本人使用汉字，对大脑的利用精细得多，左半球记认字音字义、右半球记认字形（连字义），而且左右两半球均衡协作。这就是为什么中国、日本患失读症者少的原因。

更有趣的是，美国科学家对中国儿童和美国儿童的阅读能力和某些智商做比较实验，发现中国儿童的智商要高得多。

开始他们很惊愕，但这是不可否认的事实。他们研究了各种可能原因，最后才较清楚地看到，其一个重要原因是中国儿童学的是汉语、汉字，因此他们的大脑左、右半球从小就得到更充分、更均衡的锻炼。

根据汉字跟大脑两半球的这种关系，费城的心理学家做了一个假设，能否用学汉语汉字的方法来纠正失读症呢？他们首先教这位美国少年学汉字、汉语，接着实验正式开始了：在一张纸上，上行写英语句子，下行写同意思的汉语句子，要这位美国少年看着汉字读出英语句子来。这位美国少年毫不费力便把英语句子念出来了，实验初步成功了。要知道他原来单看英语是念不出来的，所以这个实验结果是确切的。

不过这个实验有一个问题，即汉语句子只起"唤醒"英语句子的作用，不等于把病治好了。根据以后的实验表明，这一问题是可以解决的，因为在不断的"唤醒"作用下，患者能慢慢恢复英语的阅读能力。这些实验先后在法国等国家进行，都获得了初步的成功。

汉语、汉字的学习、使用，可以使人们更充分、均衡地使用大脑两半球，其意义是非常深远的。已有人提出用学习汉语、汉字的方法提高西方儿童的智能了，还有其他一些想法和研究，我们感兴趣地期待着这些研究成果。

（选自复旦大学出版社１９９６年《千字文阅读与训练》）

繁體字材料

漢語可以治病　　曉來

兩年前美國費城的心理學家公布了一例用學漢語的方法治病的實驗，引起了醫學界、心理學界、語言學界乃至信息科學界的廣泛注意。

美國費城有一少年，聰明好學，深得老師的喜愛。但一天不幸的事情發生了：他父親叫他看報上的天氣預報，他一看，報上的字一個都不認識，他痛苦地告訴父親，說看不懂。已讀小學五年級的他怎麼連天氣預報也看不懂呢？他父親不相信，帶他去看醫生，醫生經過測試實這是真的，並說孩子患了一種叫“失讀症”的病。

我們知道，人的大腦皮層有一個語言中樞，是人類語言能力的生理基礎，它的作用就是調控人類的語言行為，例如聽懂別人說話的意思，正確表達自己的思想。這個中樞一旦因腦外傷受損或因腦血管供血障礙，則人的語言行為便出現障礙，常見的有“失語症”。這種患者常常不能用語言正確表達自己的思想，說起話來顛三倒四，複雜一些的內容他們就說不出來，嚴重的甚至完全不能使用語言。“失讀症”是失語症中的一種。這個美國少年怎麼會患上這種病呢？追查的結果，證實是腦外傷造成的。

傳統的看法是，人腦的語言中樞在大腦左半球，按這個觀點推論，只要在左半球的這個中樞受損，就可能發生失語症或失讀症，不管他是哪個國家、哪個地區的人。但事實卻不全是這樣。

科學家經過調查發現，中國和日本患失讀症的人要比歐美少得多。這是為甚麼？經過多次實驗，發現了一個基本的、卻是簡單的事實：中國和日本都使用漢字。循著這條線索，科學家進一步實驗、探索，發現歐美人使用的是拼音文字，他們記認字音和字義使用的是大腦左半球，而且僅僅是左半球。但中國人、日本人使用漢字，對大腦的利用精細得多，左半球記認字音字義、右半球記認字形（連字義），而且左右兩半球均衡協作。這就是為甚麼中國、日本患失讀症者少的原因。

更有趣的是，美國科學家對中國兒童和美國兒童的閱讀能力和某些智商做比較實驗，發現中國兒童的智商要高得多。

開始他們很驚愕，但這是不可否認的事實。他們研究了各種可能原因，最後才較清楚地看到，其一個重要原因是中國兒童學的是漢語、漢字，因此他們的大腦左、右半球從小就得到更充分、更均衡的鍛煉。

　　根據漢字跟大腦兩半球的這種關系，費城的心理學家做了一個假設，能否用學漢語漢字的方法來糾正失讀症呢？他們首先教這位美國少年學漢字、漢語，接著實驗正式開始了：在一張紙上，上行寫英語句子，下行寫同意思的漢語句子，要這位美國少年看著漢字讀出英語句子來。這位美國少年毫不費力便把英語句子念出來了，實驗初步成功了。要知道他原來單看英語是念不出來的，所以這個實驗結果是確切的。

　　不過這個實驗有一個問題，即漢語句子只起"喚醒"英語句子的作用，不等於把病治好了。但以後的實驗表明，這一問題是可以解決的，因為在不斷的"喚醒"作用下，患者能慢慢恢復英語的閱讀能力。這些實驗先後在法國等國家進行，都獲得了初步的成功。

　　漢語、漢字的學習、使用，可以使人們更充分、均衡地使用大腦兩半球，其意義是非常深遠的。已有人提出用學習漢語、漢字的方法提高西方兒童的智能了，還有其他一些想法和研究，我們感興趣地期待著這些研究成果。

　　＊　　　　＊　　　　＊　　　　＊　　　　＊　　　　＊

回答下列问题

1. 什么是"失语症"？

2. 为什么中国人、日本人患"失读症"的人比其他国家少？

3. 汉语是怎样治好了美国费城一位少年的"失读症"的？

4. 这篇文章里"长句"、"短句"交叉出现。仔细看一看作者一般在什么时候用长句，什么时候用短句。为什么？

16. 中国瓷器　殷红

就那么一只瓷盘，有舞姿优美了世界，有花雨撒向人们的心灵。壮健的男子舞了几千年，撒花雨的女子撒了几千年，还是舞不完撒不完一个民族不朽的希望。

哦，中国瓷器！

瓷器上舞蹈的黄皮肤民族！

那花果的芬芳自瓷器上飘出，那米酒的醇香自瓷器里溢出，轻轻逸逸缠缠绵绵，自一条丝绸之路，自一条波浪喧响的海途，吸引了无数称美的目光。

那鲜艳的色彩，是滴漓漓的绿色滋润了春天，是玫瑰色的云霞辉煌了夏天，是流动的金光成熟了秋季，是如玉的光彩忠贞了爱情……

哦，中国瓷器！

瓷器上微笑的黑眼睛民族！

即使岁月的尘灰将你封存了几个世纪，一旦出土，仍然是生动的形象，是祖先的灵魂飞光溅彩！

那形象里，有一个民族圣洁的友谊和金色的祝福。

那光彩里，有岳飞的血液红得凝重，有李白的文彩灵气典雅城镇，有张择瑞的浓墨浓情生动山水。

有一颗古莲子，开出鲜艳的荷花……

哦，中国瓷器！

瓷器上站着的不老民族？

只要在书桌上放一件精致的中国瓷器，你会想到生活是一种艺术，因而艺术地生活，会有一片薄薄的日光月光，辉映你的生命……

（选自漓江出版社１９９１年《当代中国散文擂台赛作品选》）

繁體字材料

中國瓷器　　殷紅

就那麼一隻瓷盤，有舞姿優美了世界，有花雨撒向人們的心靈。壯健的男子舞了幾千年，撒花雨的女子撒了幾千年，還是舞不完撒不完一個民族不朽的希望。

哦，中國瓷器！

瓷器上舞蹈的黃皮膚民族！

那花果的芬芳自瓷器上飄出，那米酒的醇香自瓷器裡溢出，輕輕逸逸纏纏綿綿，自一條絲綢之路，自一條波浪喧響的海途，吸引了無數稱羨的目光。

那鮮艷的色彩，是滴滴漓的綠色滋潤了春天，是玫瑰色的雲霞輝煌了夏天，是流動的金光成熟了秋季，是如玉的光彩忠貞了愛情……

哦，中國瓷器！

瓷器上微笑的黑眼睛民族！

即使歲月的塵灰將你封存了幾個世紀，一旦出土，仍然是生動的形象，是祖先的靈魂飛光濺彩！

那形象裡，有一個民族聖潔的友誼和金色的祝福。

那光彩裡，有岳飛的血液紅得凝重，有李白的文彩靈氣典雅城鎮，有張擇瑞的濃墨濃情生動山水。

有一顆古蓮子，開出鮮艷的荷花……

哦，中國瓷器！

瓷器上站著的不老民族？

只要在書桌上放一件精緻的中國瓷器，你會想到生活是一種藝術，因而藝術地生活，會有一片薄薄的日光月光，輝映你的生命……

*　　　　*　　　　*　　　　*　　　　*　　　　*

回答下列問題

1. 在这篇"抒情文"里，作者为什么对中国瓷器抒发了那么多的感情？

2. "丝绸之路"是什么？作者为什么要提到它？

3. 这篇短文反映了抒情文的一些什么特点？

4. 在这篇抒情文里，作者用了许多没有谓语的句子，为什么？这种句子的修辞效果是什么？

5. 注意标点符号在这篇短文里的运用。

17. 四季抒情　　徐成森

春

绿色的翅膀，托举着绿色的灵魂。

当因袭的冰雪消融，天际吹来觉醒的东风的时候，新的希望的种子便在期待的泥土奋挣。那迎着最初的骄阳摇曳着的两片小小的子叶，就是它的满载着幻想的羽翼。

看啊，那绿色的心在初霁的晴空振翮翱翔。

夏

爱情在炽热的火焰里燃烧。

飓风煽动着烈火，大地也似在热情中战栗。

繁枝伸向高空，象在擎起整个天宇；根须虬绕着泥土，它要紧紧地拥抱大地。每一个叶孔都在悸动，它拼命地吸收着空气，吸收着阳光。每一条叶脉都在沸腾，它贪婪地吮吸着感情的乳汁，为的是让思想的子房变得更加充实。

烈火的洪波已经漫过了堤岸，但是别担忧，那未来的一切，正在这火的波涛中孕育。

秋

终于，风浪停息了，大海一片宁静。理智的崖岸矗立在陆地的边沿恶然沉思。

曾在风中那么热烈地喧闹过的绿叶沉默了，那争芳斗艳的百卉千花也都悄然低首，它们那快乐而又惆怅的眼泪款款飘垂在熟透了的泥土里。

只有金色的果实却从雾霭里羞涩地伸出自己的脸颊，那殷红的双唇似在等待着一次忘情的热吻。

一切都终于成熟了。在林中，在草地，在田野，在山冈，在一切有生命和呼吸的地方，都留下了欣慰的女神那欢乐的足迹……

冬

静止并不就是终结，而凝固也并非意味着死亡。

当冰雪象复活了的世纪一般沉重地压在高树和野草身上的时候，你听到的岂是它们痛苦的垂死的呻吟？

当世界上最后一枚枯叶离开了瑟缩的枝头时，我看见它用一个甜美的微笑向过去的时代告别。而在高高的枝头隐约可辨的芽苞，正储存着第二个春天的全部信息！

那么，让无情的冰雪埋葬掉陈腐的过去吧，也许，冷静的思考会带来更多的智慧和敏睿。未来将属于另一个全新的更美好的季节！

（选自陕西旅游出版社１９９２年《散文诗精品》）

繁體字材料

四季抒情　徐成森

春

綠色的翅膀，托舉著綠色的靈魂。

當因襲的冰雪消融，天際吹來覺醒的東風的時候，新的希望的種子便在期待的泥土奮掙。那迎著最初的驕陽搖曳著的兩片小小的子葉，就是它的滿載著幻想的羽翼。

看啊，那綠色的心在初霽的晴空振翮翱翔。

夏

愛情在熾熱的火焰裡燃燒。

颶風煽動著烈火，大地也似在熱情中戰慄。

繁枝伸向高空，像在擎起整個天宇；根須虯繞著泥土，它要緊緊地擁抱大地。每一個葉孔都在悸動，它拚命地吸收著空氣，吸收著陽光。每一條葉脈都在沸騰，它貪婪地吮吸著感情的乳汁，為的是讓思想的子房變得更加充實。

烈火的洪波已經漫過了堤岸，但是別擔憂，那未來的一切，正在這火的波濤中孕育。

秋

終於，風浪停息了，大海一片寧靜。理智的崖岸矗立在陸地的邊沿惘然沉思。

曾在風中那麼熱烈地喧鬧過的綠葉沉默了，那爭芳鬥艷的百卉千花也都悄然低首，它們那快樂而又惆悵的眼淚款款飄垂在熟透了的泥土裡。

只有金色的果實卻從霧靄裡羞澀地伸出自己的臉頰，那殷紅的雙唇似在等待著一次忘情的熱吻。

一切都終於成熟了。在林中，在草地，在田野，在山岡，在一切有生命和呼吸的地方，都留下了欣慰的女神那歡樂的足跡……

冬

靜止並不就是終結，而凝固也並非意味著死亡。

當冰雪像復活了的世紀一般沉重地壓在高樹和野草身上的時候，你聽到的豈是它們痛苦的垂死的呻吟？

當世界上最後一枚枯葉離開了瑟縮的枝頭時，我看見它用一個甜美的微笑向過去的時代告別。而在高高的枝頭隱約可辨的芽苞，正儲存著第二個春天的全部信息！

那麼，讓無情的冰雪埋葬掉陳腐的過去吧，也許，冷靜的思考會帶來更多的智慧和敏睿。未來將屬於另一個全新的更美好的季節！

    *   *   *   *   *   *

回答下列问题

1. "绿色的翅膀，托举着绿色的灵魂"是什么意思？

2. 在这篇歌颂四季的抒情文里，你觉得哪个季节作者写得最好？为什么？

3. 作者在这篇抒情文里运用了各种修辞手法来表达他的心情。这些修辞手法是什么？用"春"这一节来举例说明。

4. 这篇抒情文就是歌颂四季的吗？如果不是，那么作者通过四季在说明什么呢？